ANNUAL EDITIONS

P9-BYU-783

08/09

Psychology
2009 Update
Thirty-Eighth Edition

EDITOR

Karen G. Duffy
SUNY at Geneseo (Emerita)

Karen G. Duffy holds a doctorate in psychology from Michigan State University, and she is an emerita Distinguished Service Professor of State University of New York at Geneseo. Dr. Duffy continues to work on her books and research, and she is also involved in several community service projects both in the United States and Russia.

 **Higher Education**

Boston   Burr Ridge, IL   Dubuque, IA   New York   San Francisco   St. Louis
Bangkok   Bogotá   Caracas   Kuala Lumpur   Lisbon   London   Madrid   Mexico City
Milan   Montreal   New Delhi   Santiago   Seoul   Singapore   Sydney   Taipei   Toronto

The McGraw·Hill Companies

Higher Education

ANNUAL EDITIONS: PSYCHOLOGY (2009 Update), THIRTY-EIGHTH EDITION

1 2 3 4 5 6 7 8 9 0 QPD/QPD 0 9 8 7

ISBN 978–0–07339779–5
MHID 0–07–339779–2
ISSN 0272–3794

Managing Editor: *Larry Loeppke*
Managing Editor: *Faye Schilling*
Developmental Editor: *Jade Benedict*
Editorial Assistant: *Nancy Meissner*
Production Service Assistant: *Rita Hingtgen*
Permissions Coordinator: *Lenny Behnke*
Senior Marketing Manager: *Julie Keck*
Marketing Communications Specialist: *Mary Klein*
Marketing Coordinator: *Alice Link*
Project Manager: *Sandy Wille*
Design Specialist: *Tara McDermott*
Senior Administrative Assistant: *DeAnna Dausener*
Senior Production Supervisor: *Laura Fuller*
Cover Graphics: *Kristine Jubeck*

Compositor: Laserwords Private Limited
Cover Images: (background) Ann Burgraff/Corbis; (foreground) Getty Images

Library in Congress Cataloging-in-Publication Data
Main entry under title: Annual Editions: Psychology 2008/2009 (2009 update).
 1. Psychology—Periodicals. I. Duffy, Karen G., *comp.* II. Title: Psychology
658'.05

www.mhhe.com

Preface

In publishing ANNUAL EDITIONS we recognize the enormous role played by the magazines, newspapers, and journals of the public press in providing current, first-rate educational information in a broad spectrum of interest areas. Many of these articles are appropriate for students, researchers, and professionals seeking accurate, current material to help bridge the gap between principles and theories and the real world. These articles, however, become more useful for study when those of lasting value are carefully collected, organized, indexed, and reproduced in a low-cost format, which provides easy and permanent access when the material is needed. That is the role played by ANNUAL EDITIONS.

Ronnie's parents couldn't understand why he didn't want to be picked up and cuddled as did his older sister when she was a baby. As an infant, Ronnie did not respond to his parents' smiles, words, or attempts to amuse him. By the age of two, Ronnie's parents knew that he was not like other children. He spoke no English, was very temperamental, and often rocked himself for hours. Ronnie is autistic. His parents feel that some of Ronnie's behavior may be their fault. As young professionals, they both work long hours and leave both of their children with an older woman during the work week. Ronnie's pediatrician assures his parents that their reasoning does not hold merit, because the causes of autism are little understood and are likely to be biological rather than parental. What can we do about children like Ronnie? From where does autism come? Can autism be treated or reversed? Can autism be prevented?

Psychologists attempt to answer these and other complex questions with scientific methods. Researchers, using carefully planned research designs, try to discover the causes of complex human behavior—normal or not. The scientific results of psychological research typically are published in professional journals, and therefore may be difficult for the lay person to understand.

Annual Editions: Psychology 08/09 is designed to meet the needs of lay people and introductory level students who are curious about psychology. This Annual Edition provides a vast selection of readable and informative articles primarily from popular magazines and newspapers. These articles are typically written by journalists, but a few are written by psychologists with writing styles that are clear yet retain the excitement of the discovery of scientific knowledge.

The particular articles selected for this volume were chosen to be representative of the most current work in psychology. They were selected because they provide examples of the types of psychological research and issues discussed in most introductory psychology classes.

As in any science, some of the topics discussed in this collection are startling, while others confirm what we already know. Some articles invite speculation about social and personal issues; others encourage careful thought about potential misuse of research findings. You are expected to make the investment of effort and critical reasoning necessary to answer such questions and concerns.

I assume that you will find this collection of articles readable and useful. I suggest that you look at the organization of this book and compare it to the organization of your textbook and course syllabus. By examining the topic guide provided after the table of contents, you can identify those articles most appropriate for any particular unit of study in your course. Your instructor may provide some help in this effort or assign articles to supplement the text. As you read the articles, try to connect their contents with the principles you are learning from your text and classroom lectures. Some of the articles will help you better understand a specific area of psychology, while others are designed to help you connect and integrate information from diverse research areas. Both of these strategies are important in learning about psychology or any other science; it is only through intensive investigation and subsequent integration of the findings from many studies that we are able to discover and apply new knowledge.

Please take time to provide us with some feedback to guide the annual revision of this anthology by completing and returning the article rating form in the back of the book. With your help, this collection will be even better next year. Thank you.

Karen Grover Duffy

Karen Grover Duffy
Editor

Contents

UNIT 1
The Science of Psychology

UNIT 2
Biological Bases of Behavior

The concepts in bold italics are developed in the article. For further expansion, please refer to the Topic Guide.

UNIT 3
Perceptual Processes

The concepts in bold italics are developed in the article. For further expansion, please refer to the Topic Guide.

UNIT 4
Learning and Remembering

UNIT 5
Cognitive Processes

The concepts in bold italics are developed in the article. For further expansion, please refer to the Topic Guide.

UNIT 6
Emotion and Motivation

UNIT 7
Development

The concepts in bold italics are developed in the article. For further expansion, please refer to the Topic Guide.

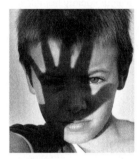

UNIT 8
Personality Processes

UNIT 9
Social Processes

The concepts in bold italics are developed in the article. For further expansion, please refer to the Topic Guide.

UNIT 10
Psychological Disorders

The concepts in bold italics are developed in the article. For further expansion, please refer to the Topic Guide.

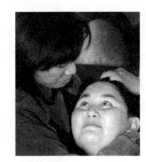

UNIT 11
Psychological Treatments

The concepts in bold italics are developed in the article. For further expansion, please refer to the Topic Guide.

Correlation Guide

This convenient guide matches the units in Annual Editions: Psychology, 38/e with the corresponding chapters in three of our best-selling McGraw-Hill Psychology textbooks by Robert S. Feldman and Michael W. Passer.

Annual Editions: Psychology, 38/e (ISBN: 007339775X)	Essentials of Understanding Psychology, 7/e (ISBN: 0073405493)	Understanding Psychology, 8/e (ISBN: 0073531936)	Psychology: The Science of Mind and Behavior, 4/e (ISBN: 0073382760)
Unit 1: The Science of Psychology	**Chapter 1:** Introduction to Psychology	**Chapter 1:** Introduction to Psychology **Chapter 2:** Psychological Research	**Chapter 1:** The Science of Psychology
Unit 2: Biological Bases of Behavior	**Chapter 2:** Neuroscience and Behavior	**Chapter 3:** Neuroscience and Behavior	**Chapter 2:** Studying Behavior Scientifically **Chapter 3:** Genes, Environment and Behavior **Chapter 4:** The Brain and Behavior
Unit 3: Perceptual Processes	**Chapter 3:** Sensation and Perception **Chapter 4:** States of Consciousness	**Chapter 4:** Sensation and Perception **Chapter 5:** States of Consciousness	**Chapter 5:** Sensation and Perception **Chapter 6:** States of Consciousness
Unit 4: Learning and Remembering	**Chapter 5:** Learning **Chapter 6:** Memory	**Chapter 6:** Learning **Chapter 7:** Memory	**Chapter 7:** Learning and Adaptation **Chapter 8:** Memory
Unit 5: Cognitive Processes	**Chapter 7:** Thinking, Language, and Intelligence	**Chapter 8:** Cognition and Language **Chapter 9:** Intelligence	**Chapter 9:** Language and Thinking **Chapter 10:** Intelligence
Unit 6: Emotion and Motivation	**Chapter 8:** Motivation and Emotion	**Chapter 10:** Motivation and Emotion	**Chapter 11:** Motivation and Emotion
Unit 7: Development	**Chapter 9:** Development **Chapter 11:** Health Psychology	**Chapter 12:** Development **Chapter 14:** Health Psychology	**Chapter 12:** Development Over the Life Span **Chapter 14:** Adjusting to Life
Unit 8: Personality Processes	**Chapter 10:** Personality	**Chapter 13:** Personality	**Chapter 13:** Personality
Unit 9: Social Processes	**Chapter 14:** Social Psychology	**Chapter 17:** Social Psychology	**Chapter 17:** Social Thinking and Behavior
Unit 10: Psychological Disorders	**Chapter 12:** Psychological Disorders	**Chapter 15:** Psychological Disorders	**Chapter 15:** Psychological Disorders
Unit 11: Psychological Treatments	**Chapter 13:** Treatment of Psychological Disorders	**Chapter 16:** Treatment of Psychological Disorders	**Chapter 16:** Treatment of Psychological Disorders

Topic Guide

This topic guide suggests how the selections in this book relate to the subjects covered in your course. You may want to use the topics listed on these pages to search the Web more easily.

On the following pages a number of Web sites have been gathered specifically for this book. They are arranged to reflect the units of this *Annual Edition*. You can link to these sites by going to the student online support site at *http://www.mhcls.com/online/*.

ALL THE ARTICLES THAT RELATE TO EACH TOPIC ARE LISTED BELOW THE BOLD-FACED TERM.

xiv

Internet References

The following Internet sites have been carefully researched and selected to support the articles found in this reader. The easiest way to access these selected sites is to go to our student online support site at *http://www.mhcls.com/online/*.

AE: Psychology 08/09

The following sites were available at the time of publication. Visit our Web site—we update our student online support site regularly to reflect any changes.

General Sources

APA Resources for the Public
http://www.apa.org/psychnet/

Use the site map or search engine to access APA Monitor, the American Psychological Association newspaper, APA books on a wide range of topics, PsychINFO, an electronic database of abstracts on scholarly journals, and the HelpCenter.

Health Information Resources
http://www.health.gov/nhic/Pubs/tollfree.htm

Here is a long list of toll-free numbers that provide health-related information. None offer diagnosis and treatment, but some do offer recorded information; others provide personalized counseling, referrals, and/or written materials.

Mental Help Net
http://mentalhelp.net

This comprehensive guide to mental health online features more than 6,300 individual resources. Information on mental disorders and professional resources in psychology, psychiatry, and social work is presented.

Psychology: Online Resource Central
http://www.psych-central.com

Thousands of psychology resources are currently indexed at this site. Psychology disciplines, conditions and disorders, and self-development are among the most useful.

School Psychology Resources Online
http://www.schoolpsychology.net

Numerous sites on special conditions, disorders, and disabilities, as well as other data ranging from assessment/evaluation to research, are available on this resource page for psychologists, parents, and educators.

Social Psychology Network
http://www.socialpsychology.org

The Social Psychology Network is the most comprehensive source of social psychology information on the Internet, including resources, programs, and research.

UNIT 1: The Science of Psychology

Abraham A. Brill Library
http://plaza.interport.net/nypsan/service.html

Containing data on over 40,000 books, periodicals, and reprints in psychoanalysis and related fields, the Abraham A. Brill Library has holdings that span the literature of psychoanalysis from its beginning to the present day.

American Psychological Society (APS)
http://www.psychologicalscience.org/about/links.html

The APS is dedicated to advancing the best of scientific psychology in research, application, and the improvement of human conditions. Links to teaching, research, and graduate studies resources are available.

Psychological Research on the Net
http://psych.hanover.edu/Research/exponnet.html

This Net site provides psychologically related experiments. Biological psychology/neuropsychology, clinical psychology, cognition, developmental psychology, emotions, health psychology, personality, sensation/perception, and social psychology are some of the areas covered.

UNIT 2: Biological Bases of Behavior

Institute for Behavioral Genetics
http://ibgwww.colorado.edu/index.html

Dedicated to conducting and facilitating research on the genetic and environmental bases of individual differences in behavior, this organized research unit at the University of Colorado leads to genetic sites, statistical sites, and the Biology Meta Index, as well as to search engines.

Serendip
http://serendip.brynmawr.edu/serendip/

Serendip, which is organized into five subject areas (brain and behavior, complex systems, genes and behavior, science and culture, and science education), contains interactive exhibits, articles, links to other resources, and a forum area.

UNIT 3: Perceptual Processes

Five Senses Home Page
http://www.sedl.org/scimath/pasopartners/senses/welcome.html

This elementary lesson examines the five senses and gives a list of references that may be useful.

Psychology Tutorials and Demonstrations
http://psych.hanover.edu/Krantz/tutor.html

Interactive tutorials and simulations, primarily in the area of sensation and perception, are available here.

UNIT 4: Learning and Remembering

Mind Tools
http://www.psychwww.com/mtsite/

Useful information on stress management can be found at this Web site.

www.mhcls.com/online/

The Opportunity of Adolescence
http://www.winternet.com/~webpage/adolescencepaper.html

According to this paper, adolescence is the turning point, after which the future is redirected and confirmed. The opportunities and problems of this period are presented with quotations from Erik Erikson, Jean Piaget, and others.

Project Zero
http://pzweb.harvard.edu

The Harvard Project Zero has investigated the development of learning processes in children and adults for 30 years. Today, Project Zero's mission is to understand and enhance learning, thinking, and creativity in the arts and other disciplines for individuals and institutions.

UNIT 5: Cognitive Processes

American Association for Artificial Intelligence (AAAI)
http://www.aaai.org/AITopics/index.html

This AAAI site provides a good starting point to learn about artificial intelligence (AI)—what artificial intelligence is and what AI scientists do.

Chess: Kasparov v. Deep Blue: The Rematch
http://www.chess.ibm.com/home/html/b.html

Clips from the chess rematch between Garry Kasparov and IBM's supercomputer, Deep Blue, are presented here along with commentaries on chess, computers, artificial intelligence, and what it all means.

UNIT 6: Emotion and Motivation

Emotional Intelligence Discovery
http://www.cwrl.utexas.edu/~bump/Hu305/3/3/3/

This site has been set up by students to talk about and expand on Daniel Goleman's book, Emotional Intelligence. There are links to many other EI sites.

John Suler's Teaching Clinical Psychology Site
http://www.rider.edu/users/suler/tcp.html

This page contains Internet resources for clinical and abnormal psychology, behavioral medicine, and mental health.

Nature vs. Nurture: Gergen Dialogue
with Winifred Gallagher
http://www.pbs.org/newshour/gergen/gallagher_5-14.html

Experience modifies temperament, according to this TV interview. The author of I.D.: How Heredity and Experience Make You Who You Are explains a current theory about temperament.

UNIT 7: Development

American Association for Child and Adolescent Psychiatry
http://www.aacap.org

This site is designed to aid in the understanding and treatment of the developmental, behavioral, and mental disorders that could affect children and adolescents. There is a specific link just for families about common childhood problems that may or may not require professional intervention.

Behavioral Genetics
http://www.ornl.gov/hgmis/elsi/behavior.html

This government-backed Web site includes helpful information on behavioral genetics.

UNIT 8: Personality Processes

The Personality Project
http://personality-project.org/personality.html

This Personality Project (by William Revelle) is meant to guide those interested in personality theory and research to the current personality research literature.

UNIT 9: Social Processes

National Clearinghouse for Alcohol and Drug Information
http://ncadi.samhsa.gov

Information on drug and alcohol facts that might relate to adolescence and the issues of peer pressure and youth culture is presented here. Resources, referrals, research and statistics, databases, and related Net links are available.

Nonverbal Behavior and Nonverbal Communication
http://www3.usal.es/~nonverbal/

This Web site has a detailed listing of nonverbal behavior and nonverbal communication sites, including the work of historical and current researchers.

UNIT 10: Psychological Disorders

American Association of Suicidology
http://www.suicidology.org

The American Association of Suicidology is a nonprofit organization dedicated to the understanding and prevention of suicide. This site is designed as a resource to anyone concerned about suicide.

Ask NOAH About: Mental Health
http://www.noah-health.org/en/mental/

Information about child and adolescent family problems, mental conditions and disorders, suicide prevention, and much more is available here.

Mental Health Net Disorders and Treatments
http://www.mentalhelp.net/

Presented on this site are hotlinks to psychological disorders pages, which include anxiety, panic, phobic disorders, schizophrenia, and violent/self-destructive behaviors.

Mental Health Net: Eating Disorder Resources
http://www.mentalhelp.net/poc/center_index.php/id/46

This mental health Net site provides a complete list of Web references on eating disorders, including anorexia, bulimia, and obesity.

National Women's Health Resource Center (NWHRC)
http://www.healthywomen.org

NWHRC's site contains links to resources related to women's substance abuse and mental illnesses.

UNIT 11: Psychological Treatments

The C.G. Jung Page
http://www.cgjungpage.org

Dedicated to the work of Carl Jung, this is a comprehensive resource, with links to Jungian psychology, news and opinions, reference materials, graduate programs, dreams, multilingual sites, and related Jungian themes.

Knowledge Exchange Network (KEN)
http://www.mentalhealth.org

Information about mental health (prevention, treatment, and rehabilitation services) is available via toll-free telephone services, an electronic bulletin board, and publications.

NetPsychology
http://netpsych.com/index.htm

This site explores the uses of the Internet to deliver mental health services. This is a basic cybertherapy resource site.

Sigmund Freud and the Freud Archives
http://plaza.interport.net/nypsan/freudarc.html

Internet resources related to Sigmund Freud, which include a collection of libraries, museums, and biographical materials, as well as the Brill Library archives, can be found here.

We highly recommend that you review our Web site for expanded information and our other product lines. We are continually updating and adding links to our Web site in order to offer you the most usable and useful information that will support and expand the value of your Annual Editions. You can reach us at: *http://www.mhcls.com/annualeditions/.*

UNIT 1

The Science of Psychology

Unit Selections

Key Points to Consider

- What is psychology? Why study psychology?

- What exactly do psychologists do? Are there different types of psychology?

- How does psychology make a difference in day-to-day life?

- How can we distinguish good science from pseudoscience?

- Can psychological research be biased? How so?

- What can we do to diminish the effects of any bias in psychological research?

Student Web Site

www.mhcls.com/online

Internet References

Further information regarding these Web sites may be found in this book's preface or online.

Abraham A. Brill Library
http://plaza.interport.net/nypsan/service.html
American Psychological Society (APS)
http://www.psychologicalscience.org/about/links.html
Psychological Research on the Net
http://psych.hanover.edu/Research/exponnet.html

Little did Wilhelm Wundt realize his monumental contribution to science when in 1879 in Germany, he opened the first psychological laboratory to examine consciousness. Wundt would barely recognize modern psychology compared to the way he practiced it.

Contemporary psychology is defined *as the science of individual mental activity and behavior.* This definition reflects the two parent disciplines from which psychology emerged: philosophy and biology. Compared to its parents, psychology is very much a new discipline. Some aspects of modern psychology are particularly biological, such as neuroscience, perception, psychophysics, and behavioral genetics. Other aspects are more philosophical, such as the study of personality, while still other areas within psychology approximate sociology, as does social psychology.

Today's psychologists work in a variety of settings. Many psychologists are academics, teaching and researching psychology on university campuses. Others work in applied settings such as hospitals, mental health clinics, industry, and schools. Most psychologists specialize in psychology only after graduate training. Industrial psychologists specialize in human performance in organizational settings, while clinical psychologists are concerned about the assessment, diagnosis, and treatment of individuals with a variety of mental disorders. Each specialty typically requires a graduate education and sometimes requires a license to practice.

Since its establishment, the field has expanded into many different areas. As mentioned above, some areas are very practical. Other areas appear to emphasize theory and research. Growing pains in the field resulted in conflict over what the agenda of the first national psychological association, the American Psychological Association, should be. Because academics perceived this association as mainly serving practitioners, academics and researchers established their own competing association, the American Psychological Society that eventually changed its name to the Association for Psychological Science. Despite its varied nature and sporadic development, psychology remains a viable and exciting field.

The first unit of the book is designed to introduce you to the study and history of psychology. An excellent article, based on an important question, begins this anthology. It asks "Why Study Psychology?" Four renowned psychologists from various areas of the discipline reveal why they became psychologists and how they currently use their knowledge of the field. Perhaps their revelations will inspire you to pursue psychology, too.

The second article addresses another cogent question, "Does Psychology Make a Significant Difference in Our Lives?" Noted psychologist Philip Zimbardo answers the question with a resoundingly affirmative answer. He suggests that we should "give away" psychology so that the general public knows more about important issues such as how to prevent AIDS and how to become better parents.

The third article by Scott O. Lilienfeld explicates the differences between science and pseudoscience and between psychology and popular psychology (as often found in the mass media). Although the article was written for professors, it is highly readable and important to beginning students of psychology because of its emphasis on exactly which dimensions produce high quality science.

The final article of this unit specifically pertains to research in the field of psychology. Morton Ann Gernsbacher casts a critical eye on some of the research. She asserts that psychological research is often filled with bias by means of the language researchers use and the slanted interpretation of their findings. The bias generally occurs against female and minority participants. Gernsbacher would be remiss if she did not offer tips about how to uncover and, importantly, how to prevent such biases from creeping into our science.

Why Study Psychology?

Why did psychology's leading researchers take that first course?
Was it the compelling advice of a master? Perhaps a sudden [epiphany]?
Why Did You Study Psychology?
There probably are as many reasons as there are people in the field.
In this series, leading psychology researchers talk about getting into science.

Developing a Supertaste

Linda M. Bartoshuk
Yale University School of Medicine
PhD 1965 from Brown University

As a kid growing up in Aberdeen, South Dakota, I read science fiction and dreamed of astronomy. Junior high had a career day; students got to interview members of the profession to which they aspired. I asked for a scientist, but was assigned to interview a secretary.

In high school, when I signed up for math and science, my guidance counselor suggested these were unrealistic choices, but relented when I agreed to take bookkeeping and typing. Fifty-four words a minute later (not bad in the world before word processors) I still preferred trigonometry.

When it came time for college, I came in second in a math contest and won a slide rule (for anyone who has never used one, they are amazing little devices). I headed to Rapid City to tour the South Dakota School of Mines and Technology. Women were welcomed but few went, and I was not attracted to the prospect. Carleton College had a telescope and an astronomy major. The cost was daunting but a National Merit Scholarship came to my aid and I was off. Again, few women turned up in math and science, but we were treated well by our instructors.

Not so in the real world. I learned that some observatories banned women from using the telescopes; those big, complex machines were too much for us. I had had it. I remember the night my roommate and I sat with the Carleton course book and discovered that a psychology major would give me credit for all the math and science I had taken. Wow! As a junior I signed up for introductory psychology taught by John Bare, the new department chair. The class scintillated. When we got to psychophysics, I knew I was home. Astronomy had taught me that measurement of the perceived brightness of stars played a role in measuring the size of the universe. The farther away the star, the dimmer it appears from earth. If we only knew how bright it was at the source, we could calculate the distance.

Discovering that some supertasters live in neon taste worlds has brought me full circle.

One of the few women in astronomy provided the missing link; some stars pulse and we can see their brightness wax and wane. Theory related the periodicity of the pulsation to the absolute brightness of the star. We had the size of the universe! John Bare sent me to Brown University to study taste with his mentor, Carl Pfaffmann. Discovering that some supertasters live in neon taste worlds compared to non tasters (like me) who live in pastel taste worlds has brought me full circle. We cannot share experiences, so how could we discover that taste is more vivid to some? The missing link was a standard. If we could find some sensation that was not correlated with taste, everyone could express taste intensities relative to that standard. Assuming any variability in perception of the standard to be roughly equal across groups, we could compare tastes across groups. To my delight, one of the best standards we have tested is the brightness of the sun.

An APS Fellow and Charter Member, Bartoshuk has served on the APS Board of Directors. She will give the Bring the Family Address at the 16th Annual Convention.

The Children Come First

Patrice Marie Miller
Salem State College
EdD 1988 from Harvard University

It is hard to choose a major or a career when you have never really been exposed to it. Thinking back, though, it seems as if the issues that I am involved in as a developmental psychologist started as early as ninth grade. At that time, I was living in Rio de Janeiro, Brazil. Rio, then as now, was a city full of natural beauty and poverty. In the ninth grade I worked on a project started by my history professor, in which we visited one of the *favelas* (the hillside slums) on Saturdays and engaged in games and crafts activities with the children. The idea was to try and have a positive impact on their development by giving them something constructive to do and some contact with other models for doing things.

Based on that experience, I decided that I wanted to do something that would have a positive impact on the lives of children, especially poor children. In high school and the early years of college, I tried different ways of having an impact on the lives of children, such as tutoring in East Harlem and working as a teacher's assistant. I enjoyed these experiences in many ways, but I felt as if we did not know enough about how children developed to know how best to help them.

I decided that I wanted to do something that would have a positive impact on the lives of children, especially poor children.

My senior year at New York University, I was still wondering what to do. I thought I might teach for a few years—perhaps back in Rio—while I figured out my future. The August before senior year, while at a psychological meeting with my mother, a school psychologist, I met a professor teaching behavior analysis at NYU. Second semester of that year, I worked with him on a research project involving autistic children. This experience pushed me into thinking of a different kind of career, one as an academic psychologist. I enjoy the problem solving involved in planning, carrying out, analyzing and writing up research. Thinking out issues and having things work out the way you had hoped is a special kind of thrill that I only experienced when I began to do research.

When I finished my BA, I still was not ready to forge ahead. First, I had to go back and learn some of the mathematics I had managed to duck. During this time, I worked on several research projects, along with my psychologist husband (surely, also, a reinforcing influence in all this). When we moved to Cambridge, Massachusetts, I obtained my doctorate in human development from Harvard's Graduate School of Education. My dissertation on very young infants' reactions to being taken care of by a stranger versus their mother was an attempt to look at whether and in what ways young infants differentiated between their mothers and other caregivers. It was the first of several projects I have been engaged in since on early social and emotional development of children. Teaching, which I also do, allows me to communicate some of my passions to newer students.

The way I think about it now is that my work ideally combines intellectual activities that I greatly enjoy, with an opportunity to work on issues in a field that, as a whole, I believe makes a difference in the lives of children.

Miller is a developmental psychologist specializing in social and emotional development.

Clinical Cognition

Teresa A. Treat
Yale University
PhD 2000 from Indiana University

Throughout my undergraduate and graduate years at Indiana University, I was inspired by Dick McFall's vision of an integrative psychological science. Dick spoke eloquently about a new generation of clinical scientists who were fully trained in both clinical and cognitive science, or in clinical and neural science, such that they were viewed as legitimate in both fields. And he wondered whether such hybrid scholars would view psychopathology from a novel vantage that might help to move forward our understanding, assessment, and treatment of psychological problems. I tested the waters by taking a mathematical psychology course with Jim Townsend during my first year in the clinical-science program. The course damn near killed me—granted, this is not an uncommon experience in a Townsend course—but Jim was unfailing in his support and encouragement, and I emerged with numerous ill-formed notions about the potential utility of formal mathematical modeling of clinically relevant cognitive processing.

In the meantime, McFall, Rick Viken, and I had begun developing photo stimulus sets that would allow us to use cognitive science models and methods to investigate men's perceptions of women's sexual interest (with implications for our understanding of acquaintance-initiated sexual aggression), as well as women's perceptions of other women's shape- and weight-related information (with implications for our understanding of eating disorders). The resulting photo stimulus sets were a far cry from the simpler, well-controlled stimuli that cognitive scientists typically used to investigate normative cognitive processes. Thus, it was unclear whether the principles and paradigms developed in this more highly controlled context would generalize to the messiness of investigations of clinically relevant individual differences in complex social perception.

As the work progressed, I became accustomed to hearing cognitive scientists insist that "those are the most uncontrolled stimuli I've ever seen!" In contrast, of course, many clinical scientists claimed that they were "the most over-controlled stimuli" they'd ever seen. Fortunately Rob Nosofsky, John Kruschke, and David MacKay—as well as two extremely gifted graduate students at the time, Tom Palmeri and Mike Erickson—worked with us every step of the way on these two lines of research and spent countless hours training me in the rudiments of multidimensional scaling, formal models of categorization and learning, and computational modeling.

Eventually, I had completed all the coursework necessary for a joint degree in clinical and cognitive science, but I had yet to declare my additional major. It felt presumptuous to call myself a clinical-cognitive scientist, because that implied that I was a "real" cognitive scientist as well as a "real" clinical scientist. The latter had been a central piece of my academic identity for years, but I had yet to recognize the former. Three years of working side by side with cognitive students in Kruschke's lab finally changed this. And then one day, when I was musing out loud in the lab about whether to declare the joint degree, one of my lab mates challenged me by saying, "What's wrong with you? You're as much a cognitive scientist as the rest of us." Soon thereafter, I remember nervously marching upstairs to the cognitive-science office to officially declare the joint major and choose a career as a clinical-cognitive scientist—long after I already was living and loving a career in McFall's "integrative psychological science."

Treat is a clinical and counseling psychologist who specializes in cognitive science.

Redefining a Career

Milton D. Hakel
Bowling Green State University
PhD 1966 from the University of Minnesota

It wasn't pretty. It wasn't easy. But especially in the perspective offered by the passage of over 40 years, choosing a major, then choosing to pursue graduate study, and then deciding study for the PhD was a chaotic, sometimes frantic, and always exciting process.

As a teen, I knew I wanted to go to college, but I had no clear direction in mind. When I was a high school junior, I wanted to go anyplace but the University of Minnesota. After investigating the costs, and considering my grades (which made me a weak competitor for scholarships), dissonance reduction worked its magic and I applied only to the University of Minnesota. It was a fortunate application (and acceptance), and I have always appreciated the excellent and challenging education I received there.

As an undergraduate beginning in 1959, I ran through a succession of 12 declared and undeclared majors, hoping to find something that could suit me for the long run. Some majors lasted as little as three weeks, until I got the results of a mid-term or final that I interpreted as a signal to apply my efforts elsewhere. Other majors lasted much longer, and I graduated with a double major in philosophy and psychology. But by my senior year I knew I wanted to pursue graduate study in psychology. Many small but significant events led to that career direction.

As a third-quarter freshman, I talked my way into a limited-enrollment honors section of an introductory laboratory course (my grades put me just below the formal cut score). The course offered hands-on experience in research. In trios we collected data to replicate a one trial learning experiment originally published by William K. Estes, and individually we analyzed and reported the findings. I concluded that I could learn how to design and conduct research. All three of us in my group eventually earned PhDs, and it was a special pleasure many years later to actually meet Estes, when he became the editor of *Psychological Science* (I was part of the original APS Publication Committee that invited him to be the founding editor).

As a junior I quit commuting and moved on campus, meeting that first day a delightful and spirited woman who became my wife within a year. I took two courses in individual differences; in retrospect, they are the most important courses I ever

had—thank you Jim Jenkins and Marv Dunnette. The issues I first studied there continue to animate scientific discourse and public policy: testing and learning, heritability, group differences. I also took a course in vocational guidance, and heard about "varch" as an attribute of a career, variety, and change. I knew this was what I wanted, and guessed that a career in research would offer it.

In defining my career I redefined a few key words: chaos, frantic, excitement.

I hung out in the psychology building, getting to know graduate students and some faculty. When an opening occurred for an undergraduate teaching assistant (they needed someone to sharpen mark-sense pencils and do other tasks too menial for graduate students), I applied and got the job, and my exposure to psychology and psychologists expanded.

As a senior in 1962–63 I did a voluntary research project under Dunnette's guidance. The work I did in that "job sample" was sufficient as a demonstration of capability to get me into graduate school. I applied to only one, but my grades and scores were borderline, so I was admitted on probation (the US Air Force was my other "employment" option, and one could already see that the Vietnam War was getting ugly). The senior project eventually became my first publication.

In graduate school to pursue a master's, I found it considerably surprising when I was invited at the end of my first year to bypass the MA and work directly toward the doctorate. I became interested in how people form impressions of others and use those impressions to make consequential decisions, such as who to hire. The topic was partly a consequence of having been interviewed by about 50 different potential employers (and being rejected by 40 of them) while looking for summer jobs. I completed the degree, and research that Dunnette and I proposed was supported by the National Science Foundation in 1966. I stayed at Minnesota for two years as a postdoc, and then moved to Ohio State, Houston, and Bowling Green.

My experiences sensitized me to the fallibility of predictors and the need to devise effective and equitable systems for 1) selecting employees/admitting students, and 2) enabling people to develop their capabilities fully. These continue to be engaging issues.

So in defining my career I redefined a few key words. Chaos—going from no direction through 12 majors to one. Frantic—marrying while still an undergraduate, having two children while in graduate school, and worrying about employment and the draft raised occasional anxieties. Excitement—enough for a lifetime, and that was just the beginning.

Hankel is an APS Fellow and Charter Member and has served on the APS Board of Directors. He is an industrial/organizational psychologist.

Does Psychology Make a Significant Difference in Our Lives?

The intellectual tension between the virtues of basic versus applied research that characterized an earlier era of psychology is being replaced by an appreciation of creative applications of all research essential to improving the quality of human life. Psychologists are positioned to "give psychology away" to all those who can benefit from our wisdom. Psychologists were not there 35 years ago when American Psychological Association (APA) President George Miller first encouraged us to share our knowledge with the public. The author argues that psychology is indeed making a significant difference in people's lives; this article provides a sampling of evidence demonstrating how and why psychology matters, both in pervasive ways and specific applications. Readers are referred to a newly developed APA Web site that documents current operational uses of psychological research, theory, and methodology (its creation has been the author's primary presidential initiative): www.psychologymatters.org.

PHILIP G. ZIMBARDO

Does psychology matter? Does what we do, and have done for a hundred years or more, really make a significant difference in the lives of individuals or in the functioning of communities and nations? Can we demonstrate that our theories, our research, our professional practice, our methodologies, our way of thinking about mind, brain, and behavior make life better in any measurable way? Has what we have to show for our discipline been applied in the real world beyond academia and practitioners' offices to improve health, education, welfare, safety, organizational effectiveness, and more?

Such questions, and finding their answers, have always been my major personal and professional concern. First, as an introductory psychology teacher for nearly six decades, I have always worked to prove relevance as well as essence of psychology to my students. Next, as an author of the now classic basic text, *Psychology and Life* (Ruch & Zimbardo, 1971), which claimed to wed psychology to life applications, I constantly sought to put more psychology in our lives and more life in our psychology (Gerrig & Zimbardo, 2004; Zimbardo, 1992). To reach an even broader student audience, I have coauthored *Core Concepts in Psychology* (Zimbardo, Weber, & Johnson, 2002) that strives to bring the excitement of scientific and applied psychology to students in state and community colleges.

In order to further expand the audience for what is best in psychology, I accepted an invitation to help create, be scientific advisor for, and narrator of the 26-program PBS TV series, *Discovering Psychology* (1990/2001). For this general public audience, we have provided answers—as viewable

instances—to their "so what?" questions. This award-winning series is shown both nationally and internationally (in at least 10 nations) and has been the foundation for the most popular telecourse among all the Annenberg CPB Foundation's many academic programs (see www.learner.org). Finally, as the 2002 president of the American Psychological Association, my major initiative became developing a compendium of exemplars of how psychology has made a significant difference in our lives. This Web-based summary of "psychology in applied action" has been designed as a continually modifiable and updateable repository of demonstrable evidence of psychological knowledge in meaningful applications. In a later section of this article, the compendium will be described more fully and some of its examples highlighted.

I was fortunate in my graduate training at Yale University (1954–1960) to be inspired by three exceptional mentors, each of whom modeled a different aspect of the relevance and applicability of basic psychology to vital issues facing individuals and our society. Carl Hovland developed the Yale Communication and Attitude Change Program after coming out of his military assignment in World War II of analyzing the effectiveness of propaganda and training programs (Hovland, Lumsdaine, & Sheffield, 1949). He went on to transform what was at that time a complex, global, and vague study of communication and persuasion into identifiable processes, discrete variables, and integrative hypotheses that made possible both experimental research and applications (Hovland, Janis, & Kelley, 1953). Neal Miller always straddled the fence between basic and applied research, despite being known for his classic experimental and theoretical formulations of motivation and reward in learning and conditioning. His World War II experience of training pilots to overcome fears so that they could return to combat was an applied precursor of his later role in developing biofeedback through his laboratory investigations of conditioning autonomic nervous system responses (N. E. Miller, 1978, 1985, 1992). The last of my Yale mentors, Seymour Sarason, moved out from his research program on test anxiety in children into the community as one of the founders of Community Psychology (Sarason, 1974). It was a daring move at that time in a field that honored only the scientific study of *individual* behavior.

Psychology of the 50s was also a field that honored basic research well above applied research, which was typically accorded second-class status, if not denigrated by the "experimentalists," a popular brand name in that era. Psychology at many major universities aspired to be "soft physics," as in the heady days of our Germanic forebears, Wundt, Fechner, Ebbinghaus, Titchner, and others (see Green, Shore, & Teo, 2001). Anything applied was seen at best as crude social engineering by tinkerers, not real thinkers. Moreover, behaviorism was still rampant, with animal models that stripped away from learning what nonsense syllable memory researchers had deleted from memory—merely the context, the content, the human meaning, and the culture of behavior. The most prominent psychologist from the 50s through the 80s, B.F. Skinner, was an anomaly in this regard. Half of him remained a Watsonian radical behaviorist who refused to admit the existence of either motivation or cognition into his psychology (Skinner, 1938, 1966, 1974). Meanwhile, the other Skinner side applied operant conditioning principles to train pigeons for military duties and outlined a behaviorist Utopia in *Walden Two* (Skinner, 1948).

Giving Psychology Away: The Call for Societal Accountability

And then along came George Miller whose American Psychological Association (APA) presidential address in 1969 stunned the psychological establishment because one of its own firstborn sons committed the heresy of exhorting them to go public, get real, get down, give it up, and be relevant. Well, that is the way I think I heard it back then when George Miller (1969) told his audience that it was time to begin "to give psychology away to the public." It was time to stop talking only to other psychologists. It was time to stop writing only for professional journals hidden away in library stacks. It was time to go beyond the endless quest for experimental rigor in the perfectly designed study to test a theoretically derived hypothesis. Maybe it was time to begin finding answers to the kinds of questions your mother asked about why people acted the way they did. Perhaps it was acceptable to start considering how best to translate what we knew into a language that most ordinary citizens could understand and even come to appreciate.

I for one applauded George Miller's stirring call to action for all these reasons. It was heady for me because I believed

that coming from such a distinguished serious theorist and researcher—not some do-gooder, liberal communitarian whom the establishment could readily dismiss—his message would have a big impact in our field Sadly, the banner raised by Miller's inspirational speech, did not fly very high over most psychology departments for many years to come. Why not? I think for four reasons: Excessive modesty about *what* psychology really had of value to offer the public, ignorance about *who* was "the public," cluelessness about *how* to go about the mission of giving psychology away, and lack of sufficient concern about *why* psychology needed to be accountable to the public.

How shall we counterargue against such reasoning? First, scanning the breadth and depth of our field makes apparent that there is no need for such professional modesty. Rather, the time has come to be overtly proud of our past and current accomplishments, as I will try to demonstrate here. We have much to be proud of in our heritage and in our current accomplishments. Second, the public starts with our students, our clients, and our patients and extends to our funding agencies, national and local politicians, all nonpsychologists, and the media. And it also means your mother whose "bubba psychology" sometimes needs reality checks based on solid evidence we have gathered. Third, it is essential to recognize that the media are the gatekeepers between the best, relevant psychology we want to give away and that elusive public we hope will value what we have to offer. We need to learn how best to utilize the different kinds of media that are most appropriate for delivering specific messages to particular target audiences that we want to reach. Psychologists need to learn how to write effective brief press releases, timely op-ed newspaper essays, interesting articles for popular magazines, valuable trade books based on empirical evidence, and how best to give radio, TV, and print interviews. Simple awareness of media needs makes evident, for example, that TV requires visual images, therefore, we should be able to provide video records of research, our interventions, or other aspects of the research or therapeutic process that will form a story's core.

"Media smarts" also means realizing that to reach adolescents with a helpful message (that is empirically validated), a brief public service announcement on MTV or an article in a teen magazine will have a broader impact than detailed journal articles or even popular books on the subject.[1] Thus, it becomes essential to our mission of making the public wiser consumers of psychological knowledge to learn how to communicate effectively to the media and to work with the media.

Finally, we can challenge the fourth consideration regarding societal accountability with the awareness that taxpayers fund much of our research as well as some of the education of our graduate students. It is imperative that we convey the sense to the citizens of our states and nation that we are responsive to society's needs and, further, that we feel responsible for finding solutions to some of its problems (Zimbardo, 1975). It has become standard operating procedure for most granting agencies now to require a statement about the potential societal value of any proposed research. That does not mean that all research must be applied to dealing with current social or individual problems because there is considerable evidence that research that originally seemed esoterically "basic" has in time found valuable applications (see Swazey, 1974). It does mean that although some of our colleagues begin with a focus on a problem in an applied domain, the others who start with an eye on theory testing or understanding some basic phenomena should feel obligated to stretch their imaginations by considering potential applications of their knowledge. I believe we have much worthy applicable psychology, basic research, theory, and methodology that is awaiting creative transformations to become valuable applied psychology.

The Profound and Pervasive Impact of Past Psychological Knowledge

Before I outline some recent, specific instances of how psychological research, theory, and methodology have been applied in various settings, I will first highlight some of the fundamental contributions psychology has already made in our lives. Many of them have become so pervasive and their impact so unobtrusively profound that they are taken for granted. They have come to be incorporated into the way we think about certain domains, have influenced our attitudes and values, and so changed the way individuals and agencies behave that they now seem like the natural, obvious way the world should be run. Psychology often gets little or no credit for these contributions—when we should be deservedly proud of them.

Psychological Testing and Assessment

One of psychology's major achievements has been the development and the extensive reliance on objective, quantifiable means of assessing human talents, abilities, strengths, and weaknesses. In the 100 years since Alfred Binet first measured intellectual performance, systematic assessment has replaced the subjective, often biased judgments of teachers, employers, clinicians, and others in positions of authority by objective, valid, reliable, quantifiable, and normed tests (Binet, 1911; Binet & Simon, 1915). It is hard to imagine a test-free world. Modern testing stretches from assessments of intelligence, achievement, personality, and pathology to domains of vocational and values assessment, personnel selection, and more. Vocational interest measures are the backbone of guidance counseling and career advising. The largest single application of classified testing in the world is the Armed Services Vocational Aptitude Battery that is given to as many as 2 million enlisted personnel annually. Personnel selection testing has over 90 years of validity research and proven utility.

We are more familiar with the SAT and GRE standardized testing, currently being revised in response to various critiques, but they are still the yardstick for admission to many colleges and universities (Sternberg, 2000). Workplace job skills assessment and training involves huge numbers of workers and managers in many countries around the world (DuBois, 1970). Little wonder, then, that such pervasive use of assessments has spawned a multibillion dollar industry. (Because I am serving here in this article in the capacity as cheerleader for our discipline, I will not raise questions about the political misuse or overuse of testing nor indeed be critical of some of the other contributions that follow; see Cronbach, 1975.)

Positive Reinforcement

The earlier emphasis in schools and in child rearing on punishment for errors and inappropriate behavior has been gradually displaced by a fundamentally divergent focus on the utility of positive reinforcement for correct, appropriate responding (Straus & Kantor, 1994). Punishing the "undesirable person" has been replaced by punishing only "undesirable behavioral acts." Time-outs for negative behavior have proven remarkably effective as a behavior-modification strategy (Wolfe, Risley, & Mees, 1965). It has become so effective that it has become a favorite technique for managing child behavior by parents in the United States. "Half the parents and teachers in the United States use this nonviolent practice and call it 'time-out,' which makes it a social intervention unmatched in modern psychology," according to the American Academy of Pediatrics' (1998) publication.

Animal training has benefited enormously from procedures of shaping complex behavioral repertoires and the use of conditioned reinforcers (such as clickers' soundings paired with food rewards). An unexpected value of such training, as reported by animal caregivers, is that they enhance the mental health of many animal species through the stimulation provided by learning new behaviors (San Francisco Chronicle, 2003). Skinner and his behaviorist colleagues deserve the credit for this transformation in how we think about and go about changing behavior by means of response-contingent reinforcement. Their contributions have moved out of animal laboratories into schools, sports, clinics, and hospitals (see Axelrod & Apsche, 1983; Druckman & Bjork, 1991; Kazdin, 1994; Skinner, 1974).

Psychological Therapies

The mission of our psychological practitioners of relieving the suffering of those with various forms of mental illness by means of appropriately delivered types of psychological therapy has proven successful. Since Freud's (1896/1923, 1900/1965) early cases documenting the efficacy of "talk therapy" for neurotic disorders, psychotherapy has taken many forms. Cognitive behavior modification, systematic desensitization, and exposure therapies have proven especially effective in treating phobias, anxiety disorders, and panic attacks, thanks to the application of Pavlovian principles of classical conditioning (Pavlov, 1897/1902, 1897/1927), first developed by Joseph Wolpe (1958). Even clinical depression is best treated with a combination of psychotherapy and medication, and psychotherapy has been shown to be as effective as the drugs alone (Hollon, Thase, & Markowitz, 2002). At a more general level, psychology has helped to demystify "madness," to bring humanity into the treatment of those with emotional and behavioral disorders, and to give people hope that such disorders can be changed (Beck, 1976). Our practitioners and clinical theorists have also developed a range of treatments designed especially for couples, families, groups, for those in rehabilitation from drugs or physical disabilities, as well as for many specific types of problems such as, addictions, divorce, or shyness.

Self-Directed Change

The shelves of most bookstores in the United States are now as likely to be filled with "self-help" books as they are with cooking and dieting books. Although many of them can be dismissed as bad forms of "pop psych" that offer guidance and salvation without any solid empirical footing to back their claims, others provide a valuable service to the general public. At best, they empower people to engage in self-directed change processes for optimal personal adjustment (see Maas, 1998; Myers, 1993; Zimbardo, 1977). In part, their success comes from providing wise advice and counsel based on a combination of extensive expert experience and relevant research packaged in narratives that ordinary people find personally meaningful.

Dynamic Development Across the Life Span

Earlier conceptions of children as small adults, as property, and later as valuable property were changed in part by the theories and research of developmental psychologists (see McCoy, 1988; Pappas, 1983). In recent times, the emerging status of "the child as person" has afforded children legal rights, due process, and self-determination, along with the recognition that they should be regarded as competent persons worthy of considerable freedom (Horowitz, 1984). Psychology has been a human service profession whose knowledge base has been translated into support for a positive ideology of children (Hart, 1991). The human organism is continually changing, ever modifying itself to engage its environments more effectively, from birth through old age. This fundamental conception has made evident that babies need stimulation of many kinds for optimal development, just as do their grandparents. There is now widespread psychological recognition that infants do experience pain; learning often depends on critical age-related developmental periods; nature and nurture typically interact in synergistic ways to influence our intelligence and many attributes; mental growth follows orderly progressions, as does language acquisition and production; and that the elderly do not lose their mental agility and competence if they continue to exercise their cognitive skills throughout life (see Baltes & Staudinger 2000; Bee, 1994; Erikson, 1963; Piaget, 1954; Pinker, 1994; Plomin & McClearn, 1993; Scarr, 1998). These are but a few of the fundamental contributions of psychology to the way our society now thinks about human development over the course of a lifetime because of decades of research by our developmentalist colleagues.

Parenting

Advice by psychologists on best parental practices has varied in quality and value over time. However, there now seems to be agreement that children need to develop secure attachments to parents or caregivers and that the most beneficial parenting style for generating an effective child-parent bond is authoritative. Authoritative parents make age-appropriate demands on children while being responsive to their needs, autonomy, and freedom (see Baumrind, 1973; Collins, Maccoby, Steinberg, Hetherington, & Bornstein, 2000; Darling & Steinberg, 1993; Maccoby, 1980, 1992, 2000).

Psychological Stress

Is there any day in our modern lives that stress does not seem to be omnipresent? We are stressed by time pressures on us, by our jobs (Maslach, 1982), by our marriages, by our friends or by our lack of them. Back when I was a graduate student, stress was such a novel concept that it was surprising when our professor Irving Janis (1958) wrote one of the first books on the subject of psychological stress. The concept of psychological stress was virtually unrecognized in medical care in the 50s and 60s. Psychosomatic disorders baffled physicians who never recognized stress as a causal factor in illness and disease. Since then, psychological research and theorizing has helped to move the notion of stress to the center of the biopsychosocial health model that is revolutionizing medical treatments (Ader & Cohen, 1993; Cohen & Herbert, 1996). Psychologists have shown that our appraisals of stress and our lifestyle habits have a major impact on many of the major causes of illness and death (see Lazarus, 1993; Lazarus & Folkman, 1984). We have made commonplace the ideas of coping with stress, reducing lifestyle risk factors, and building social support networks to enable people to live healthier and longer lives (see Coe, 1999; Cohen & Syme, 1985; Taylor & Clark, 1986).

Unconscious Motivation

Psychology brought into the public mind, as did dramatists such as William Albee, Arthur Miller, and Tennessee Williams, that what we think and do is not always based on conscious decisions. Rather, human behavior may be triggered by unconscious motivations of which we have no awareness. Another nod of thanks goes out to the wisdom of Sigmund Freud and of Carl Jung (1936/1959) for helping to illuminate this previously hidden side of human nature. In a similar vein, slips of the tongue and pen are now generally interpreted as potentially meaningful symptoms of suppressed intentions. It is relatively common in many levels of U.S. society for people to believe that accidents may not be accidental but motivated, that dreams might convey important messages, and also that we use various defense mechanisms, such as projection, to protect fragile egos from awareness of negative information.

Prejudice and Discrimination

Racial prejudice motivates a range of emotions and behaviors among both those targeted and those who are its agents of hatred. Discrimination is the overt behavioral sequeala of prejudiced beliefs. It enforces inequalities and injustices based on categorical assignments to presumed racial groups. Stereotypes embody a biased conception of the attributes people presumably possess or lack. The 1954 decision by the Supreme Court of the United States (*Brown v. Board of Education of Topeka, KS*) that formally desegregated public schools was based on some critical social psychological research. The body of empirical research by Kenneth and Mamie Clark (1939a, 1939b, 1940, 1950) effectively demonstrated for the Court that the segregated educational conditions of that era had a negative impact on the sense of self-worth of Negro (the then-preferred term) school children. The Court, and the thoughtful public since then, accepted the psychological premise that segregated education, which separates the races, can never be really equal for those being stigmatized by that system of discrimination. Imposed segregation not only is the consequence of prejudice, it contributes further to maintaining and intensifying prejudice, negative stereotypes, and discrimination. In the classic analysis of the psychology of prejudice by Gordon Allport (1954), the importance of equal status contact between the races was advanced as a dynamic hypothesis that has since been widely validated in a host of different contexts (Pettigrew, 1997).

Humanizing Factory Work

Dehumanizing factory assembly lines in which workers were forced to do the same repetitive, mindless task, as if they were robots, initially gave Detroit automakers a production advantage. However, Japanese automakers replaced such routinized assembly lines with harmonious, small work teams operating under conditions of participatory management and in-group democratic principles. The remarkable success of the Japanese automakers in overtaking their American counterparts in a relatively short time is due in part to their adaptation of the principles of group dynamics developed by Kurt Lewin, his colleagues and students at the Massachusetts Institute of Technology, and the University of Michigan (Lewin, 1947a, 1947b, 1948). Paradoxically, U.S. auto manufacturers are now incorporating this Japanese work model into their factories, decades after they should have done so. This is one way in which psychological theory can be credited with a humanizing impact on industrial work. But psychologists working in the industrial/organizational framework have done even more to help businesses appreciate and promote the importance of goal setting, worker-job fit, job satisfaction, and personnel selection and training.

Political Polling

It is hard to imagine elections without systematic polling of various segments of the electorate using sampling techniques as predictors of election outcomes. Polling for many other purposes by Gallup, Roper, and other opinion polling agencies has become big business. Readers might be surprised to learn that psychologist Hadley Cantril (1991) pioneered in conducting research into the methodology of polling in the 1940s. Throughout World War II, Cantril provided President Roosevelt with valuable information on American public opinion. He also established the Office of Public Opinion Research, which became a central archive for polling data.

How and Why Psychology Matters in Our Lives

I am proud to be a psychologist. As the 2002 APA president, one of my goals was to spread that pride far and wide among my colleagues as well as among all students of psychology. For starters, we can all be proud of the many contributions we have made collectively to enrich the way people think about the human condition, a bit of which was outlined above. I am also proud of the fact that our scientific approach to understanding the behavior of individuals has guided some policy and improved some

operating procedures in our society. We have always been one of the most vigilant and outspoken proponents of the use of the scientific method for bringing reliable evidence to bear on a range of issues (Campbell, 1969). Given any intervention or new policy, psychologists insist on raising the question, "but does it really work?" and utilizing evaluative methodologies and meta-analyses to help make that decision. Psychologists have modeled the approach to reducing errors in advancing behavior-based conclusions through random assignment, double-blind tests, and sensitivity to the many biases present in uncontrolled observations and research procedures. Many of us have also been leaders in advancing a variety of innovations in education through our awareness of principles of attention, learning, memory, individual differences, and classroom dynamics. In addition, I am proud of our discipline's dedication to relieving all forms of human suffering through effective therapeutic interventions along with promoting prevention strategies and appropriate environmental change. As psychologists, we should also be pleased by discovering that our theories, research, and methodologies are serving to influence individual and societal actions, as will be shown next.

Psychologymatters.org

The scaffolding for such pride in psychology might best be manifest in a newly developed compendium, which shows society what we have done and are doing to improve the quality of life. I wanted to have available in one easily accessible and indexed source a listing of the research and theories that have been translated into practice. Such a resource would indicate how each item is being applied in various settings, such as schools, clinics, hospitals, businesses, community services, and legal and governmental agencies. It would establish the fact that psychology makes a significant difference in our lives by means of these concrete exemplars of its relevant applications. Ideally, this compendium would indicate how psychological contributions have saved lives, reduced or prevented suffering, saved money, made money, enhanced educational goals, improved security and safety, promoted justice and fairness, made organizations operate more effectively, and more. By designing this compendium as a Web-based open file, it can be continually updated, modified, and expanded as promising research meets the criterion of acceptability as having made a practically significant difference.

This effort to devise a compendium began with the help of APA's Science Directorate, by issuing a call for submissions to many e-mail lists serving APA members and through requests in APA's *Monitor on Psychology* and on the www.apa.org Web site. The initial set of items was vetted independently by Len Mitnick (formerly of the National Institute of Mental Health) and me. A "blue-ribbon" task force of journal editors, textbook authors, and senior scientists was formed to further vet these final items, help revise them, and then to work at expanding our base.[2]

Because this compendium offers the opportunity to portray an attractive, intelligent face of psychology to the public, final drafts have been edited or rewritten by science writers in APA's Public Communication's office, ably directed by Rhea

Farberman. Ideally, the submissions appear in a jargon-free, readable style appealing to the nonpsychologist public, as well as to our professional colleagues. In addition to having the individual items categorized into many general topical domains, readily searchable by key words or phrases, we have expanded the value of this site by adding an extensive glossary of psychological terms, a historical timeline of major psychological events and contributors, and basic information on "how to be a wiser consumer of research." We will include other extensions as appropriate based on feedback from colleagues and the public we are serving.

The criteria for inclusion are that each submission be presented (a) in sufficient detail to allow an independent assessment; (b) with evidence of significant statistical effects obtained within the study; (c) with reported application or extension of the submitted research, methodology, or theory in some specific domain of relevance; and (d) with evidence of where and how it has made a significant difference, such as citation of a new law, policy, standardized procedure, or operating system that was based on the submitted item. Items with *promise* of such applicability in the future (because they were too new to have been subject to any evaluation of outcome effectiveness) are being held in a "wait-and-check-back-later" file. I should mention in passing that many submitted items described research that was interesting, including some classic studies, but they have never met the test of societal applicability.

I welcome the feedback of *American Psychologist* readers on this first phase of our efforts, while also issuing a cordial invitation to add your voice to this compendium with additional worthy submissions. The reach of these initial efforts will hopefully be extended by having this compendium serve as a model to the psychological associations of countries around the world, adding to psychology's global relevance.

Please visit us at www.psychologymatters.org. But please wait a moment before booting up your computer, until you finish reading the next section of this article, which highlights a sampling of what you will find there.

Highlights of Psychology's Real World Relevance

I want to conclude with a dozen or so examples taken from our compendium that illustrate a range of its different topics and domains of applicability. This presentation will end with one extended instance of what I consider a model collaboration of theory, research, media applicability, and global dissemination of psychological knowledge conveyed in a unique format—soap operas! It is the ingenious application of the theory of social modeling by Albert Bandura (1965, 1977) in the design of scenarios used in soap operas to encourage literacy, birth control, the education of woman, environmental sustainability, and more.

Human Factors

Traffic safety has been improved by researchers in the area of human factors and ergonomics through a better understanding of visual perception. We now know that changing the standard color of red emergency trucks to a lime-green color reduces accidents because that greenish hue is better perceived in dim light. Similarly, changing traffic sign fonts to increase their recognition at night is another safety improvement resulting from psychological research by Allen (1970), Solomon and King (1985), and Garvey, Pietrucha, and Meeker (1997).

Scott Geller's (2001, 2003) research program applies Skinnerian behavior analysis to increase safe behaviors, reduce at-risk behaviors, and prevent unintentional injuries at work and on the road. Such unintentional injury is the leading cause of death to people ages 44 years and under. The behavior-based safety (BBS) approach for increasing safety identifies critical behaviors that are targeted for change, establishes baselines, applies change interventions, and evaluates workers' change away from specific risky behaviors to more beneficial directions. This approach has been applied in thousands of organizations with great success, such as in having people wear seat belts and in occupational safety programs. The rate of reported injuries after five years of implementation of this behavioral approach decreased by as much as an average 72% across a number of organizations (for a summary of the evidence for the extent of injury reduction, see the report by Beth Sulzer-Azaroff & John Austin, 2000). One indicator of the social significance of applying behavior analysis is apparent in the *Clinical Practice Guidelines* of New York States' (1999) Department of Health, Early Intervention Program: "It is recommended that principles of applied behavior analysis (ABA) and behavior intervention strategies be included as important elements in any intervention program for young children with autism" (p. 13).

Navigational aids for the blind and visually impaired people have been developed by psychologists Roberta Klatsky and Jack Loomis, working with geographer Reginald Golledge (Loomis, Klatsky, & Golledge, 2001) over several decades. They utilize principles of spatial cognition along with those of space and auditory perception to guide locomotion. Their new technology is now in development funded by the National Institute for Disability and Rehabilitation Research.

Criminal Justice

Cognitive and social psychologists have shown that eyewitness testimony is surprisingly unreliable. Their research reveals the ease with which recall of criminal events is biased by external influences in interrogations and police line-ups. The seminal work of Beth Loftus (1975, 1979, 1992) and Gary Wells (Wells & Olson, 2003), among others, has been recognized by the U.S. Attorney General's office in drawing up national guidelines for the collection of accurate and unbiased eyewitness identification (see Malpass & Devine, 1981; Stebley, 1997).

The Stanford Prison Experiment has become a classic demonstration of the power of social situational forces to negatively impact the behavior of normal, healthy participants who began to act in pathological or evil ways in a matter of a few days (Zimbardo, Haney, Banks, & Jaffe, 1973). It added a new awareness of institutional power to the authority power of Stanley Milgram's (1974) blind obedience studies (see Blass, 1999; Zimbardo, Maslach, & Haney, 1999). The lessons of this research have gone well beyond the classroom. In part as a consequence of my testimony before a Senate judiciary committee on crime and prisons (Zimbardo, 1974), its committee chair, Senator Birch Bayh, prepared a new law for federal prisons requiring juveniles in pretrial detention to be housed separately from adult inmates (to prevent their being abused). Our participants were juveniles in the pretrial detention facility of the Stanford jail. A video documentary of the study, "Quiet Rage: The Stanford Prison Experiment," has been used extensively by many agencies within the civilian and military criminal justice system as well as in shelters for abused women. I recently discovered that it is even used to educate role-playing military interrogators in the Navy SEAR (survival, evasion, and resistance) program about the dangers of abusing their power against others role-playing pretend spies and terrorists (Annapolis Naval College psychology staff, personal communication, September 18, 2003). The Web site for the Stanford Prison Experiment gets more than 500 visitors daily and has had more than 13 million unique page views in the past four years (www.prisonexp.org). Those surprising figures should be telling us that we must focus more effort on utilizing the power of the Web as a major new medium for disseminating psychology's messages directly to a worldwide audience.

Education

Among the many examples of psychology at work in the field of education, two of my favorites naturally have a social psychological twist. Elliot Aronson and his research team in Austin, Texas, dealt with the negative consequences of desegregated schools by creating "jigsaw classrooms." Prejudice against minority children was rampant, those children were not performing well, and elementary school classes were marked by high degrees of tension. But when all students were taught to share a set of materials in small learning teams where each child has one set of information indispensable to the rest of the team, and on which tests and grades depend, remarkable things happened. All kids started to listen to the other kids, especially minority kids who they used to ignore or disparage, because such attention and cooperation is essential to getting a good grade. Not only did the self-esteem of the minority children escalate, but so did their academic performance, as prejudice and discrimination went down. The techniques of the jigsaw classroom are inexpensive for teachers to learn and to operationalize, so it is no wonder that Aronson's simple concept is now being incorporated into the curricula of hundreds of schools in many states, with similarly impressive results (Aronson, 1990; Aronson, Blaney, Stephan, Sikes, & Snapp, 1978; Aronson & Gonzalez, 1988; Aronson & Patnoe, 1997).

Teaching young children interpersonal cognitive problem solving skills, known as ICPS, reduces physical and verbal aggression, increases coping with frustrations, and promotes positive peer relationships. This research program developed by Myrna Shure and George Spivak (1982) over the past several decades is a major violence prevention approach being applied in schools and family agencies in programs called "Raising a Thinking Child" and by the U.S. Department of Education's "I Can Problem Solve" program.

Health

Environmental health is threatened by a host of toxic substances, such as lead, mercury, solvents, and pesticides. Experimental psychologists, behavioral analysts, and psychometricians have helped create the field of behavioral toxicology that recognizes the nervous system as the target for many toxins, with defects in behavior and mental processes as the symptomatic consequences. Pioneering work by psychologist Bernard Weiss (1992, 1999) and others has had a significant impact on writing behavioral tests into federal legislation, thereby better regulating the use of a wide range of neurotoxins in our environment. That research documents the vulnerability of children's developing brains to chemicals in the environment.

Among the many negative consequences of America's involvement in the Vietnam War was the explosion of the phenomenon of posttraumatic stress disorder (PTSD). Many veterans were experiencing this debilitating disorder that was uncovered during their psychotherapy treatments. The more we discovered about this delayed, persistent, intense stress reaction to violence and trauma, the more we realized that veterans of earlier wars had also experienced PTSD, but it was unlabeled. That was also the case with many civilian victims of trauma, among them rape victims and those who had experienced child abuse. PTSD has become a well-recognized and publicly acknowledged phenomenon today because it was one of the mental health consequences of the monumental trauma from the terrorist attacks on September 11, 2001, in New York City and Washington, DC. Credit for the early recognition, identification, measurement, and treatment of PTSD goes to the programs of research funded by the Veteran's Administration, which was pioneered by the research team of clinical psychologist Terry Keane (Keane, Malloy, & Fairbank, 1984; Weathers, Keane, & Davidson, 2001).

The Magic of Touch

One of the consequences of a host of amazing medical advances is saving the lives of many premature infants who would have died even just a decade ago. With modern intensive care, preemies weighing only a few pounds now survive, but the essential hospital costs are staggering, up to $10,000 a day for weeks or months! One simple solution for sending them home sooner depends on accelerating their growth by means of touch therapy. Psychologist Field extended earlier research she had done with biologist Saul Schanberg (Field, 1998; Field & Schanberg, 1990; Field et al., 1986) on massaging infant rat pups that were motherless. Just as the infant rats rapidly grew in response to that vigorous touch, so did the human preemies. Massaging them several times a day for only 15 minutes was sufficient to stimulate growth hormones. On average, such massaged infants are able to go home six days sooner than comparison preemies treated in the conventional way. Given 470,000 premature infants are born each year in the United States alone, it is evident that billions of dollars in health care costs could be saved if this simple, inexpensive treatment was made standard procedure in more hospital intensive care units (see also Meltz, 2000).

To establish the societal value of any intervention designed to save lives or enhance health and well-being, one must

systematically evaluate its cost-effectiveness. That means establishing a ratio of the benefits compared with various cost estimates of putting the intervention into operation and sustaining it over time. Such a ratio was developed for dollar costs per year of life saved and applied to more than 500 life-saving interventions (Tengs et al., 1995). Across all of these interventions, the median cost was $42,000 per year of life saved. Although some programs save more resources than they cost, others cost millions of dollars for each year of life they save and thus become of questionable social value. Using this standard measure, we discover that new neonatal intensive care for low-birth-weight infants (preemies) costs a whooping $270,000 for each year of their lives saved. By that yardstick, the inexpensive touch therapy intervention would dramatically reduce that cost-effectiveness ratio.

The puzzling issue then is why such a simple procedure is not now standard operating procedure in every such intensive care unit in the nation or the world? One goal of our compendium development team is also to investigate why some potentially useful interventions have not been applied in the venues where they could make a significant difference. For instance, social psychologists have shown convincingly that elderly patients in a home for the aged who were given a sense of control and responsibility over even minor events became healthier and lived significantly longer than comparison patients (Langer & Rodin, 1976; Rodin & Langer, 1977). Amazingly, this simple, powerful intervention has not ever been utilized—even in the institution where the research was conducted.

Undoing Dyslexia via Video Games

Treatment for dyslexia by speech therapists and counselors is a slow, long, expensive, and frustrating experience for professionals, parents, and children. Cognitive neuroscientist, Paula Tallal, is using new functional magnetic resonance imaging techniques to identify the source of reading dyslexia in brain regions that do not adequately process fast appearing sound-sight phonemic combinations. She then worked with a computer-programming agency to develop special video games that systematically shape these children's ever-faster responses to various sights and sounds in the games. With this new technology, children treat themselves in an atmosphere of entertainment and adventure, rely only on intrinsic motivation of game playing, get personalized feedback, and need minimal supervision by highly skilled professionals.

The special computerized video game is called "Fast For-Word." It provides intensive, highly individualized adaptive training across a large number of cognitive, linguistic, and reading skills that are vital for academic success. By adapting trial by trial to each child's performance, progress in aural and written language skills of children with dyslexia is reduced to but a few weeks from what had been typically years of intervention efforts. Approximately 375,000 individuals have completed such training across 2,200 public schools nationwide, and over 2,000 private practice professionals use Fast ForWord programs in their clinics (for more information, visit www.scientificlearning.com and www.brainconnection.com).

This sensitive application of psychological knowledge and new methods blended with high technology has resulted in enhanced quality of life for these children as well as their families and teachers, not to mention much money and resources saved (see Holly Fitch & Tallal, 2003; Tallal & Benasich, 2002; Tallal, Galaburda, Llinas, & Von Euler, 1993).

An Idealized Example of Psychology Applied Globally

The use of intrinsically interesting media, such as video games and Tele-Health dynamic systems, enables adults as well as children to play central roles in individualized health-management programs. The power of the media also has been extended to television as a far-reaching medium to convey vital persuasive messages about behavior changes that are essential to cope with many of the social, economic, political, and health problems facing individuals around the globe. Can psychology contribute to effectively dealing with the population explosion in many countries, increase the status and education of women, and minimize or prevent AIDS? A tall order, for sure. However, it is now happening through a remarkable collaboration of a wise TV producer, a brilliant psychologist, and an international agency that distributes their unusual messages worldwide (Bandura, 2002; Smith, 2002).

Promoting Family Planning

The explosion in population around the world is one of our most urgent global problems. Ecologically sustainable development and growth is being challenged by a variety of entwined phenomena, such as high fertility rates in many countries coupled with suboptimal birth rates in others, dramatically increased longevity in some nations along with the spread of deadly communicable diseases in others. One means of population control in overpopulated countries involves women and men actively engaged in their own family planning. However, the question is how to do so effectively and efficiently because most previous efforts have met with minimal success?

A TV producer in Mexico, Miguel Sabido, created soap operas that were serialized daily dramas, with prosocial messages about practicing family planning and also others that promote literacy and education of women. Woven into the narrative of his commercial dramas were elements taken from Albert Bandura's sociocognitive theory of the importance of social models in shaping desired behaviors (Bandura, 1965, 1977, 1986). In many Spanish-speaking countries, most family members watch soap operas fervently each day as their plots unfold over many weeks or months. Viewers identify with attractive, desirable models and dis-identify with those whose actions seem repulsive or create unwanted problems for the "good" guys. In some scenarios, there are also actors who represent "transitional models," starting off engaging in high-risk or undesirable behaviors but then changing in socially appropriate directions. After some programs, there is informational or community support for the cause being projected, by celebrities, government officials, or members of the clergy. This

13

secondary influence path for behavior change adds the key element of making connections to the viewers' personal social networks and community settings in addition to the direct path from the media message to desired changes in target behaviors.

Does it really work? After watching the Mexican programs promoting family planning, many women enrolled in family planning clinics. The 32% increase of woman starting to use this service was similar to the increase in contraceptive users. This was true even though there was never an explicit message about contraception for family planning (in deference to the negative position on this birth control issue by the Catholic Church). Another key result was that the greater the level of media exposure to these family-oriented TV soap operas, the greater was the percentage of women using contraceptives and also discussing family planning with spouses "many times" (Bandura, 2002).

Preventing the Spread of AIDS

These dramas were shown in one region of Tanzania, Africa, and their effects compared with a control region where TV viewers were not exposed to the dramas (later on they got to see the same soap operas). One of the many prosocial effects was an increase in new family planning adopters following the viewing of these dramatic serials compared with no change in the control region. Seventeen segments were included in dramas in Tanzania to prevent the spread of the AIDS virus, a special problem among truck drivers who have unprotected sex with hundreds of prostitutes working at truck stop hubs. Actors portrayed positive models who adopt safe sex practices or negative ones who do not—and then they die of AIDS! Condom distribution soared following viewing this series, whereas it remained low in the control, no soap opera region. Along with this critical change in behavior were also reports of reduced number of sexual partners, more talk about HIV infection, and changed beliefs in personal risk of HIV infection from unprotected sex. Such attitudinal and behavioral changes are vital to slowing the spread of AIDS, which is estimated to make orphans of up to 25 million children worldwide in the next half dozen years (Naik, 2002; The Straits Times, 2002).

Female Literacy

Education of women is one of the most powerful prophylaxes for limiting population growth, so these soap opera programs in many countries show stories that endorse women continuing with their education as one way of liberating young women from male and matriarchal dominance. In one village in India, there was an immediate 30% increase in women going to school after the airing of these soap operas.

A Potent Blending of Talents, Wisdom, and Resources for Social Good

So here we have the unique case of a wise person in the media borrowing ideas from a psychologist and then extending the scope of influence by pairing up with a nonprofit agency, Population

Communications International (PCI) to disseminate these dramas worldwide. PCI's "mission is to work creatively with the media and other organizations to motivate individuals and communities to make choices that influence population trends encouraging development and environmental protection" (PCI, 2002). PCI's efforts at social diffusion span more than 17 countries worldwide with radio and TV serial dramas, comic books, and videos for classroom use. Finally, there is a fourth essential component: systematic evaluation of outcomes by an independent organization of all of these entertainment-educational change programs (see www.population.org).

It is evident that these serial dramatizations use the power of narrative story telling over an extended time, which the public views voluntarily, to motivate specific behavior change in directions guided by the information conveyed in the drama, which in turn has its origins in sound psychological theory and research. What also becomes evident is that when psychologists want to give psychology away to the public, we need to collaborate with those who understand best *how* to reach the public, namely those intimately involved with the mass media. They are our gatekeepers to the audiences we want to reach and influence. We have to find ways of inviting and intriguing media with the utility of psychological knowledge for crafting entertaining stories that can make a significant difference in the quality of lives of individuals and society.

Accentuating Psychology's Positive Messages

The collaboration between psychologist Albert Bandura, media master Miguel Sabido, and the resourcefulness of the PCI agency is an ideal model for us to emulate and extend in spreading more of our positive messages. Among those new messages are the two exciting directions that psychology can be expected to take in the next decade. The emergence of Martin Seligman's (2002) revolutionary "Positive Psychology" enterprise is creating a new vital force for recognizing and enriching the talents, strengths, and virtues of even ordinary people (see Diener, 2000; Myers, 2002; Snyder & Lopez, 2002). It is shifting attention away from deficits, disabilities, and disorders toward a focus on what is special about human nature like our resilience in the face of trauma, our joys, our sense of wonder and curiosity, and our capacity for goodness and love.

The fertile field of "behavioral economics" integrates psychology with economics and neuroscience to understand the economically irrational human element in judgments under uncertainty (see Kahneman & Tversky, 1979; Simon, 1955; Tversky & Kahneman, 1974, 1986). We can anticipate that Daniel Kahneman's winning the 2003 Nobel Prize in economics has made him a role model for the next generation of professional psychologists to emulate and to enter this exciting domain of relevant inquiry.

In conclusion, I repeat the questions that got me to this point and the simple answer that I now feel is justified—and I hope readers of this article agree with its positive bias.

Does psychology matter? Can psychological research, theory, methods, and practice make a significant difference in the lives of individuals, communities, and nations? Do we psychologists

have a legacy of which we can be proud? Can we do more and better research that has significant applicable effects in the real world? Are we ready now "to give psychology away to the public" in useful, accessible ways? And finally, can we learn how better to collaborate with the media, with technology experts, with community leaders, and with other medical and behavioral scientists for psychology to make an even more significant difference in the coming decade?

My final answer is simply YES, YES indeed! May the positive forces of psychology be with you, and with our society.

Notes

1. Recognizing the importance of bringing psychology's understanding that violence is a learned behavior to the public, APA has joined with the National Association for the Education of Young Children and the Advertising Council to create a national multimedia public service advertising campaign designed to remind adults of the role they play in teaching children to use or avoid violence and then empower these adults to model and teach the right lessons. The campaign, first launched in 2000, has reached over 50 million households. At the community level, the campaign includes collaborations with local groups in a train-the-trainer model to bring early childhood violence prevention awareness and know-how to parents, teachers, and other caregivers.

2. The task force selected to identify and evaluate the research, theory, and methodology in psychology that qualified for inclusion in the Psychology Matters compendium has been ably cochaired by David Myers and Robert Bjork. Other members have included Alan Boneau. Gordon Bower, Nancy Eisenberg, Sam Glucksberg, Philip Kendall, Kevin Murphy, Scott Pious, Peter Salovey, Alana Conner-Snibbe, Beth Sulzer-Azaroff, Chris Wickens, and Alice Young. They have been assisted by the addition of Brett Pelham and David Partenheimer. Rhea Farberman and her staff in APA's Office of Public Communications have played a vital role in the development and continuing evolution of this project. The staff of the Science Directorate aided in the early development of the survey that was circulated to initiate electronic input of candidate items from APA constituent groups.

References

Ader, R., & Cohen, N. (1993). Psychoneuroimmunology: Conditioning and stress. *Annual Review of Psychology, 44,* 53–85.

Alien, M. J. (1970). *Vision and highway safety.* Philadelphia: Chilton.

Allport, G. (1954). *The nature of prejudice.* Reading, MA: Addison-Wesley.

American Academy of Pediatrics, Committee on Psychosocial Aspect of Child and Family Health. (1998). Guidance for effective discipline. *Pediatrics, 101,* 723–728.

Aronson, E. (1990). Applying social psychology to desegregation and energy conservation. *Personality and Social Psychology Bulletin, 16,* 118–132.

Aronson, E., Blaney, N., Stephan, C., Sikes, J., & Snapp, M. (1978). *The jigsaw classroom.* Beverly Hills, CA: Sage.

Aronson, E., & Gonzalez, A. (1988). Desegregation jigsaw, and the Mexican-American experience. In P. A. Katz & D. Taylor (Eds.),

Eliminating racism: Profiles in controversy (pp. 301–314). New York: Plenum Press.

Aronson, E., & Patnoe, S. (1997). *The jigsaw classroom: Building cooperation in the classroom* (2nd ed.). New York: Addison Wesley Longman.

Axelrod, S., & Apsche, H. (1983). *Effects of punishment on human behavior.* New York: Academic Press.

Baltes, P. B., & Staudinger, U. M. (2000). Wisdom: A metaheuristic (pragmatic) to orchestrate mind and virtue toward excellence. *American Psychologist, 55,* 122–136.

Bandura, A. (1965). Influence of models' reinforcement contingencies on the acquisition of imitated responses. *Journal of Personality and Social Psychology. 1,* 589–595.

Bandura, A. (1977). *Social learning theory.* Englewood Cliffs, NJ: Prentice Hall.

Bandura, A. (1986). *Social foundations of thought and action: A social cognitive theory.* Englewood Cliffs, NJ: Prentice Hall.

Bandura, A. (2002). Environmental sustainability by sociocognitive deceleration of population growth. In P. Schmuck & W. Schultz (Eds.), *The psychology of sustainable development* (pp. 209–238). Dordrecht, the Netherlands: Kluwer.

Baumrind, D. (1973). The development of instrumental competence through socialization. In A. Pick (Ed.), *Minnesota Symposium on Child Development* (Vol. 6, pp. 3–46). Minneapolis: University of Minnesota Press.

Beck, A. T. (1976). *Cognitive therapy and emotional disorders.* New York: International Universities Press.

Bee, H. (1994). *Lifespan development.* New York: HarperCollins.

Binet, A. (1911). *Les idées modernes sur les enfants* [Modern ideas about children]. Paris: Flammarion.

Binet, A., & Simon. T. (1915). *A method of measuring the development of intelligence of young children.* Chicago: Chicago Medical Books.

Blass, T. (Ed.). (1999). *Obedience to authority: Current perspectives on the Milgram Paradigm* (pp. 193–237). Mahwah, NJ: Erlbaum.

Campbell. D. T. (1969). Reforms as experiments. *American Psychologist, 24,* 409–429.

Cantril, A. H. (1991). *The opinion connection: Polling, politics, and the press.* Washington, DC: CQ Press.

Clark, K. B., & Clark, M. K. (1939a). The development of consciousness of self and the emergence of racial identification in negro preschool children. *Journal of Social Psychology, 10,* 591–599.

Clark, K. B., & Clark, M. K. (1939b). Segregation as a factor in the racial identification of negro preschool children: A preliminary report. *Journal of Experimental Education, 8,* 161–163.

Clark, K. B., & Clark, M. K. (1940). Skin color as a factor in racial identification of negro preschool children. *The Journal of Social Psychology, II,* 159–169.

Clark, K. B., & Clark, M. K. (1950). Emotional factors in racial identification and preference in negro children. *Journal of Negro Education, 19,* 341–350.

Coe, C. L. (1999). Psychosocial factors and psychoneuroimmunology within a lifespan perspective. In D. P. Keating & C. Hertzman (Eds.), *Developmental health and the wealth of nations: Social, biological, and educational dynamics* (pp. 201–219). New York: Guilford Press.

Cohen, S., & Herbert, T. B. (1996). Health psychology: Psychological factors and physical disease from the perspective of human psychoneuroimmunology. *Annual Review of Psychology, 47,* 113–142.

Cohen, S., & Syme, S. L. (Eds.). (1985). *Social support and health.* Orlando, FL: Academic Press.

Collins, W. A., Maccoby, E. E., Steinberg, L., Hetherington, E. M., & Bornstein, M. H. (2000). Contemporary research on parenting: The case for nature and nurture. *American Psychologist, 55,* 218–232.

Cronbach, L. J. (1975). Five decades of public controversy over mental testing. *American Psychologist, 30,* 1–14.

Darling, N., & Steinberg, L. (1993). Parenting style as context: An integrative model. *Psychological Bulletin, 113,* 487–496.

Diener, E. (2000). Subjective well-being: The science of happiness and a proposal for a national index. *American Psychologist, 55,* 34–43.

Discovering psychology [Television series]. (1990; updated 2001). Boston: WGBH, with the American Psychological Association. (Funded and distributed by the Annenberg CPB Foundation, Washington, DC)

Druckman. D., & Bjork, R. A. (1991). *In the mind's eye: Enhancing human performance.* Washington, DC: National Academy Press.

DuBois, P. H. (1970). *A history of psychological testing.* Boston: Allyn & Bacon.

Erikson, E. H. (1963). *Childhood and society* (2nd ed.). New York: Norton.

Field, T. (1998). Massage therapy effects. *American Psychologist, 53,* 1270–1281.

Field, T., & Schanberg, S. M. (1990). Massage alters growth and catecholamine production in preterm newborns. In N. Gunzenhauser (Ed.), *Advances in touch* (pp. 96–104). Skillman, NJ: Johnson & Johnson.

Field, T., Schanberg, S. M., Scafidi, F., Bauer, C. R., Vega-Lahr, N., Garcia, R., et al. (1986). Tactile/kinesthetic stimulation effects on preform neonates. *Pediatrics, 77,* 654–658.

Freud, S. (1923). *Introductory lectures on psycho-analysis* (J. Riviera, Trans.). London: Allen & Unwin. (Original work published 1896)

Freud, S. (1965). *The interpretation of dreams.* New York: Avon. (Original work published 1900)

Garvey, P. M., Pietrucha, M. T., & Meeker, D. (1997). Effects of font and capitalization on legibility of guide signs. *Transportation Research Record No. 1605,* 73–79.

Geller, E. S. (2001). *The psychology of safety handbook.* Boca Raton, FL: CRC Press.

Geller, E. S. (2003). Behavior-based safety in industry: Realizing the large-scale potential of behavior analysis to promote human welfare. *Applied & Preventive Psychology, 10,* 87–105.

Gerrig, R., & Zimbardo, P. G. (2004). *Psychology and life* (17th ed.). Boston: Allyn & Bacon.

Green, C. D., Shore, M., & Teo, T. (2001). *The transformation of psychology: Influences of 19th century philosophy, technology, and natural science.* Washington, DC: American Psychological Association.

Hart, S. N. (1991). From property to person status: Historical perspective on children's rights. *American Psychologist, 46,* 53–59.

Hollon, S. D., Thase, M. E., & Markowitz, J. C. (2002). Treatment and prevention of depression. *Psychological Science in the Public Interest, 3,* 39–77.

Holly Fitch, R., & Tallal, P. (2003). Neural mechanisms of language-based learning impairments: Insights from human populations and animal models. *Behavior and Cognitive Neuroscience Reviews, 2,* 155–178.

Horowitz, R. M. (1984). Children's rights: A look backward and a glance ahead. In R. M. Horowitz & J. B. Lazar (Eds.), *Legal rights of children* (pp. 1–9). New York: McGraw-Hill.

Hovland, C. I., Janis, I. L., & Kelley, H. H. (1953). *Communication and persuasion.* New Haven, CT: Yale University Press.

Hovland, C. I., Lumsdaine, A. A., & Sheffield, F. D. (1949). *Experiments on mass communication.* Princeton, NJ: Princeton University Press.

Janis, I. L. (1958). *Psychological stress: Psychoanalytical and behavioral studies of surgical patients.* New York: Wiley.

Jung, C. G. (1959). The concept of the collective unconscious. In *The archetypes and the collective unconscious, collected works* (Vol. 9, Part 1, pp. 54–74). Princeton, NJ: Princeton University Press. (Original work published 1936)

Kahneman, D., & Tversky, A. (1979). Prospect theory: An analysis of decision under risk. *Econometrica, 47,* 263–291.

Kazdin, A. E. (1994). *Behavior modification in applied settings* (5th ed.). Pacific Grove, CA: Brooks/Cole.

Keane, T. M., Malloy, P. F., & Fairbank, J. A. (1984). Empirical development of an MMPI subscale for the assessment of PTSD. *Journal of Consulting and Clinical Psychology, 52,* 138–140.

Langer, E. F., & Rodin, J. (1976). The effects of choice and enhanced personal responsibility for the aged: A field experiment in an institutionalized setting. *Journal of Personality and Social Psychology, 34,* 191–198.

Lazarus, R. S. (1993). From psychological stress to the emotions: A history of changing outlooks. *Annual Review of Psychology, 44,* 1–21.

Lazarus, R. S., & Folkman, S. (1984). *Stress, appraisal, and coping.* New York: Springer.

Lewin, K. (1947a). Frontiers in group dynamics: Concept, method and reality in social science; social equilibria and social change. *Human Relations, 1,* 5–41.

Lewin, K. (1947b). Frontiers in group dynamics: II. Channels of group life; social planning and action research. *Human Relations, 1,* 143–153.

Lewin, K. (1948). *Resolving social conflicts.* New York: Harper.

Loftus, E. F. (1975). Leading questions and the eyewitness report. *Cognitive Psychology, 7,* 560–572.

Loftus, E. F. (1979). Eyewitness testimony. Cambridge, MA: Harvard University Press. Loftus, E. F. (1992). When a lie becomes memory's truth: Memory distortion after exposure to misinformation. *Current Directions in Psychological Science, 1,* 121–123.

Loomis, J. M., Klatsky, R. L., & Golledge, R. G. (2001). Navigating without vision: Basic and applied research. *Optometry and Vision Science, 78,* 282–289.

Maas, J. (1998). *Power sleep: The revolutionary program that prepares your mind for peak performance.* New York: Villard.

Maccoby, E. E. (1980). *Social development: Psychological growth and the parent-child relationship.* San Diego, CA: Harcourt Brace Jovanovich.

Maccoby, E. E. (1992). The role of parents in the socialization of children: An historical overview. *Developmental Psychology, 28,* 1006–1017.

Maccoby, E. E. (2000). Parenting and its effects on children: On reading and misreading behavior genetics. *Annual Review of Psychology, 51,* 1–27.

Malpass, R. S., & Devine, P. G. (1981). Eyewitness identification: Lineup instructions and the absence of the offender. *Journal of Applied Psychology, 66,* 482–489.

Maslach, C. (1982). *Burnout: The cost of caring.* Englewood Cliffs, NJ: Prentice Hall.

McCoy, E. (1988). Childhood through the ages. In K. Finsterbush (Ed.), *Sociology 88/89* (pp. 44–47). Guilford, CT: Duskin.

Meltz, B. F. (2000, November 2). Do you touch your baby enough? *Boston Globe,* p. H1.

Milgram, S. (1974). *Obedience to authority.* New York: Harper & Row.

Miller, G. (1969). Psychology as a means of promoting human welfare. *American Psychologist, 24,* 1063–1075.

Miller, N. E. (1978). Biofeedback and visceral learning. *Annual Review of Psychology, 29,* 373–404.

Miller, N. E. (1985). The value of behavioral research on animals. *American Psychologist, 40,* 423–440.

Miller, N. E. (1992). Introducing and teaching much-needed understanding of the scientific process. *American Psychologist, 47,* 848–850.

Myers, D. G. (1993). *The pursuit of happiness.* New York: Avon.

Myers, D. G. (2002). *Intuition: Its powers and perils.* New Haven, CT: Yale University Press.

Naik, G. (2002, July 5). Uganda AIDS study suggests education stems spread of HIV. *Wall Street Journal,* p. A14.

New York State. (1999). *Clinical practice guidelines.* New York: Department of Health, Early Intervention Program, Autism.

Pappas. A. M. (1983). Introduction. In A. M. Pappas (Ed.), *Law and the status of the child* (pp. xxvii–lv). New York: United Nations Institute for Training and Research.

Pavlov, I. P. (1902). *The work of the digestive glands* (W. H. Thompson, Trans.) London: Griffin. (Original work published in 1897)

Pavlov, I. P. (1927). *Conditioned reflexes* (G. V. Anrep, Trans.). London: Oxford University Press. (Original work published 1897)

Pettigrew, T. F. (1997). Generalized intergroup contact effects on prejudice. *Personality and Social Psychology Bulletin, 23,* 173–185.

Piaget, J. (1954). *The construction of reality in the child.* New York: Basic Books.

Pinker, S. (1994). *The language instinct: How the mind creates language.* New York: Morrow.

Plomin, R., & McClearn, G. E. (1993). *Nature, nurture, and psychology.* Washington, DC: American Psychological Association.

Population Communications International. (2002). *15th anniversary: Keeping pace with change.* New York: Author.

Rodin, J., & Langer, E. F. (1977). Long-term effects of a control-relevant intervention with the institutionalized aged. *Journal of Personality and Social Psychology. 35,* 897–902.

Ruch, F. L., & Zimbardo, P. G. (1971). *Psychology and life* (8th ed.). Glenview, IL: Scott, Foresman.

Sarason, S. B. (1974). *The psychological sense of community: Prospects for a community psychology.* Oxford, England: Jossey-Bass.

Scarr, S. (1998). American child care today. *American Psychologist, 53,* 95–108.

Seligman, M. (2002). *Authentic happiness: Using the new positive psychology to realize your potential for lasting fulfillment.* New York: Free Press.

Shure, M. B., & Spivak, G. (1982). Interpersonal problem solving in children: A cognitive approach to prevention. *American Journal of Community Psychology, 10,* 341–356.

Simon, H. (1955). A behavioral model of rational choice. *Quarterly Journal of Economics, 69,* 99–118.

Skinner, B. F. (1938). *The behavior of organisms: An experimental analysis.* New York: Appleton-Century.

Skinner, B. F. (1948). *Walden two.* New York: Macmillan.

Skinner, B. F. (1966). What is the experimental analysis of behavior? *Journal of the Experimental Analysis of Behavior, 9,* 213–218.

Skinner, B, F. (1974). *About behaviorism.* New York: Knopf.

Smith, D. (2002). The theory heard "round the world." *Monitor on Psychology, 33,* 30–32.

Snyder, C. R., & Lopez, S. J. (2002). *Handbook of positive psychology.* New York: Oxford University Press.

Solomon, S. S., & King, J. G. (1985). Influence of color on fire vehicle accidents. *Journal of Safety Research, 26,* 47.

Stebley, N. M. (1997). Social influence in eyewitness recall: A meta-analytic review of line-up instruction effects. *Law and Human Behavior, 21,* 283–298.

Sternberg, R. J. (Ed.). (2000). *Handbook of intelligence.* Cambridge, England: Cambridge University Press.

The Straits Times. (2002, July 12). *The HIV orphan mega-crises.* Hong Kong: 14th International AIDS Conference.

Straus, M. A., & Kantor, G. K. (1994). Corporal punishment of adolescents by parents: A risk factor in the epidemiology of depression, suicide, alcohol abuse, child abuse, and wife beating. *Adolescence, 29,* 543–561.

Sulzer-Azaroff, B., & Austin, J. (2000, July). Does BBS work? Behavior-based safety and injury reduction: A survey of the evidence. *Professional Safety,* 19–24.

Swazey, J. P. (1974). *Chlorpromazine in psychiatry: A study of therapeutic innovation.* Cambridge, MA: MIT Press.

Tallal, P., & Benasich, A. A. (2002). Developmental language learning impairments. *Development and Psychopathology, 14,* 559–579.

Tallal, P., Galaburda, A. M., Llinas, R. R., & Von Euler, C. (Eds.). (1993). *Temporal information processing in the nervous system: Special reference to dyslexia and dysphasia* (Vol. 682). New York: New York Academy of Sciences.

Taylor, S. E., & Clark, L. F. (1986). Does information improve adjustments to noxious events? In M. J. Saks & L. Saxe (Eds.), *Advances in applied social psychology* (Vol. 3, pp. 1–28). Hillsdale, NJ: Erlbaum.

Tengs, T, O., Adams, M. E., Pliskin, J. S., Safan, D. G., Siegel, J. E., Weinstein, M. C., & Graham, J. D. (1995). Five-hundred life-saving interventions and their cost effectiveness. *Risk Analysis, 15,* 369–390.

Tversky, A., & Kahneman, D. (1974). Judgment under uncertainty: Heuristics and biases. *Science, 185,* 1124–1131.

Tversky, A., & Kahneman, D. (1986). The framing of decisions and the psychology of choice. *Science, 211,* 453–458.

Weathers, F. W., Keane, T. M., & Davidson, J. R. T. (2001). Clinicians' administered PTSD scale: A review of the first ten years of research. *Depression & Anxiety, 13,* 132–156.

Weiss, B. (1992). Behavioral toxicology: A new agenda for assessing the risks of environmental pollution. In J. Grabowski & G. VandenBos (Eds.), *Psychopharmacology: Basic mechanisms and applied interventions. Master lectures in psychology* (pp. 167–207). Washington, DC: American Psychological Association.

Weiss, B. (1999, May). *The vulnerability of the developing brain to chemicals in the environment.* Paper presented at the New York Academy of Medicine conference on Environmental Toxins and Neurological Disorders, New York.

Wells, G. L., & Olson, E. A. (2003). Eyewitness testimony. *Annual Review of Psychology, 54,* 277–295.

Wolfe, M. M., Risely, T. R., & Mees, H. L. (1965). Application of operant conditioning procedures to behavior problems of an autistic child. *Research and Therapy, 1,* 302–312.

Wolpe, J. (1958). *Psychotherapy by reciprocal inhibition.* Stanford, CA: Stanford University Press.

Zimbardo, P. G. (1974). *The detention and jailing of juveniles* (pp. 141–161) [Hearings before U. S. Senate Committee on the Judiciary Subcommittee to Investigate Juvenile Delinquency, September 10, 11, 17, 1973], Washington, DC: U.S. Government Printing Office.

Zimbardo, P. G. (1975). On transforming experimental research into advocacy for social change. In M. Deulsch & H. Hornstein (Eds.), *Applying social psychology: Implications for research, practice and training* (pp. 33–66). Hillsdale, NJ: Erlbaum.

Zimbardo, P. G. (1977). *Shyness: What it is, what to do about it.* Reading, MA: Addison-Wesley.

Zimbardo, P. G. (1992). *Psychology and life* (13th ed.). New York: HarperCollins.

Zimbardo, P. G., Haney, C., Banks, W. C., & Jaffe, D. (1973, April 8). The mind is a formidable jailer: A Pirandellian prison. *The New York Times Magazine,* Section 6, pp. 38–46.

Zimbardo, P. G., Maslach, C., & Haney, C. (1999). Reflections on the Stanford prison experiment: Genesis, transformations, consequences. In T. Blass (Ed.), *Obedience to authority: Current perspectives on the Milgram Paradigm* (pp. 193–237). Mahwah, NJ: Erlbaum.

Zimbardo, P. G., Weber, A. L., & Johnson, R. L. (2002). *Psychology: Core concepts* (4th ed.). Boston, MA: Allyn & Bacon.

Editor's note—Philip G. Zimbardo was president of APA in 2002. This article is based on his presidential address, delivered in Toronto, Canada, at APA's 111th Annual Convention on August 9, 2003. Award addresses and other archival materials, including presidential addresses, are peer reviewed but have a higher chance of publication than do unsolicited submissions. Presidential addresses are expected to be expressions of the authors' reflections on the field and on their terms as president. Both this address and that of Robert J. Sternberg, the 2003 APA president, were presented at this convention to catch up on the year lag that had developed in the last decade of giving presidential addresses.

Author's note—Correspondence concerning this article should be addressed to Philip G. Zimbardo, Department of Psychology, Stanford University Building 430, Mail Code 380, Stanford, CA 94305. E-mail: zim@stanford.edu

The 10 Commandments of Helping Students Distinguish Science from Pseudoscience in Psychology

Scott O. Lilienfeld

"Professor Schlockenmeister, I know that we have to learn about visual perception in your course, but aren't we going to learn anything about extrasensory perception? My high school psychology teacher told us that there was really good scientific evidence for it."

"Dr. Glopelstein, you've taught us a lot about intelligence in your course. But when are you going to discuss the research showing that playing Mozart to infants increases their I.Q. scores?"

"Mr. Fleikenzugle, you keep talking about schools of psychotherapy, like psychoanalysis, behavior therapy, and client-centered therapy. But how come you've never said a word about sensory-motor integration therapy? My mother, who's an occupational therapist, tells me that it's a miracle cure for attention-deficit disorder."

The Psuedoscience of Popular Psychology

If you're like most introductory psychology instructors, these sorts of questions probably sound awfully familiar. There's a good reason: much of the popular psychology "knowledge" that our students bring to their classes consists of scant more than pseudoscience. Moreover, our students are often fascinated by dubious claims on the fringes of scientific knowledge: extrasensory perception, psychokinesis, channeling, out-of-body experiences, subliminal persuasion, astrology, biorhythms, "truth serum," the lunar lunacy effect, hypnotic age regression, multiple personality disorder, alien abduction reports, handwriting analysis, rebirthing therapy, and untested herbal remedies for depression, to name but a few. Of course, because some of these claims may eventually be shown to contain a core of truth, we should not dismiss them out of hand. Nevertheless,

what is troubling about these claims is the glaring discrepancy between many individuals' beliefs in them and the meager scientific evidence on their behalf.

Yet many introductory psychology instructors accord minimal attention to potentially pseudoscientific topics in their courses, perhaps because they believe that these topics are of, at best, marginal relevance to psychological science. Moreover, many introductory psychology textbooks barely mention these topics. After all, there is already more than enough to cover in psychology courses, so why tack on material of doubtful scientific status? Furthermore, some instructors may fear that by devoting attention to questionable claims they will end up sending students the unintended message that these claims are scientifically credible.

Benefits of Teaching Students to Distinguish Science from Psuedoscience

So why should we teach psychology students to distinguish science from pseudoscience? As personality theorist George Kelly (1955) noted, an effective understanding of a construct requires an appreciation of both of its poles. For example, we cannot grasp fully the concept of "cold" unless we have experienced heat. Similarly, students may not grasp fully the concept of scientific thinking without an understanding of pseudoscientific beliefs, namely those that at first blush appear scientific but are not.

Moreover, by addressing these topics, instructors can capitalize on a valuable opportunity to impart critical thinking skills, such as distinguishing correlation from causation and recognizing the need for control groups, by challenging students' misconceptions regarding popular psychology. Although many students find these skills to be "dry" or even deadly dull when presented in the abstract, they often enjoy acquiring these skills in the context of lively and controversial topics (e.g., extrasensory perception) that stimulate their interest. Students often learn about such topics from various popular psychology sources that they seek out in everyday life, such as magazine articles, Internet sites, and television programs.

Indeed, for many beginning students, "psychology" is virtually synonymous with popular psychology. Yet because so much of popular psychology consists of myths and urban legends, such as most people use only 10 percent of their brains, expressing anger is usually better than holding it in, opposites attract in interpersonal relationships, high self-esteem is necessary for psychological health, people with schizophrenia have more than one personality, among a plethora of others, many students probably emerge from psychology courses with the same misconceptions with which they entered. As a consequence, they often depart college incapable of distinguishing the wheat from the chaff in popular psychology.

Teaching students to distinguish science from pseudoscience can prove immensely rewarding. Foremost among these rewards is producing discerning consumers of the popular psychology literature. Indeed, research evidence supports the efficacy of teaching psychology courses on pseudoscience and the paranormal. For example, Morier and Keeports (1994) reported that undergraduates enrolled in a "Science and Pseudoscience" seminar demonstrated a statistically significant reduction in paranormal beliefs relative to a quasi-control group of students enrolled in a psychology and law class over the same time period (see also Dougherty, 2004). They replicated this effect over a 2-year period with two sections of the course. Wesp and Montgomery (1998) found that a course on the objective examination of paranormal claims resulted in a statistically significant improvement in the evaluation of reasoning flaws in scientific articles. Specifically, students in this course were better able to identify logical errors in articles and provide rival explanations for research findings.

The 10 Commandments

Nevertheless, teaching students to distinguish science from pseudoscience brings more than its share of challenges and potential pitfalls. In my introductory psychology course (in which I emphasize strongly the distinction between science and pseudoscience in psychology) and in my advanced undergraduate seminar, "Science and Pseudoscience in Psychology," I have learned a number of valuable lessons (by first making just about every mistake about which I'll warn you).

In the following section, I summarize these teaching tips, which I refer to as the "10 Commandments" of teaching psychology students to distinguish science from pseudoscience. To avoid being accused of failing to separate Church from State, I have worded all of these injunctions in the positive rather than the negative to distinguish them from the (only slightly better known) biblical 10 Commandments. I urge readers of this column to inscribe these commandments on impressive stone tablets to be mounted outside of all psychology departments.

First Commandment

Thou shalt delineate the features that distinguish science from pseudoscience. It's important to communicate to students that the differences between science and pseudoscience, although not absolute or clear-cut, are neither arbitrary nor subjective. Instead, philosophers of science (e.g., Bunge, 1984) have identified a constellation of features or "warning signs" that characterize most pseudoscientific disciplines. Among these warning signs are:

- A tendency to invoke ad hoc hypotheses, which can be thought of as "escape hatches" or loopholes, as a means of immunizing claims from falsification.
- An absence of self-correction and an accompanying intellectual stagnation.
- An emphasis on confirmation rather than refutation.
- A tendency to place the burden of proof on skeptics, not proponents, of claims.
- Excessive reliance on anecdotal and testimonial evidence to substantiate claims.
- Evasion of the scrutiny afforded by peer review.
- Absence of "connectivity" (Stanovich, 1997), that is, a failure to build on existing scientific knowledge.
- Use of impressive-sounding jargon whose primary purpose is to lend claims a facade of scientific respectability.
- An absence of boundary conditions (Hines, 2003), that is, a failure to specify the settings under which claims do not hold.

Teachers should explain to students that none of these warning signs is by itself sufficient to indicate that a discipline is pseudoscientific. Nevertheless, the more of these warning signs a discipline exhibits, the more suspect it should become.

Second Commandment

Thou shalt distinguish skepticism from cynicism. One danger of teaching students to distinguish science from pseudoscience is that we can inadvertently produce students reflexively dismissive of any claim that appears implausible. Skepticism, which is the proper mental set of the scientist, implies two seemingly contradictory attitudes (Sagan, 1995): an openness to claims combined with a willingness to subject these claims to incisive scrutiny. As space engineer James Oberg (see Sagan, 1995) reminded us, we must keep our minds open but not so open that our brains fall out. In contrast, cynicism implies close-mindedness. I recall being chastised by a prominent skeptic for encouraging researchers to keep an open mind regarding the efficacy of a novel psychotherapy whose rationale struck him as farfetched. However, if we foreclose the possibility that our preexisting beliefs are erroneous, we are behaving unscientifically. Skepticism entails a willingness to entertain novel claims; cynicism does not.

Third Commandment

Thou shalt distinguish methodological skepticism from philosophical skepticism. When encouraging students to think critically, we must distinguish between two forms of skepticism: (1) an approach that subjects all knowledge claims to scrutiny with the goal of sorting out true from false claims, namely methodological (scientific) skepticism, and (2) an approach that denies the possibility of knowledge, namely philosophical skepticism. When explaining to students that scientific knowledge is inherently tentative and open to revision, some students may mistakenly conclude that genuine knowledge is impossible. This view, which is popular in certain postmodernist circles, neglects to distinguish knowledge claims that are more certain from those that are less certain. Although absolute certainty is probably unattainable in science, some scientific claims, such as Darwin's theory of natural selection, have been extremely well corroborated, whereas others, such as the theory underpinning astrological horoscopes, have been convincingly refuted. Still others, such as cognitive dissonance theory, are scientifically controversial. Hence, there is a continuum of confidence in scientific claims; some have acquired virtual factual status whereas others have been resoundingly falsified. The fact that methodological skepticism does not yield completely certain answers to scientific questions and that such answers could in principle be overturned by new evidence does not imply that knowledge is impossible, only that this knowledge is provisional. Nor does it imply that the answers generated by controlled scientific investigation are no better than other answers, such as those generated by intuition (see Myers, 2002).

Fourth Commandment

Thou shalt distinguish pseudoscientific claims from claims that are merely false. All scientists, even the best ones, make mistakes. Sir Isaac Newton, for example, flirted with bizarre alchemical hypotheses throughout much of his otherwise distinguished scientific career (Gleick, 2003). Students need to understand that the key difference between science and pseudoscience lies not in their content (i.e., whether claims are factually correct or incorrect) but in their approach to evidence. Science, at least when it operates properly, seeks out contradictory information and—assuming that this evidence is replicable and of high quality—eventually incorporates such information into its corpus of knowledge. In contrast, pseudoscience tends to avoid contradictory information (or manages to find a way to reinterpret this information as consistent with its claims) and thereby fails to foster the self-correction that is essential to scientific progress. For example, astrology has changed remarkably little over the past 2,500 years despite overwhelmingly negative evidence (Hines, 2003).

Fifth Commandment

Thou shalt distinguish science from scientists. Although the scientific method is a prescription for avoiding confirmatory bias (Lilienfeld, 2002), this point does not imply that scientists are free of biases. Nor does it imply that all or even most scientists are open to evidence that challenges their cherished beliefs. Scientists can be just as pigheaded and dogmatic in their beliefs as anyone else. Instead, this point implies that good scientists strive to become aware of their biases and to counteract them as much as possible by implementing safeguards against error (e.g., double-blind control groups) imposed by the scientific method. Students need to understand that the scientific method is a toolbox of skills that scientists have developed to prevent themselves from confirming their own biases.

Sixth Commandment

Thou shalt explain the cognitive underpinings of pseudoscientific beliefs. Instructors should emphasize that we are all prone to cognitive illusions (Piatelli-Palmarini, 1994), and that such illusions can be subjectively compelling and difficult to resist. For example, class demonstrations illustrating that many or most of us can fall prey to false memories (e.g., Roediger & McDermott, 1995) can help students to see that the psychological processes that lead to erroneous beliefs are pervasive. Moreover, it is important to point out to students that the heuristics (mental shortcuts) that can produce false beliefs, such as representativeness, availability, and anchoring (Tversky & Kahneman, 1974), are basically adaptive and help us to make sense of a complex and confusing world. Hence, most pseudoscientific beliefs are cut from the same cloth as accurate beliefs. By underscoring these points, instructors can minimize the odds that students who embrace pseudoscientific beliefs will feel foolish when confronted with evidence that contradicts their beliefs.

Seventh Commandment

Thou shalt remember that pseudoscientific beliefs serve important motivational functions. Many paranormal claims, such as those concerning extrasensory perception, out-of-body experiences, and astrology, appeal to believers' deep-seated needs for hope and wonder, as well as their needs for a sense of control over the often uncontrollable realities of life and death. Most believers in the paranormal are searching for answers to profound existential questions, such as "Is there a soul?" and "Is there life after death?" As psychologist Barry Beyerstein (1999) noted (in a play on P.T. Barnum's famous quip), "there's a seeker born every minute" (p. 60). Therefore, in presenting students with scientific evidence that challenges their paranormal beliefs, we should not be surprised when many of them become defensive. In turn, defensiveness can engender an unwillingness to consider contrary evidence.

One of the two best means of lessening this defensiveness (the second is the Eighth Commandment) is to gently challenge students' beliefs with sympathy and compassion, and with the understanding that students who are emotionally committed to paranormal beliefs will find these beliefs difficult to question, let alone relinquish. Ridiculing these beliefs can produce reactance (Brehm, 1966) and reinforce students' stereotypes of science teachers as close-minded and dismissive. In some cases, teachers who have an exceptionally good rapport with their class can make headway by challenging students' beliefs with good-natured humor (e.g., "I'd like to ask all of you who believe in psychokinesis to please raise my hand"). However, teachers must ensure that such humor is not perceived as demeaning or condescending.

Eighth Commandment

Thou shalt expose students to examples of good science as well as to examples of pseudoscience. In our classes, it is critical not merely to debunk inaccurate claims but to expose students to accurate claims. We must be careful not merely to take away student's questionable knowledge, but to give them legitimate knowledge in return. In doing so, we can make it easier for students to swallow the bitter pill of surrendering their cherished beliefs in the paranormal. Students need to understand that many genuine scientific findings are at least as fascinating as are many scientifically dubious paranormal claims. In my own teaching, I have found it useful to intersperse pseudoscientific information with information that is equally remarkable but true, such as lucid dreaming, eidetic imagery, subliminal perception (as opposed to subliminal persuasion, which is far more scientifically dubious), extraordinary feats of human memory (Neisser & Hyman, 2000), and appropriate clinical uses of hypnosis (as opposed to the scientifically unsupported use of hypnosis for memory recovery; see Lynn, Lock, Myers, & Payne, 1997). In addition, we should bear in mind the late paleontologist Stephen Jay Gould's (1996) point that exposing a falsehood necessarily affirms a truth. As a consequence, it is essential not only to point out false information to students, but also to direct them to true information. For example, when explaining why claims regarding biorhythms are baseless (see Hines, 2003), it is helpful to introduce students to claims regarding circadian rhythms, which, although often confused with biorhythms, are supported by rigorous scientific research.

Ninth Commandment

Thou shalt be consistent in one's intellectual standards. One error that I have sometimes observed among skeptics, including psychology instructors who teach critical thinking courses, is to adopt two sets of intellectual standards: one for claims that they find plausible and a second for claims that they do not. The late psychologist Paul Meehl (1973) pointed out that this inconsistency amounts to "shifting the standards of evidential rigor depending on whose ox is being gored" (p. 264). For example, I know one educator who is a vocal proponent of the movement to develop lists of empirically supported therapies, that is, psychological treatments that have been shown to be efficacious in controlled studies. In this domain, he is careful to draw on the research literature to buttress his assertions regarding which psychotherapies are efficacious and which are not. Yet he is dismissive of the research evidence for the efficacy of electroconvulsive therapy (ECT) for depression, even though this evidence derives from controlled studies that are every bit

as rigorous as those conducted for the psychotherapies that he espouses. When I pointed out this inconsistency to him, he denied emphatically that he was adhering to a double standard. It eventually became apparent to me that he was casting aside the evidence for ECT's efficacy merely because this treatment struck him as grossly implausible. Why on earth, he probably wondered, should inducing an epileptoid seizure by administering electricity to the brain alleviate depression? But because surface plausibility is a highly fallible barometer of the validity of truth claims, we must remain open to evidence that challenges our intuitive preconceptions and encourage our students to do so as well.

Tenth Commandment

Thou shalt distinguish pseudoscientific claims from purely metaphysical religious claims. My final commandment is likely to be the most controversial, especially for skeptics who maintain that both pseudoscientific and religious beliefs are irrational. To appreciate the difference between these two sets of beliefs, we must distinguish pseudoscience from metaphysics. Unlike pseudoscientific claims, metaphysical claims (Popper, 1959) cannot be tested empirically and therefore lie outside the boundaries of science. In the domain of religion, these include claims regarding the existence of God, the soul, and the afterlife, none of which can be refuted by any conceivable body of scientific evidence. Nevertheless, certain religious or quasi-religious beliefs, such as those involving "intelligent design" theory, which is the newest incarnation of creationism (see Miller, 2000), the Shroud of Turin, and weeping statues of Mother Mary, are indeed testable and hence suitable for critical analysis alongside of other questionable naturalistic beliefs. By conflating pseudoscientific beliefs with religious beliefs that are strictly metaphysical, instructors risk (a) needlessly alienating a sizeable proportion of their students, many of whom may be profoundly religious; and (b) (paradoxically) undermining students' critical thinking skills, which require a clear understanding of the difference between testable and untestable claims.

Conclusion

Adherence to the Ten Commandments can allow psychology educators to assist students with the crucial goal of distinguishing science from pseudoscience. If approached with care, sensitivity, and a clear understanding of the differences between skepticism and cynicism, methodological and philosophical skepticism, the scientific method and the scientists who use it, and pseudoscience and metaphysics, incorporating pseudoscience and fringe science into psychology courses can be richly rewarding for teachers and students alike. In a world in which the media, self-help industry, and Internet are disseminating psychological pseudoscience at an ever-increasing pace, the critical thinking skills needed to distinguish science from pseudoscience should be considered mandatory for all psychology students.

References

Beyerstein, B. L. (1999). Pseudoscience and the brain: Tuners and tonics for aspiring superhumans. In S. D. Sala (Ed.), *Mind myths: Exploring popular assumptions about the mind and brain* (pp. 59–82). Chichester, England: John Wiley.

Brehm, J. (1966). *A theory of psychological reactance.* New York: Academic Press.

Bunge, M. (1984, Fall). What is pseudoscience? *Skeptical Inquirer, 9,* 36–46.

Dougherty, M. J. (2004). Educating believers: Research demonstrates that courses in skepticism can effectively decrease belief in the paranormal. *Skeptic, 10*(4), 31–35.

Gilovich, T. (1991). How we know what isn't so: *The fallibility of human reason in everyday life.* New York: Free Press.

Gleick, J. (2003). *Isaac Newton.* New York: Pantheon Books.

Gould, S. J. (1996, May). Keynote address, *"Science in the age of (mis)information."* Talk presented at the Convention of the Committee for the Scientific Investigation of Claims of the Paranormal, Buffalo, New York.

Hines, T. (2003). Pseudoscience and the paranormal: A critical examination of the evidence. Buffalo, NY: Prometheus.

Kelly, G. A. (1955). *The psychology of personal constructs, Vols. 1 and 2.* New York: Norton.

Lilienfeld, S. O. (2002). When worlds collide: Social science, politics, and the Rind et al. child sexual abuse meta-analysis. *American Psychologist, 57,* 176–88.

Lilienfeld, S. O., Lohr, M., & Morier, D. (2001). The teaching of courses in the science and pseudoscience of psychology. *Teaching of Psychology, 28,* 182–191.

Lilienfeld, S. O., Lynn, S. J., & Lohr, J. M. (2003). *Science and pseudoscience in clinical psychology.* New York: Guilford.

Lynn, S. J., Lock, T. G., Myers, B., & Payne, D. G. (1997). Recalling the unrecallable: Should hypnosis be used to recover memories in psychotherapy? *Current Directions in Psychological Science, 6,* 79–83.

Meehl, P. E. (1973). Psychodiagnosis: Selected papers. Minneapolis, MN: University of Minnesota Press.

Miller, K. (2000). *Finding Darwin's God: A scientist's search for common ground between God and evolution.* New York: Cliff Street Books.

Morier, D., & Keeports, D. (1994). Normal science and the paranormal: The effect of a scientific method course on students' beliefs in the paranormal. *Research in Higher Education, 35,* 443–453.

Myers, D. G. (2002). *Intuition: Its powers and perils.* New Haven: Yale University Press.

Neisser, U., & Hyman, I. E. (2000). *Memory observed: Remembering in natural contexts.* New York: Worth Publishers.

Piatelli-Palmarini, M. (1994). *Inevitable illusions: How mistakes of reason rule our minds.* New York: John Wiley & Sons.

Popper, K. R. (1959). *The logic of scientific discovery.* New York: Basic Books.

Roediger, H. L., & McDermott, K. B. (1995). Creating false memories: Remembering words not presented in lists. *Journal of Experimental Psychology: Learning, Memory, and Cognition, 21,* 803–814.

Ruscio, J. (2002). *Clear thinking with psychology: Separating sense from nonsense.* Pacific Grove, CA: Wadsworth.

Sagan, C. (1995). *The demon-haunted world: Science as a candle in the dark.* New York: Random House.

Shermer, M. (2002). *Why people believe weird things: Pseudo-science, superstition, and other confusions of our time.* New York: Owl Books.

Stanovich, K. (1997). *How to think straight about psychology* (4th ed.). New York: HarperCollins.

Tversky, A., & Kahneman, D. (1974). Judgment under uncertainty: Heuristics and biases. *Science, 185,* 1124–1131.

Wesp, R., & Montgomery, K. (1998). Developing critical thinking through the study of paranormal phenomena. *Teaching of Psychology, 25,* 275–278.

How to Spot Bias in Research

Morton Ann Gernsbacher

A 1924 article published in the *American Journal of Psychiatry* reported the results of the following laboratory task: "A meaningless picture was produced by pouring India-ink of different intensities on a piece of thick limed paper and then pressing the paper under a glass plate. In addition some abstract lines were drawn by chance on the picture and a few pieces of white paper cut also by chance pasted on the same."

Two genetically distinct groups of 25 human participants were shown the meaningless picture and asked to talk, for two minutes, about any objects in the picture that they recognized. One group of participants was more prone to articulate what the researcher deemed "insignificant" statements, such as "I really don't see any objects" or, in the case of one participant, "If you are a photographer, doctor, I'd like to tell you that you had better change professions." The other group was more likely to talk about objects such as dogs, elephants, and steamships. Because the first group had a higher ratio of "insignificant" to "significant" statements, that group was also deemed "talkative."

An article published just last year in the same journal reported the results of the following laboratory task: "A target force was applied to the subject's left index finger by a torque motor. Subjects were then required to reproduce the force they just experienced, either directly by pressing with the index finger of their right hand or indirectly by using a joystick controlling the torque motor."

The data from the study's two groups of 20 participants are shown in Figure 1. Both groups "reproduced the original force much more accurately" when using the joystick to control the torque motor than when using only their index finger. And when using the joystick, the two groups did not differ. In contrast, when using their index fingers to control the torque motor, the group represented in blue was significantly "more accurate at the task;" that group's ability to match the target force more closely resembled "perfect performance."

These results were interpreted by the researchers as supporting the hypothesis that one group was characterized by "a dysfunction in their ability to predict the sensory consequences of their actions." Indeed, the title of the article was "Evidence for Sensory Prediction Deficits" among this group of participants. Which group? The blue group.

One last example. Using the Deese-Roediger-McDermott "false memory" paradigm, two groups of participants were presented auditorily with lists of semantically related words (e.g., *bed, rest, awake, tired,* and *dream*), and later asked to discriminate between words they'd heard and words they hadn't heard, including words that were semantically associated to words they'd heard (e.g., *sleep*). As shown in Figure 2, the green group demonstrated significantly better memory discrimination than the purple group; the green group was less likely to falsely recognize words they hadn't heard, despite the false words' semantic association with words they'd heard.

The green group's better memory discrimination was attributed to their mentally representing words "in an aberrant manner," even though a concurrent—and direct—test of semantic clustering found no differences between the green and purple groups. The green group's aberrant semantic mental representations was hypothesized to stem from "anatomic abnormalities . . . or as a result of an as-yet unknown pathology."

When another research team reported no difference between green- and purple-type participants in either false recall or false

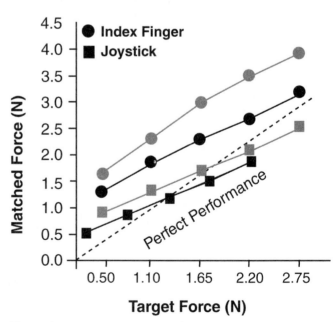

Figure 1

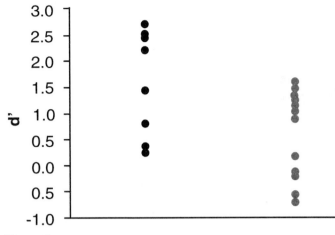

Figure 2

in one study was interpreted as the result of an as-yet unknown pathology, and whose equivalent performance in another study was interpreted as frontal executive impairment.

Confused? If I told you that the group interpreted as providing insignificant and talkative descriptions comprised "normal females," the group interpreted as unable to predict the sensory consequences of their actions comprised persons diagnosed with schizophrenia, and the group interpreted as having aberrant mental representations and frontal executive impairment comprised persons diagnosed with autism, would it help? It shouldn't.

Maggio (1991) recommends that we test our writing for bias by substituting our own group for the group we are discussing. If we feel offended, then our writing is biased. I recommend that we test our interpretations for bias by peeling off the labels, as I've done here. If our interpretations make little sense, then our science is biased.

Reference

Maggio, R. (1991). *The bias-free word finder: A dictionary of nondiscriminatory language.* Boston: Beacon Press.

MORTON ANN GERNSBACHER is the Vilas Research Professor and Sir Frederic C. Bartlett Professor of Psychology at the University of Wisconsin-Madison. She can be reached via email at mgernsbacher@ psychologicalscience.org.

recognition, the authors of the study that had observed the green group's better discrimination interpreted the other study's lack of a between-group difference to the green group also having "frontal-executive impairment."

So, we have a group of individuals whose more factual descriptions of a meaningless picture were interpreted as insignificant and talkative. We have a group whose more accurate tactile matching was interpreted as sensory prediction deficits. And we have a group whose heightened memory discrimination

UNIT 2

Biological Bases of Behavior

Unit Selections

Key Points to Consider

- What is meant by the terms "nature" and "nurture?"

- What contributes more to an individual's psychological being—nature or nurture?

- How does the environment contribute to an individual's psychological being?

- How do genes influence human psychological characteristics and behaviors?

- How has genetic research advanced our understanding of various psychological disorders?

- Do nature and nurture interact in some way?

Student Web Site

www.mhcls.com/online

Internet References

Further information regarding these Web sites may be found in this book's preface or online.

Institute for Behavioral Genetics
  http://ibgwww.colorado.edu/index.html
Serendip
  http://serendip.brynmawr.edu/serendip/

As a child, Angelina vowed she did not want to turn out like either of her parents. Angelina's mother was very passive and acquiescent about her father's drinking. When Dad was drunk, Mom always called his boss to report that Dad was "sick" and then acted as if there was nothing wrong at home. Angelina's childhood was a nightmare. Her father's behavior was erratic and unpredictable. If he drank just a little bit, most often he was happy. If he drank a lot, which was usually the case, he frequently but not always became belligerent.

Despite vowing not to become her father, as an adult Angelina found herself in the alcohol rehabilitation unit of a large hospital. Angelina's employer could no longer tolerate her on-the-job mistakes or her unexplained absences from work. Angelina's supervisor therefore referred her to the clinic for help. As Angelina pondered her fate, she wondered whether her genes pre-ordained her to follow in her father's inebriated footsteps, or whether the stress of her childhood had brought her to this point in her life. After all, being the child of an alcoholic is not easy.

Just as Angelina, psychologists also are concerned with discovering the causes of human behavior. Once the cause is known, treatments for problematic behaviors can be developed. In fact, certain behaviors might even be prevented when the cause has been pre-identified. But for Angelina, prevention was too late.

One of the paths to understanding humans is to understand the biological underpinnings of their behavior. Genes and chromosomes, the body's chemistry (as found in hormones, neurotransmitters, and enzymes), and the nervous system comprised of the brain, spinal cord, nerve cells, and other parts are all implicated in human behavior. All represent the biological aspects of behavior and ought, therefore, to be worthy of study by psychologists.

Physiological psychologists and psychobiologists are often the ones who examine the role of biology in behavior. The neuroscientist is especially interested in brain functioning; the psychopharmacologist is interested in the effects of various pharmacological agents or psychoactive drugs on behavior.

These psychologists often utilize one of a handful of techniques to understand the biology-behavior connection. Animal studies involving manipulation, stimulation, or destruction of certain parts of the brain offer one method of study; these studies remain controversial with animal rights activists. There is also a second available technique that includes the examination of unfortunate individuals whose brains are malfunctioning at birth or are damaged later by accidents or disease.

We can also use animal models to understand genetics; with animal models we can control reproduction as well as manipulate and develop various strains of animals if necessary. Such tactics with humans would be considered extremely unethical and are often disdained by animal rights activists. Also, by studying an individual's behavior in comparison to both natural and adoptive parents, or by studying identical twins reared together or apart, we can begin to understand the role of genetics and the environment in human behavior.

The articles in this unit are designed to familiarize you with the knowledge psychologists have gleaned by using these and other techniques to study physiological processes and other underlying mechanisms in human behavior. Each article should interest you and make you more curious about the role of biology in human psychological functioning.

The Amazing Brain

Is Neuroscience the Key to What Makes Us Human?

RICHARD RESTAK

While in medical school, V. S. Ramachandran, director of the Center for Brain and Cognition at the University of California at San Diego, encountered a patient given to episodes of alternately weeping and laughing uncontrollably. This display of emotional mercuriality struck Ramachandran as a replay of the human condition. "Were these just mirthless joy and crocodile tears, I wondered? Or was he actually feeling alternately happy and sad, the same way a manic-depressive might, but on a compressed scale?"

During his professional career as a neurologist and researcher, Ramachandran has retained his curiosity and formulated about his patients the "kinds of very simple questions that a schoolboy might ask but are embarrassingly hard for experts to answer."

For example, "Why does this patient display these curious symptoms? What do the symptoms tell us about the working of the normal brain?" In the process, Ramachandran has learned that many patients with damage in a localized part of the brain often suffer a highly selective loss of one specific function with other functions remaining unaffected—an indication that the damaged area is normally involved somehow in mediating the impaired function. Further, some of these selective impairments can be both fascinating and informative.

Consider David, a patient of Ramachandran's who emerged from a coma mentally intact, with the exception of the bizarre delusion that his mother had been replaced by an impostor.

Further evaluation revealed an important distinction: Although David couldn't recognize his mother when encountering her face to face, he had no trouble identifying her when talking to her on the telephone. What could account for such an anomaly?

It turns out that separate pathways lead from the auditory and visual regions of the brain to the amygdala, an important component of the brain's emotional circuitry. In David's case, the fibers connecting the visual center to the amygdala were no longer functioning normally. As a result, whenever he looked at his mother he no longer got that warm feeling of recognition that normally accompanies seeing one's parent. He therefore accused her of being an impostor.

The auditory fibers in David's brain, in contrast, retained their normal connections with the amygdala. Consequently, the emotional linkage of voice and person remained intact and David recognized his mother's voice.

"This is a lovely example . . . of neuroscience in action; of how you can take a bizarre, seemingly incomprehensible neurological syndrome . . . and then come up with a simple explanation in terms of the known neural pathways in the brain," writes Ramachandran.

Other bizarre but informative disorders taken up in this wide-ranging book include phantom limb (the sensation that an amputated arm or leg is still present); synesthesia (a condition in which the senses are mingled so that the affected person tastes a shape, or sees a color in a sound or a number); and achromotopsia (seeing the world in shades of gray, like a black-and-white film).

"By studying neurological syndromes which have been largely ignored as curiosities or mere anomalies, we can sometimes acquire novel insights into the functions of the normal brain," the author writes. Moreover, he suggests, "the study of patients with neurological disorders has implications for the humanities, for philosophy, maybe even for aesthetics and art."

While all this sounds reasonable, Ramachandran sometimes comes across like the proverbial carpenter who approaches all issues as resolvable via the use of hammer and nail. Specifically, he claims that neuroscience can answer (or soon will) "some lofty questions that have preoccupied philosophers since the dawn of history: What is free will? What is body image? What is art? What is the self? Who am I?"

At times, his reductionism pushes the envelope a bit: "We recognize that life is a word loosely applied to a collection of processes—DNA replication and transcription, Krebs cycle, Lactic acid cycle, etc., etc." At another point, after naming several brain structures he asserts, "Know how they perform their individual operations, how they interact, and you will know what it means to be a conscious human being."

Despite such extravagant and hubristic statements, no one so far has been able to perform the alchemical conversion whereby "To be or not to be" can be understood in terms of neurotransmitters and brain structures. Nor is such a conversion ever likely since, as philosopher Gilbert Ryle pointed out, it would invoke the category mistake: intermingling separate and distinct orders of discourse.

For example (Ryle's own example, incidentally), the university that I attended cannot be equated except associatively with the buildings comprising it. True, the buildings when considered together may loosely be referred to as "the university"; but the entity defined by that word is far more nuanced than just real estate.

Likewise, can the mind be explained totally in terms of the brain? Ramachandran thinks so and while, on the whole, I tend to agree with him, I also have to admit to a trace of agnosticism on the question.

Not surprisingly, when discussing mental illness, Ramachandran is strictly in the neuropsychiatric camp: Neurology and psychiatry are so interpenetrated that future treatments and cures can only come about via increased knowledge about the brain. As a neurologist and neuropsychiatrist myself, I certainly don't disagree with that claim. Many psychiatrists, however, may find Ramachandran's phrasing of the matter a bit off-putting ("it is only a matter of time before psychiatry becomes just another branch of neurology").

But his heart is in the right place. Freudianism and other guru-driven "isms" are dead, replaced by an emphasis on the brain. Indeed, so much has been learned about mental illness in the past two decades as a result of brain research that it's difficult to imagine any alternative approach.

My principal criticism of this book concerns its odd arrangement: 112 pages of text accompanied by 44 pages of endnotes. As he mentions in his introduction, Ramachandran holds a rather quirky notion about endnotes ("the real book is in the endnotes"). Perhaps that's true, but the delegation of large parts of the narrative to the endnotes presents several difficulties.

For one, this text-endnote dichotomy makes it too easy for both author and editor to forsake their most important duty: organizing the material into a free-flowing narrative. Second, on occasion—such as his description of the more exotic forms of synesthesia—the endnotes prove even more interesting than the main text.

Finally, material in the text is sometimes repeated in the endnotes, such as Ramachandran's explanation of the origin of the ear. And given this emphasis on the endnotes, why are the notes corresponding to the last two citations in the final chapter missing?

Admittedly, these are minor quibbles that detract not at all from a perfectly marvelous book. Overall, reading Ramachandran in *A Brief Tour of Human Consciousness* is like listening to a John Coltrane solo: The man is here, there, and everywhere; he's inventive, inspired, wildly speculative, and yet disciplined by the demands of his craft. Give him a fact about the brain and he'll link it with a quote from Shakespeare; a nanosecond later he'll suggest an experiment that you can carry out in your living room to learn more about the fact.

To Ramachandran, the brain is more than an enchanted loom, and wider than the sky; it's an endless source for manic excitement, intriguing questions, profound reflections and a zany humor ("our brains . . . if raised in a culture-free environment like Texas would barely be human"). And like Coltrane, Ramachandran leaves you marveling at how he does it; wondering how he's learned all that he knows; and spinning like a top from the effort of trying to absorb all the wonderful things that he's telling you.

A Brief Tour of Human Consciousness is well worth the effort. You'll be entertained, provoked, amused and—most important of all—eager to learn more.

RICHARD RESTAK a neurologist and neuropsychiatrist, is the author of *Poe's Heart and the Mountain Climber: Exploring the Effects of Anxiety on Our Brains and Our Culture*, 2004.

Genetic Influence on Human Psychological Traits

A Survey

There is now a large body of evidence that supports the conclusion that individual differences in most, if not all, reliably measured psychological traits, normal and abnormal, are substantively influenced by genetic factors. This fact has important implications for research and theory building in psychology, as evidence of genetic influence unleashes a cascade of questions regarding the sources of variance in such traits. A brief list of those questions is provided, and representative findings regarding genetic and environmental influences are presented for the domains of personality, intelligence, psychological interests, psychiatric illnesses, and social attitudes. These findings are consistent with those reported for the traits of other species and for many human physical traits, suggesting that they may represent a general biological phenomenon.

THOMAS J. BOUCHARD, JR.

Among knowledgeable researchers, discussions regarding genetic influences on psychological traits are not about whether there is genetic influence, but rather about how much influence there is, and how genes work to shape the mind. As Rutter (2002) noted, "Any dispassionate reading of the evidence leads to the inescapable conclusion that genetic factors play a substantial role in the origins of individual differences with respect to all psychological traits, both normal and abnormal" (p. 2). Put concisely, all psychological traits are heritable. Heritability (h^2) is a descriptive statistic that indexes the degree of population variation in a trait that is due to genetic differences. The complement of heritability ($1 - h^2$) indexes variation contributed by the environment (plus error of measurement) to population variation in the trait. Studies of human twins and adoptees, often called behavior genetic studies, allow us to estimate the heritability of various traits. The name behavior genetic studies is an unfortunate misnomer, however, as such studies are neutral regarding both environmental and genetic influences. That they repeatedly and reliably reveal significant heritability for psychological traits is an empirical fact and one not unique to humans. Lynch and Walsh (1998) pointed out that genetic influence on most traits, as indexed by estimates of heritability, is found for all species and observed that "the interesting questions remaining are, How does the magnitude of h^2 differ among characters and species and why?" (p. 175).

Why Study Genetic Influences on Human Behavioral Traits?

A simple answer to the question of why scientists study genetic influences on human behavior is that they want a better understanding of how things work, that is, better theories. Not too many years ago, Meehl (1978) argued that "most so-called 'theories' in the soft areas of psychology (clinical, counseling, social, personality, community, and school psychology) are scientifically unimpressive and technologically worthless" (p. 806). He listed 20 fundamental difficulties faced by researchers in the social sciences. Two are relevant to the current discussion: heritability and nuisance variables. The two are closely related. Nuisance variables are variables assumed to be causes of group or individual differences irrelevant to the theory of an investigator. Investigators seldom provide a full theoretical rationale in support of their choice of nuisance variables to control. As Meehl pointed out, removing the influence of parental socioeconomic status (SES; i.e., treating it as a nuisance variable) on children's IQ, when studying the causes of individual differences in IQ, makes the assumption that parental SES is exclusively a source of environmental variance, as opposed to being confounded with genetic influence. Meehl argued that this example "is perhaps the most dramatic one but other less emotion-laden examples can be found on all sides in the behavioral sciences" (p. 810). His point was that knowledge of how genetic factors influence any given measure (e.g., SES) or trait (e.g., IQ) will allow scientists to develop more scientifically impressive and worthwhile theories about the sources of individual differences in psychological traits.

Evidence of genetic influence on a psychological trait raises a series of new questions regarding the sources of population variance for that trait. All the questions addressed in quantitative genetics (Lynch & Walsh, 1998) and genetic epidemiology (Khoury, 1998) become relevant. What kind of gene action is involved? Is it a simple additive influence, with the effects of genes simply adding up so that more genes cause greater expression of the trait, or is the mode of action more complex? Are the effects of genes for a particular trait more pronounced in men or women? Are there interactions between genes and the environment? For example, it has been known for a long time that stressful life events lead to depression in some people but not others. There is now evidence for an interaction. Individuals who carry a specific genetic variant are more susceptible to depression when exposed to stressful life events than individuals who do not carry the genetic variant (Caspi et al., 2003). Are there gene-environment correlations? That is, do individuals with certain genetic constitutions seek out specific environments? People who score high on measures of sensation seeking certainly, on average, tend to find themselves in more dangerous environments than people who score low for this trait. McGue and I have provided an extended list of such questions (Bouchard & McGue, 2003).

Estimates of the Magnitude of Genetic Influence on Psychological Traits

Table 1 reports typical behavior genetic findings drawn from studies of broad and relatively representative samples from affluent Western societies. In most, but not all, of these studies, estimates of genetic and environmental influences were obtained from studies of twins. Because the studies probably undersampled people who live in the most deprived segment of Western societies, the findings should not be considered as generalizable to such populations. (Documentation for most of the findings can be found in Bouchard & McGue, 2003.)

Personality

Psychologists have developed two major schemes for organizing specific personality traits into a higher-order structure, the Big Five and the Big Three. As Table 1 shows, the findings using the two schemes are much the same. Genetic influence is in the range of 40 to 50%, and heritability is approximately the same for different traits. There is evidence of nonadditive genetic variance. That is, genes for personality, in addition to simply adding or subtracting from the expression of a trait, work in a more complex manner, the expression of a relevant gene depending to some extent on the gene with which it is paired

on a chromosome or on genes located on other chromosomes. Research has yielded little evidence for significant shared environmental influence, that is, similarity due to having trait-relevant environmental influences in common. Some large studies have investigated whether the genes that influence personality traits differ in the two sexes (sex limitation). The answer is no. However, sometimes there are sex differences in heritability.

Mental Ability

Early in life, shared environmental factors are the dominant influence on IQ, but gradually genetic influence increases, with the effects of shared environment dropping to near zero (see the twin studies in Table 1). Although not reported here, adoption studies of (a) unrelated individuals reared together and (b) adoptive parents and their adopted offspring have reported similar results—increasing genetic influence on IQ with age and decreasing shared environmental influence. Results from two twin studies of IQ in old age (over 75) are reported in Table 1. Both studies found a substantial level of genetic influence and little shared environmental influence. The results do, however, suggest some decline in heritability when compared with results for earlier ages. There is no evidence for sex differences in heritability for IQ at any age.

Psychological Interests

Heritabilities for psychological interests, also called vocational or occupational interests, are also reported in Table 1. These heritabilities were estimated using data gathered in a single large study that made use of a variety of samples (twins, siblings, parents and their children, etc.) gathered over many years. All respondents completed one form or another of a standard vocational interest questionnaire. There is little variation in heritability for the six scales, with an average of .36. As with personality traits, there is evidence for nonadditive genetic influence. Unlike personality, psychological interests show evidence for shared environmental influence, although this influence is modest, about 10% for each trait.

Psychiatric Illnesses

Schizophrenia is the most extensively studied psychiatric illness, and the findings consistently suggest a very high degree of genetic influence (heritability of about .80), mostly additive genetic influence, with no shared environmental influence. There do not appear to be gender differences in the heritability of schizophrenia. Major depression is less heritable (about .40) than schizophrenia. Men and women share most, but not all, genetic influences for depression. Panic disorder, generalized anxiety disorder, and phobias are moderately heritable, and the effect is largely additive, with few if any sex differences. The heritability of alcoholism is in the range of .50 to .60 mostly because of additive genetic effects. Findings regarding the possibility of sex differences in the heritability of alcoholism are mixed.

Antisocial behavior has long been thought to be more heritable in adulthood than childhood. The results of a recent analysis do not support that conclusion. The genetic influence is additive

Table 1 Estimates of Broad Heritability and Shared Environmental Influence and Indications of Nonadditive Genetic Effects and Sex Differences in Heritability for Representative Psychological Traits

Trait	Heritability	Nonadditive genetic effect	Shared environmental effect	Sex differences in heritabilily
Personality (adult samples)				
Big Five				
Extraversion	.54	Yes	No	Perhaps
Agreeableness (aggression)	.42	Yes	No	Probably not
Conscientiousness	.49	Yes	No	Probably not
Neuroticism	.48	Yes	No	No
Openness	.57	Yes	No	Probably not
Big Three				
Positive emotionality	.50	Yes	No	No
Negative emotionality	.44	Yes	No	No
Constraint	.52	Yes	No	No
Intelligence				
By age in Dutch cross-sectional twin data				
Age 5	.22	No	.54	No
Age 7	.40	No	.29	No
Age 10	.54	No	.26	No
Age 12	.85	No	No	No
Age 16	.62	No	No	No
Age 18	.82	No	No	No
Age 26	.88	No	No	No
Age 50	.85	No	No	No
In old age (>75 years old)	.54–.62	Not tested	No	No
Psychological interests				
Realistic	.36	Yes	.12	NA
Investigative	.36	Yes	.10	NA
Artistic	.39	Yes	.12	NA
Social	.37	Yes	.08	NA
Enterprising	.31	Yes	.11	NA
Conventional	.38	Yes	.11	NA
Psychiatric illnesses (liability estimates)				
Schizophrenia	.80	No	No	No
Major depression	.37	No	No	Mixed findings
Panic disorder	.30–.40	No	No	No
Generalized anxiety disorder	.30	No	Small female only	No
Phobias	.20–.40	No	No	No
Alcoholism	.50–.60	No	Yes	Mixed findings
Antisocial behavior				
Children	.46	No	.20	No
Adolescents	.43	No	.16	No
Adults	.41	No	.09	No
Social attitudes				
Conservatism				
Under age 20 years	.00	NR	Yes	NR
Over age 20 years	.45–.65	Yes	Yes in females	Yes
Right-wing authoritarianism (adults)	.50–.64	No	.00–.16	NA
Religiousness				
16-year-olds	.11–.22	No	.45–.60	Yes
Adults	.30–.45	No	.20–.40	Not clear
Specific religion	Near zero	NR	NA	NR

Note. NA = not available: NR = not relevant.

and in the range of .41 to .46. Shared environmental influences decrease from childhood to adulthood, but do not entirely disappear in adulthood. There are no sex differences in heritability.

Social Attitudes

Twin studies reveal only environmental influence on conservatism up to age 19; only after this age do genetic influences manifest themselves. A large study (30,000 adults, including twins and most of their first-degree relatives) yielded heritabilities of .65 for males and .45 for females. Some of the genetic influence on conservatism is nonadditive. Recent work with twins reared apart has independently replicated these heritability findings. Conservatism correlates highly, about .72, with right-wing authoritarianism, and that trait is also moderately heritable.

Religiousness is only slightly heritable in 16-year-olds (.11 for girls and .22 for boys in a large Finnish twin study) and strongly influenced by shared environment (.60 in girls and .45 in boys). Religiousness is moderately heritable in adults (.30 to .45) and also shows some shared environmental influence. Good data on sex differences in heritability of religiousness in adults are not available. Membership in a specific religious denomination is largely due to environmental factors.

A Note on Multivariate Genetic Analysis

In this review, I have addressed only the behavior genetic analysis of traits taken one at a time (univariate analysis). It is important to recognize that it is possible to carry out complex genetic analyses of the correlations among traits and compute genetic correlations. These correlations tell us the degree to which genetic effects on one score (trail measure) are correlated with genetic effects on a second score, at one or at many points in time. The genetic correlation between two traits can be quite high regardless of whether the heritability of either trait is high or low, or whether the correlation between the traits is high or low. Consider the well-known positive correlation between tests of mental ability, the evidentiary base for the general intelligence factor. This value is typically about .30. The genetic correlation between such tests is, however, much higher, typically closer to .80. Co-occurrence of two disorders, a common finding in psychiatric research, is often due to common genes. The genetic correlation between anxiety and depression, for example, is estimated to be very high. Multivariate genetic analysis of behavioral traits is a very active domain of research.

Concluding Remarks

One unspoken assumption among early behavior geneticists, an assumption that was shared by most for many years, was that some psychological traits were likely to be significantly influenced by genetic factors, whereas others were likely to be primarily influenced by shared environmental influences. Most behavior geneticists assumed that social attitudes, for example, were influenced entirely by shared environmental influences, and so social attitudes remained largely unstudied until relatively recently. The evidence now shows how wrong these assumptions were. Nearly every reliably measured psychological phenotype (normal and abnormal) is significantly influenced by genetic factors. Heritabilities also differ far less from trait to trait than anyone initially imagined. Shared environmental influences are often, but not always, of less importance than genetic factors, and often decrease to near zero after adolescence. Genetic influence on psychological trails is ubiquitous, and psychological researchers must incorporate this fact into their research programs else their theories will be "scientifically unimpressive and technologically worthless," to quote Meehl again.

At a fundamental level, a scientifically impressive theory must describe the specific molecular mechanism that explicates how genes transact with the environment to produce behavior. The rudiments of such theories are in place. Circadian behavior in humans is under genetic influence (Hur, Bouchard, & Lykken, 1998), and some of the molecular mechanisms in mammals are now being revealed (Lowrey & Takahashi, 2000). Ridley (2003) and Marcus (2004) have provided additional examples of molecular mechanisms that help shape behavior. Nevertheless, the examples are few, the details are sparse, and major mysteries remain. For example, many behavioral traits are influenced by nonadditive genetic processes. These processes remain a puzzle for geneticists and evolutionists, as well as psychologists, because simple additive effects are thought to be the norm (Wolf, Brodie, & Wade, 2000). We also do not understand why most psychological traits are moderately heritable, rather than, as some psychologists expected, variable in heritability, with some traits being highly heritable and others being largely under the influence of the environment. It seems reasonable to suspect that moderate heritability may be a general biological phenomenon rather than one specific to human psychological traits, as the profile of genetic and environmental influences on psychological traits is not that different from the profile of these influences on similarly complex physical traits (Boomsma, Busjahn, & Peltonen, 2002) and similar findings apply to most organisms.

Note

1. See Evans (2004, Fig. 1) for a recent commission of this error.

References

Boomsma, D. I., Busjahn, A., & Peltonen, L. (2002). Classical twin studies and beyond. *Nature Reviews: Genetics, 3,* 872–882.

Bouchard, T. J., Jr., & McGue, M. (2003). Genetic and environmental influences on human psychological differences. *Journal of Neurobiology, 54,* 4–45.

Caspi, A., Sugden, K., Moffitt, T. E., Taylor, A., Craig, I. W., Harrington, H., McClay, J., Mill, J., Martin, J., Braiwaite, A., & Poulton, R. (2003). Influence of life stress on depression: Moderation by a polymorphism in the 5-HTT gene. *Science, 301,* 386–389.

Evans, G. W. (2004). The environment of childhood poverty. *American Psychologist, 59,* 77–92.

Hur, Y.- M., Bouchard, T. J., Jr., & Lykken, D. T. (1998). Genetic and environmental influence on morningness-eveningness. *Personality and Individual Differences, 25,* 917–925.

Khoury, M. J. (1998). Genetic epidemiology. In K. J. Rothman & S. Greenland (Eds.), *Modem epidemiology* (pp. 609–622). Philadelphia: Lippincott-Raven.

Lowrey, P. L., & Takahashi, J. S. (2000). Genetics of the mammalian circadian system: Photic entrainment, circadian pacemaker mechanisms, and posttranslational regulation. *Annual Review of Genetics, 34,* 533–562.

Lynch, M., & Walsh, B. (1998). *Genetics and analysis of quantitative traits.* Sunderland. MA: Sinauer.

Marcus, G. (2004). *The birth of the mind: How a tiny number of genes creates the complexities of human thought.* New York: Basic Books.

Meehl, P. E. (1978). Theoretical risks and tabular asterisks: Sir Karl, Sir Ronald, and the slow progress of soft psychology. *Journal of Consulting and Clinical Psychology, 46,* 806–834.

Ridley, M. (2003). *Nature via nurture: Genes, experience and what makes us human.* New York: HarperCollins.

Rutter, M. (2002). Nature, nurture, and development: From evangelism through science toward policy and practice. *Child Development, 73,* 1–21.

Wolf, J. B., Brodie. E. D. I., & Wade. M. J. (Eds.).6 (2000). *Epistasis and the evolutionary process.* New York: Oxford University Press.

From Discovery to Translation
New Directions in Research

Dr. Thomas Insel

Introduction

I think the time has come for us to set the bar higher in what we expect, both for treatments and for the way we diagnose mental illnesses. We are still at the stage where we diagnose by symptoms; we diagnose and treat on an episodic basis, rather than having a coordinated, longitudinal approach to what are really chronic illnesses.

Comparatively, mental illness lags behind other areas of medicine. Biomedical research is having an impact for heart disease and cancer; what has research delivered so far for mental illnesses?

As far as I can tell, the prevalence for autism, schizophrenia, bipolar disorder, major depressive disorder, and all of the anxiety disorders has not decreased over the last 30 years.

Decade of the Brain

The 1990s were proclaimed by Congress and then-President Bush as the "Decade of the Brain." Research began to focus us for the first time on this idea that mental life could be understood as a life of the brain. That is, mental events could be understood as neural events, and this separation between mind and body that's been around since Descartes needed to be resolved, as we began to think about the mind as really an expression of the brain.

This leads to a biological understanding of mental illness. As soon as you say these are brain disorders, it means the science you have to focus on isn't simply psychology, it's biology, and you have to bring in a whole new range of tools.

One example of using such new tools is a study that was done in children within the intramural program here at the National Institute of Mental Health. In this work, Judy Rappaport and colleagues studied a rare form of schizophrenia that starts very early in life, called *childhood onset,* that starts before age 14. Initially when she saw this group of 70-plus children, she did a comparison in age-match controls, using structural MRI scans to look at brain structures between children with schizophrenia at age nine or 10, and those without.

In the three views of their brains as a composite shown here, representing the average across all 70 children, areas in red or orange and some yellow show where there is thinning of the gray matter of the cortex of the brain. The key here is the lower row, where—when we look at the same children five years later compared to the same controls—we can see that this is very progressive brain disease. Five years later we find very profound reductions in gray matter across most of the brain.

We're not talking about a neurological disease like Parkinson's or Huntington's. In schizophrenia, we find a disorder of whole brain systems. It's more diffuse, rather than a problem of a specific focus. That is what separates this group from the brain disorders most of us think about when we talk about neurology.

Decade of Discovery

Currently, we are in a "Decade of Discovery." We're getting to some of the basic principles of how the brain is put together and how it develops. I compare where we are going now in mental illness research to where astronomy has been in recent years. Whole new worlds are being discovered because there are tools to look deep into outer space. In human brain research, we now have tools to look deep into inner space. We can do that at the level of genes, where for the first time we are identifying, learning about a whole range of players we didn't know about five years, or, in some cases, six months ago.

The Human Genome

At the genomic end, the big event has been the completion, in 2003, of a map of all the genes in the human genome. Here is one way to understand this achievement: if you have a very long book filled with lots of letters, the Genome Map tells you what all the letters are, what their order is, and which of those letters form words. The map is spread out over 46 chapters, or chromosomes. There are about 3 billion "letters" across those 46 chromosomes, but only about 23,000 genes, that is, 23,000 words where the text actually spells something that makes something—in this case, protein.

Like having the white pages of the phone book, if you knew what you wanted, you could use this to look up the address. That was terrific, but actually what we needed was the yellow pages, because when something goes wrong, you want to know who are the electricians, the mechanics, and so on. The kinds of questions that we want to ask of the genome are about where to look for something that has gone wrong in the brain or in some cell in the body. For that, we will need to know much more than we do now.

The second, really critical piece, which was not talked about in 2003, when this received so much media attention, was that the genome published was in fact of a single person. But unless you have an identical twin, there is no one on the planet who has exactly your sequence. And we didn't then appreciate fully how much variation there is in the sequence of the genome. About one out of every 1,000 bases is different between any two of us, so understanding that variation is going to be a huge challenge.

The HapMap

Now, that challenge of understanding the variation has changed very dramatically, because this year we have another genome project that has been completed: the *Hap-Map*. This was launched soon after the publication of the genome in 2003. People all over the world, in about 12 different centers, set out to discover where all this variation is, and what parts of the variation really matter.

With 3 billion bases, even with variation in only one of every thousand, you are left with 3 million expected points of variation to investigate. So, it would seem untenable to attempt to identify all of them. However, it turns out it's much easier to take on this question than we had thought, because you don't need to measure them all. The points of variation tend to cluster together, so if you identify one, you can usually predict the next six or seven that are nearby. So in fact, you don't need to measure all 3 million bases that are unique points of variation; you need to measure only about 10 percent or less of those.

From about the time this was recognized, in late 2005, a whole series of new tools have started becoming available, which allow us to measure sequences—what we call "genotyping"—quickly and cheaply.

Here is an example of how this has helped speed up research in this area. If we were to ask—before the discovery mentioned above that points of variation cluster—why one person develops schizophrenia and her brother doesn't, we would have had to identify all of these 3 million common points of variation. We call them *snips* (SNPs), which stands for "single nucleotide polymorphisms," and a SNP is a point of variation, a place in the genome where one of the letters has flipped from one to another. Up until a few months ago, we would have needed to measure all 3 million. We would have had to collect a thousand people with schizophrenia and a thousand people without, and genotype all of their DNA to get a sense of all of the points of variation. That's about 6 billion genotypes. The cost would be about $3 billion to answer the question. Possible, but unless you were as wealthy as Bill Gates, you likely would not do it.

But look at where we are today. Instead of 3 million bases, you now have to identify only 300,000, because of the HapMap. About one out of every 10 gives you what you need. You would still need a thousand cases and a thousand controls, and you would genotype all of the polymorphisms as before. But now instead of 6 billion sequences, you need 600 million.

That will still take a lot of money, but it's much less than before. Also, the cost to genotype a sequence has dropped; rather than fifty cents per genotype, the cost is less than a cent. Suddenly, it has become feasible: for $3 million, you can answer the question. And we will answer that question over the next couple of years, as we get all of the samples together and run them through these very powerful and, now, not-so-expensive methods for understanding what aspects of variation in the human genome confer a risk for having one of these disorders.

In human brain research, we now have tools to look deep into inner space.

Understanding the Mechanisms

This technique has already begun to pay off. To name one example: age-related macular degeneration. This is the most common cause of adult-onset blindness. Early in 2006, four groups simultaneously reported an association between one particular gene and its variations and the risk for this disease. There are two amazing things about this. First, no one thought about this as a genetic disease before. Although there were some known familial aspects, scientists did not expect to find genes of large effect.

We are just learning who the big players are, but genomics will take us in that direction.

The second amazing thing was that the gene was a complement gene; that is, important for the immune system, and no one had been looking at the immune system as a cause for this particular disease. Two months later, another group reported yet another immune system complement gene. When you put these two together, you can explain 74 percent of the risk for developing age-related macular degeneration.

One year ago at this time we didn't even realize that this was a heavily genetic disease, and already with the help of the Hap Map and these large data sets we're able to predict with 74 percent reliability who is vulnerable. This is happening in type 2 and type 1 diabetes, hypertension, and other heart diseases. We will do this in mental illnesses, and I think it will happen fairly rapidly. We haven't done the full-scale studies that need to be done. We are just learning who the big players are, but genomics will take us in that direction.

The treatments we have for schizophrenia now have all been developed by serendipity or are knock-offs of drugs we already have. None of them is adequate. The major disability experienced by individuals living with schizophrenia has to do with the cognitive deficits that come with this illness, and we don't have treatment for that symptom yet.

But now we have a path we can follow to change this situation.

Understanding the mechanisms—that is, at the molecular level how someone develops this disorder—will tell us where to pinpoint interventions as we develop new treatments. That's how scientists discovered the drug Gleevec, that cures certain kinds of myeloid leukemia.

Neuroimaging Tools

Neuroimaging tools have made exciting new things possible in research on mental illnesses. PET scans, MRI scans, and related kinds of technology have become much better in the last year or so, particularly in spatial resolution; we can see details we couldn't see two years ago. We can measure things quickly, almost in real time, which was not even a possibility we considered up until the last two or three years.

In depression, we've found an area of the brain is involved that we were never even looking for. Much to everyone's surprise, a study examining brain metabolism in people with either bipolar or unipolar depression compared to people without those illnesses showed an area (highlighted in red, and the surrounding area in yellow [in slide 17; that seemed to be reduced in its metabolic rate.) That is, in people with either illness, this area seems to be less active than it should be.

This area was such a frontier in the brain that it didn't even have a name yet. It was identified in old maps of the cortical surface only with a number, *cingulate area 25*. We all still simply call it *area 25,* but this area that, three years ago, nobody had really bothered to explore is, in 2006, the hottest story for the study of depression.

Here is why. It appears that area 25 is involved not only in the way we modulate sadness and depression, but also in the way an individual person responds to treatment. If we look at PET scans showing the metabolic rate in different brain areas, the areas in red show increased metabolic rate; the areas in blue, decreased metabolic rate.

We can look at a group of people who have been treated with paroxetine (Paxil) successfully—people who had very high depression scores before treatment and then were essentially recovered when they were studied three months later. If we then look at people who were successfully treated with cognitive behavior therapy—equally effectively treated, in this group—what we see is that this one area seems to change, the same area we saw in the study of unipolar and bipolar depression: cingulate area 25.

When we ask people who have experienced depression to simulate sadness and to remember what that was like, what we observe during transient sadness is that activity in this same area increases; it is the same region that has high levels of metabolic activity when depression is present and that becomes less active with treatment.

Perhaps even more remarkable is that when you look at people who have been treated but have not recovered, it's the failure to show the change in this area that seems to indicate who is not going to recover with the treatment (in the case of this study, with fluoxetine, or Prozac).

Interestingly, this set of observations comes from Dr. Helen Mayberg, who is not a psychiatrist but a neurologist, who had been interested in Parkinson's disease and who has now attacked depression in much the way neurologists had attacked Parkinson's. In doing so, she has come up with this very interesting picture of the circuitry of depression.

PET scans, MRI scans, and related kinds of technology have become much better. We can see details we couldn't see two years ago.

It turns out these changes that accompany the recovery from depression don't depend on the type of treatment, whether it is treatment with one of the SSRI medications, like paroxetine or fluoxetine, or with a placebo, with transcranial magnetic stimulation, or with ECT. Whatever the treatment may be, if a person experiencing depression improves, this area of the brain seems to show the change. There are many other changes in the brain, but this is the one they seem to have in common.

Moreover, there is evidence that there is an actual structural change in people who are at risk for depression.

This is perhaps the most extraordinary finding of all. Some people have a particular genetic variant in the serotonin transporter which puts them at risk for depression. We have studied people who have experienced a number of life events that are stressful, comparing those with the variant that is thought to make them vulnerable to those who have the variant that appears to make people more resilient; doing structural scans on a hundred such people, we asked a computer what was different between the brains of these two groups. The one place that popped out was, again, this frontier area, *area 25*.

This is extraordinary. We now have the beginning of a circuitry for depression in a way that we believe we have for the circuitry for Parkinson's disease. It gives us a nodal point to work from. Dr. Mayberg and her colleagues have begun to map out this circuitry of the brain. We can begin to understand not only the different nodes in these complicated circuits, but what those different nodes might be responsible for. Some nodes might be responsible for the somatic or vegetative aspects of depression; some for the emotional aspects, the sense of helplessness; and some for the memory problems or the loss of vitality. These aspects of the illness may all be associated with different circuits, and require different kinds of interventions. We could begin to map and understand this illness at that level of detail.

Biological Understanding

To get to new, better treatments, what we really need is what we call in science the pathophysiology of these illnesses. We need to understand their basic biology, the way we are getting to understand that of cancer, for example.

We are getting there. We may soon have the tools to practice bio-diagnostics, that is, tools with which to make a diagnosis and then develop treatments that target core aspects of the illness.

Whatever the treatment may be, if a person experiencing depression improves, this area of the brain seems to show the change.

Decade of Translation: Translating Research into Practice

Perhaps the most important point in all of this is personalized care. I often say that researchers are in love with the mean, while patients and families feel the variants. That is, we researchers spend so much time studying 100 people or 1,000 people and finding out that a new treatment makes 30 percent of them 40 percent better. But an individual person with an illness, or a family member, or a doctor treating a patient want to know which treatment is going to be best for this particular person.

Beyond the decade of discovery, we need to enter a "Decade of Translation," bringing all this exciting research activity into our practice.

In recent years the NIMH has been very involved in some of the several large-scale trials that have been asking important questions about how we treat these illnesses. Over the last seven years, about 10,000 people at 200 sites have been participating in trials focused on this question: how do we personalize care? How do we figure out which treatment is best for which person?

To summarize very briefly what we have been learning from these trials, this message has come through: medications are generally helpful, and necessary in many cases, but they are absolutely not sufficient.

How does a large study connect to personalized care? Consider the CATIE study—a large double-blind study examining the long-term effects and usefulness of antipsychotic medications in persons with schizophrenia. Seventy-five percent of the people who went into the study on any given medication discontinued that medication within the 18 months of the trial's duration. A 75 percent dropout rate tells you something about the medication, not about the illness.

This CATIE finding points to the urgent need for personalized care. The idea of treating schizophrenia with just a medication visit of ten or 15 minutes once each month is unacceptable. We need to bring down that 75 percent rate, and to do it individual by individual, with personalized care.

It may turn out that schizophrenia is not a single illness but a handful of distinct illnesses—a little bit like hypertension. There are lots of ways to get this increase in blood pressure: a tumor in your kidney, something in your pituitary, or a vascular problem. I wouldn't be surprised if at the end of the day that were true for schizophrenia; knowing the underlying causes of the symptoms will help us treat the illness much more effectively.

How do we use these new tools to translate research into practice? The STAR*D study looked at 4,000 people,

Research Study Seeks to Improve Depressive Symptoms Quickly

Several medications are effective for treating depression. However, they can take weeks or months to achieve their full effects. The National Institute of Mental Health (NIMH) is studying whether a particular drug can cause a rapid antidepressant effect in patients with bipolar or unipolar depression. The study also tries to see if it can sustain the results with another medication in certain patients. Understanding how this works may help the understanding of depression and the design of better antidepressants.

NIMH is seeking people the ages of 18 and 65 with depression (unipolar or bipolar) who are:

- Free of other serious medical conditions
- Willing to participate in a minimum of a 12-day inpatient stay

Research medications provided free of charge. Compensation and transportation reimbursement is provided. *Atendemos pacientes de habla hispana.* Contact: (301) 496-5645 (TTY: 1 (866) 411-1010) or Libby Jolkovsky, M.S., at (301) 402-9347 or http://patientinfo.nimh.nih.gov.

who were experiencing major depressive disorder and went on citalopram, an SSRI. About 30 percent got well during the study's 12 weeks of treatment with citalopram (Celexa) Later, we looked at everyone's DNA and asked: Is there a way to predict which people will get well?

Sure enough, a gene variation popped up that explains a great deal of the variance of who will or won't respond to citalopram. Now we've identified four or five such genes that explain about 50 percent of the variation in response. As it happens, one gene variation that is associated with response or failure to respond to citalopram is far more common—three times more common—in African Americans, so it may be a factor in explaining a trend that has been observed for a while, that African Americans who experience major depressive disorder may be less responsive to SSRIs. Here, then, is one instance of a finding that can help us understand something better, and rather than simply observe it, to improve our treatment of individuals.

A 75 percent dropout rate tells you something about the medication, not about the illness. We need to bring down that rate with personalized care.

So, we're getting there—closer to the point where we don't have to wait 12 weeks to tell somebody they shouldn't be on this medication. In the next year or so we're looking at having the kinds of tools that would let us predict who will and won't respond, and who might have adverse events, while taking a given medication for depression.

Cure Therapeutics

As I said earlier, if you are a person with an illness, or a family member, or a health care provider, you want to know which treatment is going to be best or which might involve too many risks for this particular person. Personalized care takes us to that question in two ways.

First, it takes us to what I call *cure therapeutics,* that is, beyond just recovery. We want to talk about getting to the point we now talk about with cancer or diabetes or hypertension. It's about not just making people get better; it's making people well. That ought to be the bar that we set. We may not make it to that point, but if we don't set that as the standard, we're certainly not going to make it.

Strategic Prevention

The other aspect of this is what we call *strategic* prevention, a concept familiar to many people because it's at the heart of modern cardiology and of dealing with certain forms of cancer, as well. *Strategic* prevention means understanding which people are specifically at risk and developing interventions long before the disease does its damage. If you are a cardiologist in America, you're spending most of your time with people who've never had a heart attack. You don't wait for someone to have the first episode before you put them into treatment—you've got lifestyle changes, diet, statins.

But in mental illness, we wait until there is a first psychotic break and then we see what we can do. That is not where to set the bar or where we want to be.

Rather, we need to translate our expanding knowledge into not just medicines or treatments for acute symptoms, but into tools for strategic prevention. Furthermore, we need to apply these tools now, but we also need to apply them in the right way. If we have really terrific high-tech treatments that aren't available or can't be paid for, we will have failed miserably.

But I think that if we at NIMH can demonstrate not only that something works, but that it is cost-effective, as we're doing now for the treatment of depression in the workplace, people will begin to respond to that. First you've got to have the intervention; then you've got to demonstrate its very real effectiveness; and then you can really lobby for change. And that's an area where NAMI can have an impact.

On June 28, 2006, **DR. THOMAS INSEL,** Director of the National Institute of Mental Health, spoke at NAMI's annual convention. After 15 years as a researcher at NIMH, Dr. Insel served at Emory University as director of the Yerkes Regional Primate Research Center, 1994–1999. He then was founding director of the Center for Behavioral Neuroscience, 1999–2002, before returning to NIMH in his current capacity. Dr. Insel's talks have been a highlight of recent NAMI conventions, and this year his keynote address was particularly welcome, with its focus on the hope and promise offered by new advances in research on mental illnesses. The preceeding excerpts from Dr. Insel's discussion and slides highlight some of the areas he touched upon.

The Structure of the Human Brain

Precise studies of the size and shape of the brain have yielded fresh insights into neural development, differences between the sexes and human evolution.

JOHN S. ALLEN, JOEL BRUSS, AND HANNA DAMASIO

I f you lived in the 19th century, your entire character—attributes such as ambition, tenderness, wit and valor—might have been judged by the size and shape of your skull. This practice, called phrenology, was developed by Franz Joseph Gall and Johann Spurzheim in Vienna during the early 1800s. Adherents claimed different mental "faculties" were localized to different parts of the brain, and these regions would be bigger if you possessed the traits in abundance. Phrenologists also believed the brain determined the shape of the skull, so they reasoned an external examination of the cranium would detect regional brain development. This led to the popular (arid not inaccurate) characterization of phrenology as the "science" of bumps on the head.

We are right to be skeptical of these early explorations of brain size and its functional correlates. However, there was a nugget of truth in the phrenological view of world: Brain structure is a fundamental aspect of neuroscience because brain functions take place in specific combinations of brain regions. In complex animals, the size and shape of the brain reflect a host of evolutionary, developmental, genetic, pathological and functional processes that interact to produce an individual organism.

Because many factors influence neural structures, the study of brain volume, or volumetrics, has the potential to offer insights from many perspectives. In an evolutionary context, studies of brain volume across species can link anatomical, behavioral and ecological data. Species that have unpredictably large or small brains are useful for studying the forces of evolution that influence brain size. For example, Katharine Milton at the University of California, Berkeley has suggested that fruit-eating primates have a higher brain-to-body mass ratio than leaf-eating primates because locating widely dispersed, seasonally available fruit makes greater cognitive demands than finding more convenient foods, such as leaves. Volumetrics can also illuminate developmental patterns within and across species, which in turn suggest how evolution might be constrained by implicit rules of neurological growth. The study of neurological diseases also depends on a systematic analysis of brain size and shape. For instance, some children with autism have atypically large brains, and Alzheimer's disease causes progressive brain atrophy. In both cases, the pathological processes that underlie these conditions manifest as changes in brain volume. So volumetric studies are both a means to understanding brain function and an end in themselves.

Tools of the Trade

Neuroanatomy has undergone a resolution in the past 30 years. The leap became possible with the introduction of new imaging technologies such as x-ray computed tomography (CT, also called CAT scanning), magnetic resonance imaging (MRI) and positron emission tomography (PET). With these tools, scientists can view the structure and activity of the living human brain in unprecedented detail. For the structural and volumetric study of the brain, CT and MRI have been of critical importance.

Computed tomography is the older technology. It uses the variable absorption of x-rays by different brain components to visualize structures inside the skulls of living subjects. A single CT image is the product of thousands of individual measurements, which are made as the x-ray source swivels in a full circle around the head.

Unlike CT, MRI does not use x rays, relying instead on powerful magnets to momentarily align the nuclei of hydrogen atoms in body tissues, most of which are within water molecules. When the magnet is turned off, the infinitesimal spinning (or resonating) nuclei fall back to a normal state, releasing energy in the form of radio waves. The frequency of these waves provides a measure of local hydrogen concentration, which varies according to tissue type, such as bone or fat. This produces a very fine-grained map—often as good as a postmortem analysis. The technique clearly distinguishes gray matter (mostly neuronal cell bodies), white matter (mostly nerve fibers insulated by fatty myelin, plus supporting cells) and cerebrospinal fluid or CSF (the liquid that fills the spaces within and around the brain). In addition, individual MR scans can be stacked to form a virtual three-dimensional model, then resliced along any plane or angle.

Draw the Line

The process of dividing the brain into different regions is known as *parcellation,* and there are many ways to do it depending on the goals of the investigators and the methods available. MRI parcellation uses visible anatomical landmarks, such as the sulci (folds) and gyri (bulges) on the surface of the brain to create "regions of interest" or ROIs. They can include broad structural divisions—for example, the temporal, parietal and occipital lobes—as well as smaller structures such as the hippocampus or corpus callosum. The locations of specific brain activities, when they are known, can also guide anatomical parcellation.

A three-dimensional MR scan is made from a series of separate, contiguous images. A typical high-resolution analysis might have a slice thickness of 1.5 millimeters, meaning that an average brain would be compiled from more than 100 sections. Specialized image-processing software can then "extract" the brain from the skull and visualize it as a solid object. It can be sliced in any plane, rotated or resized to match a standard model. At this point, ROIs can be defined by marking the boundary limits of the structure on the surface of the brain. These marks are then transferred to "coronal" slices (parallel to the plane of a person's face) to define the region on each image. The ROI volume (area multiplied by slice thickness) from each section is summed to give an overall value. The studies mentioned in this article, like others in the field, were done through a laborious process of manually tracing ROIs onto each image. Several methods are currently being developed to automate this painstaking process, but to date none exists that can match the precision of hand tracing with expert knowledge of anatomy.

One of the most useful aspects of an MR scan for imaging neural structures is that it sharply defines gray matter, white matter and cerebrospinal fluid. Many research groups are studying the relative gray:white composition of various structures, aided by automated methods (which do work well for this purpose) for segmenting MRIs into these categories.

Genes and Brains

Genetic processes underlie the development and evolution of the brain, and several research teams are studying the genetics of human brain volume and structure. One strategy is to use MRI to look at the brain volumes of identical and fraternal twins. The studies indicate that human cranial capacity is a strongly inherited trait, and most of the variation in total or hemispheric volume can be explained by genetic factors. In one report, by William Baaré and his colleagues at the University Medical Center of Utrecht in the Netherlands, genes accounted for the large majority of brain volume differences: 90 percent for the brain as a whole, 82 percent for gray matter and 88 percent for white-matter.

However, two major neuroanatomical features appear to be free of strong genetic control. In the same paper, Baaré stated that the lateral ventricles—CSF-filled cavities inside the brain—were only mildly influenced by heredity. A separate study by Alycia Bartley and her colleagues at the National Institute of Mental Health explained how patterns of sulci and gyri were more similar in monozygotic (identical) twins than in dizygotic (fraternal) twins. Interestingly, siblings from both groups were still very different from each other, especially in the smaller sulci. Thus, while overall volumes of major brain sectors are under strong genetic control, smaller regions may be more responsive to environmental influence. These insights into the relative contributions of genes and environments to this phenotype are useful in framing another area of volumetrics research—the evolution of the modern human brain.

Lobe Row over Low Brows

Scientists have debated for decades the hypothesis that frontal lobe expansion accelerated during hominid evolution. When we compare our own high foreheads to the low brows of our closest living kin (the chimpanzee) and extinct cousins (the Neandertals), the idea seems obvious. In terms of brain functions in which parts of the frontal lobe play a critical role, language, prediction and judgment represent important cognitive differences between us and other animals. So the idea that the frontal lobe expanded disproportionately during hominid evolution makes intuitive sense.

The equation of a big frontal lobe with intelligence is also embedded in the popular imagination. The 1955 science-fiction movie This Island Earth featured three intelligent species: humans, Metalunan aliens (similar to humans but more advanced, with unnervingly large foreheads) and the menacing but highly advanced Zagons. The mutant alien brains of the Zagons had apparently become so large that they literally burst through their foreheads. The implicit notion in this hierarchy is that brain size is linked with mental acuity. More specifically, the increasing size of the foreheads (especially in the humanlike Metalunans) highlights a belief that cognitive ability is tied to the frontal regions. But is this assumption true?

Several recent studies have turned the tools of neuroimaging to the issue of relative frontal lobe expansion during hominid evolution. Our colleague Katerina Semendeferi, now at the University of California, San Diego, used MRI to compare the proportional size of the frontal lobe in people and other primates. She found that the frontal cortex (gray matter) and the entire frontal lobe (including gray and white matter) had very similar relative proportions in humans, orangutans, gorillas and chimpanzees. In these four species the frontal lobe as a whole comprised between 33 and 36 percent of the total volume of the cerebrum, and the frontal cortex made up 36 to 39 percent of the cerebral gray matter. Although the human brain is approximately three times larger than the brains of the great apes, regression analyses of the data indicated that the proportion of the frontal lobe is not greater than expected for an ape with our size brain. By contrast, our brain proportions are different than those of a "lesser ape" (the small-bodied gibbon) and two monkey species (rhesus macaque and cebus monkey), which have significantly smaller frontal lobes.

Semendeferi suggests the evolution of a proportionally larger frontal lobe happened after the human and great ape lineage split off from the other anthropoid primates (20 to 25 million years ago), but before the divergence of hominids during the late Miocene (5 to 10 million years ago). Therefore, frontal lobe expansion is not a recent development in humans. She offers several hypotheses about the evolutionary origins of brain enlargement and cognitive change in the hominid line. These traits may have arisen from cortical reorganization within small subsectors of the lobe, enriched connectivity between selected regions, regional changes in cytoarchitecture or some combination of these features. The evidence from comparative anatomy supports all three possibilities.

Lobal Forming

Our most recent work on proportionate volume also relates to the debate over frontal lobe expansion. We found that variation in total brain size is much greater than variation in the proportions of the major lobes. In other words, people vary more in brain size than in how the major regions of the brain are apportioned. This is strikingly evident when we compare men and women. Although men have larger brains, the proportions of the major lobes are similar. In both sexes, the frontal lobe comprises about 38 percent of the hemisphere (ranging from 36 to 43 percent), the temporal lobe 22 percent (ranging from 19 to 24 percent), the parietal lobe 25 percent (ranging from 21 to 28 percent), and the occipital lobe 9 percent (ranging from 7 to 12 percent). (Note that these values differ slightly from those of Semendeferi because of a parcellation scheme in this study that includes more of the white matter core.)

Comparing frontal- and parietal-lobe volumes has added another twist to the story. As we expected, people with large frontal lobes also have large parietal lobes, since they both reflect large overall brain size. However, after controlling for overall dimensions, we found that there was a highly significant, negative correlation between frontal and parietal lobe volume: People with larger frontal lobes had smaller parietal lobes and vice versa. We concluded that this inverse relation probably reflects genetic rather than environmental factors, because the boundary between these lobes, the central sulcus, appears early in the developing brain, and its course and position are strongly influenced by inheritance.

The negative correlation indicates that frontal lobe expansion during hominid evolution likely would have come at the cost of a smaller parietal lobe. And the contraction of the parietal lobe makes little sense from a cognitive standpoint. After all, association cortices in the parietal lobe serve many important language functions, and tool use, a hallmark of hominid cognitive evolution, depends on the connections between parietal and frontal lobes. Thus it is possible that there could have been selection *against* relative frontal lobe expansion if it compromised the functions of the parietal lobe. In light of this evidence, the frontal lobe probably grew at the same time as other major regions of the cerebrum during the past 2 million years.

A third perspective on frontal lobe evolution comes from a CT study of the skulls of several hominid fossils from the past half-million years. Fred Bookstein at the University of Michigan and his colleagues compared the skulls of our extinct hominid cousins with those of modern human beings. Archaic members of genus *Homo* are characterized by cranial capacities

that equal or exceed those of modern *Homo sapiens sapiens*. However, the bones of the cranium and face are very thick and strong, and most specimens have large brow ridges and some degree of mid-facial prognathism (protruding nose), which together give the impression of a low, sloping forehead. But despite these external differences, Bookstein et al. showed that the inside of the cranial vault was identical by using a statistical method known as Procrustes analysis. This strategy uses a series of floating intervals between fixed anatomical landmarks to standardize the measurement of size, position, orientation and, ultimately, shape. (Procrustes was the highwayman of Greek mythology who forced each victim to fit the same terrible bed—stretching or axing the unfortunates as necessary.) The authors determined that the interior shape of the frontal bone (and presumably the shape of the frontal lobe itself) had not changed over the past 500,000 years—despite substantial changes in the external morphology of the face.

Sex in the Brain

Postmortem and MRI studies show that on average, men's brains are larger than women's brains, even after correcting for body size. This dimorphism is unlikely to be a recently evolved trait, as other primates have similar patterns. But size is not the only difference. It turns out that women tend to have a higher proportion of gray matter than men.

We recently published a pair of papers that examined differences in brain structures of men and women. On average, male brains (mean 1,241 cubic centimeters) were about 12 percent larger than female brains (mean 1,100 cubic centimeters), although there was significant overlap between the two groups. This dissimilarity did not seem to involve sex-specific differences in hemispheric volume, as the majority of men and women had larger right hemispheres. In general, sex differences for each of the major lobes of the brain reflected those of the brain as a whole. However, the occipital lobe, which processes visual information, was less sexually dimorphic than other regions.

Our segmentation of the brain into gray and white matter revealed that women have a mean gray:white ratio of 1.35 compared with 1.26 for men. This higher ratio in women appears to be caused by less white matter rather than more gray matter. Men had, on average, 9.3 percent more gray matter than women, but the increase in white matter volume was almost twice as big—17.4 percent. When we analyzed the covariance in this data set, the ratio difference disappeared with white matter volume normalized. This analysis indicated that the variability in white-matter volume had the most influence on sex differences.

Of all brain structures, the corpus callosum has probably drawn the most attention over the years for putative differences between the sexes. This large band of white matter connects the right and left hemispheres, and early research suggested that it might be larger in women than men. However, the current generation of studies has found the opposite to be true—it is actually larger in men, reflecting the greater overall size of male brains. In our ongoing studies, we observe that the corpus callosum is about 10 percent larger in men; however, it constitutes a significantly greater percentage of the total white matter in women (2.4 percent versus 2.2 percent).

This detail suggests an explanation for why men have a greater proportion of white matter. In MR images, most white matter includes myelinated axon fibers, glial cells and blood vessels. By contrast, the white matter of the corpus callosum is mostly just fiber tracts. Therefore, if the callosum is an index of the axonal fraction of white matter, then men may have more non-axonal components (glia, blood vessels) in the overall makeup of their white matter. In other words, the "excess" white matter in men (underlying the lower gray:white ratio) probably doesn't represent a big step up in the connectivity of male brains.

Dispelling an Old Cliché

What do these differences in brain volume tell us about the way that male and female brains actually work? When the sexually dimorphic corpus callosum was first suggested in the early 1980s, many scientists speculated that the "larger" band in women meant they had a greater degree of communication between the two hemispheres. This idea seemed to support the cliché that in women, the "emotional" "analytical" left side were more "in touch" with each other. Of course, we now know that women do not have larger corpus callosa than men. This fact doesn't preclude greater functional connectivity between the hemispheres (as the stereotype would have it), but there is no anatomical evidence for the claim.

On average, the brains of men and women differ by more than 100 cubic centimeters, or about two and a half golf balls. Should we expect this difference to have direct cognitive effects? Not necessarily, for several important reasons. First, although the sex difference in brain volume is present after correction for body size, some of the variation can be attributed to a person's physical dimensions. In a careful MRI study (in which equal attention was paid to both brain and body size parameters), Michael Peters of the University of Guelph and his colleagues found that the difference in brain volume between the sexes dropped by two-thirds after height was included as a covariate.

Next, volume differences between the sexes are distributed fairly evenly throughout the major lobes of the brain; there is no "sex-specific" region that accounts for an undue share of the difference in total brain volume. This diffuse pattern indicates that it will be difficult to find a functional sex difference that correlates with differences in total brain volume. Furthermore, a similar pattern of sexual dimorphism is seen in several other primate species: the human sex difference in brain volume evolved before the profound changes in brain size and cognition that occurred during hominid evolution.

Although we have argued against a strong functional explanation for sexual dimorphism in total brain volume—indeed, it may reflect primate ancestry rather than cognitive adaptations—we do not suggest that there are no structural-functional differences in brain anatomy between men and women. Rather, we would expect the changes to exist in more subtle ways—

particular regions or networks of the brain that are associated with specific behaviors (for example, visual-spatial tasks) that exhibit sexual dimorphism.

The Mark of Silence

Heschl's gyrus (HG) is a small structure on the top of the temporal lobe, buried within the Sylvian fissure. It is important because it marks the approximate position of the primary auditory cortex—the place in the brain where sound is initially processed. But how would HG develop in people who had never heard sounds in their lives?

The examination of HG in deaf individuals is related to a series of now classic animal studies that proved the requirement for sensory information during critical periods of neural development. When the animal's sensory input was blocked (by covering one eye, for example), the brain structures that normally received those projections failed to develop. Obviously, such experiments cannot be conducted in people, so we have little direct information on sensory deprivation and the development of the human brain. With this in mind, we collaborated with Karen Emmorey at the Salk Institute to record gray and white matter volumes of HG in hearing and congenitally deaf individuals using high-resolution MRI.

We measured the volume of HG and other regions in the brains of 25 congenitally deaf individuals and 25 age and sex-matched controls. One of these areas, the planum temporale, borders HG and is involved with secondary processing of sound. This structure is one of the most reliably asymmetric parts of the human brain, being larger in the left hemisphere than the right. In fact, many scientists once thought that the asymmetry might have evolved with spoken language. However, a similar pattern also exists in chimpanzees, so hemispheric language functions must have developed within the context of preexisting lateralization (at least in this area).

The planum temporale proved to be the same in deaf and hearing subjects, indicating that the structure of this region is not critically influenced by sensory input. However, HG did change: The gray:white ratio was significantly higher in deaf subjects compared to hearing controls. This increase was caused by a reduction in white matter volume, as the amount of gray matter (after normalization) varied little between deaf and hearing subjects. We speculated that the auditory deprivation from birth might have led to a combination of less myelination, fewer connections with the auditory cortex and the gradual decay of unused axonal fibers. This part of the brain is not dead—it responds to nonauditory stimuli, according to functional imaging studies. But our results do indicate that exposure to sound may influence the anatomical development of this primary sensory region.

Mind the Gap

Given the complexity of the subject matter and the number of issues that need to be addressed, the volumetric study of the human brain is still in its infancy We have not yet ascertained the full scope of human-brain variability, and more normative research is necessary. And despite the fact that MKI has been used in hundreds of studies of schizophrenia, Alzheimer's disease and autism, quantitative volumetric data is not yet a standard component of clinical diagnoses. We anticipate the next generation of higher-resolution MRI studies will add even more analytical power to further elucidate the links between brain structure and function.

Bibliography

Allen, J. S., H. Damasio and T. J. Crabowski. 2002. Normal neuroanatomical variation in the human brain: An MRI-volumetric study. *American Journal of Physical Anthropology* 118:341–358.

Allen, J. S., H. Damasio, T. J. Grabowski, J. Bruss and W. Zhang. 2003. Sexual dimorphism and asymmetries in the gray-white composition of the human cerebrum. *NenroImage* 18:880–894.

Baaré, W. F. C., H. E. Hulshoff Pol, D. I. Boomsma, D. Posthuma, E. J. C. de Geus, H. G. Schnack, N. E. M. van Haren, C. J. van Oel and R. S. Kahn. 2001. Quantitative genetic modeling of variation in human brain morphology. *Cerebral Cortex* 11:816–824.

Bartley, A. J., D. W. Jones and D. R. Weinberger. 1997. Genetic variability of human brain size and cortical gyral patterns. *Brain* 120:257–269.

Bookstein, F., K. Schäfer, H. Prossinger, H. Seid-ler, M. Fieder, C. Stringer, G. W. Weber, J.-L. Arsuaga, D. E. Slice, F. J- Rohlf, W. Recheis, A. J. Mariam and L. F. Marcus. 1999. Comparing frontal cranial profiles in archaic and modern *Homo* by morphometric analysis. *Anatomical Record (New Anatomist)* 257:217–224.

Emmorey, K., J. S. Allen, J. Bruss, N. Schenker and H. Damasio. 2003. A morphometric analysis of auditory brain regions in congenitally deaf adults. *Proceedings of the National Academy of Sciences of the U.S.A.* 100:10049–10054.

Grabowski, T. J., R. J. Frank, N. R. Szumski, C. K. Brown and H. Damasio. 2000. Validation of partial tissue segmentation of single-channel magnetic resonance images of the brain. *NeuroImage* 12:640–636.

Holloway, R. L. 1980. Within-species brain-body weight variability: A reexamination of the Danish data and other primate species. *American Journal of Physical Anthropology* 53:109–121.

Milton, K. 1981. Distribution patterns of tropical plant foods as an evolutionary stimulus to primate mental development. *American Anthropologist* S8:534–548.

Peters, M., L. Jancke, J. F. Staiger, G. Schlaug, Y. Huang and H. Steinmetz. 1998. Unsolved problems in comparing brain sizes in *Homo sapiens. Brain and Cognition* 37:254–285.

Semendeferi, K. and H. Damasio. 2000. The brain and its main anatomical subdivisions in living hominoids using magnetic resonance imaging, *Journal of Human Evolution* 38:317–332.

Semendeferi, K., A. Lu, N. Schenker and H. Damasio. 2002. Humans and great apes share a large frontal cortex. *Nature Neuroscience* 5:272–276.

JOHN S. ALLEN is a biological anthropologist who received his Ph.D. from the University of California, Berkeley in 1989. He is a research scientist and adjunct associate professor in the Department of Neurology, University of Iowa College of Medicine. **JOEL BRUSS** is a research assistant in the Human Neuroanatomy and Neuroimaging Laboratory at the University of Iowa College of Medicine. **HANNA DAMASIO** received her M.D. from the University of Lisbon School of Medicine. She is the University of Iowa Foundation Distinguished Professor of Neurology, and director of the human Neuroanatomy and Neuorimaging laboratory. Address for Allen: Department of Neurology, 2 RCP, University of Iowa Hospitals and Clinics, 200 Hawkins Drive, Iowa City, IA 52242. Internet: john-s-allen@uiowa.edu

UNIT 3
Perceptual Processes

Unit Selections

Key Points to Consider

- How does sensation differ from perception?

- Why is it important to keep our senses sharp? How can we assure we care for our sense organs?

- What senses are most important to humans and why?

- How does noise affect us?

- What are altered states of consciousness?

- Why are sleeping and dreaming so important to psychologists?

Student Web Site

www.mhcls.com/online

Internet References

Further information regarding these Web sites may be found in this book's preface or online.

Five Senses Home Page
   http://www.sedl.org/scimath/pasopartners/senses/welcome.html
Psychology Tutorials and Demonstrations
   http://psych.hanover.edu/Krantz/tutor.html

Sean Justice/CORBIS

Marina and her roommate have been friends since freshman year. Because they share so much in common, they decided to become roommates in their sophomore year. They both want to travel abroad one day. Both date men from the same college, both are education majors, and both want to work with young children after graduation from college. Today they are at the local art museum. As they walk around the galleries, Marina is astonished at her roommate's taste in art. Whatever her roommate likes, Marina hates. The paintings and sculptures that Marina admires are the very ones to which her roommate turns

up her nose. "How can our tastes in art be so different when we share so much in common?" Marina wonders.

What Marina and her roommate are experiencing is a difference in perception—the interpretation of the sensory stimulation provided by the artwork. Perception and its sister area of psychology, sensation, are the focus of this unit.

For many years, it was popular for psychologists to consider sensation and perception as two distinct processes. Sensation was defined in passive terms as the simple event of some stimulus energy (i.e. a sound wave) impinging on the body or on a specific sense organ that then reflexively transmitted appropriate information to the central nervous system. With regard to the concept of sensation, in the past both passivity and simple reflexes were stressed. Perception, on the other hand, was defined as an integrative and interpretive process that the higher centers of the brain supposedly accomplish based on sensory information and available memories for similar events.

The Gestalt psychologists, early German researchers, were convinced that perception was a higher order function compared to sensation. The Gestalt psychologists believed that the whole stimulus was more than the sum of its individual sensory parts; Gestalt psychologists believed this statement was made true by the process of perception.

For example, some of you listen to a song and hear the words, the loudness, and the harmony as well as the main melody. However, you do not really hear each of these units; what you hear is the whole song. If the song is pleasant to you, you proclaim that you like the song and even buy the CD or download it to your MP3 player. If the song is raucous to you, you perceive that you do not like it and hope it ends soon. However, even the songs you first hear and do not like may become likeable after repeated exposure to those songs. Hence perception, according to these early Gestalt psychologists, was a more advanced and complicated process than sensation.

The strict dichotomy of sensation and perception is no longer widely accepted by today's psychologists. The revolution came in the mid-1960s when a psychologist published a then-radical treatise in which he reasoned that perceptual processes included *all* sensory events that he believed were directed by an actively searching central nervous system. Also, this viewpoint provided that certain perceptual patterns, such as recognition of a piece of artwork, may be species-specific. That is, all humans, independent of learning history, should share some of the same perceptual repertoires. This unit on perceptual processes is designed to further your understanding of these complex and interesting processes.

Sensational Tune-Ups

Fifteen ways to improve your vision, hearing, taste, and sense of smell.

SID KIRCHHEIMER

Are people around you mumbling more often these days? Does food seem to need an extra splash of Tabasco to please the palate? Would the newspaper be easier to read if your arms were just a few feet longer and the print a bit bigger?

Welcome to the club. By the time we hit middle age, most of us suffer from some decline of the senses. But don't despair. There are ways to protect—and even improve—your ability to see, hear, smell, and taste all of life's offerings. Experts we consulted recommend the following senses-sharpening strategies:

Sight

Only reading glasses or other special eyewear can foil the common cause of weakened vision: presbyopia, the so-called aging eyes that result when the lens of the eye loses its flexibility, making it harder to focus clearly on close objects. But you can take measures to stave off some of the leading causes of age-related blindness. See if these work for you:

Pop five a day A National Eye Institute study shows that one of the best ways to arrest macular degeneration is by following a simple five-pill supplement regimen: daily doses of 500 mg of vitamin C, 400 international units of vitamin E, 15 mg of beta carotene, 80 mg of zinc oxide, and 2 mg of cupric oxide. "You really need to take these in supplement form because there is no way you could get these amounts from food alone," says National Eye Institute researcher Emily Chew, M.D.

Loosen up A study in the *British Journal of Ophthalmology* finds that a tight necktie may increase risk of glaucoma by constricting neck veins, boosting fluid pressure inside the eyes to dangerous levels. "No one says you have to strangle yourself," says study author Robert Ritch, M.D., of the New York Eye and Ear Infirmary. "If you can't get your finger in between your neck and your collar easily, it's too tight."

Keep your specs on The mainstay material in prescription eyewear—polycarbonate lenses—helps block harmful ultraviolet light, a key cause of cataracts, says ophthalmologist William Lloyd, M.D., of UC Davis Medical Center. So keep your glasses on whenever you're outdoors (or don prescription sunglasses). And if you're 20/20, look for nonprescription sunglasses at the drugstore or mall that are labeled to protect against both UVA and UVB rays.

Plow into power plants Some of the disease-protecting chemicals naturally found in fruits and vegetables also shield these plants from UV rays and other environmental pollutants that can damage your vision. While most types of produce are beneficial, peas, peppers, and green leafy vegetables such as kale, romaine lettuce, and spinach stand out because they're rich in lutein and other key vision-protecting nutrients.

Get an early start Eye-harming environmental pollutants—smog, in plain English—are at their lowest levels early in the day. To limit your exposure to toxins in the air, Lloyd suggests doing yard work, exercise, and other outdoor activities early in the morning.

Hearing

While illness, injury, overuse of certain drugs, and genetics can all lead to hearing loss, the primary reason most aging Americans go deaf is their past exposure to noise. With every noise that is loud or long enough, some of the 16,000 or so tiny hairs inside each ear that allow sound waves to be heard are permanently damaged, causing a gradual hearing loss that becomes noticeable in middle age and beyond. Some sound advice:

Plug 'em Wearing ear protection is the obvious way to protect these sensitive hair cells, but you don't have to look like an airport baggage handler while doing it. Small foam plugs that discreetly fit in your ear may actually be better than the bulky, padded earmuff types, says David Nielsen, M.D., of the American Academy of Otolaryngology–Head and Neck Surgery. These plugs reduce noise by about 20 decibels compared with the 15-decibel protection you get from more expensive padded earmuffs. "Plus, the plugs are cooler," he points out.

Work out in silence Regular exercise keeps hearing sharp by improving or maintaining good blood flow to the inner ear. But during exercise, when more blood is feeding muscles, less may get to nerves that control hearing, making them more vulnerable to noise-caused damage. Some studies indicate that loud music or noise heard during exercise may be more damaging than noise heard at the same volumes when you're sedentary. Researchers are not unanimous about this, "but unless you need to listen to loud music while you exercise, you probably shouldn't," says Nielsen.

Don't be a blowhard Strenuous nose blowing can cause temporary or permanent hearing loss by rupturing the delicate structures inside the eardrum. To relieve nasal congestion, advises Nielsen, gently blow one nostril at a time.

Spark Your "Sixth" Sense

Just for fun, we asked leading experts what can be done to maintain or enhance the "sixth sense"—abilities such as ESP, telepathy, and clairvoyance. It turns out psychic abilities may actually benefit from aging. "Conditions that are more conducive for psychic experiences seem to occur more readily in older people than in younger ones," says researcher Emily Williams Kelly, Ph.D., of the University of Virginia's division of personality studies, which studies psychic phenomena. How better to get in touch with the "other side"? Consider the following:

- **Use the quiet** When the house is absent of yelling kids, blaring music, and other immediate distractions, you're more likely to be able to focus on the beyond. "These events seem to occur more readily in those who have them with quiet, solitude, and meditation," says Kelly.
- **Watch for signs** "People who are extroverted and open to the idea of having these experiences are more likely to show ESP abilities," says Kelly. And their "glass is half full" attitude includes taking clues from everyday events. "Signs are everywhere," adds Lisa Nash, a clairvoyant and online psychic reader at Global Psychic, Inc. "Pay attention to what you see while you are driving. It may be an indication of what's in your life's path. A dead deer on the side of the road might indicate that you are neglecting your inner power that comes from gentleness."
- **Eat for illumination** Nash says many psychics eat healthfully, avoiding alcohol and drugs as well as caffeine, sugar, and processed foods in order to maintain mental focus and clarity. Meanwhile, recent research shows that one of the omega-3 fatty acids found in heart-healthy fish such as salmon and mackerel can prevent age-related damage to a part of the brain where cells responsible for learning and memory communicate with one another.

—S.K.

Get screened If you have diabetes, you're more likely to suffer earlier and faster hearing loss, probably because of impeded blood flow to nerves that control hearing. "If you have diabetes in particular, you really should consider getting a yearly hearing test, just as you get annual tests for vision, kidney function, and other possible diabetes complications," says Nancy Vaughan, Ph.D., a researcher at the National Center for Rehabilitative Auditory Research in Portland, Oregon, who has investigated the diabetes-early-hearing-loss link. Those with high blood pressure or high cholesterol could also benefit from regular hearing screenings, she adds.

Watch your aspirin Aspirin is among the 200 or so medications that can cause hearing loss by damaging hearing hair cells and nerves that carry sounds to the brain. This is not to say you should ditch your daily aspirin therapy. But it does mean you should be diligent about following the typical recommended dosages for heart health and pain—and not take much higher doses. You'll know you're taking too much aspirin if your ears "ring" but the ringing stops when you stop taking aspirin.

Smell and Taste

When smell is impaired, an inability to taste usually follows. This not only makes eating less pleasurable; it can also lead to other problems. "Smell and taste get the digestive process rolling by triggering saliva and gastric juices to help digest food," says Marcia Levin Pelchat, Ph.D., a scientist at Monell Chemical Senses Center in Philadelphia, the nation's leading institute for smell and taste research. "Before food is even eaten, these senses allow the body to anticipate food and make absorption more efficient." And when you can't smell or taste food, you're less likely to eat it, risking malnutrition. Chew over the following strategies for preserving the flavor in your life:

Breathe in If you're sitting down for a hot meal, says Alan Hirsch, M.D., director of the Smell and Taste Treatment and Research Foundation in Chicago, take advantage of the cool fact that "it's good to sniff food before you eat because heat aerates odor molecules that you'll perceive as taste."

Hit the showers A less practical but equally effective variation on the above principle: "The heat and humidity of a warm shower clears sinuses and helps dissolve molecules that facilitate the ability to smell," says Hirsch. Plus, you'll be nice and clean for dinner.

Manage your sniffles People with recurrent colds or allergy problems are more vulnerable to smell and taste impairment because they often develop nasal polyps that block the sense receptors inside the top of the nose, Hirsch adds. "It's most noticeable while they have a cold or allergies, but frequent nasal or sinus problems can lead to chronic problems in the ability to smell."

. . . But rethink that cold remedy A zinc deficiency is one suspected cause of smell problems, but that doesn't mean cold remedies containing this nutrient are a cure-all. "Zinc lozenges such as Cold-Eeze and zinc nose sprays that you can buy over the counter actually cause a temporary distortion in smell and taste, especially in sweet sensations," says Pelchat. "When you stop using them, your normal senses of smell and taste usually return."

Buckle up The single most common cause of a complete smell impairment? "Head injury, like that sustained in a car accident," says Hirsch. "Perhaps the easiest thing you can do to protect your senses of smell and taste is to always wear a seat belt while driving."

SID KIRCHHEIMER last wrote for *AARP The Magazine* about scams ("Rip-off Alert," July–August 2004). He is also the author of a forthcoming action guide that collects hundreds of tips on how to avoid consumer rip-offs (AARP Books/Sterling, spring 2006).

Extreme States

Out-of-body experiences? Near-death experiences? Researchers are beginning to understand how they occur and how they may alter the brain.

Steven Kotler

I was 17 years old and terrified. The whole "let's go jump out of an airplane" concept had been dreamed up at a Friday night party, but now I was Saturday-morning sober and somehow still going skydiving. To make matters worse, this was in 1984, and while tandem skydiving was invented in 1977, the concept had yet to make its way to the airfield in mid-Ohio where I had wound up. So my first jump wasn't done with an instructor tethered to my back handling any difficulties we might encounter. Instead, I jumped alone 2,000 feet, my only safety net an unwieldy old Army parachute, dubbed a "round."

Thankfully, nobody expected me to pull my own rip cord. A static line, nothing fancier than a short rope, had been fixed between my rip cord and the floor of the airplane. If everything went according to plan, 15 feet from the plane, when I reached the end of my rope, it would tug open the chute. *Getting* to this point was more complicated.

As the plane flew along at 100 miles per hour, I had to clamber out a side door, ignore the vertiginous view, step onto a small metal rung, hold onto the plane's wing with both hands, and lift one leg behind me, so that my body formed a giant T. From this position, when my instructor gave the order, I was to jump. If all this wasn't bad enough, when I finally leaped out of the plane, I also leaped out of my body.

It happened the second I let go of the wing. My body started falling through space, but my consciousness was hovering about 20 feet away, watching me descend. During training, the instructor had explained that rounds opened, closed, and opened again in the first milliseconds of deployment. He had also mentioned that it happened too fast for the human eye to see and that we shouldn't worry about it. Yet in the instant I began falling, I was worried. I was also watching the chute's open-close-open routine, despite knowing that what I was watching was technically impossible to see.

My body began to tip over, tilting into an awkward position that would produce quite a jerk when the chute caught. In what might best be described as a moment of extracorporeal clarity, I told myself to relax rather than risk whiplash. In the next instant, my chute caught with a jerk. The jerk snapped my consciousness back into my body, and everything returned to normal.

Out-of-body experiences belong to a subset of not-so-garden-variety phenomena broadly called the paranormal, although the dictionary defines that word as "beyond the range of normal experience or scientific explanation," and out-of-body experiences are neither. This type of experience has been reported in almost every country in the world for centuries. Mystics of nearly every faith, including all five of the world's major religions, have long told tales of astral projection. But this phenomenon is not reserved for only the religious. The annals of action sports are packed with accounts of motorcyclists who recall floating above their bikes, watching themselves ride, and pilots who occasionally find themselves floating outside their airplane, struggling to get back inside. However, most out-of-body tales do not take place within the confines of an extreme environment. They transpire as part of normal lives.

The out-of-body experience is much like the near-death experience, and any exploration of one must include the other. While out-of-body experiences are defined by a perceptual shift in consciousness, no more and no less, near-death experiences start with this shift and then proceed along a characteristic trajectory. People report entering a dark tunnel, heading into light, and feeling an all-encompassing sense of peace, warmth, love, and welcome. They recall being reassured along the way by dead friends, relatives, and a gamut of religious figures. Occasionally, there's a life review, followed by a decision of the "should I stay or should I go?" variety. A 1990 Gallup poll of American adults found that almost 12 percent of Americans, roughly 30 million individuals, said they have had some sort of near-death experience.

Both phenomena have had a serious credibility problem. Much of it stems from the scientists who did the earliest investigations. Charles Tart, a psychologist at the University of California at Davis, who did the first major study of out-of-body experiences in 1969, and Raymond Moody, a psychiatrist recently retired from the University of Nevada at Las Vegas who did the same for near-death experiences in the early 1970s, designed experiments of questionable rigor and made matters worse by ignoring the peer-review process and publishing their results in best-selling books. Both Tart and Moody later wrote follow-up books partially debunking and partially recanting their previous ones.

Unfortunately, many researchers studying these extreme states of consciousness are unaware of these follow-up books and still point to the original work as evidence that none of this should be taken seriously. Simultaneously, many skeptics are unaware of much of the research done since then. But forget for the moment this troubled history and concentrate on more recent work. And there is plenty.

In 1982, while a children's brain cancer researcher and finishing his residency in pediatrics at Children's Hospital in Seattle, Melvin Morse was also moonlighting for a helicopter-assisted EMT service. One afternoon he was flown to Pocatello, Idaho, to perform CPR on 8-year-old Crystal Merzlock, who had apparently drowned in the deep end of a community swimming pool. When Morse arrived on the scene, the child had been without a heartbeat for 19 minutes; her pupils were already fixed and dilated. Morse got her heart restarted, climbed into the chopper, and went home. Three days later Crystal regained consciousness.

A few weeks passed. Morse was back at the hospital where Crystal was being treated, and they bumped into each other in the hallway. Crystal pointed at Morse, turned to her mother, and said, "That's the guy who put the tube in my nose at the swimming pool." Morse was stunned. "I didn't know what to do. I had never heard of OBEs [out-of-body experiences] or NDEs [near-death experiences]. I stood there thinking: How was this possible? When I put that tube in her nose, she was brain dead. How could she even have this memory?"

Morse decided to make a case study of Crystal's experience, which he published in the *American Journal of Diseases of Children*. He labeled the event a fascinoma, which is both medical slang for an abnormal pathology and a decent summary of the state of our knowledge at the time. He was the first to publish a description of a child's near-death experience.

He started by reviewing the literature, discovering that the classic explanation—delusion—had been recently upgraded to a hallucination provoked by a number of different factors, including fear, drugs, and a shortage of oxygen to the brain. But it was drugs that caught Morse's eye. He knew that ketamine, used as an anesthetic during the Vietnam War, frequently produced out-of-body experiences and that other drugs were suspected of being triggers as well. Morse decided to study halothane, another commonly used anesthetic, believing his study might help explain the many reports of near-death experiences trickling out of emergency rooms. "It's funny to think of it now," he says, "but really, at the time, I set out to do a long-term, large-scale debunking study."

Morse's 1994 report, commonly referred to as the Seattle study and published in *Current Problems in Pediatrics*, spanned a decade. During that period, he interviewed 160 children in the intensive care unit at Children's Hospital in Seattle who had been revived from apparent death. Every one of these children had been without a pulse or sign of breathing longer than 30 seconds. Some had been in that state for as long as 45 minutes; the average apparent death lasted between 10 and 15 minutes. For a control group, he used hundreds of other children also in intensive care, also on the brink of death, but whose pulse

and breathing hadn't been interrupted for more than 30 seconds. That was the only difference. In other dimensions—age, sex, drugs administered, diseases suffered, and setting—the groups were the same. In setting, Morse not only included the intensive care unit itself but also scary procedures such as insertion of a breathing tube and mechanical ventilation. These are important additions because fear has long been considered a trigger for a near-death experience (and might have been the trigger responsible for what happened when I skydived).

Morse graded his subjects' experiences according to the Greyson scale, a 16-point questionnaire designed by University of Virginia psychiatrist Bruce Greyson that remains the benchmark for determining whether or not an anomalous experience should be considered a near-death experience. Using this test, Morse found that 23 out of 26 children who experienced apparent death—the cessation of heartbeat and breathing—reported a classic near-death experience, while none of the other 131 children in his control group reported anything of the kind.

Morse later videotaped the children recalling their experiences, which included such standard fare as long tunnels, giant rainbows, dead relatives, and deities of all sorts. But many descriptions—augmented by crayon drawings—included memories of the medical procedures performed and details about doctors and nurses whose only contact with the child occurred while the child was apparently dead.

Other scientists have duplicated Morse's findings. Most recently, cardiologist Pim van Lommel, a researcher at Rijnstate Hospital in Arnhem, the Netherlands, conducted an eight-year study involving 344 cardiac-arrest patients who seemed to have died and were later revived. Out of that total, 282 had no memories, while 62 reported a classic near-death experience. Just as in Morse's study, van Lommel examined the patients' records for any factors traditionally used to explain near-death experiences—such as setting, drugs, or illness—and found no evidence of their influence. Apparent death was the only factor linked to near-death experiences. He also found that one person in his study had difficult-to-explain memories of events that happened in the hospital while he was presumed dead.

Possible clues to the biological basis of these unusual states turned up in studies conducted in the late 1970s, when the Navy and the Air Force introduced a new generation of high-performance fighter planes that underwent extreme acceleration. Those speeds generated tremendous g-forces, which pulled too much blood out of the pilots' brains, causing them to black out. The problem, known as G-LOC, for g-force-induced loss of consciousness, was serious, and James Whinnery, a specialist in aerospace medicine, was in charge of solving it.

Over a 16-year period, working with a massive centrifuge at the Naval Air Warfare Center in Warminster, Pennsylvania, Whinnery spun fighter pilots into G-LOC. He wanted to determine at what force tunnel vision occurred. More than 500 pilots accidentally blacked out during the study, and from them Whinnery learned how long it took pilots to lose consciousness under acceleration and how long they remained unconscious after the acceleration ceased. By studying this subset he also learned how long they could be unconscious before brain damage started.

He found that G-LOC could be induced in 5.67 seconds, that the average blackout lasted 12 to 24 seconds, and that at least 40 of the pilots reported some sort of out-of-body experience while they were unconscious. Not knowing anything about out-of-body experiences, Whinnery called these episodes dreamlets, kept detailed records of their contents, and began examining the literature on anomalous unconscious experiences. "I was reading about sudden-death episodes in cardiology," Whinnery says, "and it led me right into near-death experiences. I realized that a smaller percentage of my pilots' dreamlets, about 10 to 15 percent, were much closer in content to a classic NDE."

When Whinnery reviewed his data, he noted a correlation: The longer his pilots were knocked out, the closer they got to brain death. And the closer they got to brain death, the more likely it was that an out-of-body experience would turn into a near-death experience. This was the first hard evidence for what had been long suspected—that the two states are not two divergent phenomena, but two points on a continuum.

Whinnery found that G-LOC, when gradually induced, produced tunnel vision. "The progression went first to grayout (loss of peripheral vision) and then to blackout," he explains, and the blindness occurred just before a person went unconscious. "This makes a lot of sense. We know that the occipital lobe (the portion of the brain that controls vision) is a well-protected structure. Perhaps it continued to function when signals from the eyes were failing due to compromised blood flow. The transition from grayout to unconsciousness resembles floating peacefully within a dark tunnel, which is much like some of the defining characteristics of a near-death experience. The pilots also recalled a feeling of peace and serenity as they regained consciousness.

The simplest conclusion to draw from these studies is that, give or take some inexplicable memories, these phenomena are simply normal physical processes that occur during unusual circumstances. After all, once scientists set aside the traditional diagnosis of delusion as a source of these unusual mental states and began looking for biological correlates, there were plenty of possibilities. Compression of the optic nerve could produce tunnel vision; neurochemicals such as serotonin, endorphins, and enkephalins could help explain the euphoria; and psychotropics like LSD and mescaline often produce vibrant hallucinations of past events. But no one has directly tested these hypotheses.

What researchers have studied is the effect of a near-death experience. Van Lommel conducted lengthy interviews and administered a battery of standard psychological tests to his study group of cardiac-arrest patients. The subset that had had a near-death experience reported more self-awareness, more social awareness, and more religious feelings than the others.

Van Lommel then repeated this process after a two-year interval and found the group with near-death experience still had complete memories of the event, while others' recollections were strikingly less vivid. He found that the near-death experience group also had an increased belief in an afterlife and a decreased fear of death compared with the others. After eight years he again repeated the whole process and found those two-year effects significantly more pronounced. The near-death experience group was much more empathetic, emotionally vulnerable, and often showed evidence of increased intuitive awareness. They still showed no fear of death and held a strong belief in an afterlife.

Morse, too, did follow-up studies long after his original research. He also did a separate study involving elderly people who had a near-death experience in early childhood. "The results were the same for both groups," says Morse. "Nearly all of the people who had had a near-death experience—no matter if it was 10 years ago or 50—were still absolutely convinced their lives had meaning and that there was a universal, unifying thread of love which provided that meaning. Matched against a control group, they scored much higher on life-attitude tests, significantly lower on fear-of-death tests, gave more money to charity, and took fewer medications. There's no other way to look at the data. These people were just transformed by the experience."

Morse has gone on to write three popular books about near-death experiences and the questions they raise about the nature of consciousness. His research caught the attention of Willoughby Britton, a doctoral candidate in clinical psychology at the University of Arizona who was interested in post-traumatic stress disorder. Britton knew that most people who have a close brush with death tend to have some form of post-traumatic stress disorder, while people who get that close and have a near-death experience have none. In other words, people who have a near-death experience have an atypical response to life-threatening trauma. No one knows why.

B ritton also knew about work done by legendary neurosurgeon and epilepsy expert Wilder Penfield in the 1950s. Penfield, one of the giants of modern neuroscience, discovered that stimulating the brain's right temporal lobe—located just above the ear—with a mild electric current produced out-of-body experiences, heavenly music, vivid hallucinations, and the kind of panoramic memories associated with the life review part of the near-death experience. This helped explain why right temporal lobe epilepsy was a condition long defined by its most prominent symptom: excessive religiosity characterized by an intense feeling of spirituality, mystical visions, and auditory hallucinations of the voice-of-God variety. And given what Whinnery has found, it is possible that his pilots' near-death-like dreamlets were related to brief episodes of compromised blood flow in the temporal lobe.

Britton hypothesized that people who have undergone a near-death experience might show the same altered brain firing patterns as people with temporal lobe epilepsy. The easiest way to determine if someone has temporal lobe epilepsy is to monitor the brain waves during sleep, when there is an increased likelihood of activity indicative of epilepsy. Britton recruited 23 people who had a near-death experience and 23 who had undergone neither a near-death experience nor a life-threatening traumatic event. Then, working at a sleep lab, she hooked up her subjects to electrodes that measured EEG activity all over the brain—including the temporal lobes—and recorded everything that happened while they slept.

She then asked a University of Arizona epilepsy specialist who knew nothing about the experiment to analyze the EEGs.

Two features distinguished the group with near-death experience from the controls: They needed far less sleep, and they went into REM (rapid eye movement) sleep far later in the sleep cycle than normal people. "The point at which someone goes into REM sleep is a fantastic indicator of depressive tendencies," says Britton. "We've gotten very good at this kind of research. If you took 100 people and did a sleep study, we can look at the data and know, by looking at the time they entered REM, who's going to become depressed in the next year and who isn't."

Normal people enter REM at 90 minutes. Depressed people enter at 60 minutes or sooner. Britton found that the vast majority of her group with near-death experience entered REM sleep at 110 minutes. With that finding, she identified the first objective neurophysiological difference in people who have had a near-death experience.

Britton thinks near-death experience somehow rewires the brain, and she has found some support for her hypothesis regarding altered activity in the temporal lobe: Twenty-two percent of the group with near-death experience showed synchrony in the temporal lobe, the same kind of firing pattern associated with temporal lobe epilepsy. "Twenty-two percent may not sound like a lot of anything," says Britton, "but it's actually incredibly abnormal, so much so that it's beyond the realm of chance."

She also found something that didn't fit with her hypothesis. The temporal lobe synchrony wasn't happening on the right side of the brain, the site that had been linked in Penfield's studies to religious feeling in temporal lobe epilepsy. Instead she found it on the left side of the brain. That finding made some people uncomfortable because it echoed studies that pinpointed, in far more detail than Penfield achieved, the exact locations in the brain that were most active and most inactive during periods of profound religious experience.

Over the past 10 years a number of different scientists, including neurologist James Austin from the University of Colorado, neuroscientist Andrew Newberg, and the late anthropologist and psychiatrist Eugene D'Aquili from the University of Pennsylvania, have done SPECT (single photon emission computed tomography) scans of the brains of Buddhists during meditation and of Franciscan nuns during prayer. They found a marked decrease in activity in the parietal lobes, an area in the upper rear of the brain. This region helps us orient ourselves in space; it allows us to judge angles and curves and distances and to know where the self ends and the rest of the world begins. People who suffer injuries in this area have great difficulties navigating life's simplest landscapes. Sitting down on a couch, for example, becomes a task of Herculean impossibility because they are unsure where their own legs end and the sofa begins. The SPECT scans indicated that meditation temporarily blocks the processing of sensory information within both parietal lobes.

When that happens, as Newberg and D'Aquili point out in their book *Why God Won't Go Away*, "the brain would have no choice but to perceive that the self is endless and intimately interwoven with everyone and everything the mind senses. And this perception would feel utterly and unquestionably real." They use the brain-scan findings to explain the interconnected cosmic unity that the Buddhists experienced, but the results could also explain what Morse calls the "universal, unifying thread of love" that people with near-death experience consistently reported.

These brain scans show that when the parietal lobes go quiet, portions of the right temporal lobe—some of the same portions that Penfield showed produced feelings of excessive religiosity, out-of-body experiences, and vivid hallucinations—become more active. Newberg and D'Aquili also argue that activities often found in religious rituals—like repetitive chanting—activate (and deactivate) similar areas in the brain, a finding that helps explain some of the more puzzling out-of-body experience reports, like those of the airplane pilots suddenly floating outside their planes. Those pilots were as intensely focused on their instrumentation as meditators focused on mantras. Meanwhile, the sound of the engine's spinning produces a repetitive, rhythmic drone much like tribal drumming. If conditions were right, says Newberg, these two things should be enough to produce the same temporal lobe activity to trigger an out-of-body experience.

Neuropsychologist Michael Persinger of Laurentian University in Sudbury, Ontario, has conducted other studies that explore the generation of altered mental states. Persinger built a helmet that produces weak, directed electromagnetic fields. He then asked over 900 volunteers, mostly college students, to wear the helmets while he monitored their brain activity and generated variations in the electromagnetic field. When he directed these fields toward the temporal lobes, Persinger's helmet induced the sort of mystical, free-of-the-body experiences common to right temporal lobe epileptics, meditators, and people who have had near-death experiences.

None of this work is without controversy, but an increasing number of scientists now think that our brains are wired for mystical experiences. The studies confirm that these experiences are as real as any others, because our involvement with the rest of the universe is mediated by our brains. Whether these experiences are simply right temporal lobe activity, as many suspect, or, as Britton's work hints and Morse believes, a whole brain effect, remains an open question. But Persinger thinks there is a simple explanation for why people with near-death experience have memories of things that occurred while they were apparently dead. The memory-forming structures lie deep within the brain, he says, and they probably remain active for a few minutes after brain activity in the outer cortex has stopped. Still, Crystal Merzlock remembered events that occurred more than *19 minutes* after her heart stopped. Nobody has a full explanation for this phenomenon, and we are left in that very familiar mystical state: the one where we still don't have all the answers.

A Matter of Taste

Are you a supertaster? Just stick out your tongue and say "yuck".

MARY BECKMAN

There's good taste, and according to scientists, there's supertaste. Blue food coloring is going to tell me where I lie on the continuum. Armed with a bottle of blue dye No. 1 and a Q-tip, I paint my tongue cobalt, swish some water in my mouth and spit into the bathroom sink. In the mirror I see a smattering of pink bumps—each hiding as many as 15 taste buds apiece—against the lurid blue background. Now I'm supposed to count how many of those bumps, called fungiform papillae, appear inside a circle a quarter-inch in diameter, but I don't need to do that. Obviously, I have fewer than the 30 that would qualify me as having an extraordinary palate. I am not a supertaster. Thank goodness.

Normally, people prize highly acute senses. We brag about twenty-twenty vision or the ability to eavesdrop on whispers from across the room. But taste is not so simple: supertaste may be too much of a good thing, causing those who have it to avoid bitter compounds and find some spicy foods too hot to handle. This unusual corner of perception science has been explored by Linda Bartoshuk of Yale University, who first stumbled upon supertasting about 15 years ago while studying saccharin. While most people found the sugar substitute sweet and palatable, others sensed a bitter aftertaste. She went on to test hundreds of volunteers with a host of chemicals found in food. About one in four, she discovered, qualified as supertasters, a name she coined.

To find what made them special, Bartoshuk zeroed in on the tongue's anatomy. She found that people have different numbers of fungiform papillae, with tongue topography ranging from, say, sparse cactus-pocked deserts to lush lawns. To qualify for supertasterdom, which is a genetically inherited trait, a person has to have wall-to-wall papillae on his or her tongue and also have an ability to readily taste PROP, a bitter synthetic compound also known as 6-n-propylthiouracil, which is used as a thyroid medication.

As it happens, Bartoshuk is a non-taster—she's among another one in four who can't detect PROP at all—and likes it that way. "I prefer the dumb, happy life I lead," she says. "'Super' connotes superiority, but supertaste often means sensory unpleasantness." In the course of her research she has relied on volunteers and colleagues to perceive what she cannot, such as the difference in creaminess between skim and 2 percent milk. "PROP tastes like quinine," says Laurie Lucchina, a supertaster who made this discovery about ten years ago when she worked with Bartoshuk. Another person in the lab, Valerie Duffy, now at the University of Connecticut, is a medium taster. Bartoshuk routinely tested "the junk food of the month," sent to the lab through a food subscription service, on the two women. "Once she brought in a cookie that she thought was very bland. But to me, it tasted just right," recalls Lucchina.

"Mother's milk reflects the culture into which babies are born."

Perhaps not surprisingly, supersensitive taste influences what people eat. Bartoshuk and other researchers found that supertasters tend to shun or restrict strong-flavored foods and drinks—coffee, frosted cake, greasy barbequed ribs, hoppy hand-crafted ales. Also, supertasters tend to crave neither fats nor sugars, which probably helps explain why researchers have found that supertasters also tend to be slimmer than people without the sensitivity. When it comes to rich desserts, Lucchina says, "I usually eat just a bite or two and then I'm done."

Taste sensitivity may also affect health. According to recent studies, supertasters have better cholesterol profiles than the norm, helping reduce their risk of heart disease. Yet supertasting may also have a downside. Some scientists have speculated that supertasters don't eat enough bitter vegetables, which are believed to protect against various types of cancer. And in a still-preliminary study of 250 men by Bartoshuk and co-workers, nontasters had fewer colon polyps, a risk factor for colon cancer, than did medium tasters or supertasters. To be sure, not everyone is convinced that supertasters put themselves in harm's way by skimping on vegetables. Adam Drewnowski, a nutrition scientist at the University of Washington, says a dollop of butter or maybe a splash of cheese sauce may be all a supertaster needs to find spinach or broccoli palatable. Still, the new data intrigue medical researchers, who don't usually consider taste an inherited factor in disease risk.

Of course, there's more to satisfaction than meets the tongue. Flavors are a combination of taste and odors, which float up through the back of our mouths to activate a suite of smell receptors in the nose. (Hold your nose while tasting a jellybean. You can tell it's sweet but not what flavor it is. Then unplug your nose. See?) Each smell tingles a different constellation of neurons in the brain, and with experience we learn what these different patterns mean—it's bacon sizzling in the kitchen, not liver. Nature may dictate whether or not we're supertasters, but it's nurture that shapes most of our food preferences.

And taste training starts earlier than one might think—during breast-feeding or even in the womb, according to biopsychologist Julie Mennella of the Monell Chemical Senses Center in Philadelphia. She asked pregnant women and breast-feeding mothers to drink carrot juice for three weeks. In both cases, when it came time to switch to solid food, babies of these mothers liked carrots better than babies whose mothers never drank the stuff. "These are the first ways they learn what foods are safe," Mennella says. "Mother's milk reflects the culture into which babies are born."

Learning can even trump innate good sense, according to a study Mennella reported this past April. She found that 7-month-old babies normally disliked bitter and sour flavors, and when given a bottle with a slightly bitter, sour formula, they pushed it away and wrinkled their angelic faces in disgust. But 7-month-olds who had been introduced to the bitter formula months earlier happily drank it again. In another study of babies who'd never been fed carrots, she found that those who'd been exposed to a variety of other vegetables clearly enjoyed carrots more than did babies who'd dined on a more monotonous diet. She suggests that early exposure to a diversity of flavors enables babies to trust new foods later in life. "Clearly experience is a factor in developing food habits," says Mennella. "But we don't know how that interacts with genetics."

Beyond genes and even learning lies a more ineffable aspect of taste: its emotional content. Certain foods can bring back unpleasant experiences; it may take only one rotten hot dog to put you off franks for life. Other tastes unlock happy memories. To an extent that researchers are still trying to understand, learning which foods are safe to eat while in the security of mother's arms may be the source of some of our most enduring desires. This learning process could be, Mennella says, "one of the foundations of how we define what is a comfort food."

MARY BECKMAN, a freelance writer in Idaho, specializes in the life sciences.

What Dreams Are Made Of

Technologies that reveal the inner workings of the brain are beginning to tell the sleeping mind's secrets.

Marianne Szegedy-Maszak

Strange images appear from long-forgotten memories. Or out of nowhere: You're roller-skating on water; your mother flashes by on a trapeze; your father is in labor; a friend dead for years sits down at the dinner table. Here are moments of unspeakable terror; there, moments of euphoria or serenity. Shakespeare wrote, "We are such stuff as dreams are made on," and 300 years later, Sigmund Freud gave the poetry a neat psychoanalytic spin when he called dreams "the royal road to the unconscious." The movies that unfold in our heads some nights are so powerfully resonant they haunt us for days—or inspire us. Mary Shelley dreamed of Frankenstein before she created him on paper; the melody to "Yesterday" came to Paul McCartney as he slept.

Everybody dreams—yet no one, throughout history, has fully grasped what the dreaming mind is doing. Are the nightly narratives a message from the unconscious to the conscious mind, as Freud believed? Or are they simply the product of random electrical flashes in the brain? Today, researchers aided by powerful technologies that reveal the brain in action are concluding that both schools of thought hold truth. "This is the greatest adventure of all time," says Harvard psychiatrist and dream researcher J. Allan Hobson. "The development of brain imaging is the equivalent of Galileo's invention of the telescope, only we are now exploring inner space instead of outer space."

Freud saw dreams as buried wishes disguised by symbols.

Mind-brain dance. The dream researchers' new tools, functional magnetic resonance imaging and positron emission tomography (PET) scanning, have been used for some time to capture the waking brain at work—making

decisions, feeling frightened or joyous, coping with uncertainty. And those efforts have shown clearly that psychology and physiology are intimately related: In someone suffering from an anxiety disorder, for example, the fear center of the brain—the amygdala—"lights up" as neurons fire in response to images that trigger anxiety; it flickers in a minuet with the center of memory, the hippocampus. Scanning people who are sleeping, too, suggests that the same sort of mind-brain dance continues 24 hours a day.

"Psychology has built its model of the mind strictly out of waking behavior," says Rosalind Cartwright, chair of the department of behavioral science at Rush University Medical Center in Chicago, who has studied dreams for most of her 83 years. "We know that the mind does not turn off during sleep; it goes into a different stage." Brain cells fire, and the mind spins. Problems find solutions; emotional angst seems to be soothed; out-of-the-box ideas germinate and take root.

> The door between the kitchen and the garage was split, so you could open the top half without opening the bottom half. It was the only safe way of doing it, because we had a rhinoceros in the garage. The garage was a lot bigger, though; it was also sort of a basement, and led underneath the rest of the house. My mother was cooking dinner, and I went into the bathroom where my brother Stuart was. The rhinoceros punched a hole in the floor with his horn.
>
> **Madeline,** third grade

What to make of young Madeline's dream? To Freud, had he met her, Madeline's rhinoceros horn would almost certainly have symbolized a penis, and the animal's violence would have been an expression of normal but threatening sexual feelings toward her brother—or perhaps of a fear of men in general. Freud saw dreams as deeply

Frankenstein and Mary Shelley

A Dream Come True

Can man create life? A talk on evolution that considered the possibility so disturbed Mary Godwin that she went to bed and dreamed up Frankenstein. She and three other writers, including her soon-to-be-husband, Percy Shelley, were staying at Lake Geneva in Switzerland during that summer of 1816, entertaining one another by telling and competing to write the best ghost stories. Shelley's vivid dream, in which she saw a "hideous phantasm of a man stretched out" and a scientist using a machine to try to bring him to life, inspired hers. She began to write the next day.

—Betsy Querna

Joseph and a Word from God

A Dream Come True

When Joseph discovered that Mary was pregnant during their engagement, he was "just crushed," says Father Gerald Kleba, a Roman Catholic priest in St. Louis who wrote the historical novel *Joseph Remembered*. Assuming that she had committed adultery, Joseph figured he would have to leave her. But an angel visited him in a dream, according to the Bible, and told him not be afraid. Mary had conceived through the Holy Spirit and would bear a special child. That "huge aha moment" shaped the rest of Joseph's life, says Kleba, and still speaks to many Christians of the power of faith.

—B.Q.

buried wishes disguised by symbols, a way to gratify desires unacceptable to the conscious mind. His ideas endured for years, until scientists started systematically studying dream content and decided that actually, something less exotic is going on.

"Dreams do enact—they dramatize. They are like plays of how we view the world and oneself in it," says William Domhoff, who teaches psychology and sociology at the University of California-Santa Cruz. "But they do not provide grandiose meanings." Domhoff bases his view on a study of themes and images that recur in a databank of some 16,000 dreams—including Madeline's—that have been collected as oral narratives and are held at Santa Cruz. (The narratives can be read at www.dreambank.net.)

Post-Freudians might argue that the monsters lurking in children's dreams signal a growing awareness of the world around them and its dangers. Young children describe very simple and concrete images, while the dreams of 9- and 10-year-olds get decidedly more complex. A monster that goes so far as to chase or attack might represent a person who is frightening to the child during waking hours. "Dreaming serves a vital function in the maturation of the brain and in processing the experiences of the day," says Alan Siegel, professor of psychology at UC-Berkeley and author of *Dream Wisdom.*

The experience of dreaming is as universal as a heartbeat.

Nonsense. Physiology purists, who would say that Madeline's brain is simply flashing random images, got their start in 1953 with the discovery of rapid eye movement sleep. Using primitive electroencephalograms,

researchers watched as every 90 minutes, sleepers' eyes darted back and forth and brain waves surged. Then, in 1977, Harvard psychiatrists Hobson and Robert McCarley reported that during sleep, electrical activity picked up dramatically in the most primitive area of the brain—the pons—which, by simply stimulating other parts of the brain, produced weird and disconnected narratives. Much like people looking for meaning in an inkblot, they concluded, dreams are the brain's vain attempt to impose coherence where there is none.

Or maybe that's not the whole story, either, said a young neuropsychologist at the Royal London School of Medicine 20 years later, when his findings hinted that dreaming is both a mental and a physical process. Mark Solms showed that dreams can't be explained as simple physical reactions to flashes from the primitive pons, since some of the most active dreamers in his study had suffered brain damage in that area. On the other hand, in those with damage to regions of the brain associated with higher-order motivation, passionate emotions, and abstract thinking, the nightly movies had stopped. That seemed a sign that dreams might indeed express the mind's ideas and motivations. "It is a mistake to think that we can study the brain using the same concepts we use for the liver," says Solms.

"From my perspective, dreaming is just thinking in a very different biochemical state," says Deirdre Barrett, who teaches psychology at Harvard and is editor of the journal *Dreaming*. The threads can be "just as complex as waking thought and just as dull. They are overwhelmingly visual, and language is less important, and logic is less important."

I am a traveler carrying one light bag and looking for a place to spend the night. I . . . discover a hostel of a sort in a large indoor space big enough to house a gymnasium. I find a spot near a corner and

Paul McCartney and "Yesterday"

A Dream Come True

"I woke up with a lovely tune in my head," Paul McCartney recalled to his biographer, Barry Miles. "I thought, 'That's great. I wonder what that is?'" He got up that morning in May 1965, went to the piano, and began playing the melody what would become "Yesterday." At first, lacking lyrics, he improvised with "Scrambled eggs, oh my baby, how I love your legs." While he really liked the tune, he had some reservations: "Because I'd, dreamed it, I couldn't believe I'd written it." Today, with more than 1,600 covers, that song holds the Guinness world record for most recorded versions.

—B.Q.

prepare for bed. I think to myself, "Luckily, I have my high-tech pillow." I take out of my bag a light, flat panel about 8 by 10 inches and the thickness of a thick piece of cardboard. "It works by applying a voltage," I say. "There's a new kind of material which fluffs up when you apply a voltage." On the face of the panel is a liquid-crystal display with two buttons, one labeled "on" and one labeled "off." I touch the "on" button with my index finger, and the flat panel magically inflates to the dimensions of a fluffy pillow. I lay it down on the ground and comfortably go to sleep.

Chuck, scientist (from Dreambank.net)

If Chuck's experience is an example of logic gone to sleep, no wonder dreamers so often wake up shouting, "Eureka!" Indeed, history is filled with examples of inspiration that blossomed during sleep and eventually led to inventions or works of art or military moves. Exactly what happens to inspire creativity is unclear, but the new technology is providing clues.

Crazy smart. Brain scans performed on people in REM sleep, for example, have shown that even as certain brain centers turn on—the emotional seat of the brain and the part that processes all visual inputs are wide awake—one vital area goes absolutely dormant: the systematic and clear-thinking prefrontal cortex, where caution and organization reside. "This can explain the bizarreness you see in dreams, the crazy kind of sense that your brain is ignoring the usual ways that you put things together," says Robert Stickgold, associate professor of psychiatry at Harvard and director of the Center for Sleep and Cognition at Beth Israel Deaconess Medical Center. "This is what you want in a state in which creativity is enhanced. Creativity is nothing more and nothing less than putting

memories together in a way that they never have been before."

No wonder dreamers so often wake up shouting, "Eureka!"

Putting memories together is also an essential part of learning; people integrate the memory of new information, be it how to tie shoelaces or conjugate French verbs, with existing knowledge. Does dreaming help people learn? No one knows—but some sort of boost seems to happen during sleep. Many studies by sleep researchers have shown that people taught a new task performed it better after a night of sleep.

A study of how quickly dreamers solve problems supports Stickgold's theory that the sleeping mind can be quite nimble and inventive. Participants were asked to solve scrambled word puzzles after being awakened during both the REM phase of sleep and the less active non-REM phase. Their performance improved by 32 percent when they worked on the puzzles coming out of REM sleep, which told researchers that that phase is more conducive to fluid reasoning. During non-REM sleep, it appears, our more cautious selves kick into gear.

Indeed, PET scans of people in a non-REM state show a decline in brain energy compared with REM sleep and increased activity in those dormant schoolmarmish lobes. Does this affect the content of dreams? Yes, say researchers from Harvard and the Boston University School of Medicine.

Since people should theoretically be more uninhibited when the controlling prefrontal cortex is quiet, the team tracked participants for two weeks to see if their REM dreams were more socially aggressive than the ones they reported during non-REM sleep. The REM dreams, in fact, were much more likely to involve social interactions and tended to be more aggressive.

I had a horrible dream. Howard was in a coffin. I yelled and screamed at his mom that it was all her fault. I kicked myself that I hadn't waited to become a widow rather than a divorcée in order to get the insurance. I woke up feeling miserable, the dream was so icky.

Barb (from Dreambank.net)

To many experts, Barb's bad dream would be a good sign, an indication that she would recover from the sorrow of her divorce. A vivid dream life, in which troubled or anxious people experience tough emotions while asleep, is thought to act, in the words of Cartwright, as "a kind of internal therapist."

59

Saddam and His Winning Strategy

A Dream Come True

Saddam Hussein used his dreams to guide policy, sometimes to the befuddlement of his closest advisers. The dictator's personal secretary told U.S. military investigators in an interview in 2003 that Hussein would sleep on difficult problems and report the solutions the next morning. One time that his dream got it right: During the Iran-Iraq War of the 1980s, Hussein dreamed that the Iranians would launch an offensive through a large marshland, so he ordered more troops there. His generals thought the move illogical but acquiesced. The Iranians attacked there, and the Iraqis prevailed.

—B.Q.

Jack Nicklaus and His Grip

A Dream Come True

In the summer of 1964, Jack Nicklaus was in a slump: "It got to the point where a 76 looked like a great score to me," the golfer told the Cleveland *Plain Dealer*. One night, during the Cleveland Open, he dreamed he was hitting the ball with a different grip—and it worked better. So he tried it the next day, shot a 68, then a 65, and ended the tournament tied for third place. For the year, he shot about a 70 average, the lowest in professional golf. "I'm almost embarrassed to admit how I changed my grip this week," he told the reporter at the time. "But that's how it happened. It's kinda crazy, isn't it?"

—B.Q.

The enduring and vexing question is: How much of value do dreams say? Despite all the efforts to quantify, to measure, no one has an answer yet. But dreams have played a role in psychotherapy for over a century, since Freud theorized that they signal deep and hidden motivations. "A dream is the one domain in which many of a patient's defenses are sufficiently relaxed that themes emerge that ordinarily would not appear in waking life," says Glen Gabbard, professor of psychiatry and psychoanalysis at Baylor College of Medicine.

A vivid dream life is thought to act as an "internal therapist."

Sometimes, dreams can be a helpful diagnostic tool, a way of taking the emotional temperature of a patient. The dreams of clinically depressed people are notable for their utter lack of activity, for example.

Might there be a physiological reason? Eric Nofzinger, director of the Sleep Neuroimaging Research Program at the University of Pittsburgh medical school, has studied PET scans of depressed patients and has found that the difference between their waking and sleeping states is far less dramatic than normal. On the one hand, he says, "we were shocked, surprised, and amazed at how much activity" there was in the emotional brain of healthy people during sleep. In depressed patients, by contrast, the vigilant prefrontal cortex, which normally is not active during sleep, worked overtime. Never surrendering to the soothing power of dreams, the brain is physically constrained, and its dream life shows it.

Healing power. Is it possible that dreaming can actually heal? "We know that 60 to 70 percent of people who

go through a depression will recover without treatment," says Cartwright, who recently tested her theory that maybe they are working through their troubles while asleep. In a study whose results were published this spring in the journal *Psychiatry Research,* she recruited 30 people going through a divorce and asked them to record their dreams over five months. Depressed patients whose dreams were rich with emotion—one woman reported seething while her ex-husband danced with his new girlfriend—eventually recovered without the need for drugs or extensive psychotherapy. But those whose dreams were bland and empty of feeling were not able to recover on their own.

> I've sat straight up in bed many times, reliving it, reseeing it, rehearing it. And it's in the most absurd ways that only a dream could depict . . . the one that comes to mind most, dreaming of a green pool in front of me. That was part of the radarscope. It was a pool of gel, and I reached into the radarscope to stop that flight. But in the dream, I didn't harm the plane. I just held it in my hand, and somehow that stopped everything.

Danielle O'Brien, air traffic controller for American Airlines Flight 77, which crashed into the Pentagon on Sept. 11, 2001 (in an interview with ABC News)

Many clinicians working with traumatized patients have found that their nightmares follow a common trajectory. First, the dreams re-create the horrors; later, as the person begins to recover, the stories involve better outcomes. One way to help victims of trauma move on is to encourage them to wake themselves up in the midst of a horrifying dream and consciously take control of the narrative, to take action, much as O'Brien appears to have done in her dream. This can break the cycle of nightmares by offering a sense of mastery. "If you can change the dream content," says Harvard's Barrett, author of *Trauma and Dreams,* "you see a reduction in all the other post-traumatic symptoms."

Cartwright recalls helping a rape victim who came in suffering from nightmares in which she felt an utter lack of control; together, they worked to edit the young woman's dreams of being in situations where she was powerless—of lying on the floor of an elevator without walls as it rose higher and higher over Lake Michigan, for example. "I told her, 'Remember, this is your construction. You made it up, and you can stop it,'" says Cartwright, who coached the woman to recognize the point at which the dream was becoming frightening and try to seize control. At the next session, the woman reported that, as the elevator rose, she decided to stand in her dream and figure out what was happening. The walls rose around her until she felt safe.

A window? A royal road? A way for the brain to integrate today with yesterday? While definitive answers remain elusive, the experience of dreaming is clearly as universal as a heartbeat and as individual as a fingerprint—and rich with possibilities for both scientist and poet.

UNIT 4
Learning and Remembering

Unit Selections

Key Points to Consider

- What are learning and remembering? How are they related?

- In what types of jobs do people need good learning ability and fine-tuned memories? What we can learn from these individuals?

- Are "knowing" and "remembering" the same thing?

- What is intelligence? Why is it important? How is it related to learning and remembering?

- What is the theory of multiple intelligences? Is it a viable and respected theory?

Student Web Site
www.mhcls.com/online

Internet References
Further information regarding these Web sites may be found in this book's preface or online.

Mind Tools
   http://www.psychwww.com/mtsite/
The Opportunity of Adolescence
   http://www.winternet.com/~webpage/adolescencepaper.html
Project Zero
   http://pzweb.harvard.edu

Don Mason/Brand X Pictures/Jupiter Images

Do you remember your first week of classes at college? There were so many new buildings and so many people's names to remember. You had to recall accurately where all your classes were as well as your professors' names. Just remembering your class schedule was problematic enough. For those of you who lived in residence halls, the difficulties multiplied. You had to remember where your residence was, recall the names of individuals living on your floor, and learn how to navigate from your room to other places on campus, such as the dining halls and library. Then came examination time. Did you ever think you would survive college exams? The material, in terms of difficulty level and amount, was perhaps more than you thought you could manage.

What a stressful time you experienced when you first came to campus! Much of what created the stress was the strain on your learning and memory systems, two complicated processes unto themselves. Indeed, most of you survived just fine—and with your memories, learning strategies, and mental health intact.

Two of the processes you depended on when you first came to college are the processes of learning and of memorizing, some of the oldest psychological processes studied by psychologists. Today, with their sophisticated experimental techniques, psychologists have distinguished several types of memory processes and have discovered what makes learning more complete so that subsequent memory is more accurate. We also have discovered that humans aren't the only organisms capable of these processes. All types of animals can learn, even if the organism is as simple as an earthworm or amoeba.

Psychologists know, too, that rote learning and practice are not the only forms of learning. For instance, at this point in time in your introductory psychology class, you might be studying operant and classical conditioning, two very simple but nonetheless important forms of learning of which humans and even simple organisms are capable. Both types of conditioning can occur without our awareness or active participation in them. The articles in this unit examine the processes of learning and remembering (or its reciprocal, forgetting) in some detail.

What might underpin learning and memory abilities is intelligence, another all-important but controversial concept in psychology. With regard to intelligence, one persistent problem has been the difficulty of defining just what intelligence is. David Wechsler, author of several of the most popular intelligence tests in current clinical use, defines intelligence as *the global capacity of the individual to act purposefully, to think rationally, and to deal effectively with the environment.* Other psychologists have proposed more alternative or more complex definitions.

The definitional problem arises when we try to develop tests that validly and reliably measure such abstract, intangible concepts. A valid test is one that measures what it purports to measure. A reliable test yields the same score for the same individual over and over again. Because defining and assessing intelligence has been so controversial and so difficult, historian Edward Boring once suggested that we define intelligence as whatever it is that an intelligence test measures! Let's look at learning, remembering, and intelligence.

Teaching for Understanding

TOM SHERMAN AND BARBARA KURSHAN

W iggins' view of understanding requires students to integrate facts, information, knowledge, and applications to develop understanding. Understanding, from this perspective, is an extensive web of interrelated ideas, experiences, and beliefs that transforms information from simple, memorized facts into knowledge that can be the basis for action. Recent research and theory have provided a relatively clear picture of how technologies can support classroom teaching and learning that leads to this genuine understanding. Moreover, teaching for understanding appears to result in students passing or scoring higher on high stakes tests.

Over the past 8–10 years scientists, teachers, and behavioral investigators have synthesized research and practice to explain how to develop the intellectual tools and learning strategies needed to acquire the knowledge that allows people to think productively. These scientists believe that learners construct their knowledge from their experiences, a perspective that generates many implications for how to teach students to understand.

Psychologist John Bransford and his colleagues propose three strongly supported findings that capture the essence of this evidence for teaching and learning:

1. Preconceptions influence all learning.
2. Understanding comes from knowing facts and principles.
3. Metacognition is essential for understanding.

Teachers and learners can use technology in many ways to support these findings on human learning. Technology can help teachers discover students' preconceptions and provide a broad range of instructional options to meet diverse learner needs. Technology is a tool for teachers to more effectively and accurately create profiles of each learner's experiences and background and how students learn and then develop technology-based instruction consistent with each student's needs. For learners, technologies can open alternatives to mastering ideas, concepts, processes, and outcomes. Learners can employ technology to expose misconceptions, simulate solution applications, test facts, and respond to problem-solving challenges. Integrating technology into instructional practices often improves student achievement; presents relevant, timely, and appropriate remediation; and provides content that can be crafted to meet different learning styles. We examine specific ways that technologies can contribute to meeting the findings of modern learning psychology.

Preconceptions Influence All Learning

Students come to school with well-formed ideas about how the world works. Called preconceptions, existing ideas that children hold are central to constructing new learning. Humans begin learning right from birth, and even very young children form ideas about their worlds based on observations and experiences. These preconceptions have powerful and enduring effects on how children learn new information as well as how they will remember and use new knowledge.

A main challenge for teachers is to use these preconceptions as the foundation for helping learners expand or modify their existing understandings. Another challenge is to correct misconceptions. Until recently, the impact of misconceptions has not been well understood, and they were generally thought to be easily corrected. However, most misconceptions are relatively firmly held beliefs based on observations of natural events and have practical explanatory power or are effective in limited applications.

For example, a flat earth theory is intuitive because the earth looks flat and we have no experience that contradicts the idea of a flat earth. And, a flat earth conception works very well with most experiences we have, for instance, building a small house. However, flat earth thinking becomes problematic for long-range navigation, as well as understanding geography and other sciences. It is not unusual for people to operate cognitively from a flat earth theory even though they know intellectually that the earth is not flat.

Classroom instruction is rarely designed to correct students' incorrect assumptions. Generally, the instructional approach is to teach the correct answer and problem-solving strategy. Misconceptions cannot be ignored because new and accurate information inconsistent with these misconceptions is likely to be learned superficially, recalled only for tests, and then forgotten.

Perhaps practicing teachers' most frequent question about students' prior knowledge is, "How is it possible to assess every student's prior knowledge?" One answer is to use technology to assist with this critical task by allowing students to reveal their preconceptions on well-designed assessments that focus on commonly held misconceptions. Technology tools provide teachers the ability to assess students' misconceptions. Recent applications on handhelds and PCs can be used to aggregate class responses, test knowledge, and provide feedback to the class. Discourse, published by

ETS (Educational Testing Service), lets teachers know instantly if each and every student in the class is following the lesson. (Editor's note: For company contact information, see Resources on p. 11.) With instant feedback, instruction can be modified as it occurs for every student. Similarly, Classroom Performance System from eInstruction Corporation provides a nonthreatening environment allowing all students to participate and teachers to give immediate feedback and aggregate results.

Technologies also offer great potential to integrate preconceptions with new knowledge by providing learners with many examples of concepts to be taught from which students can choose the most salient for them. Concept mapping tools enable students to visually see their misconceptions and correct them, leading to increased understanding and retention of content. CTOOLS, from Michigan State University and developed through an NSF grant, provides a Web-based problem-solving environment for exploring concepts in science. WebLearn, developed by the computer science department of RMIT University in Australia, focuses on identifying students' misconceptions in learning college mathematics. If an answer specified is incorrect, commonly occurring misconceptions are checked for and appropriate feedback is provided to the student.

Students benefit because they have the option of choosing examples that are most consistent with their personal backgrounds and knowledge. In addition, an array of examples allows students to test applications of their understandings in different and unfamiliar situations. When students engage their understanding through these examples, they can examine the relationships between their beliefs and outcomes. Students and teachers can develop a stronger sense of the intellectual strategies that may be helpful in developing more extensive and accurate understandings.

Finally, technology-assisted learning tools can provide simulated intellectual challenges through which students can confront the inconsistencies between the knowledge they have and the new knowledge in a lesson. For example, students who misunderstand a concept such as retrograde motion of stars is a product of distance and the earth's rotation rather than the varying speeds of stars can manipulate models of the solar system to see the consequences of varying speed. Students who hold views such as welfare mothers never get off the dole can explore databases with accurate statistical information as well as primary sources. By creating this disequilibrium, teachers can motivate students to learn and focus their attention on critical features of the concept being taught.

Understanding Comes from Knowing Facts and Principles

Understanding evolves from a combination of learning factual knowledge and general principles. Learning factual information is essential, because without facts students have nothing to understand. However, isolated facts are difficult to learn and unlikely to be recalled. Although this may appear obvious, the ways that facts should be connected is often not well understood. The relation between facts, concepts, and principles requires multiple interactions between the learners existing and new facts and more general or higher-level conceptualization that provides a framework for making these facts meaningful.

Students must develop extensive conceptual frameworks to organized facts into knowledge in their memories much like a

well organized file cabinet makes facts easy to retrieve. When knowledge is extensively connected with other concepts and well organized, it is much more accessible and more accurately used. Organization facilitates applying knowledge in different situations and on novel problems, a process called transfer.

To present the facts and guide students to develop the broad frameworks to organize the facts, teachers must have a strong mastery of the material they are teaching and recognize how students typically learn that material.

Computer-based programs can provide students with a menu of choices from which they can develop experience with varying applications of ideas drawn from examples embedded in multiple contexts. For example, if the goal of instruction was to teach students how the concept of transportation can explain the formation of population centers, students can search maps looking for potential sites based on geographical features. Once sites are selected, the map can reveal where cities actually formed. Students will be challenged to explain both their accurate and inaccurate choices. The SimCity program published by Electronic Arts is one example of software that can leverage the power of technology to facilitate thinking about the accuracy of held beliefs.

A variety of experiences coupled with collaborative discussions enables students to use and organize facts. In addition, as they build experience, students can develop broader conceptions. Finally, technology-based concept maps can show students other ways to organize their understandings and allow them to compare their concept structures. Software that helps learners to brainstorm, organize, plan, and create is valuable for supporting development of concepts. Products, such as Inspiration (Inspiration Software Inc.) and MindMapper (The Bosley Group) graphically present these skills and promote the development of visual learning strategies.

Metacognition Is Essential for Understanding

Students must be aware of and control their thinking. Metacognition describes the personal awareness of individuals to choose, monitor, and adjust the thinking strategies they use to learn and solve problems. In other words, students select and control their mental processes so that they can think efficiently and effectively. It is well known that successful learners have more thinking skills and use their intellectual abilities differently than less successful learners.

Genuine understanding is most likely when students are cognitively managing the interaction between what they know and what they are learning. Because learning begins with learners' existing conceptions, growth comes from changing and expanding their existing beliefs. Teachers help students learn to monitor their understanding by using cognitive skills such as reflection and summarizing. In this way, students master the material and the thinking strategies needed to understand. We have developed a site called Study Smart that illustrates how online programs can teach the metacognitive intellectual tools, skills, strategies, and attitudes that are characteristic of successful learners. Many programs integrate these kinds of thinking strategies and provide the opportunity to summarize and reflect on knowledge. Two that effectively engage learners while teaching these skills are the Zoombinis series developed by TERC (distributed by Riverdeep) and BrainCogs developed by Fablevision.

Although metacognition may seem intuitive, developing good metacognitive strategies is difficult for most learners. The most effective ways to teach these cognitive management skills is to provide many models and continuous opportunities. Teachers are one good source of models, but technologies can also encourage students to address the disequilibrium created by the differences between current and new information.

Simulations and dramatizations of events and situations as well as strategies to solve problems let learners compare, contrast, and experiment with new and old ways of thinking in a variety of settings. For example, in science, a common misconception is that a ball thrown in the air has energy that propels it upward. Using technologies, students can manipulate the variables acting on the ball and compare the outcomes with their predictions. Computer simulations and animations can clearly depict and simulate learning situations and also provide the tools for exploring the concepts through "what if" strategies. The Logal Science Explore Series, published by Riverdeep, includes computer simulations that help students more effectively discover and understand scientific concepts. With the simulations, students develop problem-solving skills as they form hypotheses, manipulate variables, generate and collect data, analyze relationships, and draw conclusions.

Another example that promotes higher order thinking skills and lasting conceptual understanding is the series of research-based interactive math and science simulations called Gizmos from Explore-learning. These knowledge interactions help students to build stronger understandings and to identify ways to manipulate their cognitive actions to stimulate more active thinking.

Summary

These three findings summarize the basic premise that human learning is a complex interaction between existing understandings and new knowledge. Changing beliefs is often difficult because our inclination is to fit new ideas into existing conceptual frameworks. Information, whether observed or presented by a teacher, that does not fit existing frameworks is usually forgotten because it is either irrelevant or incorrect.

Successfully modifying existing beliefs comes from discovering that a current belief is inadequate to explain new information or as a result of a purposeful quest to expand or to challenge an existing conceptual framework. Although teachers can devise these events for students, it is essential for students to engage personally to change their understandings. And, students who are aware of thinking strategies and are open to new ideas are much more likely to understand in new ways. One of the appeals of technologies is to entice learners to think differently and more expansively.

Technologies can be used to present new knowledge in carefully crafted learning environments that stimulate students to examine their beliefs and revise what and how they think based on new facts and expanded conceptual frameworks.

Because technology is powerful and responsive, it can be used to assess students' existing knowledge so teachers have a clear picture of student needs. In addition, technology-based programs can present students with situations that are inconsistent with their existing conceptions, allowing multiple opportunities to confront misconceptions and to identify and experiment with alternative conceptions.

From a pedagogical perspective, teaching involves creating situations in which students can confront their misconceptions, enhance their incomplete knowledge, improve their intellectual abilities, and construct ever more accurate representations of ideas and processes. As they mature as knowers, learners not only build more extensive and accurate understandings but also develop more sophisticated learning skills and strategies. Thus, the two-fold general goals of teaching are for students to master content and to develop the skills, strategies, and attitudes characteristic of successful learners. There are many technologies that can be among teachers' pedagogical tools to meet both goals.

Consider your teaching and how you can integrate technology to better teach for understanding. We suggest you begin by considering your beliefs about teaching and learning. Current thinking about learning indicates that there are substantial differences in the ways we teach if we want the majority of students to learn beyond only recalling facts. Understanding requires a more significant and intense interaction between learners and content so that new ideas are processed deeply and extensively connected to existing and new knowledge. One practical advantage of a well developed and evidence-based theory such as constructivism is that you can make purposeful decisions about using technology in teaching. This is in marked contrast, for example, to using technologies merely because it is possible to expose students to a program or Web site. The benefits of exposure increase markedly when the technology application fits with a purpose consistent with how people learn. Here we have suggested a variety of technology-based applications that are consistent with well developed theoretical propositions to transform classrooms to be more consistent with the conditions that promote learning. In addition, it appears that technologies can be valuable resources for teachers to respond to the increasing demands for students to get passing marks on high stakes tests. Although certainly not magic, technologies can be an important pedagogical tool that increases the ability for teachers to successfully teach all students to learn with understanding.

THOMAS M. SHERMAN is a professor of education in the College of Liberal Arts and Human Sciences at Virginia Tech. He teaches courses in educational psychology, evaluation, and instructional design and has written more than 100 articles for professional publications. Tom works regularly with practicing teachers and students in the areas of learning improvement and teaching strategies. He is also active in civic affairs, serving on local and state committees. **DR. BARBARA KURSHAN** is the president of Educorp Consulting Corporation. She has a doctorate in education with an emphasis on computer-based applications. She has written numerous articles and texts and has designed software and networks to meet the needs of learners. She works with investment banking firms and venture groups on companies related to educational technology. She serves on the boards of Fablevision, Headsprout, and Medalis, and is currently on the advisory boards of Pixel, WorldSage, and Tegrity.

What Studies of Actors and Acting Can Tell Us About Memory and Cognitive Functioning

The art of acting has been defined as the ability to live truthfully under imaginary circumstances. Our many years of researching theatrical expertise have produced findings relevant to text comprehension, learning theory, cognitive aging, and expert memory. In this article, we first discuss how large amounts of dialogue, learned in a very short period, can be reproduced in real time with complete spontaneity. We then turn to abstracting the essence of acting and applying it to diverse undertakings, from discovering optimal learning strategies to promoting healthy cognitive aging. Finally, we address the implications of acting expertise on current theories of embodied cognition.

HELGA NOICE AND TONY NOICE

Actors report that the question they are asked most frequently is, "How do you learn all those lines?" However, actors themselves rarely consider memorization a defining skill. Rather they are concerned about giving honest, spontaneous performances, ones that focus on communicating the meanings underlying the literal words. Indeed, when actors do mention memory, it is usually within the context of forgetting the lines until they are needed to communicate the feeling of the moment. The fine British actor, Michael Caine, summed up the process:

> You must be able to stand there *not* thinking of that line. You take it off the other actor's face. Otherwise, for your next line, you're not listening and not free to respond naturally, to act spontaneously. (Caine, 1990, pp. 28–29)

How do actors achieve this freedom to live in the present moment while speaking memorized dialogue, and what light can this process shed on human cognition? We have been investigating actors' processes for almost 20 years. That inquiry has taken place in three (sometimes overlapping) phases.

The First Phase: Learning the Role

We started examining actors' script-acquisition strategies by means of protocol analysis (i.e., we collected and compared actors' descriptions of their working processes during the performance of a task). Because the standard playwright's contract calls for the replacement of any actor who deviates from the script's exact wording, actors learn dialogue with a high degree of precision. Although rote repetition is widely assumed to be the strategy of choice for word-for-word retention, we found that professional actors rarely acquire their roles by rote. One actor described the process this way:

> What I don't do: I don't memorize right away. And, in fact, if I have a problem, it's in keeping myself from memorizing too soon. Most of the time I memorize by magic—and that is, I don't really memorize. There is no effort involved. There seems to be no process involved: It just happens. One day early on, I know the lines. (Noice & Noice, 1997, p. 13)

A series of further studies used empirical methodology (investigation of various learning techniques in controlled experiments) in addition to protocol analysis. These studies revealed that actors unwittingly employ most of the learning principles identified by cognitive researchers (e.g., Noice & Noice, 1997) by employing devices such as extensive elaboration (imaginative embellishment), perspective taking (adopting the perspective of one character in a narrative), self-referencing (relating material personally to oneself), self-generation (remembering one's own ideas better than ideas of others), mood congruency (matching one's mood to the emotional valence of the material), and distinctiveness (considering details that render an item unique). Actors also determine the goal of every utterance of the character, breaking down scripts into what they call "beats" (the smallest goal-directed chunks of dialogue). These beats lay out the entire role as a causal chain. For example, one actor divided a half page of dialogue into three successive beats: "to flatter," "to draw him out," and "to allay his fears." That is, the character first flattered the other character; then, when the flattery appeared to work, she drew him out, which, in turn, allowed her to allay his fears (Noice & Noice, 1997).

Establishing this causal chain often entails generating multiple elaborations for a few words of dialogue. (A well-established cognitive concept is that additional elaboration leads to greater recall; e.g., Graesser & Clark, 1985). Here is an example from the play, *The Front* Page (Hecht & MacArthur, 1950): The mayor confronts a reporter, saying: "Don't pester me now, please" (p. 69). One actor's protocol revealed that he inferred from the use of the word *pester* that the mayor considered the reporter to be like a bothersome child, since the term is generally used with children. The rest of the sentence was processed at similar depth: The actor realized that the mayor, not wanting to alienate a potentially useful reporter, is careful to say "now," indicating that future discussions are possible. Furthermore, he softens the whole statement by adding, "please." In addition, the mayor's ego would probably make him proud of this use of alliteration, further ensuring recall of the line, "Don't pester me now, please." This procedure is repeated for every successive goal (or subgoal) of the character, so that a link is forged between almost every word or phrase and the goal that caused the character to utter it (Noice & Noice, 1997). A consistent finding in the text-comprehension literature is that goal statements are better recalled than non-goal statements (e.g., Trabasso & van den Broek, 1985). Processing the script at such depth produces a great deal of verbatim retention without rote memorization.

It is important to note that retention of the script is just the preparatory part of the actor's work. When the words have been learned, the actor must then mean them each time he or she says them, so that every performance is identical yet unique. That is, what is said remains the same, but how it is said depends on the mental, physical, and emotional interactions between the actors at every moment of the play or film. This double process was one of the aspects of acting most often mentioned in the more than 100 protocols we collected. Actors analyze the role prior to rehearsal; but during rehearsal, they try to devote all their conscious awareness to remaining in the present moment by attending to the other actors, only glancing down at the script when necessary. Eventually, they find they are "off book."

The Second Phase: Teaching the Technique

One question not answered by the specification of actors' script-processing approaches was whether their rapid acquisition of dialogue was a product of their many years of experience in learning theatrical roles or was based on an explicit strategy that could be taught to nonactors. To answer this, we tried to train undergraduates in the actors' strategy (Noice & Noice, 1997). Assuming that the first part of the process (the deep processing of the script) was responsible for an actor's highly efficient memory, we taught students to elaborate on a text the way actors do by asking goal-directed questions (e.g., "Am I flirting with her when I say this?"). Consistent with previous findings,

students who elaborated by questioning the underlying meaning remembered more than did controls who read the same text purely for comprehension. (Indeed, most of the early investigations of cognitive learning principles had employed read-only controls.) However, we then tried to make the conditions more stringent by having the controls deliberately memorize the same material using any strategy they had found successful in the past. If the actors' strategy still produced more retention, it would suggest that we had found an optimal means of studying verbal material. Unfortunately, the deliberate-memorization controls outperformed the students who used the actors' analytic strategy. (The memorization strategy produced 57% retention; the actors' analytic strategy, only 33%.)

After much thought, we turned to the other half of the actors' process, the one they use for rehearsal and performance. Instead of instructing the students to analyze the text, we had them read the material, imagining someone they knew who needed this information. Indeed, we specifically told them not to try to remember the words but to put all their concentration on meaning them (i.e. actively using them to gain a specific end such as warning a friend). Suddenly, the results were reversed: Meaning the words produced greater retention than memorizing them did, with 50% retention for the memorization strategy but 60% for the actors' performance strategy. This finding has been replicated repeatedly using different populations and procedures and various types of materials. We coined the term *active experiencing* (AE) to refer to this process in which participants are asked to use all physical, mental, and emotional channels to communicate the meaning of material to another person, either actually present or imagined (for a review, see Noice & Noice, 2004; for an example, see Figure 1).

In addition to improving the speed and accuracy with which specific material can be learned, the AE principle turned out

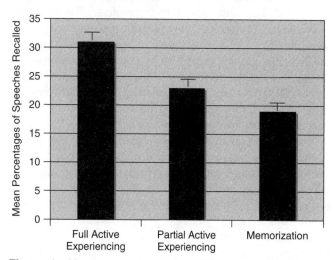

Figure 1 Mean percentage of speeches recalled by participants using active experiencing (AE) or other strategies. Undergraduates with no acting training or experience were randomly assigned to one of three conditions: a) full AE including both motivated verbal communication and motivated movement; b) partial AE using verbal communication only; c) deliberate memorization. Participants in the first two conditions were given brief procedural coaching (Noice & Noice, 2001).

to have application to a far thornier problem: cognitive aging. Previous research (e.g., Wilson & Bennett, 2003) had shown that enhanced cognitive health and the delayed onset of Alzheimer's were observed in participants who had engaged in the performance of activities requiring mentally effortful processing. However, research on such activities generally tracked participation over many years. A number of short-term studies were also performed, but they were usually targeted to specific cognitive abilities such as being able to recognize drawings of abstract figures when they were shown in different orientations on the page (e.g., Willis, Cornelius, Blow, & Baltes, 1983). In such studies, although improvement was often found, it was limited to the specific skill trained, and did not generalize to other cognitive areas.

Therefore, we performed a series of 4-week, controlled interventions, using pre- and post-testing to assess change on various cognitive tasks (e.g., word recall, problem solving) and also to assess any increase in life satisfaction. The participants (aged 65 to 90 years) were recruited through talks in senior organizations and follow-up newsletter notices. The participants in the experimental condition knew that the program would consist of some form of instruction to improve cognition; but, in order to avoid self-selection, they did not know they would be studying acting until they arrived at the first training session. The intervention contained (in a highly concentrated form) elements such as novelty, effort, and complexity, which have frequently been shown to enhance cognition in older adults (e. g., Hultsch, Hertzog, Small, & Dixon, 1999). A professional theater director presented a series of progressively more difficult exercises in which participants became cognitively, emotionally, and physically involved in the performance. Thus, if the exercise called for one participant to demand attention from another, there would be observable changes in the first participant. These might include increased sternness of facial expression, harshness of tone of voice, and aggressiveness of body language. The instructor monitored the performances to make sure that observed changes were byproducts of a participant's imaginative involvement in the dramatic situation and not the result of simply trying to imitate the outward characteristics of the behavior, a process that actors call "indicating." (Distinguishing between true involvement and indicating is a defining skill possessed by almost all professional directors and acting teachers.)

These interventions produced gains in multiple measures of cognitive and affective performance, even though no part of the instruction was targeted to the test instruments. That is, participants were never provided with specific strategies to improve test performance. Therefore, any improvement would appear to result from the mental stimulation inherent in the course (see Figure 2). The results were obtained in comparison with no-treatment and alternate-intervention (art appreciation) controls (Noice, Noice, & Staines, 2004).

Some studies have provided evidence that biological mechanisms underlie the effects of behavioral interventions. Wilson and Bennett (2003) suggested that cognitive activity may help maintain the health of interconnected neural systems, and Park (2002) used imaging studies to show strong activation of certain brain areas when participants were directed to think about

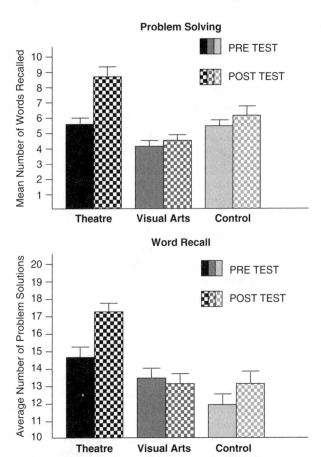

Figure 2 Pretest and posttest results for word recall and problem-solving ability by older adults given a 4-week course in acting or art appreciation or no training (control). The acting course was devoted mainly to cognitive stimulation through the active-experiencing principle. Besides the gains in word recall and problem solving, acting training also produced a marginally significant improvement in working memory and a significant increase in perceived quality of life (Noice, Noice, & Staines, 2004). These gains persisted for 4 months without reinstatement of the training.

meaning. (This is particularly pertinent to our results because all acting, by its nature, involves the communication of meaning.)

The Third Phase: Back to Theory

Implicit in the AE principle is that cognitive processing is but one element of performance. Feelings are also communicated, and both thoughts and feelings affect physiology in terms of facial expressions, vocal inflections, and quality and speed of movements. The latter aspects turned out to have some strong implications for memory theory. Since the early 1970s, dozens of experiments on subject-performed tasks (SPTs) have shown that short action phrases such as "move the cup" or "lift the pen" are better remembered when the actions are actually performed than when the phrases are studied under standard verbal-learning instructions (for a review, see Nilsson, 2000). One widely accepted theoretical explanation involves the establishment of motoric codes. (When information is encoded, many theorists believe that some sort of memory record or "code" is established, a visual code for a picture, a verbal code for a word, a motoric code for a movement.) An alternate explanation offered for the SPT phenomenon is that actually performing an action such as hitting the table increases the mental association between the action (hitting) and the agent (the one doing the hitting). However, almost all SPT experiments have used literal enactment of short action phrases. Such literal enactment virtually never occurs in theatre or film. That is, rarely would a theatrical script require an actor to walk toward the door while saying, "I'm walking toward the door." Instead, actors' movements are non-literal. For example, a character might be asked to leave the room; he replies, "I'm perfectly happy here," while sitting down in a nearby chair. Obviously, there is no literal connection between the verbal phrase ("I'm perfectly happy here") and the action of sitting, but there is a goal-directed one: Both the statement and the physical action are attempts to defy the person who requested the character to leave. We have found that such nonliteral action during a theatre performance produces the same movement-enhanced verbal memory found in SPT experiments, including the fact that movements do not have to be repeated during testing. The latter finding would appear to cast doubt on encoding specificity as an explanation. (Encoding specificity is the theory that memory is enhanced when conditions at retrieval match those at encoding.) We have also replicated the nonliteral phenomenon in a lab with undergraduates after only a few minutes of procedural coaching (Noice & Noice, 2001).

The theoretical position that appears most consistent with our findings is that of embodied cognition (e.g., Glenberg & Kaschak, 2002). According to this view, thought, memory, and language are based on actual perceptual (i.e., motor and sensory) experience: "Knowledge is embodied to the extent that (a) it depends on activity in systems also used for perception, action, and emotion, and (b) reasoning using that knowledge (including combining information from language and action) requires use of those systems" (A.M. Glenberg, personal communication, November 21, 2005). Our data certainly fit this view. In a play, for dramatic effect, some lines of dialogue are spoken when the actors are moving about the stage, and some while actors are sitting or standing in one spot. In one experiment (Noice, Noice, & Kennedy, 2000), actors produced superior recall for dialogue originally spoken while moving, even though the movements were not duplicated at the time of testing.

To account for this in terms of embodied cognition, consider this situation: A character crosses the stage, picks up a bottle, and says, "This is how I solve my problems." Obviously, the actor has to know why the character makes that utterance because it will affect how he walks and picks up the bottle. That is, the quality of the actions will be different if the man intends to dump the contents, or throw the bottle at the other's head, or greedily take a drink. According to Glenberg's version of embodiment theory, these potential actions are called affordances (i.e., the bottle affords these different action possibilities), and the meaning of any situation is derived from the meshing of the available affordances. When such a situation is retrieved from memory, the perceptual characteristics of the experience are simulated by neuronal activity in the brain. But the manner in which the

actions were originally performed necessarily constrains the meaning of the accompanying utterance. The resulting specificity of an actor's stored perceptual experience aids recall of the literal words and movements, in keeping with Glenberg's view that memory and comprehension are grounded in bodily action (e.g., Glenberg & Kaschak, 2002).

Conclusion

At present, we are performing an intervention with even older adults who reside in state-supported housing and have not had the advantage of higher education. This population has been shown to be at increased risk of cognitive decline (e.g., Springer, McIntosh, Winocur, & Grady, 2005). In addition, we have refined our intervention to compare two types of theater performance: dramatic and musical.

The next logical step is to investigate the neural mechanisms underlying acting. Brain-imaging studies have identified the areas implicated in such diverse tasks as performing motor movement, reacting to pleasant or unpleasant pictures, and processing meaning (e.g., Park, 2002). We are pilot testing short dramatic phrases that trained actors would tend to process with their usual AE strategy. We hypothesize that when actors and non-actors encode these phrases, the patterns of cortical activation will reveal the differences between brain mechanisms normally used for text processing and the cognitive-motoricemotive mechanisms elicited by AE. Such a finding could add physiological support to the existing behavioral evidence that bodily action and emotional response, in addition to semantic analysis, can enhance human memory. These results could also bring us one small step closer to the scientific understanding of aesthetic experience.

References

Caine, M. (1990). *Acting in film: An actor's take on movie making.* New York: Applause Theatre Books.

Glenberg, A.M., & Kaschak, M.P. (2002). Grounding language in action. *Psychonomic Bulletin & Review, 9,* 558–565.

Graesser, A.C., & Clark, L.F. (1985). *Structures and procedures of implicit knowledge.* Norwood, NJ: Ablex.

Hecht, B., & MacArthur, C. (1950). *The front page.* New York: Samuel French.

Hultsch, D.F., Hertzog, C., Small, B.J., & Dixon, R.A. (1999). Use it or lose it: Engaged lifestyle as a buffer of cognitive decline in aging. *Psychology of Aging, 14,* 245–263.

Nilsson, L-G. (2000). Remembering actions and words. In E. Tulving & F.I.M. Craik (Eds.), *The Oxford handbook of memory* (pp. 137–148). New York: Oxford University Press.

Noice, H., & Noice, T. (2001). Learning dialogue with and without movement. *Memory and Cognition, 29,* 820–828.

Noice, H., Noice, T., & Kennedy, C. (2000). The contribution of movement on the recall of complex material. *Memory, 8,* 353–363.

Noice, H., Noice, T., & Staines, G. (2004). A short-term intervention to enhance cognitive and affective functioning in older adults. *Journal of Aging and Health, 16,* 1–24.

Noice, T., & Noice, H. (1997). *The nature of expertise in professional acting: A cognitive view.* Mahwah, NJ: Erlbaum.

Noice, T., & Noice, H. (2004). A cognitive learning principle derived from the role acquisition strategies of professional actors. *Cognitive Technology, 9,* 1–24.

Park, D.D. (2002). Judging meaning improves function in the aging brain. *Trends in Cognitive Sciences, 6,* 227–229.

Springer, M.V., McIntosh, A.R., Winocur, G., & Grady, C.L. (2005). The relation between brain activity during memory tasks and years of education in young and older adults. *Neuropsychology, 19,* 181–192.

Trabasso, T., & van den Broek, P.W. (1985). Causal thinking and the representation of narrative events. *Journal of Memory and Language, 24,* 612–630.

Willis, S.L., Cornelius, S.W., Blow, F.C., & Baltes, P.B. (1983). Training research in aging: Attentional processes. *Journal of Educational Psychology, 75,* 257.

Wilson, R.S., & Bennett, D.A. (2003). Cognitive activity and risk of Alzheimer's disease. *Current Directions in Psychological Science, 12,* 87–91.

Address correspondence to Helga Noice, Department of Psychology, Elmhurst College, 190 Prospect Ave, Elmhurst, IL 60126; e-mail: helgan@elmhurst.edu.

Elmhurst College, Indiana State University

Memory Flexibility
A Workout for Working Memory

New research suggests that mental exercises might enhance one of the brain's central components for reasoning and problem-solving.

SADIE F. DINGFELDER

People may be able to remember a nearly infinite number of facts, but only a handful of items—held in working memory—can be accessed and considered at any given moment. It's the reason why a person might forget to buy an item or two on a mental grocery list, or why most people have difficulty adding together large numbers. In fact, working memory could be the basis for general intelligence and reasoning: Those who can hold many items in their mind may be well equipped to consider different angles of a complex problem simultaneously.

If psychologists could help people expand their working-memory capacity or make it function more efficiently, everyone could benefit, from chess masters to learning-disabled children, says Torkel Klingberg, MD, PhD, an assistant cognitive neuroscience professor at the Karolinska Institute in Sweden. Children with attention-deficit hyperactivity disorder (ADHD), for example, might especially benefit from working-memory training, says Rosemary Tannock, PhD, a psychologist and psychiatry professor at The Hospital for Sick Children in Toronto.

"It could be that working-memory problems give rise to observable behavioral symptoms of ADHD: distractibility and also poor academic achievement," she says. Working-memory deficits might also underpin some reading disabilities, as it controls the ability to recall words read earlier in a sentence, says Tannock.

But how—or even if—working memory can be expanded through training remains a topic of hot contention among psychologists. Some argue that working memory has a set limit of about four items, and that individual differences in working memory arise from the ability to group small bits of information into larger chunks. However, new research suggests that working-memory capacity could expand with practice—a finding that could shed new light on this central part of the mind's architecture, as well as potentially lead to treatments for ADHD or other learning disabilities.

Functional Limitations

One such study—by researchers at Syracuse University—hit upon the potential trainability while attempting to resolve a debate in the literature on the limits of working memory.

Since the 1950s, psychologists have found one aspect of working memory—sometimes referred to as the focus of attention—to have severe limitations. For example, George Miller, PhD—a founder of cognitive psychology and a psychology professor at Princeton University—established that people generally can't recall lists of numbers more than seven digits long. Those who exceeded that limit tended to make smaller groups of numbers into larger ones, using a process called "chunking." For example, people familiar with U.S. intelligence agencies would see the letter group "FBICIA" as two chunks, rather the six letters, and that set of letters would only occupy two slots in a person's memory, rather than six.

If psychologists could help people expand their working-memory capacity or make it function more efficiently, everyone could benefit, from chess masters to learning-disabled children.

In recent years, however, evidence is mounting that the limitation of working memory is somewhere between one and four information chunks. The downward revision results from new techniques to keep people from chunking information, which can create the illusion of greater fundamental storage capacity, says Nelson Cowan, PhD, a psychology professor at the University of Missouri–Columbia. In one common chunking-prevention method, participants repeat meaningless phrases over and over while performing working memory tasks such as memorizing lists of numbers.

A recent literature review by Cowan, published in *Behavioral and Brain Sciences* (Vol. 24, No. 1, pages 87–185), makes the case that a variety of working-memory measures all converge on a set limit of four items.

Other researchers have suggested that working-memory capacity is limited even further—to just a single item. In a study by Brian McElree, PhD, a psychology professor at New York University, participants underwent a test of working memory called "n-back." In the task, the participants read a series of numbers, presented one at a time on a computer screen. In the easiest version of the task, the computer presents a new digit, and then prompts participants to recall what number immediately preceded the current one. More difficult versions might ask participants to recall what number appeared two, three or four digits ago.

McElree found that participants recalled the immediately preceding numbers in a fraction of the time it took them to recall numbers presented more than one number ago—a finding published in the *Journal of Experimental Psychology: Learning, Memory and Cognition* (Vol. 27, No. 1, pages 817–835).

"There is clear and compelling evidence of one unit being maintained in focal attention and no direct evidence for more than one item of information extended over time," says McElree.

In an attempt to reconcile the two theories, psychology professor Paul Verhaeghen, PhD, and his colleagues at Syracuse University replicated McElree's experiment, but tracked participants' response times as they practiced at the task for 10 hours over five days.

"We found that by the end of day five . . . their working memory [capacity] had expanded from one to four items, but not to five," says Verhaeghen. "It seems that both theories are correct."

The focus of attention might expand as other working-memory processes become automated, Verhaeghen says. Perhaps practice improves the process of attaching a position to a number, freeing up the mind to recall up to four numbers, he notes.

Some researchers believe the practice effect uncovered by Verhaeghen reflects more efficient information encoding rather than expanded working-memory capacity. According to McElree, the response time measures used by Verhaeghen do not provide pure measures of memory-retrieval speed, and the changes in response time with practice could indicate that participants in his study simply became more practiced at encoding numbers vividly, he says.

If Verhaeghen's findings can be replicated using other tasks, it could change how scientists conceptualize working-memory limitations. Rather than there being a set limitation, working-memory capacity could improve through practice—suggesting that those with working-memory problems could improve their capacities through repetition. However, practice would need to occur on a task-by-task basis, says Verhaeghen, and, as he points out, "It is doubtful that practice on n-back generalizes to anything in real life."

Stretching the Limits

New research on children with ADHD, however, might show tasks such as n-back can improve working memory in general, and could help children with the condition.

People with ADHD tend to have difficulty with working-memory capacity, and that deficit could be responsible for their tendency to be distracted and resulting problems at school, says Tannock.

Seeking to alleviate such difficulties with his research, Klingberg ran a randomized controlled trial of 53 children with ADHD in which half of the participants practiced working-memory tasks that gradually increased in difficulty. The other half completed tasks that did not get harder as the children became better at them. Both groups of children—who were 7 to 12 years old—practiced tasks such as recalling lists of numbers for 40 minutes a day over five weeks.

The children who practiced with increasingly difficult memory tasks performed better on two working memory tests—which were different than the practice tasks—than the control group, reported Klingberg in the *Journal of the American Academy of Child & Adolescent Psychiatry* (Vol. 44, No. 2, pages 177–186.) In addition, the parents of children with memory training reported a reduction in their children's hyperactivity and inattention three months after the intervention, while the parents of the control group participants did not.

Subsequent, yet-unpublished experiments build on those results, Klingberg says.

"We have looked at other groups too: adults with stroke, young adults without ADHD, children with . . . traumatic brain injuries," he says. "A general pattern [we've found] is as long as you have working-memory problems and you have the ability to train, you can improve your abilities."

Some researchers suggest that memory training may have more of an effect on motivation than working memory.

"It seems to me that children in the training group may have learned to have a better attitude toward the testing situation, whereas children in the control group—who repeated easy problems—may have learned that the testing situation was boring and uninteresting," says Cowan. "The differences that emerged on a variety of tasks could be the result of better motivation and attitude rather than a basic improvement in working memory."

Or, says Klaus Oberauer, PhD, a psychology professor and memory researcher at the University of Bristol in England, the practice effect in both Klingberg's studies might result from people learning to use their limited working-memory capacity more efficiently—perhaps by grouping information into larger chunks or by enlisting long-term memory.

"I think the practice effect [they found] basically is just an ordinary practice effect, in that everything gets faster" he says.

So, even if working memory can't be expanded, adults with grocery lists and children with ADHD may be able to make better use of what little space is available by practicing the task itself or repeating tests of general working memory. And, in the end, the milk gets bought and the reading assignment finished.

Further Readings

Cowan, N. (2005). Working-memory capacity limits in a theoretical context. In C. Izawa & N. Ohta (Eds.), *Human learning and memory: Advances in theory and application: The 4th Tsukuba International Conference on Memory.* (pp. 155–175). Mahwah, NJ: Erlbaum.

Klingberg, T., Fernell, E., Olesen, P.J., Johnson, M., Gustafsson, P., Dahlstrom, K., et al. (2005). Computerized training of working memory in children with ADHD—A randomized, controlled trial. *Journal of the American Academy of Child & Adolescent Psychiatry, 44*(2), 177–186.

Martinussen, R., Hayden J., Hogg-Johnson, S., & Tannock, R. (2005). A meta-analysis of working memory components in children with Attention-Deficit/Hyperactivity Disorder. *Journal of the American Academy of Child & Adolescent Psychiatry, 44*(4), 377–384.

McElree, B. (2001). Working memory and focal attention. *Journal of Experimental Psychology: Learning, Memory, & Cognition, 27*(3), 817–835.

Pernille, J.O., Westerberg, H., & Klingberg, T. (2004). Increased prefrontal and parietal activity after training in working memory. *Nature Neuroscience, 7*(1), 75–79.

Verhaeghen, P., Cerella, J., & Basak, C. (2004). A working memory workout: How to expand the focus of serial attention from one to four items in 10 hours or less. *Journal of Experimental Psychology: Learning, Memory, & Cognition, 30*(6), 1322–1337.

Two Web sites offer free programs for working out working memory: www.memorise.org/memoryGym.htm and www.easysurf.us/menu.htm.

Can You Force Yourself to Forget?

One psychologist says he's discovered a mechanism that could explain how people suppress unwanted memories; others disagree.

LEA WINERMAN

All of us have memories we'd prefer to forget. That foot-in-the-mouth moment at a party last summer, that embarrassing performance in our high-school talent show . . .

When memories like those come unwittingly to mind—prompted, say, by a run-in with someone who witnessed the moment—we might try to push the thought quickly away. But could such repeated suppressions actually make us less likely to remember the event years later?

Yes, quashing memories could impede our recall, suggests a recent series of studies by University of Oregon psychologist Michael Anderson, PhD, and his colleagues. Anderson says that his laboratory model—which taps the executive control processes that people use to concentrate and overcome interference during memory tasks—could in principle explain how people, over time, suppress distracting, unwanted or even traumatic memories.

His work could possibly help explain post-traumatic stress disorder and even, controversially, repressed memories of childhood trauma. But some researchers remain unconvinced and question whether his lab-based results will translate to real-world memory.

The Experiments

Psychologists have been debating the existence of repressed memories—first suggested by Sigmund Freud—for years. And Anderson hasn't shied away from the controversial implications of his work. In his very first paper on the topic, published in 2001 in the journal *Nature* (Vol. 410, No. 6826, pages 366–369), he begins the abstract by acknowledging that "Freud proposed that unwanted memories can be forgotten by pushing them into the unconscious, a process called repression. The existence of repression has remained controversial for more than a century."

At the end of the paper, he writes that his study bolsters the evidence that suppression is real: "These findings thus support a suppression mechanism that pushes unwanted memories out of awareness, as posited by Freud."

In the study, which used what Anderson has termed the "think/no-think" paradigm, he asked 32 college student participants to memorize pairs of unrelated words, like "ordeal, roach." Then he showed the participants the first word in each pair and asked them to either think of the second word or to consciously try to avoid thinking of it.

Finally, in the recall phase of the study, Anderson showed the participants the first words again and asked them to recall the second words. He found that participants were nearly 20 percent more likely to remember words that they had been asked to think about than words they'd been asked to avoid thinking about.

"Obviously this research is proof of principle," Anderson says. "In the past, people have said that there's no mechanism for memory suppression . . . and here's a mechanism."

Anderson also wanted to make sure that the participants had actually forgotten the target words and were not simply continuing to come up with diverting thoughts when they saw the cue word. So in a second experiment, he showed them related clues (like "insect R___" for roach) and asked them to recall the target word that best fit that clue. Again, participants were less likely to remember the words that they had been instructed to avoid thinking about.

Curious about the neural underpinnings of the phenomenon, Anderson and his colleagues decided to repeat the experiment while examining participants using functional magnetic resonance imaging. In the resulting study, published in 2004 in *Science* (Vol. 303, No. 5655, pages 232–235), he found that the hippocampus—which is generally active when people retrieve memories—was not active when participants were trying to suppress thoughts of the target word. On the other hand, the dorsolateral prefrontal cortex—an area that helps inhibit motor activity—was more active than usual. This suggests that people may be using the prefrontal cortex to overcome memory processes in the hippocampus, Anderson says.

Of course, in the real world people rarely try to suppress a thought as simple as a single word. Given this, other researchers have picked up and are extending Anderson's work. University of Colorado at Boulder psychologist Marie Banich, PhD, for example, is investigating whether Anderson's think/no-think paradigm will work for nonverbal as well as verbal stimuli, and for emotional stimuli. In a study in press at *Psychological Science*, she and her colleagues used the same research design that Anderson did, but instead paired pictures of faces with pictures of different scenes—some neutral, like a hippo in a lake, and some emotional, like the aftermath of a car crash.

As in Anderson's study, Banich had her participants memorize the face/scene pairs, then showed them the faces and asked them to either think about or avoid thinking about the associated scene.

She found two things: First, the think/no-think paradigm worked—participants recalled the scenes they'd been asked to think about better than the scenes they'd been asked not to think about. Second, it actually worked *better* for scenes with emotional content than for scenes with nonemotional content.

This result makes sense, Banich says: "Emotional regulation requires us to have cognitive control over things that are difficult for us to think about."

"Obviously this research is proof of principle," Anderson says. **"In the past people have said that there's no mechanism for memory suppression . . . and here's a mechanism."**

Michael Anderson
University of Oregon

The Controversy

Despite these results, some researchers remain skeptical of Anderson's work. In an upcoming issue of the journal *Memory & Cognition*, Washington University psychologist Henry L. Roediger III, PhD, and graduate student John Bulevich will report that they haven't been able to replicate Anderson's results.

Bulevich says that he began the studies—part of his master's thesis—intending to replicate Anderson's study and then expand it to implicit memory tests. However, his project stalled when he failed to replicate the original results.

"Inhibitory paradigms are notoriously fragile," he says. "I'm still interested in this, but I have nothing planned right now, until Anderson or his colleagues can pin down what makes this paradigm difficult to deal with."

Anderson—who helped Bulevich and Roediger with their study—says he's unconcerned with the team's failure to replicate his results. There are, he says, many variables that can go awry if not carefully controlled. For example, in the real world, we don't need to be reminded not to think about the things we don't want to think about. But, Anderson says, in the experiment it's crucial to ensure that the participants really are trying their hardest to avoid thoughts of the suppressed target words. And, he says, he has conducted a meta-analysis of the more than 1,000 participants he's tested in all his think/no-think studies, and he's found a strongly significant effect.

"I think that Roediger's paper will be useful in the long run," he says, "and it does remind us that there are factors here that are yet to be understood."

Other psychologists question whether Anderson's results, even if replicable, really mean what he thinks they mean.

In a letter to the journal *Trends in Cognitive Sciences* (Vol. 6, No. 12, page 502) and in an upcoming book chapter, University of California, Berkeley, psychologist John Kihlstrom, PhD, argues that Anderson's mechanism involves *conscious* suppression, while Freud's theories posited *unconscious* repression.

And, of course, the debate about whether repressed memories of childhood trauma are credible has raged for more than a decade—and those who believe they aren't find Anderson's work hard to take.

"There is no evidence that traumatized people repress memories of traumatic events," Kihlstrom says.

Anderson acknowledges that his studies are only the beginning of what will need to be many more years of research—but he says he thinks that such work will be worthwhile. "Whether or not what I've found could be scaled up to explain intense emotional memories is an empirical question that should be researched," he says. "But it's premature to conclude that it's not relevant—we just don't know enough yet."

Feelings' Sway over Memory

New research suggests that emotions can strengthen and shape memory.

Sadie F. Dingfelder

Where were you during the terrorist attacks of 9/11? For most, recalling this information is easier than remembering, for example, the details of Wednesday morning last week. This phenomenon—along with more than two decades of experimental evidence—has led many psychologists to posit that emotions can enhance memory and recall. (See May *Monitor*, page 10.)

However, new research suggests a more complicated picture, says Daniel Reisberg, PhD, a psychology professor at Reed College in Oregon. Some psychologists are finding that the stress associated with an emotion may affect how deeply an event is etched into memory, he notes.

Additionally, the type of emotion felt may determine what details people recall from an event, says University of California, Irvine, psychology professor Linda Levine, PhD.

"People don't just feel 'emotional.' They feel sad, scared, angry, happy," says Levine. "Those emotions have different functions, and they influence information processing and memory in different ways."

For example, people generally feel anger when something is keeping them from reaching their goals, she notes. As a result, angry people tend to focus on what they perceive to be the obstacle and may retain obstacle-related information particularly well, Levine says. In contrast, happiness signals that all is well, and happy people will perceive—and recall—a scene broadly without focusing in on particular details, found Levine and Susan Bluck, PhD, a University of Florida psychology professor, in a recent study in *Cognition and Emotion* (Vol. 18, No. 4, pages 559–574.)

In addition to adding to psychologists' understanding of the inner workings of memory, such research may also help judges and juries evaluate the testimony of eyewitnesses—who typically experience high levels of emotion when watching a crime, says Reisberg.

Tunnel Memory

People who witness an armed robbery often demonstrate how negative emotion can narrow attention and memory, says Reisberg. Such witnesses tend to recall the gun in great detail, but not the particulars of the perpetrator's appearance.

"You focus your attention on the weapon because, quite obviously, whether or not it is pointing at you is very important," says Reisberg.

Even when not in immediate peril, people experiencing negative emotions tend to focus in on specific details, while happy people take in a situation more broadly, found Levine and Bluck in their 2004 study.

To test their hypothesis, the researchers took advantage of an unusual situation: the televised announcement of the 1995 O.J. Simpson murder trial verdict. The event offered a unique opportunity to study the effect of different emotions on memory because a large number of people witnessed the same footage, says Levine. Moreover, many people experienced strong positive or negative emotions, depending on whether they deemed the defendant guilty or innocent, she says.

Seven days after the verdict, the researchers asked 156 undergraduate students how they felt about the trial's result. About half of the students were angry or sad about the verdict, a quarter were happy and a quarter did not care. Fourteen months after the verdict, the researchers tested the participants' memory of the announcement by asking them which items on a list of events occurred during the announcement. Half of the events listed actually happened—such as Simpson mouthing the words "thank you" to the jury. The other half were made up by the researchers—such as the defendant giving a "thumbs up" to his lawyer.

As the researchers expected, the students who felt happy about the verdict tended to recall the entire scene better than the sad, angry or neutral students. However, the happy students also tended to make more errors of commission—saying that events happened that did not. Students flooded with negative emotions tended to recall less about the verdict announcement overall, but they also made fewer errors in which they recalled details that did not happen.

> "Emotions have different functions, and they influence information processing and memory in different ways."
>
> Linda Levine
> University of California, Irvine

77

"The happy people and the people who felt negative made opposite types of errors, so there was no overall difference in accuracy," says Levine. However, the happier or angrier the person felt about the event, the more vivid their memory of it, she says.

The results suggest that happiness works like a broad-tipped highlighter, illuminating an event in memory and capturing many details, says Levine. However, unlike a highlighter, happy memories also can include events that did not occur but seem plausible, Levine says. Negative emotions tended to act like a narrow highlighter, accentuating particular details at the expense of others, she notes.

Memory Illusions

Other researchers, such as David Rubin, PhD, have found that intensity of emotion matters more than an emotion's kind. In one study, published in *Memory & Cognition* (Vol. 32, No. 1, pages 1,118–1,132), Rubin—a psychology professor at Duke University in North Carolina—and his collaborators found that when recalling episodes in their own lives, people tended to recall emotional memories equally vividly regardless of whether they were happy, sad, angry or fearful at the time. However, he notes, the detailed nature of such memories could be illusory.

"After an important event, you tell a story about it, and you eventually come to believe your own story," he says.

For example, many people talked for days or months after 9/11 about where they were and how they felt at the time of the attacks. As people fill in missing details, it can lead to a false sense of accuracy about a memory, notes Rubin.

However, if future studies support Levine's theory that strong emotions—happiness in particular—can lead to broadly remembered events, people may be able to harness their emotions to aid memory, says Bluck. However, such practices could go against memory's primary function, she says.

"People in the classroom and the courtroom are of course concerned with complete accuracy, but it is not clear that the memory system has accuracy as its primary goal in everyday life," she notes.

Specifically, memory helps people use their experiences to inform their future actions, says Bluck. By highlighting important information or even including things that did not happen, emotion-bound memory may allow us to make better decisions than a picture-accurate memory would, she notes.

The Culture of Memory

Researchers are discovering that our culture helps shape how we remember our past—and how far back our memory stretches.

LEA WINERMAN

Ask an American his or her earliest memory, and you'll probably hear something like this: "My cousin's wedding, I was 3." Or perhaps: "Sitting on the beach, making a sandcastle with my brother. I was almost 4."

Any earlier than about 3.5 years is, for most of us, a blank slate. We all have what Freud first called "childhood amnesia"—an inability to remember our earliest childhood.

Ask a Maori New Zealander about his or her earliest memory, though, and you might find that the childhood amnesia ended a bit sooner. A Maori's first memory might be of attending a relative's funeral at 2.5 years old. A Korean adult, on the other hand, might not remember anything before age 4.

Of course, memory varies widely from person to person. But over the past decade, researchers have also found that the average age of first memories varies up to two years between different cultures

"We think that this is a function of the meaning of memory within a particular cultural system," says Michelle Leichtman, PhD, a psychologist at the University of New Hampshire who studies childhood memory. In other words, the way parents and other adults discuss—or don't discuss—the events in children's lives influences the way the children will later remember those events.

People who grow up in societies that focus on individual personal history, like the United States, or ones that focus on personal family history, like the Maori, will have different—and often earlier—childhood memories than people who grow up in cultures that, like many Asian cultures, value interdependence rather than personal autonomy, says Leichtman.

Now, she and other researchers are working to understand the nuances of these differences and the particular factors that shape memory in different cultures.

How Old Were You?

In 1994, psychologist Mary Mullen, PhD, published the first research comparing the ages of first memories across cultures. In a study in the journal *Cognition* (Vol. 52, No. 1, pages 55–79), she asked more than 700 Caucasian and Asian or Asian-American undergraduates to describe their earliest memories. Mullen—a Harvard University graduate student at the time—found that on average the Asian and Asian-American students' memories happened six months later than the Caucasian students' memories.

The next year Mullen repeated the study with Caucasian Americans and native Koreans, and she found an even bigger difference: Nearly 16 months separated the two, according to the study published in *Cognitive Development* (Vol. 10, No. 3, pages 407–419).

"Those papers were really the springboard from which we began," says Harlene Hayne, PhD, a psychologist who studies culture and memory at the University of Otago in Dunedin, New Zealand.

Hayne has looked at earliest memories among Caucasian, Asian and Maori New Zealanders. In a 2000 study in the journal *Memory* (Vol. 8, No. 6, pages 365–376), she found that on average, as in Mullen's studies, Asian adults' first memories were later than Caucasians' (57 months as compared with 42 months). But she also found that Maori adults' memories reached even further back, to 32 months on average.

These differences can be explained by the social-interaction model developed by Katherine Nelson, PhD, a psychologist at the City University of New York, says Leichtman. According to this model, our autobiographical memories don't develop in a vacuum; instead, as children, we encode our memories of events as we talk over those events with the adults in our life. The more those adults encourage us to spin an elaborate narrative tale, the more likely we are to remember details about the event later.

This model applies within as well as between cultures, Leichtman says. She and colleague David Pillemer, EdD, have examined the effect that "high-elaborative" versus "low-elaborative" mothers have on their children. High-elaborative mothers spend a lot of time talking to their children about past events and encourage their children to give them detailed stories about daily life. Low-elaborative mothers, on the other hand, talk less about past events and tend to ask closed rather than open-ended questions.

In a 2000 study in *Cognitive Development* (Vol. 15, No. 1, pages 99–114), Leichtman arranged for a preschool teacher who'd been on maternity leave to come back and visit her class. The next day, Leichtman and her colleagues observed the mothers of the students talk to their children about the visit and coded the degree to which the mothers used a high-elaborative or low-elaborative style of speaking. Three weeks later, the researchers asked the children what they remembered about the visit—and the children with high-elaborative mothers remembered more details.

In general, Leichtman says, parents in Asian cultures have a more low-elaborative style than parents in the United States. In contrast, Maori culture is even more focused on personal history and stories than American culture, Hayne says.

"In Maori culture there's a very strong emphasis on the past—both the personal past and the family's past," she explains. "They look backward with an eye to the future." And hence they remember more of their own past as well.

"In Maori culture there's a very strong emphasis on the past—both the personal past and the family's past. They look backward with an eye to the future."

Herlene Haryne
University of Otago

We Remember What We Need

Leichtman and the other researchers emphasize that their studies do not imply that Caucasians or Maoris have "better" memories than Asians. Instead, Leichtman explains, people have the types of memories that they need to get along well in the world they inhabit. In the United States, she says, it's adaptive to have detailed narratives of childhood to relate.

"That's the way we bond with each other, by telling stories of our personal past," she says. "It's consistent with our independently oriented culture, where the emphasis is on standing out and being special and unique. In more interdependently oriented cultures, the focus is more on interpersonal harmony and making the group work, and the way in which people connect to each other is less often through sharing memories of personal events."

In other cultures, she says, the attitude is different: "They might think 'If both of you were at an event, then what would be the purpose of rehashing it between you?'"

To many Americans, she says, this lack of interest in ones own or others' personal pasts violates what we think of as a truism—that the fundamental thing that makes us who we are is our personal memories. But in some cultures she's examined, personal memory isn't nearly as important as it is to Americans. In an unpublished study of adults in rural India, for example, she found that, during a scripted interview, only 12 percent of the participants identified a specific memory from childhood. A specific memory might be "the day my father fell down a well," as opposed to a general memory like "I went to school," Leichtman explains. In comparison, 69 percent of American participants related a specific memory.

Future Directions

That there are cultural differences in memory is by now fairly well established, says Leichtman, and researchers are beginning to untangle the nuances of what causes those differences.

For example, Cornell University psychologist Qi Wang, PhD, is studying Chinese-American immigrants to see how their early childhood memories compare with those of native Chinese and native Americans. Leichtman is examining the differences between rural and urban Indians to see whether patterns of how people discuss the past, and thus early memory, are changing in that culture.

Pillemer, of the University of New Hampshire, is taking a slightly different tack on early-memory research. In a recent study in press at the journal *Memory*, he and graduate student Kate Fiske asked Caucasian and Asian participants about their earliest memories of a dream.

"Dreams are private, so the only way someone else would know about it is if you talked to them about it," he says, "so it's an interesting test of the social-interaction model." The researchers found that, as they had hypothesized, Caucasians' average age for their first remembered dream was almost one year younger than that of Asians—5.6 years old compared with 6.4 years.

Overall, Leichtman says, "It's not yet an old idea" that culture influences memory. "Right now we're really refining it and working out the wide variety of mechanisms that cause it."

Mending Memory

Psychologists are exploring memory enhancers that exploit the latest research in brain function.

RACHEL ADELSON

B rain injury, such as that from an accident or stroke, or a memory-draining disease such as Alzheimer's, can leave people struggling with everything from cooking dinner to knowing their own children. What's more, as the number of older adults in America grows, so will the number with age-related dementia, boosting the prevalence of this frustrating and usually invisible disability.

As the need for intervention grows, U.K. neuropsychologist Barbara Wilson, PhD, an authority on memory rehabilitation at the Medical Research Council's Cognition and Brain Sciences Unit in Cambridge and the Oliver Zangwill Centre for Neuropsychological Rehabilitation in Ely, says that due to lack of specialists and insurance barriers, few are being shown how best to keep their handicap from hurting everyday functioning. Yet much more is possible. "We can help people adapt to, understand, bypass and compensate for their memory difficulties," Wilson says.

Thanks to new scientific insights, the field of memory rehabilitation made remarkable strides in its first 25 years, says Allen Heinemann, PhD, president of APA's Div. 22 (Rehabilitation) and a rehabilitation psychologist with Northwestern University and the Rehabilitation Institute of Chicago. Now, says Heinemann, "the challenge is to apply what modern imaging techniques have shown about localization of memory function."

Accordingly, psychologists are studying everything from memory-related brain-activation patterns to mobile Internet devices, searching for ways to support independent living and even help the brain repair itself.

Heinemann expects the next decade to bring more clinical trials of various behavioral interventions, a growing cadre of investigators and a greater number of high-quality outpatient services and inpatient facilities providing cognitive rehab. "Our research investment will start to bear fruit," he predicts.

From Finding Keys to Greeting Friends

Although most people think that good memory means good retrieval, good memory is actually good learning—forming a strong association when acquiring new information, say rehab experts. That's why they often advise memory-impaired people to systematically take note of things. For example, they can learn to habitually take a mental snapshot when they put down their keys—say, next to the fruit bowl on the kitchen table.

Thus, Keith Cicerone, PhD, clinical director of cognitive rehabilitation at the JFK-Johnson Rehabilitation Institute in Edison, N.J., and his clinical team teach people with early-stage dementia and similar forms of memory loss—who are still capable of learning—to pay attention to routine, actively process information, avoid being distracted and write notes.

Using a similar approach is neuropsychologist Linda Clare, PhD, of University College London and the Dementia Services Development Centre Wales. Clare and her associates help patients with early-stage dementia to set goals that are relevant to daily life, for them and their families. Sample goals include:

- Learning names of familiar people they meet socially so that they do not feel awkward when they go out.
- Using a memory aid such as a calendar or memory board instead of asking family members the same question over and over again.
- Remembering family information so that it is easier to join in conversations at home.
- Identifying different types of coins to make it easier to pay for things.

In a 2002 study reported in APA's *Neuropsychology* (Vol. 16, No. 4, pages 538–547), Clare found that patients with mild Alzheimer's benefit in a lasting way from simple, systematic memory training that may enlist the still-intact neocortex. Participants were able to learn people's names by using mnemonic devices, "vanishing cues" (filling in more and more letters in a name until recall kicks in) and "expanding rehearsal" (testing themselves in spaced intervals over time). This kind of training doesn't rely on faulty parts of the brain, such as the hippocampus. Clare speculated at the time that, "If other brain areas can take over some of the functions of damaged areas, then this opens up new directions for rehabilitation."

When providing rehab services, memory experts employ a powerful approach called "errorless learning," which minimizes mistakes during training. Wilson and Clare have demonstrated in, among other journals, the *Journal of Clinical and Experimental Neuropsychology* (Vol. 22, No. 1, pages 132–146) that people with severe deficits learn better with confidence-boosting errorless training. Fostering awareness of memory loss also appears to aid therapy.

Cognitive support is central, but living with memory loss involves the whole person, says Suzanne Corkin, PhD, a neuroscientist with the Massachusetts Institute of Technology's brain and cognitive sciences department.

"Rehabilitation [also] teaches ways to keep people's mood up by taking the memory-impaired person out for lunch, to museums, for walks, by giving them a healthy level of mental stimulation," she says.

Memory Technologies

For people with mild to moderate memory loss, assistive technologies essentially take what was lost or compromised about memory on the inside and put it on the outside—in the form of everything from digital watches to computerized schedules, pagers programmed with streams of reminders and wireless personal digital assistants (PDAs), which take patients step-by-step through complex tasks.

In a controlled study published in 2001 in the *Journal of Neurology, Neurosurgery and Psychiatry* (Vol. 70, No. 4, pages 477–482), Barbara Wilson and her colleagues found that a paging system helped patients become significantly more successful in carrying out everyday activities. As if they were asking for a wake-up call, patients picked the messages and listed routine appointment dates and times in advance.

Things get more futuristic at the University of Michigan Health Systems in Ann Arbor, where rehabilitation psychologist Ned Kirsch, PhD, director of adult neurorehabilitation programs, is using PDAs and laptop computers with wireless Internet connections to help with complex functional tasks. For example, in one study, published in *Rehabilitation Psychology* (Vol. 49, No. 3, pages 200–212), Kirsch's team used a wireless PDA to help one patient who could not remember the way from one room to another in the treatment center to follow large colored circles on the walls. In this special treasure hunt, he taps the screen each time he finds a circle; progressive instructions guide him to the next one and enable him to navigate independently through his therapy day. Kirsch adds that once a home has broadband, it's cheap and easy to set up a wireless node. This type of technological approach to treatment will also become increasingly available in the community as city-wide wireless Internet installations spread, Kirsch notes.

Assistive technology has limits: For example, people with weak memories may have problems learning to use these devices, or they may lose them. And, notes Cicerone, "You have to remember to use it." People who never liked technology probably still won't; "early adopters" may be more proficient. Better interfaces should help, he notes.

> ## "We can help people adapt to, understand, bypass and compensate for their memory difficulties."
>
> Barbara Wilson
> U.K. Medical Research Council

Some may grow out of research projects under way at the Rehabilitation Engineering and Research Center for Advancing Cognitive Technologies, a new program established in 2004 by the National Institute on Disability and Rehabilitation Research and housed at the University of Colorado.

Cicerone says that some private companies have developed proprietary devices specifically for neurological support, but the evidence of their effectiveness is anecdotal only. There's also limited evidence that so-called memory-building software works: "People get good at playing that particular game, but it doesn't transfer," he adds.

The Future of Memory

Meanwhile, even though drug companies are pouring resources into memory drugs because of the huge market, pharmaceutical options for improving memory are meager. First-generation antidementia drugs called cholinesterase inhibitors haven't been shown to support significant improvement in everyday life; they may help a subset of patients in a limited way. Still, Corkin is intrigued by drugs under development that are directed at toxic forms of the amyloid protein and could limit the proliferation of amyloid plaques, which are a neuropathological hallmark of Alzheimer's disease.

On the imaging front, at the University of Illinois Medical School in Chicago, psychologist Linda Laatsch, PhD, and her colleagues in neurology and rehabilitation are using functional magnetic resonance imaging (fMRI) to gather information on normal brain-activation patterns during simple memory tasks. Conceivably, fMRI could help differentiate patients whose brains respond to cognitive rehab from those who should stick with external cues, and help follow progress via changes in brain activation. She says, "If we could reach for the stars, we'd give feedback on activation patterns during imaging"—the ultimate in biofeedback.

Theory of Multiple Intelligences
Is It a Scientific Theory?

This essay discusses the status of multiple intelligences (MI) theory as a scientific theory by addressing three issues: the empirical evidence Gardner used to establish MI theory, the methodology he employed to validate MI theory, and the purpose or function of MI theory.

JIE-QI CHEN

How Is the Credibility of a Scientific Theory Established?

Of critical importance to the scientific establishment of a theory is the methodology by which the theory is created and developed (Kuhn, 1962). This principle became clearer as the fields of the history and philosophy of science matured. Before the mid-20th century, philosophers of science such as Karl Popper (1959) attempted to define an objective and universally applicable methodology for all sciences. Such an attempt inevitably failed because it did not recognize the necessary interconnection between methodologies and the objects of study. By the 1960s, scholars in the history and philosophy of science agreed that the methodologies of science both shape and are shaped by the subjects they are applied to. Thus, the absolute objectivity of any methodology is illusionary (Kuhn, 1962). The history of this debate about methodology parallels the debate regarding the scientific credibility of MI theory.

Since the inception of MI theory, some scholars in the field of cognitive psychology have questioned its status as a scientific theory. Specific criticisms of the theory include the following: "This looks like pop psychology"; "There has been no empirical data to validate the theory"; and "The independence of multiple intelligences has not been tested empirically." In the process of developing MI theory, Gardner (1993a) considered the range of adult end-states that are valued in diverse cultures around the world. To identify the abilities that support these end-states, he examined empirical data from disciplines that had not been considered previously for the purpose of defining human intelligence. The results of Gardner's analyses consistently supported his emerging notion of specific and relatively independent sets of cognitive abilities. His examination of these data sets also yielded eight criteria for identifying an intelligence. To be

defined as an intelligence, an ability has to be tested in terms of the following eight criteria:

- An intelligence should be isolable in cases of brain damage and there should be evidence for its plausibility and autonomy in evolutionary history. These two criteria were derived from biology.
- Two criteria came from developmental psychology: An intelligence has to have a distinct developmental history with a definable set of expert end-state performances and it must exist within special populations such as idiot savants and prodigies.
- Two criteria emerged from traditional psychology: An intelligence needs to demonstrate relatively independent operation through the results of specific skill training and also through low correlation to other intelligences in psychometric studies.
- Two criteria were derived from logical analysis: An intelligence must have its own identifiable core operation or set of operations and must be susceptible to encoding in a symbol system such as language, numbers, graphics, or musical notations.

Although Gardner (1993a) did not base his theory on testing of children and statistical analyses of the results, the primary method used by psychometricians to establish the credibility of the construct of IQ, he did ground the theory on analysis of empirical data. The eight criteria used to identify intelligences are not the reverie of a giant mind. Rather they are derived from Gardner's comprehensive, thorough, and systematic review of empirical data from studies in biology, neuropsychology, developmental psychology, and cultural anthropology.

Because MI theory is based on the conception of human cognitive functioning in diverse real-life situations, its scientific establishment is grounded in empirical data that describe the functioning of multiple abilities in diverse situations. For example, MI theory better accounts for data that describe the cognitive functions of special populations than intelligence defined as IQ does. Exhibiting differentiated profiles of specific abilities, these populations include those who have suffered brain injury as well as prodigies and savants. MI theory also better describes various learning profiles that teachers and educators encounter on a daily basis. Finally, MI theory better explains the diverse abilities required to succeed in different professions.

Clearly, the scientific evidence used to support the psychometric notion of intelligence as IQ and the evidence used to establish MI theory are radically different. Referring back to lessons learned from the history of science, there can and should be more than one way to study human intelligence. If we limit studies by relying on a single standard for the acceptable measurement of intelligence, our understanding of this most central capacity of human beings will be significantly restrained.

What Methods Are Used to Validate a Theory?

In the field of psychology, a theory of intelligence is typically validated by establishing two psychometric properties of tests based on the theory: validity and reliability. *Validity* refers to the degree to which a test measures its intended attributes or desired outcomes. Although there are many kinds of validity, the most commonly reported in the manual of standardized intelligence tests is concurrent validity. It is usually established by comparing scores on one test with scores of other standardized tests of the same nature. *Reliability* refers to the consistency of a test's result over time and is usually determined by using one or more of the following methods: test-retest, equivalent-form, and split-half. Correlation is the statistical technique that almost all standardized intelligence tests use to report the degree of validity and reliability.

Validity and reliability are useful measures for testing the theoretical construct that human intelligence is a general ability that remains stable over time. If human intelligence is a general ability, different measures of the ability should be positively correlated (validity). Since the general ability is stable, measures of it at different times should be correlated as well (reliability). Defining and measuring intelligence using IQ tests makes it possible to rank order individuals based on a single numerical score that is expected to remain constant. Scores on IQ tests can also be used to categorize individuals based on the amount of intelligence they possess.

The means used to validate a theory are shaped by the constructs and uses of the theory. Gardner (1993a) argues that human intelligence is not a general ability. Rather, it is a biopsychological potential with an emergent, responsive, and pluralistic nature. To validate this theoretical construct, one has to develop means radically different from intelligence tests. As Vygotsky (1978) argued, "Any fundamentally new approach to a scientific problem inevitably leads to new methods of investigation and analysis. The invention of new methods that are adequate to the new ways in which problems are posed requires far more than a simple modification of previously accepted methods" (p. 58).

If we were developing a psychological assessment to test multiple intelligences what would its critical features be? For one, accurate assessment of multiple intelligences demands a range of measures that tap the different facets of each intellectual capacity. Also, intelligence-fair instruments are needed to assess the unique faculties of each intelligence. Intelligence-fair instruments engage the key components of particular intelligences, allowing one to look directly at the functioning of each intellectual capacity. Further, the assessment must be an ongoing process based on multiple samples of an individual's abilities over time in different contexts, taking into consideration the child's educational and cultural experiences. Finally, assessments of multiple intelligences are designed to identify and build on individuals' strengths by creating rich educational environments with learning opportunities that match children's specific abilities and interests (Chen & Gardner, 1997). Needless to say, the development of such assessments requires concerted efforts over a long period of time to produce quality instruments and to carefully train individuals who can administer and interpret them in a sensitive manner (Adams, 1993; Hsueh, 2003; Krechevsky, 1998; McNamee, Chen, Masur, McCray, & Melendez, 2003; Shearer, 1996; Yoong, 2001).

The methods used to validate MI theory are not limited to the development of new psychological assessments. MI theory can also be validated by evaluating the results of applying the theory in a range of educational settings. Many articles in this volume indicate that both teachers and parents have consistently reported that MI theory has given them more accurate perceptions of children's intellectual potentials and more specific methods for supporting and developing these potentials. Kornhaber and her colleagues at Harvard University's Project Zero studied 41 elementary schools in the United States that had applied MI theory to school-based practices for at least 3 years. Among schools that reported improvements in standardized-test scores, student discipline, parent participation, or the performance of students with learning differences, the majority linked the improvements to MI-based interventions (Kornhaber, 1999; Kornhaber, Veenema, & Fierros, 2003). The effectiveness of these applications is an important source for the validation of MI theory.

What Is the Purpose or Function of a Theory?

Whether a theory has value to a specific field or society depends on the explanatory power and the generative power of the theory (Kuhn, 1962; Losee, 1980). A theory that has high explanatory power can account for a wide range of observations. It brings order and coherence to information, clarifying the relations of parts to whole, and describing underlying mechanisms. A theory that has high generative power orients investigators to the future by offering new frameworks for studying unknowns and contributing new knowledge to the field. It stimulates new ideas, provides new questions, and leads to new ways of understanding the world.

Both the explanatory and the generative power of MI theory are high. As described earlier, the amount and range of empirical evidence that Gardner (1993a) cites and synthesizes in making his case for MI theory is substantial. Further, MI theory makes sense to practitioners and fits their experience about individuals' intellectual strengths and weaknesses. That it makes sense is clear evidence of the explanatory power of MI theory.

Although not all psychologists agree with Gardner's theory of eight relatively independent intelligences, Gardner's claim that the nature of the human intelligences is emergent, responsive, and pluralistic is no longer a novel idea in the field of cognitive psychology. MI theory has contributed to changing our perception and understanding of human intelligences. Due to its high generative power, MI theory has stimulated countless new ideas and practices in the field of education (Campbell, Campbell, & Dickinson, 1996; Chen, 1993; Chen, Krechevsky, & Viens, 1998; Kornhaber, 1999; Kornhaber, Veenema, & Fierros, 2003; Lazear, 1994; New City School, 1994).

In the area of curriculum development, for example, MI-based curricula encompass a broad range of subject areas that include but go beyond skill development in reading, writing, and arithmetic. Because all intelligences are equally valuable, subjects such as visual arts and creative movement are also included in the curriculum. According to MI theory, the talented artist and the developing dancer are just as intelligent as the excellent reader, and each has an important place in society. Also, an authentic MI-based approach goes beyond learning factual knowledge. It also stresses the importance of promoting in-depth exploration and real understanding of the key concepts essential to a domain (Gardner, 2000).

Educators who work with at-risk children have been particularly drawn to the application of MI theory because it offers an approach to intervention that focuses on strengths instead of deficits. By the same token, MI theory extends the concept of the gifted child beyond those who excel in linguistic and logical pursuits to include children who achieve in a wide range of domains.

MI theory can be applied to the development of instructional techniques as well. For example, a teacher can provide multiple entry points to the study of a particular topic by using different media and encouraging students to express their understanding of the topic through diverse representational methods such as writing, three-dimensional models, or dramatizations. Such instructional approaches make it possible for students to find ways of learning that are attuned to their predispositions and therefore increase their motivation and engagement in the learning process. Use of these approaches also increases the likelihood that every student will attain some understanding of the topic at hand.

In summation, in discussions of whether MI theory is a scientific theory, two points warrant special attention. First, intelligence is not a tangible object that can be measured; it is a construct that psychologists define. As theoretical hypotheses differ, so does the methodology used to develop the theory and the evidence cited to validate the theory. Any attempt to apply a uniform standard for establishing the credibility and value of a theory at best fails to consider the possibility of alternative approaches, and at worst impedes the development of new

ideas by constraining the use of new methodologies. Second, theories, particularly theories in the social sciences, are rarely proved or disapproved decisively, regardless of the methodology used to test the theoretical construct. A theory is not necessarily valuable because it is supported by the results of experimental tests. Rather, its value depends on the contributions it makes to understanding and to practice in the field. The value of MI theory has been clearly established by its many successful applications in the field.

References

Adams, M. (1993). *An empirical investigation of domain-specific theories of preschool children's cognitive abilities.* Unpublished doctoral dissertation, Tufts University, Medford, MA.

Campbell, L., Campbell, B., & Dickinson, D. (1996). *Teaching and learning through multiple intelligences.* Needham Heights, MA: Allyn & Bacon.

Chen, J. Q. (1993, April). *Working with at-risk children through the identification and nurturance of their strengths.* Paper presented at the biennial conference of the Society for Research of Child Development, New Orleans, LA.

Chen, J. Q., & Gardner, H. (1997). Alternative assessment from a multiple intelligences theoretical perspective. In D. P. Flanagan, J. L. Genshaft, & P. L. Harrison (Eds.), *Beyond traditional intellectual assessment: Contemporary and emerging theories, tests, and issues* (pp. 105–121). New York: Guilford.

Chen, J. Q., Krechevsky, M., & Viens, J. (1998). *Building on children's strengths: The experience of Project Spectrum.* New York: Teachers College Press.

Gardner, H. (1993a). *Frames of mind: The theory of multiple intelligences* (10th-anniversary ed.). New York: Basic Books.

Gardner, H. (1993b). *Multiple intelligences: The theory in practice.* New York: Basic Books.

Gardner, H. (1999). *Intelligence reframed: Multiple intelligences for the 21st century.* New York: Basic Books.

Gardner, H. (2000). *The disciplined mind: Beyond facts and standardized tests, the K–12 education that every child deserves.* New York: Penguin Books.

Hsueh, W. C. (2003, April). *The development of a MI assessment for young children in Taiwan.* Paper presented at the annual meeting of the American Educational Research Association, Chicago, IL.

Kornhaber, M. (1999). Multiple intelligences theory in practice (pp. 179–191). In J. Block, S. T. Everson, & T. R. Guskey (Eds.), *Comprehensive school reform: A program perspective.* Dubuque, IA: Kendall/Hunt Publishers.

Kornhaber, M., Veenema, S., & Fierros, E. (2003). *Multiple intelligences: Best ideas from research and practice.* Boston: Allyn and Bacon.

Krechevsky, M. (1998). *Project Spectrum preschool assessment handbook.* New York: Teachers College Press.

Kuhn, T. (1962). *The structure of scientific revolution.* Chicago: University of Chicago Press.

Lazear, D. (1994). *Seven pathways of learning: Teaching students and parents about multiple intelligences.* Tucson, AZ: Zephyr.

Losee, J. (1980). *A historical introduction to the philosophy of science* (2nd ed.). Oxford: University Press.

McNamee, G., Chen, J. Q., Masur, A., McCray, J., & Melendez, L. (2002). Assessing and teaching diverse learners. *Journal of Early Childhood Teacher Educators, 23*(3), 275–282.

New City School. (1994). *Multiple intelligences: Teaching for success.* St. Louis, MO: Author.

Popper, K. (1959). *The logic of scientific discovery.* London: Hutchison.

Shearer, B. (1996). *The MIDAS: professional manual.* Kent, OH: MI Research and Consulting.

Vygotsky, L. S. (1978). *Mind in society: The development of higher psychological processes* (M. Cole, V. John-Steiner, S. Scribner, & E. Souberman, Trans.). Cambridge, MA: Harvard University Press.

Yoong, S. (2001, November). *Multiple intelligences: A construct validation of the MIDAS Scale in Malaysia.* Paper presented at the International Conference on Measurement and Evaluation in Education, Penang, Malaysia.

JIE-QI CHEN is Associate Professor of Child Development and Early Education at Erikson Institute in Chicago. Her research interests involve the development of diverse cognitive abilities in young children, linking assessment to curriculum and instruction, and the use of computer technology in early childhood classrooms. She currently holds a position of Fulbright senior specialist and is coauthor of *Building on Children's Strengths* (Teachers College Press) and *Effective Partnering for School Change: Improving Early Childhood Education in Urban Classrooms* (Teachers College Press), editor of *Early Learning Activities* (Teachers College Press), and contributor to the *Multiple Intelligences* entry for *The Encyclopedia of Education* (2nd ed, McMillan Reference).

UNIT 5
Cognitive Processes

Unit Selections

Key Points to Consider

- What is consciousness? Is consciousness purely human?

- What is responsible for the development of conscious thought—the environment (e.g. schools) or something biological (e.g. genes or evolution)?

- With regard to thinking and cognition, do even experts make mistakes? Why? How?

- What is culture? In general, how does it affect us psychologically?

- How does culture affect the way we think, problem solve, perceive, and pay attention?

Student Web Site
www.mhcls.com/online

Internet References
Further information regarding these Web sites may be found in this book's preface or online.

American Association for Artificial Intelligence (AAAI)
http://www.aaai.org/AITopics/index.html
Chess: Kasparov v. Deep Blue: The Rematch
http://www.chess.ibm.com/home/html/b.html

As Rashad watches his four-month-old, he is convinced that the baby possesses some understanding of the world around her. In fact, Rashad is sure he has one of the smartest babies in the neighborhood. Although he is indeed a proud father, he keeps these thoughts to himself so as not to alienate his neighbors whom he perceives as having less intelligent babies.

Gustav lives in the same neighborhood as Rashad. Gustav doesn't have any children, but he does own two fox terriers. Despite Gustav's most concerted efforts, the dogs never come to him when he calls them. In fact, the dogs have been known to run in the opposite direction on occasion. Instead of being furious, Gustav accepts his dogs' disobedience because he is sure the dogs are just dumb beasts and don't know any better.

Both of these vignettes illustrate important and interesting ideas about cognition or thought processes. In the first vignette, Rashad ascribes cognitive abilities and high intelligence to his child; in fact, Rashad perhaps ascribes too much cognitive ability to his four-month old. On the other hand, Gustav assumes that his dogs are incapable of thought—more specifically, incapable of premeditated disobedience—and therefore forgives the dogs.

Few adults would deny the existence of their cognitive abilities. Some adults, in fact, think about thinking, something which psychologists call metacognition. Cognition is critical to our survival as adults. But are there differences in mentation in adults? And what about other organisms? Can young children—infants for example—think? If they can, do they think like adults? And what about animals; can they think and solve problems? These and other questions are related to cognitive psychology and cognitive science, showcased in this unit.

Cognitive psychology has grown faster in the past 45 years than most other specialties in psychology. Much of this has occurred in response to new computer technology as well as to the growth of the field of cognitive science. Computer technology has prompted an interest in artificial intelligence, the mimicking of human intelligence by machines. Similarly, the study of cognition has prompted the study of concept formation, problem solving, decision-making, thinking, and language processing.

The McGraw-Hill Companies, Inc./John Flournoy, photographer

Shouldn't There Be a Word . . . ?

The holes in our language and the never-ending search for words to fill them.

BARBARA WALLRAFF

I magine being the first person in the world ever to say anything. What fun it would be to fill a language with words: *tree, dog, wolf, fire, husband, wife, kiddies.* But putting names to things quickly gets complicated. For instance, if I call my husband *husband,* what should I call my friend's husband? Just for the sake of argument, let's say I name him *man.* So is my husband still only *husband,* or is he, too, man? Maybe he could go by both names. If we let him have more than one name, he can also be *father*—and *hunter-gatherer.* Let's make up words for actions as well as for things: The tree *grows* new leaves. The dog *runs*—he runs *away* from the wolf and *toward* the fire. You know what? This pastime has possibilities.

That isn't really how languages developed, of course. But in the beginning there weren't any words, and now, obviously, there are millions of them, in thousands of languages. Our own language, if we count all the terms in all the specialized jargons attached to English, has millions of words. Between prehistory and the present came a long period in which people who didn't know a word for something usually had no way of finding out whether any such word already existed. Suppose you wanted to know a plant's name—the name of a particular shrub that could be used medicinally as a sedative but could also be lethal in high doses. If you asked around and nobody knew what it was called, you'd have little choice but to make up a name. Let's say *hemlock.* Why *hemlock* and not some other word? Nobody knows anymore. The *Oxford English Dictionary* says *hemlock* and its antecedents in Middle English and Old English are "of obscure origin: no cognate word is found in the other lang[uage]s."

William Shakespeare lived and wrote toward the end of that long period, during which English was taking shape but had not been gathered into dictionaries. His writing not only shows the richness the language had already achieved but also that Shakespeare was a prolific word coiner. *Besmirch, impede, rant,* and *wild-goose chase* are a few of the more than 1,000 words and phrases that he evidently added to our language. His coinages tend to be more a matter of tinkering or redefining than of plucking words out of thin air (or *ayre,* as he spelled the word in the phrase "into thin ayre," in *The Tempest).* For instance, *smirch* was a verb before Shakespeare added the prefix *be-* to it. *Impediment,* derived from Latin, was in use in English for

at least 200 years before Shakespeare came up with *impede.* But as scholars of Elizabethan English acknowledge, only a limited amount of writing survives from Shakespeare's time, apart from his own. Many of the words whose first recorded use appears in one of Shakespeare's plays may have been familiar to writers or conversationalists of his day. It's also possible that in conversation Shakespeare coined many more words than we know—but because he didn't write them down, they've been lost to history.

The English language kept swallowing up, digesting, and drawing energy from other languages' words. As English grew, word lists of various kinds were compiled and circulated. Lists appeared in *The Egerton Manuscript,* from about 1450, and in *The Book of St. Albans,* printed in 1486. But the first comprehensive English dictionary, compiled by Nathan Bailey, was not published until 1730. Samuel Johnson did a bit of cribbing from Bailey to create his famous dictionary of 1755—even though the word *copyright* was by then in use. Still, it took about another half century for the word to make its way into Johnson's dictionary.

**aquadextros (ak' wa•dek' strus), *adj.*
possessing the ability to turn the bathtub
faucet on and off with one's toes**

In 1783, a 25-year-old Noah Webster began publishing *The American Spelling Book,* which more than a million copies annually for years—an astonishing number considering that in 1790, according to the first United States Census, the nation's total population was less than four million. Far from resting on his laurels, Webster kept working away until he had finished his masterwork, the two-volume *American Dictionary of the English Language,* published in 1828. After that, Americans as well as Britons had fewer excuses to invent words.

Of course, coining words to meet real needs continued—and it continues today, particularly in specialized realms like medicine, technology, fashion, cooking, cartooning, and online games. Sometimes what constitutes a need for a term is subjective. Why do we need *myocardial infarction* when we already have *heart attack*? Physicians think we do. Why do we need *bling-bling* when we already *have flashy jewelry?* Movie stars and rap musicians think we do. New words coined to meet needs—objective or subjective, real or perceived—have been with us since the beginning.

From the usual point of view, a new word is successful if it catches on—with a subculture or with everyone—and eventually finds its way into dictionaries. But the impulse to coin words runs so deep that we coin many more words than we really need, most of which will never catch on. These words are not failures; they're pleasures. Coining words is like sex in that it's necessary to our species—but rarely do people engage in it for the sake of keeping humankind going. We do it because it's fun.

C redit for being the first to neologize publicly on purpose, for no serious purpose, is usually given to two Englishmen, Lewis Carroll and Edward Lear, for their nonsense verse. "Twas brillig, and the slithy toves / Did gyre and gimble in the wabe," Carroll wrote, in his poem "Jabberwocky," published in *Through the Looking Glass* in 1872. *Brillig? Slithy? Gyre? Gimble? Wabe?* Carroll (whose *non*-nom de plume *was* Charles Lutwidge Dodgson) coined them all.

In 1867, Lear wrote, "The Owl and the Pussy-cat went to sea / In a beautiful pea-green boat, / . . . / They dined on mince, and slices of quince, / Which they ate with a runcible spoon." Behold the world's first use of *runcible spoon.* But what is such a thing? According to the *Oxford English Dictionary,* it is "a kind of fork used for pickles, etc., curved like a spoon and having three broad prongs of which one has a sharp edge." But, the *OED* notes, "the illustrations provided by Lear himself for his books of verse give no warrant for this later interpretation."

Though many nonsense words might seem arbitrary—can you guess from looking at *brillig* or *runcible* what it means?—a number of Lewis Carroll's coinages have a special property. Humpty Dumpty explains this to Alice a bit further on in *Through the Looking Glass,* when she asks for his help with the unfamiliar words in "Jabberwocky":

> *"'Brillig' means four o'clock in the afternoon—the time when you begin broiling things for dinner."*
>
> *"That'll do very well," said Alice; "and 'slithy'?"*
>
> *"Well, 'slithy' means 'lithe and slimy.' 'Lithe' is the same as 'active.' You see it's like a porunanteau—there are two meanings packed up into one word."*

Portmanteau words—eureka! With this idea, Carroll bestowed a versatile gift on the world of recreational neologizing. Because portmanteau words are derived from dictionary words, they tend to be less opaque than other new coinages. In fact, *chortle,* another portmanteau word that Carroll coined in "Jabberwocky," became a dictionary word because people readily understood how to use it. The *Oxford English Dictionary* explains *chortle* roots like this: "app[arently] with some suggestion *of chuckle,* and of *snort."* Unfortunately, the portmanteau

itself ("a large leather suitcase that opens into two hinged compartments," as the *American Heritage Dictionary* defines it) is now found only in museums and antiques shops. It's probably time to hunt up a less anachronistic term to carry the meaning into the future. (Among the few suggestions I've heard for this, my favorite is *twone—two* portmanteaued with *one.)*

We owe a debt to Carroll and Lear, and what they did is delightful, but it is not exactly what I would call "recreational word coining." Carroll and Lear invented their words for literary purposes—much as Shakespeare did. Literary figures from James Joyce (*bababadalgharaghtakamminarronnkonnronnlonnerronntuonnthunntrovarrhounailmskawntoohoohoordnenthumuk!*) and George Orwell (*Newspeak*) to J. R. R. Tolkien (*hobbit*) and J. K. Rowling (*quidditch*) have made up words the better to convey worlds largely of their invention. Recreational word coining, however, describes odd coining of the world we know.

Recreational redefining is a related field, which also describes the world we know. Therefore, before we get acquainted with the first true recreational word coiner, who came a bit later, let's meet the pioneer on this linguistic front—the American writer Ambrose Bierce. Bierce was a near contemporary of Carroll and Lear. In 1875 he finished a freelance manuscript that included 48 English words and his redefinitions of them. This, the first sulfurous spark of what would become *The Devils Dictionary,* failed to set the world on fire. Six years later, Bierce was named editor of *Wasp,* a new satirical journal, and he immediately began writing and publishing a feature that offered "twisty new definitions of shopworn old words," as Roy Morris Jr. explains in his introduction to the current Oxford edition of *The Devil's Dictionary.* Many of the words from *Wasp* also took their place among the 998 redefined words that ultimately made up Bierce's best-known book. An *admiral,* he wrote, is "that part of a war-ship which does the talking while the figure-head does the thinking." A *habit* is "a shackle for the free." *Zeal* is "a certain nervous disorder afflicting the young and inexperienced. A passion that goeth before a sprawl." In 1912, not long before Bierce lit out for Mexico and disappeared off the face of the earth, he published 12 volumes of his *Collected Works,* including *The Devils Dictionary.* Since then, the book has never been out of print.

The first true recreational word coiner was another American: Gelett Burgess. Like Carroll and Lear in England, Burgess published nonsense verse—one of his claims to fame is the poem "The Purple Cow." More to the point, in 1914 he published a spurious diclionan. *Burgess Unabridged: A New Dictionary of Words You Have Always Needed.* Among the words in it is *blurb*—another of Burgess's claims to fame, for this creation of his is still in use, with roughly the meaning he assigned it. Alas, few of his other words ever caught on—not without reason, as we shall see.

After a decades-long pause, a spate of books featuring recreational word coining began to appear. For instance, *An Exaltation of Larks,* which in 1968 began as a collection of venerable terms of venery ("a *pride* of lions," "a *murder* of crows," "a *gam* of whales"), has over several revisions incorporated more and more terms that the author, James Lipton (now better known as the host *of Inside the Actors Studio,* on the Bravo channel), either coined himself or found in the work of contemporary writers: "a *phalanx* of flashers," Kurt Vonnegut; "a *mews* of cathouses," Neil Simon; "an *om* of Buddhists," George Plimpton.

The 1983 book *The Meaning of Liff and* its 1990 expanded edition *The Deeper Meaning of Liff* by the British writers Douglas Adams author of the 1979 best seller *The Hitchhiker's Guide to the Galaxy* and John Lloyd, merrily misappropriated geographic names from *Aasleagh* ("a liqueur made only for drinking at the end of a revoltingly long bottle party when all the drinkable drink has been drunk") to *Zeal Monachorum* ("[Skiing term.] To ski with 'zeal monachorum' is to descend the top three-quarters of the mountain in a quivering blue funk, but on arriving at the gentle bit just in front of the restaurant to whizz to a stop like a victorious slalom-champion").

Between the publication of *Liff's* first and second editions, sniglets gave *Liff* some stiff competition. Rich Hall, a writer and cast member on HBO's comedy show *Not Necessarily the News,* came up with the idea of a *sniglet* as "any word that doesn't appear in the dictionary, but should." Sniglets fans sent Hall words like *aquadextrous,* "possessing the ability to turn the bathtub faucet on and off with your toes," and *profanitype,* "the special symbols used by cartoonists to replace swear words (points, asterisks, stars, and so on)." From 1984 to 1989 five books of sniglets were published.

Next came a more serious and high-minded variation on the theme. The writer Jack Hitt asked a number of writers and artists "if they had ever had the experience of running across a meaning for which there is no word," and he turned the words they proposed into a piece published in *Harper's Magazine* in 1990.

This was so well received that Hitt expanded the article into a 1992 book. *In a Word.* Its contributors ranged from Katharine Hepburn to Cynthia Ozick, Lou Reed to Lionel Tiger.

Today there's *The Washington Post's* Style Invitational contest, which has been running every week for nearly 13 years. Sometimes the week's contest has to do with neologizing or redefining existing words. For instance, readers are occasionally invited to "take any word, add, subtract or alter a single letter, and redefine the word." The published responses to this request include *diddleman,* "a person who adds nothing but time to an effort"; *nominatrix,* "a spike-heeled woman who controls the selection of candidates for party whip"; and *compenisate,* "to buy a red Porsche for reasons you don't quite understand."

There's my own "Word Fugitives" column, which appears in *The Atlantic Monthly.* Readers write in seeking words, other readers respond, I choose my favorite suggestions and publish them in the column, and we've all done our little bit to move civilization forward. But I've also accumulated a private stash of peoples questions that I've never, until now, gotten around to publishing.

What kinds of words do people want? Do the holes in our language tell us anything about our society? The requests I get for words easily sort themselves into six categories.

Words About Our Unruly Inner Lives

In a sense, of course, all gaps in our language tell us something about our inner lives. Some linguists say that language organizes experience. But language itself is hideously disorganized, especially the English language. Sometimes we have plenty of synonyms or near synonyms to choose from: *idea, concept, thought, inspiration, notion, surmise, theory, impression, perception, observation, mental picture.* More specialized meanings get specialized words. If, say, you're looking for a word that can mean either "a phantom" or "an ideal"—why, *eidolon* stands ready to serve. And yet some fairly common things and phenomena remain nameless. For instance, what would you call the experience of hearing about something for the first time and then starting to notice it everywhere?

That particular hole in the language is worthy of note, because once you're aware of it, if you begin rooting around in coined words, you'll start noticing words intended to fill it. It was one of the first requests published in "Word Fugitives"; *déjà new* took top honors. As I discovered later, essentially the same question had been asked by the writer Lia Matera in *In a Word;* Matera suggested we call the experience *toujours vu.* The 2001 book *Wanted Words 2,* edited by Jane Farrow, also asked the question and presented more than a dozen possible answers, including *newbiquitous and coincidently.*

Let's look at a couple of examples of inner-life-related questions. If you want answers, you'll have to supply your own, because, again, these haven't previously been published.

What would be a word for wanting to get someone's voice mail but getting the person instead? (submitted by C. Murphy, Medfield, Mass.)

I would like a word for the opposite of déjà vu—a word that would describe the feeling of learning something a hundred times but never being able to remember it. (A. Felcher, Portland, Ore.)

Words about *them*. Why is it that there never seem to be enough words in the dictionary to cover everyone we dislike? To make things worse, new kinds of dislikable people keep cropping up. For instance:

> *We need a word to describe a person who, owing to his life circumstances, clearly is not competent to provide advice but insists on doing so anyway. For example, an unemployed person who gives job-seeking advice to a person considering competing professional offers, or a receptionist who unabashedly offers medical advice to a roomful of doctors. (M. Kennet, Kibbutz Manara, Israel)*

> *I have a desperate need for a word that conveys the essential meaning of the phrase trailer trash without maligning innocent dwellings. (K. Cox, Austin, Tex.)*

Words about the material world. A sizable majority of the words that lexicographers add to our dictionaries are names for things. People just won't stop inventing things and perceiving old things in new ways. And things need names: *blogs, infinity pools, conflict diamonds*. A separate issue is commercial products, with their expensively, extensively negotiated and marketed names. Standard dictionaries exclude most product and brand names, but the proportion of "new" words that name things rises even higher if you count preexisting words and phrases that have been turned into brands: *Tiger* (computer

operating system), *Magic Hat* (beer), *Juicy Couture* (sportswear), *BlackBerry* (portable communication device).

And yet it's relatively rare for one to get requests for coinages to name things. The obvious explanation would be that things already have names. Consider *aglets* (the tiny plastic wrappers at the ends of shoelaces) and *altocumulus undulatus* (the clouds in a herringbone sky) and *chads* (you remember: the little spots of paper that fall off punch cards). There is scarcely a thing so small or ethereal or insignificant or transient that someone somewhere has not named it. Nonetheless, here are two requests:

> *I seek a word or phrase to describe a cheap plastic thing that is better for a task than its expensive metal counterpart. (B. Gibson, Concrete, Wash.)*

> *We need a word for food that hasn't quite gone bad—the things you aren't sure whether you ought to throw them out. (A. Bernays and J. Kaplan, Cambridge, Mass.)*

Words about tribulations. This is a popular category. Granted, the annoyances that people write to me about tend to be petty—for instance, being terrible at transcribing numbers (if the problem is phone numbers, would that be *dialexia*) or finding oneself standing in the supermarket's slowest line (*misalinement?*). But just because they're petty is no reason to suffer them in silence. Somehow, putting a name to what happened—preferably a name no one else has ever heard—can be satisfying. The affliction is special, possibly unique. As in:

> *My name is Todd, but throughout my life, people—both close to me and mere acquaintances—have incorrectly called me Scott. The people who do this are unrelated to one another. I mentioned this during a luncheon gathering recently, and to my surprise another person at the table claimed a similar thing happens to his wife. I figure this phenomenon must occur with sufficient frequency to warrant a name of its own. Suggestions?" (S. Nichols [just kidding!—of course he's T. Nichols], Shorewood, Minn.)*

> *Is there a term for concentrating so hard on not saying the worst possible thing in a situation that it comes out? For instance, greeting a newly mal-coiffed friend: "Your hair!" (K. Lewin, Henderson, Nev.)*

Words about words. The words in this category are undeniably ethereal. Here many old words have fallen into disuse. We as a society would be better off if everyone knew what words like *pronoun, adjective,* and *preposition* mean. I believe this because I find it nearly impossible to talk about language and how it works its wonders without employing at least basic grammatical terms. If everyone had these words down, we could move on to complaining that nowadays no one understands the likes of *meiosix* ("the use of understatement not to deceive, but to enhance the impression on the hearer," as H. W. Fowler explains in his *Modern English Usage*) and *tmesis* ("separation of the parts of a compound word by another word inserted between them"—for instance, *um-freaking-believable*). But let's not go there. Plenty of words about words remain to be coined. Here are two requests:

> *I am looking for a word to describe the deliberate misspelling of words and phrases for marketing purposes. For example, Citibank, Rite-Aid, Kool-Aid, and Krispy Kreme. It drives me crazy! (M. Harris, Brooklyn, N.Y.)*

> *Is there a term for those metaphorical insults like "She's one sandwich short of a picnic" and "He's not the sharpest knife in the drawer"? (J. Blum, San Francisco)*

Miscellany. Nouns, verbs, and a sprinkling of adjectives: these make up nearly all the words that show up on our culture's "Most Wanted" poster. Years ago, on the Word Fugitives Web site, I asked for help in inventing a one-word preposition that would mean "in spite of or perhaps because of"; you'd be surprised how often that wordy locution comes up. But, nobody bit, as I recall, and now that Web page itself has gone missing.

Here are a couple of miscellaneous requests that remain:

> *There ought to be a word, parallel to "gossiping," for having social conversations about technological things: comparing kinds of new televisions or the merits of digital cameras or cell phones. (H. Shields, Hamilton, Mass.)*

> *I find it quite astonishing that in English there is no word for the sound produced by a camel. As you know, the camel is the most important animal in the Muslim world. In the midst of so much talk about the clash of civilizations, wouldn't coining such a word help, albeit in a small way, to create a discourse?" (M. A. Moftah, Cairo, Egypt)*

What are the characteristics of a great recreational coinage? It's complicated, because just about any syllable or series of syllables could mean just about anything in English. *Bumbershoot, gamp, ombrifuge, rundle*—these are venerable dictionary words, all of which happen to mean "umbrella." But are they any more plausible carriers of that meaning than the non-dictionary words *rainbrella* and *dunolly*? (*Rainbrella* was coined by a child, and *dunolly* was plucked from a map and redefined as "an improvised umbrella" in *The Deeper Meaning of Liff*.) Furthermore, given that such seeming arbitrariness is more the rule than the exception in English, what are we doing when we rack our brains trying to come up with a brilliant coinage? What sets a keeper apart from a discard?

A number of shortcomings common to discards leap to mind. First is that the coinage is cryptic, opaque, impenetrable. For example, why should *culp*—a word coined by Gelett Burgess, in *Burgess Unabridged*—mean "a fond delusion; an imaginary attribute"? Why should *nulkin*—another of Burgess's

words—mean "the core or inside history of any occurrence"? It's true that many dictionary words are of unknown origin and that many others reached their current meanings by circuitous, even bizarre, routes. In fact, Burgess's inventions often mimic dictionary words accurately. But most of them fail to satisfy. Pretend words are more fun when they illuminate the mental processes that brought them into being.

Portmanteau words tend to have this problem licked. It's not hard to figure out that *chortle* means "chuckle" and "snort"; that the 1923 word *guesstimate* is a combination of "guess" and "estimate"; that the more recent *Spanglish* mingles "Spanish" and "English." Sometimes, though, two old words in combination look as if they should be pronounced differently from the two words spoken separately—and then the portmanteau word becomes impenetrable. (Because I'll be finding fault with the words that follow, I'm going to be nice and not identify their coiners.) For instance, the useful modern coinage *eyelie*, meaning "to pretend not to see someone," wants to be pronounced "I-lee," doesn't it? Hyphenated—*eye-lie*—it looks inauthentic. But if you try to respell it *(eyelye)* so that readers will know how to pronounce it, the sense of its origin and what it means will be lost.

---

diddleman (did • 'l • man), *n.*
a person who adds nothing but time
to an effort

Sometimes, too, a portmanteau word, like *arrowneous* ("the quality of one who drives against the arrow in a parking lot"), is pronounced so much like one of the words it comes from that it would be incomprehensible in speech. With rare exceptions, discard. Other portmanteaus fall short because they have associations they shouldn't. For instance, *hozone* is supposed to mean "the place where one sock in every laundry load disappears"— but unfortunately, nowadays the *ho* part of that word suggests prostitutes as readily as hosiery.

A similar potential flaw is the intentional irrelevant allusion, which naïve word coiners sometimes mistake for a pun. For instance, the responses I got to a request for a word to mean "going through the dirty-clothes hamper to find something clean enough to wear" included *cull-da-sack. Cull,* check: the word wanted has to do with culling, in the sense of selecting. *Sack,* check: the dirty clothes could just as well be in a laundry bag, or sack, as in a hamper. But what does the overall idea have to do with a cul-de-sac, or dead-end street? Uncheck. Discard. (What would be a better term for ransacking the hamper? How about *dry gleaning*.)

Some of the least appealing irrelevant allusions are naughty ones. For some reason, no matter what I ask for, I always get plays on *premature ejaculation* and *coitus interruptus.* Har-har-har! Similarly unappealing are irrelevant—or even relevant—allusions to Alzheimer's disease, schizophrenia, bipolar disorder, paraplegia, and so forth.

Another common flaw results from a failure to think the word through and craft it well. For instance, I like almost everything about *blabrynth* to fit the definition "the elaborate maze of voice-mail menus and prompts encountered when phoning businesses or government offices." But *labyrinth,* to which *blabrynth* is obviously meant to be related, has its *y* in the middle and an *i* in the last syllable. So shouldn't *blabrynth* be *blabberinth* or *blabyrinth?* Another example is "*petonic,* adj.: One who is embarrassed to undress in front of a household pet." We understand the *pet* part. But *onic?* Is that like in *catatonic?* But that's not "embarrassed"—that's immobilized. Furthermore, is *petonic* an adjective, or does it mean "one who . . . ," in which case it's a noun? Discard.

Two other flaws I often notice are nearly each other's opposites. On the one hand, there are supposed holes in the language that no one has ever stumbled into. Suppose the definition is "not wasteful of parsnips" or "a person who sticks up to plants." In these cases, who cares how cute the coinage is. *Parsnipmonions* and *photosycophant* aren't words that anyone could conceivably need; they don't describe the world we live in. On the other hand, there are supposed holes in the language for which perfectly good mainstream words already exist. For instance, *lexicaves* was coined to mean the indentations on the side of a dictionary, but in reality they are named *thumb indexes. Lobsterine* was coined to mean the green stuff that oozes from the center of a lobster, but the real name for this is *tomalley.*

If you avoid all those pitfalls and let inspiration strike, might your coinage eventually enter the mainstream to become a dictionary word? This is a fond hope that many people have for their brainchildren, but, alas, it is now my duty to dash it. The great majority of words coined for fun aren't real and never will be.

Allan Metcalf, the executive secretary of the American Dialect Society (ADS), has a lot of experience in delivering this particular bad news. Since 1990, Metcalf has overseen the society's annual selection of "Words of the Year." It used to bother him that even though the ADS's members are as well informed about English as anyone anywhere, the words they choose almost invariably lack staying power. Wanting to understand why, Metcalf undertook a study. The result was his 2002 book *Predicting New Words: The Secrets of Their Success.* "Successful new words," he wrote, "are alike in ways that promote their success, while unsuccessful new words are alike in ways that promote their failure."

dialexia (dı ' å • lek si • å), *n.*
being terrible at transcribing phone numbers

You might imagine that the main thing successful new words would have in common is that they fill conspicuous gaps in our language, but that's pretty much beside the point, according to

Metcalf. I interviewed him by e-mail, and he wrote me: "To mix a few metaphors: If a newly minted word is bright and shiny, it is almost certain to crash, burn, go up in smoke, and vanish into thin air. Whole volumes of clever words proposed by the cleverest coiners have evaporated in this manner."

For instance, consider Rich Hall's five books of sniglets. Metcalf wrote, "These hugely popular books contained ingenious inventions like *flirr* 'a photograph that features the camera operator's finger in the corner,' and *tacangle,* 'the position of one's head while biting into a taco.' Of the hundreds of sniglets invented by Hall, his admirers, and his imitators, the only one that has made its way into a modicum of permanency is *sniglet* itself."

Misalinement (mis • á • līn • ment), *n.*
finding oneself standing in the supermarket's slowest line

Metcalf also brought up a collection of coinages intended seriously: the 2001 book *Dictionary of the Future: The Words, Terms and Trends That Define the Way We'll Live, Work and Talk,* by the futurologist Faith Popcorn and the consumer-marketing expert Adam Hanft. "It includes words like GENEology, 'the study of one's genetic history,' and *atmos-Fear,* to describe nervousness about pollution and attacks on our air, water, and food," Metcalf wrote. "Although Popcorn is famous as the inventor of *cocooning,* the name for a staying-at-home trend she discerned in 1986, since then all the labels she's affixed to her predictions (right or wrong) have peeled off."

Hall and Popcorn may be among the world's most famous word coiners, and yet they've had minimal success at getting their words into dictionaries. Metcalf wrote me:

> *What are we to make of so many failures? It is a sad story, documented in detail in my* Predicting New Words. *In that book I discuss five qualities that allow a new word to flourish. The most important of the five is "unobtrusiveness." To become part of our standard vocabulary, a new word has to look old. An example is heads-up—not the long-familiar exclamation of warning, "Heads up!," or the adjective heads-up meaning "alert" or "competent," but the noun that means something like "advance information." Americans have been giving each other this kind of heads-up since the late twentieth century, but only now are the dictionaries beginning to recognize it. It is perfectly camouflaged in the form of its predecessor.*

So there you have the Catch-22 of word coining: If a word is clever enough that people will notice it and admire you for coining it, it's too clever to earn a place in our language for real. Is this bad news for us recreational neologizers? No doubt it will come as a blow to anyone who believes in elves and

Tinkerbell. It may also upset the kind of person who, having won a game of Monopoly, is disappointed that the real estate and the money aren't real and his or hers to keep. (What would we call someone like that? Surely such a person is too rare to deserve a name.)

Not without reason did I say that my subject is coining words just for fun. Even if the lives of our young words are short, long live the pastime—game, diversion, entertainment, addiction—of coining words!

BARBARA WALLRAFF is a contributing editor of *The Atlantic Monthly,* a syndicated newspaper columnist, and the author of *Word Court* and *Your Own Words.* This article is adapted from her new book, *Word Fugitives.*

What Was I Thinking?

Kahneman explains how intuition leads us astray.

ERIC JAFFE

This is a story without an ending. And that's not the only thing wrong with it.

In fact, there were a number of flaws in Nobel Laureate Daniel Kahneman's lecture "A Perspective of Flawed Thought," in March 2004 at the National Institutes of Health. Quite purposefully, the entire talk was full of them.

"I specialize in flaws," Kahneman said.

However appropriate that self-deprecating remark was to the topic, it hardly applied to the speaker's celebrated accomplishments. In addition to the 2002 Nobel Prize, which he received for his work applying psychologically realistic models to economic theory, APS Fellow Kahneman, Princeton University, has received most every award possible to a psychologist, including the 1990 APS William James Fellow Award.

Part of Kahneman's intent was to show that flawed thinking plays no favorites. Sure enough, despite his vast understanding of the subject, Kahneman himself claimed to be susceptible to misleading intuition, a realization he made while looking at the latest gallop poll, in which President George W. Bush's approval rating had shifted a statistically insignificant 2 percent from the previous week.

"I was influenced by this completely irrelevant data," he said. "I could not help myself from drawing inferences like, 'What happened this week?' or 'What's the explanation?' I was working on this intuitively and contrary to my better statistical judgment."

According to Kahneman, some human intuition is good, and some is erroneous. And like the incorrigible habit of the knuckle cracker, the bad ones are very difficult to correct.

One reason flawed intuition is allowed to permeate human thinking is its accessibility. For example, if the multiplication problem 17 times 24 is shown for only a moment before its answer, 408, is revealed, few solve it without a formal, lengthy act of computation. On the contrary, if the word "vomit" is displayed and immediately followed by the word "disgusting," it seems the accessible, almost instantaneous extension of the viewer's thinking.

"Intuitive impressions come to mind without explicit intention, and without any confrontation, and this is one of their distinctive aspects," he said.

To better understand the reasons for this accessibility, Kahneman has focused much of his research on expert intuitions. Expert intuitions are able to deal swiftly and decisively with a difficult matter—such as making a quick chess move or fighting a fire—that would seem to require extensive deliberation. Most of the time, a person with expert intuition is not really conscious of making a decision, but rather acts as though their instinctive choice is the only natural outcome of a circumstance.

"You can have a master chess player walking by a complicated chess position and, without slowing down, this player will say, 'White mates in three,'" Kahneman said. In the case of firefighters making perhaps life or death decisions, "something that is very close to the best solution came to mind, and nothing else."

> **APS Fellow Daniel Kahneman received the Nobel Prize in 2002 for his work applying psychologically realistic models to economic theory.**

However, unless certain conditions of expertise—namely, prolonged practice and rapid, unequivocal feedback—are fulfilled, what develops is little more than the exigent knowledge of experience. This can lead to false impressions and overconfident experts, a subject explored by Kahneman and his longtime research partner, the late Amos Tversky.

"People jump to statistical conclusions on the basis of very weak evidence. We form powerful intuitions about trends and about the replicability of results on the basis of information that is truly inadequate," Kahneman said. For this reason, a person who is not an expert, even if thoroughly versed in a field of study, might make an intuitive mistake.

Kahneman leaned heavily on the closely related argument made by another, prominent psychologist, the late Paul Meehl. In the mid-1950s, Meehl gave clinicians personality information about individuals and asked that they predict behavioral outcomes. For example, the clinician might have been asked to decide whether a released prisoner would violate parole. The predictions were then compared to statistical models based on the subset of information available to the clinician.

In a study that still holds up over 50 years later, Meehl found that when the clinician competed with the statistical formula, the formula won almost every time. This finding has served as the basis for Kahneman's theory about overconfident experts.

"What you find is a great deal of confidence in the presence of very poor accuracy," Kahneman explained. "So the confidence people have is not a good indication of how accurate they are."

Overconfidence is accentuated by the failure of people to, in general, learn from their mistakes. "When something happens that a person has not anticipated, . . . they remain convinced that what they had predicted, although it didn't happen, almost happened," he said. The overconfidence is then propagated while the accuracy remains the same, and the cycle begins again.

In order to trace the roots of flawed intuition, Kahneman divided all thought into a two-system model, intuition and deliberate computation, whose particular attributes are almost completely opposite. Intuition is fast, uncontrolled, and, most importantly, effortless. Computation, on the other hand, is slow, governed by strict rules, and effortful.

"Most judgments in actions are governed by [intuitive thought]," he said. "Most of our mental life is relatively effortless." This is why effortful work, such as trying to remember a phone number of five years ago, is more susceptible to interference, and therefore less accessible.

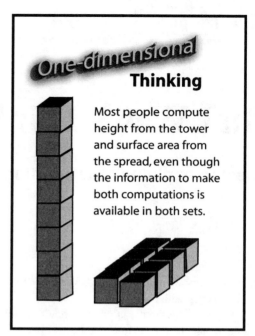

One-dimensional Thinking

Most people compute height from the tower and surface area from the spread, even though the information to make both computations is available in both sets.

"A **fully rational** agent would find it possible to answer both questions equally easily, regardless of the display," Kahneman said. "We do not use all the information that is actually available."

A bat and a ball together costs $1.10. The bat costs a dollar more than the ball. How much does the ball cost?

Interference is often enabled by poor monitoring, a shortcoming that results from our normally unconditional acceptance of intuition. Not surprisingly, according to Kahneman, **50 percent of Princeton students** incorrectly answered 10 cents when given this problem. "What happens to Princeton students is they don't check," said Kahneman. "It happens to MIT students too, though at a slightly lower rate," he joked (The answer for Princeton readers, is five cents.)

Interference is often enabled by poor monitoring, a shortcoming that results from our normally unconditional acceptance of intuition. In one study, Kahneman ran the following scenario past Princeton students: A bat and a ball together cost $1.10. The bat costs a dollar more than the ball. How much does the ball cost? Not surprisingly to Kahneman, 50 percent of Princeton students incorrectly answered 10 cents when given this problem in writing, because they unconditionally accepted their intuitions.

"What happens to Princeton students is they don't check," said Kahneman. "It happens to MIT students too, though at a slightly lower rate," he joked.

Take another common question eliciting intuitive flaw: When people were asked to guess how many murders there were in Michigan in a given year, and how many there were in Detroit, the median answers were 100 and 200, respectively.

"This by itself is not an error, but something is going on here that is not quite right," he said, referring to the presence of intuitive flaw. Occasionally someone asked about Michigan remembered Detroit is in Michigan, and their answer tended more toward 200, a meta-analytic process that reveals to Kahneman the ability of flawed thinking to mend itself if it recognizes all aspects of a situation.

"Accessibility, or the ease with which thoughts come to mind, has an influence not only on the operation of intuition—it almost defines intuition—but on the operations of computation," he said. "Our ability to avoid errors depends on what comes to mind, and whether the corrected thought comes to mind adequately."

But "what comes to mind" might actually be what does *not* come to mind. When looking at two sets of an equal number of cubes, one arranged vertically into a tower and the other spread flat, most people compute height from the tower and surface area from the spread, even though the information to make both computations is available in both sets.

"A fully rational agent would find it possible to answer both questions equally easily, regardless of the display," he said. "That's not what happens. We don't compute everything we could compute. We do not use all the information that is actually available."

For this reason, Kahneman argued that intuitive activities are very similar to perceptual activities, such as seeing and hearing. "These processes of perception are going to guide us in understanding intuition," he said. Take, for example, the following display sets, which are actually less defined than they appear:

Even though the B and the 13 are physically composed of the same elements, they are given context by association, and are rarely considered outside of this context. Though at the time this single-minded assessment doesn't seem wrong, it is in truth about as rational as peeking through the keyhole of a glass door, and grossly limits our understanding of the world. Flawed intuition occurs with similar blinders.

"When people make decisions, they tend to suppress alternative interpretations," Kahneman said. "We become aware only of a single solution—this is a fundamental rule in perceptual processing. All the other solutions that might have been considered by the system—and sometimes we know that alternative solutions have been considered and rejected—we do not become aware of. So consciousness is at the level of a choice that has already been made."

But despite all this understanding, Kahneman steered clear of offering a direct solution to flawed thinking—after all, he remained flummoxed by the gallop poll despite his 35 years studying flawed intuition. Besides, relying on computation instead of intuition would, according to Kahneman, create a slow, laborious, difficult, and costly world. What he did advocate is paying closer attention to the onset of faulty intuition.

"The alternative to thinking intuitively is mental paralysis," he said. "Most of the time, we just have to go with our intuition, [but] we can recognize situations in which our intuition is likely to lead us astray. It's an unfinished story." He paused. "So, it's an unfinished story, so . . ." Kahneman hesitated for words. Something made a succinct peroration inaccessible, but the audience intuited the talk was over, and was correct—most likely.

The Culture-Cognition Connection

Recent research suggests that Westerners and East Asians see the world differently—literally.

LEA WINERMAN

W hen you look at a picture [of a train] on the computer screen, where do your eyes linger longest? Surprisingly, the answer to that question might differ depending upon where you were raised. Americans stare more fixedly at the train in the center, while Chinese let their eyes roam more around the entire picture, according to research by psychologist Richard Nisbett, PhD.

That difference reflects a more general divide between the ways that Westerners and East Asians view the world around them, says Nisbett, who heads the Culture and Cognition Program at the University of Michigan. He and his colleagues explore how people's cultural backgrounds affect their most basic cognitive processes: categorization, learning, causal reasoning and even attention and perception.

The researchers have found increasing evidence that East Asians, whose more collectivist culture promotes group harmony and contextual understanding of situations, think in a more holistic way. They pay attention to all the elements of a scene, to context and to the relationships between items. Western culture, in contrast, emphasizes personal autonomy and formal logic, and so Westerners are more analytic and pay attention to particular objects and categories.

The idea that culture can shape the way people think at these deep levels is a departure for psychology, which as a field traditionally assumed that basic cognitive processes are universal, according to Nisbett. But it's an idea that has gained traction over the past decade or two.

Now, Nisbett and others are investigating the cognitive effects of the more subtle cultural variations between, for example, different areas of East Asia. They hope that these new studies will also help explain more precisely how and why culture and cognition interact.

Train Spotting

In a recent study, Nisbett and graduate student Hannah Faye Chua used a tracking device to monitor the eye movements of 25 American and 27 Chinese participants—all graduate students at Michigan—while the students stared for three seconds at pictures of objects against complex backgrounds. The 36 pictures included, among others, a train, a tiger in a forest and an airplane with mountains in the background.

The researchers found that the Americans focused on the foreground object 118 milliseconds sooner, on average, than the Chinese participants did, and then continued to look at the focal object longer. The Chinese tended to move their eyes back and forth more between the main object and the background, and looked at the background for longer than the Americans did.

The study, which was published in the *Proceedings of the National Academy of Sciences* in August (Vol. 102, No. 35, pages 12,629–12,633), complements earlier research that suggested—in a more general way—that Westerners and East Asians focus on different aspects of scenes.

In a 2001 study, for example, Nisbett and then-graduate student Takahiko Masuda, PhD, showed Japanese and American participants animated underwater vignettes that included focal objects—three big fish—and background objects like rocks, seaweed and water bubbles. When they asked participants to describe the scenes, Americans were more likely to begin by recalling the focal fish, while Japanese were more likely to describe the whole scene, saying something like "it was a lake or pond." Later, the Japanese participants also recalled more details about the background objects than the Americans did.

"Americans immediately zoomed in on the objects," Nisbett says. "The Japanese paid more attention to context."

Cognitive differences between Westerners and Asians show up in other areas as well. For example, in tests of categorization, Americans are more likely to group items based on how well the items fit into categories by type—so, say, a cow and a chicken might go together because they are both animals. Asians, in contrast, are more likely to group items based on relationships—so a cow and grass might go together because a cow eats grass.

Another difference between Westerners and Asians regards the fundamental attribution error—a mainstay psychological theory for the last 30 years that, it turns out, may not be so fundamental after all. The theory posits that people generally overemphasize personality-related explanations for others' behavior, while underemphasizing or ignoring contextual factors. So, for example, a man may believe he tripped and fell because of a crack in the sidewalk, but assume that someone else fell because of clumsiness.

But, it turns out, most East Asians do not fall prey to this error—they are much more likely to consider contextual factors when trying to explain other people's behavior. In a 1994 study, for example, psychologist Kaiping Peng, PhD, analyzed American and Chinese newspaper accounts of recent murders. He found that American reporters emphasized the personal attributes of the murderers, while Chinese reporters focused more on situational factors.

Frontier Spirit

Although such studies provide convincing evidence of cognitive differences between Asians and Westerners, says Nisbett, they don't explain why those differences occur.

"Our assertion is that these cognitive differences come from social differences," he says. "But that's a very tenuous connection. There's no direct evidence for it yet."

To find that evidence, psychologist Shinobu Kitayama, PhD—who co-chairs Michigan's culture and cognition program with Nisbett—is examining other cultures to determine how their different takes on collectivism, interdependence and other social attributes affect cognition. Kitayama is studying the cognitive style of residents of Hokkaido, Japan—what he calls Japan's "Wild West."

Settlers from the rest of Japan arrived there in the mid-19th century to seek their fortune in the wilderness. If this frontier spirit is associated with a kind of American-style individualism, Kitayama reasoned, then perhaps Hokkaido Japanese might look more like Americans than like other Japanese in their cognitive processes.

And indeed, in a study recently accepted for publication in the *Journal of Personality and Social Psychology,* he and his colleagues found that Hokkaido residents were nearly as likely as Americans to commit the fundamental attribution error.

"The frontier doesn't really exist anywhere anymore," Kitayama says, "but its myth and discourse are still powerful."

Another strand of evidence comes from Asian Americans, who often are raised with some blend of Asian and Western cultural traditions.

"In studies that look at Asians, European Americans and Asian Americans, Asian Americans usually fall somewhere in between the other two," Nisbett says.

Finally, Nisbett is beginning a series of studies that will examine cognitive differences between people in cultures that are quite similar in many ways, but differ in their degree of collectivism.

For example, Eastern and Western Europe, and Northern and Southern Italy—Eastern Europe and Southern Italy being generally more collectivist societies than Western Europe and Northern Italy.

"We've only done a couple of categorization tests," Nisbett says, "but so far we're finding the expected differences."

Why It Matters

In an increasingly multicultural world, these culture-induced cognitive differences can have practical implications, according to University of California, Santa Barbara, psychologist Heejung Kim, PhD. Kim, who is from South Korea, found her research inspiration in her experience as an international graduate student in the United States. In her graduate seminar classes, her inclination was to listen quietly and absorb what was going on around her—but she felt pressured to speak up.

"After struggling for a while, I began to think that someone should question whether the process of talking is valuable for everyone," she says, "because it certainly wasn't for me."

She decided to test European-American and first-generation Asian-American students by giving them a complex logic problem to solve. Control-group members solved the problem silently, while members of the experimental group had to talk out loud and explain their reasoning as they worked. Kim found that European Americans who talked out loud solved the problem just as well as those who stayed silent, but being forced to talk seriously undermined the Asian students' performance.

In general, Kim says, Asians may think and reason in a less readily "verbalizable" way than Westerners.

"It's more intuitive and less linear," she says. "So when you have to talk aloud, European Americans just vocalize their thoughts, but Asian Americans—on top of solving the problem—have to translate their thoughts into words."

In general, Nisbett says, he expects that over the next few decades work by researchers like Kim—and other Asian and Asian-American psychologists—will profoundly influence the way psychologists think about which aspects of thinking are universal and which are culture-specific.

"They're going to be bringing very different ways of thinking about cognitive psychology, social psychology, developmental psychology," he says. "They're going to change the field."

UNIT 6
Emotion and Motivation

Unit Selections

Key Points to Consider

- What is an emotion? Are emotions expressed solely by humans? Is one emotion more important than another?

- What are some positive emotions and some negative emotions of interest to psychologists?

- How are emotion and motivation related to each other?

- What is emotional or social intelligence? Why is it important?

- Why are some people more motivated (i.e. more likely to succeed) than others?

- How is eating related to motivation? Why do some people overeat? Can psychologists help them change their habits?

Student Web Site
www.mhcls.com/online

Internet References
Further information regarding these Websites may be found in this book's preface or online.

Emotional Intelligence Discovery
http://www.cwrl.utexas.edu/~bump/Hu305/3/3/3/
John Suler's Teaching Clinical Psychology Site
http://www.rider.edu/users/suler/tcp.html
Nature vs. Nurture: Gergen Dialogue with Winifred Gallagher
http://www.pbs.org/newshour/gergen/gallagher_5-14.html

Goodshoot/PictureQuest

Jasmine's sister was a working mother and always reminded Jasmine about how exciting life on the road as a sales representative was. Jasmine herself stayed home because she loved her children, two-year old Min, four-year-old Chi'Ming, and newborn Yuan. One day, Jasmine was having a difficult time with the children. The baby, Yuan, had been crying all day from colic. The other two children had been bickering over their toys. Jasmine, realizing that it was already 5:15 and her husband would be home any minute, frantically started preparing dinner. She wanted to fix a nice dinner so that she and her husband could eat after the children went to bed, then relax and enjoy each other.

This was not to be. Jasmine sat waiting for her no-show husband. When he finally walked in the door at 10:15, Jasmine was furious. His excuse that his boss had invited the whole office for dinner didn't reduce Jasmine's ire. Jasmine reasoned that her husband could have called to say that he wouldn't be home for dinner; he could have taken five minutes to do that. He said he did but the phone was busy. Jasmine berated her husband. Her face was taut and red with rage. Her voice wavered as she escalated her decibel level. Suddenly, bursting into tears, she ran into the living room. Her husband retreated to the safety of their bedroom and the respite that a deep sleep would bring.

Exhausted and disappointed, Jasmine sat alone and pondered why she was so angry with her husband. Was she just tired? Was she frustrated by negotiating with young children all day and simply wanted another adult around once in a while? Was she secretly worried and jealous that her husband was seeing another woman and had lied about his whereabouts? Was she combative because her husband's and her sister's lives seemed so much fuller than her own life? Jasmine was unsure just how she felt and why she exploded in such rage at her husband, someone she loved dearly.

This story, while sad and gender stereotypical, is not necessarily unrealistic when it comes to emotions. There are times when we are moved to deep emotion. On other occasions when we expect waterfalls of tears, we find that our eyes are dry or simply a little misty. What are these strange things we call emotions? What motivates us to rage at someone we love? And why do Americans seem to autopsy our every mood?

These questions and others have inspired psychologists to study emotions and motivation. The above episode about Jasmine, besides introducing these topics to you, also illustrates why these two topics are usually interrelated in psychology. Some emotions are pleasant, so pleasant that we are motivated to keep experiencing them. Pleasant emotions are exemplified by love, pride, and joy. Other emotions are terribly draining and oppressive—so negative that we hope they will be over as soon as possible. Negative emotions are exemplified by anger, grief, and jealousy. Emotions and motivation and their relationship to each other are the focus of this unit.

The Structure of Emotion
Evidence From Neuroimaging Studies

One common point of debate in the study of emotion is whether the basic, irreducible elements of emotional life are discrete emotion categories, such as *anger, fear, sadness,* and so on, or dimensions such as approach and avoidance. Resolving this debate will identify the basic building blocks of emotional life that are the most appropriate targets of scientific inquiry. In this paper, we briefly review meta-analytic work on the neuroimaging of emotion and examine its potential for identifying "natural kinds" of emotion in the brain. We outline criteria for identifying such natural kinds, summarize the evidence to date on category and dimensional approaches, and suggest ways in which neuroimaging studies could more directly address fundamental questions about the nature of emotion.

LISA FELDMAN BARRETT[1] AND TOR D. WAGER[2]

"In nature's infinite book of secrecy/A little I can read."

—Shakespeare, *Antony & Cleopatra*

What are the basic building blocks of emotional life that a science of emotion should focus on? This question is almost as old as psychology itself, and it remains unanswered. The "basic emotion" approach argues that certain categories of emotion, described by such English words as *anger, sadness, fear, happiness,* and *disgust,* are biologically basic—inherited, reflex-like modules that cause a distinct and recognizable behavioral and physiological pattern (e.g., Ekman, 1972; Panksepp, 1998). The "dimensional" approach argues that anger, sadness, fear, and so on are categories that characterize more highly elaborated responses constructed from more fundamental, biological properties such as *valence* (pleasure/displeasure) and *arousal* (high activation/low activation; Russell & Barrett, 1999), *positive* and *negative activation* (e.g., Watson & Tellegen, 1985), or *approach* and *withdrawal* (e.g., Lang, Bradley, & Cuthbert, 1990). The pressing question is which typology is given by nature and consists of "natural kinds," such that it is possible to make inductive discoveries about them?

Natural kinds give psychobiological evidence of their existence. Neuroimaging techniques (functional magnetic resonance imaging, or fMRI, and positron emission tomography, or PET) have recently opened the door to searching directly for the circuitry that supports emotional processing in humans. To indicate a natural kind, patterns of neural activation must be consistent (i.e., show increased activation regardless of the induction method used) and

specific (e.g., a fear circuit should be architecturally separable from an anger circuit even though the two may share some brain areas in common). To the degree that consistency and specificity criteria are satisfied, an emotion category or affect dimension can be said to have a "brain marker." In principle, it should be possible to map patterns of activity within a connected set of brain areas, but in practice, most of the imaging research to date has searched only for the most salient or distinctive feature (e.g., brain area) in the circuitry for a given emotion construct.

Meta-analytic summaries (statistical summaries of empirical findings across many studies) of the first 10 years or so of research are now available (Murphy, Nimmo-Smith, & Lawrence, 2003; Phan, Wager, Taylor, & Liberzon, 2002; Wager, Phan, Liberzon, & Taylor, 2003) and allow us to begin to search for evidence of natural kinds. The meta-analyses of Murphy et al. and Phan et al. focused on the neural activations for the five emotion categories—happiness, sadness, anger, fear, and disgust. Wager et al., along with Murphy et al., focused on the neural activations for two affective dimensional models (positive/negative affect and approach/withdrawal motivation). None of the meta-analyses assessed the valence/arousal affective model, in part because many neuroimaging studies fail to measure arousal separately. There were many potential methodological issues in conducting these meta-analyses (e.g., the sole reliance on reporting the peak activation within a broader area of activation, the inherent limitations in the signal-source resolution and spatiotemporal resolution of current neuroimaging techniques, and the heterogeneity of the studies included). Nonetheless, these meta-analyses provide a starting point for evaluating whether categories or dimensions capture natural kinds of emotional phenomena in the brain. They also highlight issues that will help make the results of future studies more cohesive and interpretable.

[1]Boston College and [2]Columbia University

Evidence for Basic Emotions in the Brain

The main findings of the emotion-category–brain-location analyses from Murphy et al. (2003) and Phan et al. (2002) are summarized in Table 1. Both meta-analyses agreed that right and left amygdalae were preferentially activated with fear, and that rostral (or forward) portions of the anterior cingulate cortex (ACC) were preferentially activated by sadness. These findings are in agreement with lesion and animal studies that have linked fear and depression to the amygdala and to the subcallosal portion of the ACC (i.e., the rostral portion of the ACC that is below the corpus callosum), respectively (e.g., LeDoux, 2000). Both analyses suggested that disgust produced frequent activation in the basal ganglia (particularly the globus pallidus). Murphy et al. also reported disgust-specific activations in the insula, a large cortical region in the frontal lobes adjacent to orbitofrontal cortex, that contains processing regions for taste, smell, and somatic as well as visceral activity, whereas Phan et al. found that insula activity was associated with negative emotions generally. At first glance, then, these findings seem to suggest that certain basic emotion categories may be natural kinds in the brain.

Consistency

The fear–amygdala correspondence was the most consistent finding across both studies, yet Phan et al. (2002) reported that only 60% of studies involving fear showed increased activation in the amygdala, and Murphy et al. (2003) reported just under 40%. Small sample sizes and stringent statistical thresholds may account for these modest percentages, but the consistency of these emotion–brain correspondences is called into question by the additional observation that increases in amygdala activation were reliably related to the method by which emotions were induced. For example, in humans, the amygdala is particularly responsive to faces and other visual stimuli (Phan et al., 2002). In fact, if one considers only studies in which participants viewed facial caricatures of fear, the fear–amygdala correspondence increases by about 20% in each meta-analysis. These findings call into question the conclusion that activation of the amygdala in humans reflects engagement of a core "fear system" in the brain.

A similar case can be made for sadness. The percentage of studies that showed a sadness–anterior cingulate correspondence (60% in Phan et al., 2002, and 50% in Murphy et al., 2003) was modest, and the sadness–ACC correspondence may be accounted for by induction method. Many of the studies involving sadness stimuli (e.g., at least 10 of the 14 studies summarized in Murphy et al.) involved cognitive demand. Phan et al. reported that cognitively demanding emotional tasks (such as being asked to remember a sad event to induce a feeling of sadness, or rating emotional stimuli) specifically engaged rostral portions of the ACC, as compared to passive emotional tasks (where stimuli are merely viewed and experienced). Thus, these activations may not reflect sadness per se but something more complex about the cognitive and motivational processes involved in interacting with emotionally valenced stimuli.

Specificity

The emotion-category–brain-localization correspondences were not only inconsistent; there is mounting evidence against their specificity. Given space constraints, we turn to the fear–amygdala correspondence for illustrative purposes. A number of studies are now available to show that the amygdala is engaged by positive objects and rewards or novelty (for a discussion, see Barrett, 2006a). Simple perceptual cues (e.g., eye gaze; Adams, Gordon, Baird, Ambady, & Kleck, 2003) modulate whether or not viewing facial caricatures of fear elicits amygdala activation, and even those with amygdala damage can correctly identify those caricatures when attention is directed toward the eyes of the stimulus caricature (Adolphs et al., 2005). Taken together, the findings are more consistent with the view that the amygdala is involved with computing the affective significance of a stimulus (i.e., the extent to which the stimulus predicts an impending threat or reward; for a discussion, see Barrett, 2006a).

Table 1 Summary of Emotion Category–Brain-Area Activation Correspondences Found in Two Studies (Phan, Wager, Taylor, & Liberzon, 2002; Murphy, Nimmo-Smith, & Lawrence, 2003)

	Phan et al. (2002)		Murphy et al. (2003)	
	N	**Brain activations**	**N**	**Brain activations**
Anger	5	None	8	Lateral orbitofrontal cortex
Sadness	14	Subcallosal anterior cingulate cortex (ACC)	14	Rostral supracallosal anterior cingulate and dorsomedial prefrontal cortex
Disgust	5	Basal ganglia	7	Insula/operculum and globus pallidus
Fear	13	Amygdala	26	Amygdala
Happiness	11	Basal ganglia	11	Rostral supracallosal anterior cingulate/ dorsomedial prefrontal cortex

Note. Sample sizes from Murphy et al. (2003) were taken from Fig. 3, which reports the number of studies included in follow-up chi-square analyses (Murphy, personal communication, 2004). The subcallosal ACC is considered the "visceral" part of the ACC; it is connected to the medial orbital frontal cortex and is associated with autonomic control. The supracallosal ACC is considered to the "cognitive" aspect of the ACC; it is connected to the dorsomedial prefrontal cortex and dorsolateral prefrontal cortex and is associated with attention and working-memory functions. The globus pallidus is part of the basal ganglia.

Evidence for Broad Affective Dimensions in the Brain

The main findings from affect-location analyses from both meta-analyses are presented in Table 2.

Consistency

Differences in analytic strategy make a detailed comparison of the Wager et al. (2003) and Murphy et al. (2003) meta-analyses impossible, but several broader observations are possible. Both analyses observed greater left-sided activations (left-lateralization) for approach- (vs. withdrawal-) related affect (localized to the frontal cortex in Wager et al.). Wager et al. reported a number of activation foci for withdrawal-related affect that were not observed by Murphy et al., including regions in the amygdala, the left medial prefrontal cortex and anterior cingulate, the basal ganglia, and the insula. Both PET and fMRI imaging methods produced identical results. Moreover, there was a dissociation between approach-active and withdrawal-active regions in the medial prefrontal cortex.

The two meta-analyses showed less consistency in their assessment of the positive versus negative activation model. Murphy et al. (2003) reported null effects. Wager et al. (2003) reported findings similar to (but considerably weaker than) those observed for the approach/avoidance model.

Specificity

The most striking observation from Wager et al. (2003) is that many of the same regions showing emotion-category effects also showed specialization for the broader category of withdrawal-related affects. For example, fear-related stimuli may activate the dorsal (or top) portion of the amygdala because they are part of a broader class of aversive stimuli that engage this region. The obvious next questions are whether affect dimensions or emotion categories better predict the observed patterns of activation, and whether another potential function, perhaps based on stimulus salience, fits the pattern of data better. This would be an important direction for future research.

Toward an Understanding of Emotion in the Brain

Every emotional event has neural correlates, and discovery of these correlates is a major task of science. An important step is to determine whether discrete emotion categories, such as fear, and/or broader affective categories, such as approach and avoidance, have consistent and specific neural correlates—brain markers—that justify thinking of them as natural kinds. A conservative approach to the existing evidence precludes drawing firm conclusions about natural emotion kinds in the human brain, but it is possible to offer several tentative observations.

Thus far, emotion category–location correspondences are neither consistent nor specific. This observation is largely consistent with evidence from other instrument-based measures of emotion in humans indicating that it is currently not possible to characterize each emotion category by a biological signature (Barrett, 2006a). Although there is good evidence from the animal literature that specific behaviors (e.g., freezing) may depend on specific nuclei (groups of neurons) in the amygdala and brainstem (e.g., LeDoux, 2000; Panksepp, 1998), there currently is insufficient evidence that these form the basis for basic emotion circuits (because each behavior is not necessarily associated with any single emotion category). Of course, it is possible to find caveats to explain why evidence for basic emotion kinds has not materialized (e.g., human research may fail to elicit strong and differentiated emotional responses in the lab), and distinct, natural kinds of emotions might reveal themselves if only scientists could find the right eliciting stimuli, employ better measurement tools, or use more sophisticated and precise research designs. Nonetheless, the available imaging research highlights an important observation: While one may not want to reject the idea of emotions as natural kinds defined by neural circuits in the brain, it is not prudent to accept that idea too quickly either.

The limitations of emotion research notwithstanding, neuroimaging studies do show some consistent effects across studies. Of the three existing dimension models, there is emerging evidence from the Murphy et al. (2003) and Wager et al. (2003) analyses for the reliability of the approach/withdrawal model, but aspects of its consistency (e.g., variations across induction method) and specificity have not been fully tested. Furthermore, the valence/arousal model remains to be meta-analytically evaluated, and dimension-specific activation patterns need to be tested for specificity against nonemotional categories such as salience and self-relevance.

Future research will undoubtedly clarify, and perhaps even reshape, the empirical landscape that we have mapped. First, the human brain is being visualized with ever-increasing precision, allowing the study of functional regions within the brain that are much smaller than the very broad regions that were the focus of Phan et al.'s (2002) and Murphy et al.'s (2003) emotion-category analyses. For example, the higher-resolution analysis of Wager

Table 2 Summary of Affect Dimension–Location Correspondences in Two Studies (Murphy, Nimmo-Smith, & Lawrence, 2003; Wager, Phan, Liberzon, & Taylor, 2003)

	Murphy et al. (2003)	Wager et al. (2003)
Positive affect	No difference in activation patterns	Left lateral frontal cortex, basal ganglia
Negative affect	No difference in activation patterns	Insula
Approach	Greater left- than right-sided activations across anterior and posterior regions	Left lateral frontal cortex, anterior medial prefrontal cortex
Withdrawal	No lateralization differences	Amygdala, left medial prefrontal cortex and rostral anterior cingulate, right striatum (basal ganglia), left insula, left fusiform and superior occipital cortices

et al. (2003) provided the observation that separate, nearby areas in the rostral medial prefrontal cortex were frequently activated by approach- and withdrawal-related affect (a finding replicated in a meta-analysis of the orbitofrontal cortex by Kringelbach & Rolls, 2004), and may explain why Murphy et al. found medial prefrontal cortex correspondences for both happiness and sadness. Furthermore, finer-grained analysis of the cortex (e.g., single-neuron activations, neurochemical analyses, more fine-grained temporal analyses) as well as PET imaging of the brainstem and other subcortical areas may help to resolve the question of which emotion structure reflects what actually occurs in the brain.

Second, researchers need to move from studying singular brain areas to identifying circuits, because a given brain area may be involved in more than one functional circuit. Studies that examine the functional connectivity between brain areas, supplemented by neuroanatomical studies of neuronal circuitry in humans and primates, allow the possibility of investigating whether the pattern of information transfer, rather than architectural distinctiveness, characterizes distinct emotion circuits. In this respect, neuroimaging plays a unique and complementary role to lesion studies in animals, because neuroimaging alone allows the simultaneous measurement of the entire brain and reveals dynamic patterns of functional connectivity across diverse systems.

Third, researchers are beginning to take more care in measuring or controlling for variables (e.g., the autonomic arousal, motor-response tendencies, and cognitive demand associated with emotional stimuli in a given processing instant) that may confound, or obscure, the evidence on emotion structure. Without such controls, activations may result more from the idiosyncratic demands of the tasks than from the emotional or affective state being induced.

Fourth, researchers must work to formalize the inferential process before neuroimaging data can be used to clarify key debates in the psychological literature. The "brain mapping" approach is typically designed to test the probability of activation in a brain area given a certain emotion or affect (e.g., what parts of the brain activate with fear?), but it is also necessary to test the probability that an emotion (or affect) is present given activation in a given brain area (e.g., given amygdala activation, is there fear?). Claims about the psychological meaning of activation are made in virtually every neuroimaging study, and these claims are often made based on general ideas about what brain areas "do," leading to intuitive, rather than empirical, tests of specificity.

Finally, progress in understanding the structure of emotion not only requires conducting better studies with better research tools; it may also require learning to ask different sorts of questions about emotion. While it is important to ask questions like "how many emotions are there?" and "what is the brain marker for fear," it may also be important to consider the possibility that emotion words, such as *fear, anger, sadness, disgust,* and *happiness,* do not refer to specific mechanisms in the mind or the brain (Barrett, 2006b). If emotions are psychological events like memories, then they are best thought of as products of distinct but interacting psychological processes with accompanying neural systems, and scientists might begin to design experiments to systematically map how instances of emotion are synthesized from component psychological processes that we know to be implemented in the human brain. Doing so may provide us with a better translation of the pages of "nature's infinite book" that are the workings of the brain, and allow us to answer the age-old question of what emotions really are.

References

Adams, R.B., Gordon, H.L., Baird, A.A., Ambady, N., & Kleck, R.E. (2003). Effects of gaze on Amygdala sensitivity to anger and fear faces. *Science, 300,* 1536–1537.

Adolphs, R., Gosselin, F., Buchanan, T.W., Tranel, D., Schyns, P., & Damasio, A.R. (2005, January). A mechanism for impaired fear recognition after amygdala damage. *Nature, 433,* 68–72.

Barrett, L.F. (2006a). Are emotions natural kinds? *Perspectives on Psychological Science, 1,* 28–58.

Barrett, L.F. (2006b). Solving the emotion paradox: Categorization and the experience of emotion. *Personality and Social Psychology Review, 10,* 20–46.

Ekman, P. (1972). Universals and cultural differences in facial expressions of emotion. In J. Cole (Ed.), *Nebraska Symposium on Motivation* (pp. 207–283). Lincoln: University of Nebraska Press.

Kringelbach, M.L., & Rolls, E.T. (2004). The functional neuroanatomy of the human orbitofrontal cortex: Evidence from neuroimaging and neuropsychology. *Progress in Neurobiology, 72,* 341–372.

Lang, P.J., Bradley, M.M., & Cuthbert, B.N. (1990). Emotion, attention, and the startle reflex. *Psychological Review, 97,* 377–398.

LeDoux, J.E. (2000). Emotion circuits in the brain. *Annual Review of Neuroscience, 23,* 155–184.

Murphy, F.C., Nimmo-Smith, I., & Lawrence, A.D. (2003). Functional neuroanatomy of emotion: A meta-analysis. *Cognitive, Affective, & Behavioral Neuroscience, 3,* 207–233.

Panksepp, J. (1998). *Affective neuroscience: The foundations of human and animal emotions.* New York: Oxford University Press.

Phan, K.L., Wager, T.D., Taylor, S.F., & Liberzon, I. (2002). Functional neuroanatomy of emotion: A meta-analysis of emotion activation studies in PET and fMRI. *Neuroimage, 16,* 331–348.

Russell, J.A., & Barrett, L.F. (1999). Core affect, prototypical emotional episodes, and other things called emotion: Dissecting the elephant. *Journal of Personality and Social Psychology, 76,* 805–819.

Wager, T.D., Phan, K.L., Liberzon, I., & Taylor, S.F. (2003). Valence, gender, and lateralization of functional brain anatomy in emotion: A meta-analysis of findings from neuroimaging. *Neuroimage, 19,* 513–531.

Watson, D., & Tellegen, A. (1985). Towards a consensual structure of mood. *Psychological Bulletin, 98,* 219–235.

Acknowledgments—We thank K. Luan Phan and Fionnuala Murphy for providing us with additional information about their meta-analysis. We also thank Michael Ross, Kevin Ochsner, James Russell, David DeSteno, and Christopher Wright for their helpful comments on earlier drafts of this article. This article was supported by NIMH Grant K02 MH001981 to Lisa Feldman Barrett.

Address correspondence to Lisa Feldman Barrett, Department of Psychology, Boston College, Chestnut Hill, MA 02167; e-mail: barretli@bc.edu.

Feeling Smart: The Science of Emotional Intelligence

A new idea in psychology has matured and shows promise of explaining how attending to emotions can help us in everyday life.

DAISY GREWAL AND PETER SALOVEY

Over the past decade almost everyone tuned in to American popular culture has heard the term *emotional intelligence*. As a new concept, emotional intelligence has been a hit: It has been the subject of several books, including a best seller, and myriad talk-show discussions and seminars for schools and organizations. Today you can hire a coach to help you raise your "EQ," your emotional quotient—or your child's.

Despite (or perhaps because of) its high public profile, emotional intelligence has attracted considerable scientific criticism. Some of the controversy arises from the fact that popular and scientific definitions of emotional intelligence differ sharply. In addition, measuring emotional intelligence has not been easy. Despite these difficulties, research on emotional intelligence has managed to sustain itself and in fact shows considerable promise as a serious line of scientific inquiry. It turns out that emotional intelligence can indeed be measured, as a set of mental abilities, and that doing so is an informative exercise that can help individuals understand the role of emotions in their everyday lives.

Ten years after the appearance of that bestselling book and a *TIME* magazine cover that asked "What's your EQ?" it seems sensible to ask what is known, scientifically, about emotional intelligence. In the history of modern psychology, the concept represents a stage in the evolution of our thinking about the relation between passion and reason and represents an important outgrowth of new theories of intelligence. Work in this subfield has produced a four-factor model of emotional intelligence that serves as a guide for empirical research. In this article we will explain ways of assessing emotional intelligence using ability-based tests and some of the findings that have resulted from this method.

Before "Emotional Intelligence"

Philosophers have debated the relation between thought and emotions for at least two millennia. The Stoics of ancient Greece and Rome believed emotion far too heated and unpredictable to be of much use to rational thought. Emotion was also strongly associated with women, in their view, and therefore representative of the weak, inferior aspects of humanity. The stereotype of women as the more "emotional" sex is one that persists today. Even though various romantic movements embraced emotion over the centuries, the Stoic view of emotions as more or less irrational persisted in one form or another well into the 20th century.

But many notions were upended during the rapid development of modern psychology in the 20th century. Setting the stage for a new way of thinking about emotions and thought, psychologists articulated broader definitions of intelligence and also new perspectives on the relation between feeling and thinking. As early as the 1930s, psychometrician Robert Thorndike mentioned the possibility that people might have a "social intelligence"—an ability to perceive their own and others' internal states, motivations and behaviors, and act accordingly. In 1934 David Wechsler, the psychologist whose name today attaches to two well-known intelligence tests, wrote about the "nonintellective" aspects of a person that contribute to overall intelligence. Thorndike's and Wechsler's statements were, however, speculations. Even though social intelligence seemed a definite possibility, Thorndike admitted that there existed little scientific evidence of its presence. A similar conclusion was reached by psychometric expert Lee Cronbach, who in 1960 declared that, after half a century of speculation, social intelligence remained "undefined and unmeasured."

But the 1980s brought a surge of new interest in expanding the definition of intelligence. In 1983 Howard Gardner of Harvard University became famous overnight when, in the book *Frames of Mind,* he outlined seven distinct forms of intelligence. Gardner proposed an "intrapersonal intelligence" very similar to the current conceptualization of emotional intelligence. "The core capacity at work here," he wrote, "is access to one's own feeling life—one's range of affects or emotions: the capacity instantly to effect discriminations among these feelings and, eventually, to label them, to enmesh them in symbolic codes, to draw upon them as a means of understanding and guiding one's behavior."

Is "emotional intelligence," then, simply a new name for social intelligence and other already-defined "intelligences"? We hope to clear up this thorny question by explaining just what we attempt to measure when assessing emotional intelligence. Certainly it can be seen as a type of social intelligence. But we prefer to explicitly focus on the processing of emotions and knowledge about emotion-related information and suggest that this constitutes its own form of intelligence. Social intelligence is very broadly defined, and partly for this reason the pertinent skills involved have remained elusive to scientists.

Emotional intelligence is a more focused concept. Dealing with emotions certainly has important implications for social relationships, but emotions also contribute to other aspects of life. Each of us has a need to set priorities, orient positively toward future endeavors and repair negative moods before they spiral into anxiety and depression. The concept of emotional intelligence isolates a specific set of skills embedded within the abilities that are broadly encompassed by the notion of social intelligence.

Emotion and Thinking

New understandings of the relation between thought and emotion have strengthened the scientific foundation of the study of emotional intelligence. Using a simple decision-making task, neurologist Antonio R. Damasio and his colleagues at the University of Iowa have provided convincing evidence that emotion and reason are essentially inseparable. When making decisions, people often focus on the logical pros and cons of the choices they face. However, Damasio has shown that without feelings, the decisions we make may not be in our best interest.

In the early 1990s Damasio had people participate in a gambling task in which the goal is to maximize profit on a loan of play money. Participants were instructed to select 100 cards, one at a time, from four different decks. The experimenter arranged the cards such that two of the decks provided larger payoffs ($100 compared to only $50) but also doled out larger penalties at unpredictable intervals. Players who chose from the higher-reward, higher risk decks lost a net of $250 every 10 cards; those choosing the $50 decks gained a net of $250 every 10 cards.

One group of participants in this study had been identified as having lesions to the ventromedial prefrontal cortex of the brain. Patients with this type of brain damage have normal intellectual function but are unable to use emotion in making decisions. The other group was normal, meaning that their brains were fully intact. Because there was no way for any of the players to calculate precisely which decks were riskier, they had to rely on their "gut" feelings to avoid losing money.

Damasio's group demonstrated that the brain-lesion patients failed to pay attention to these feelings (which he deems "somatic markers") and subsequently lost significantly more money than the normal participants. Therefore, defects in the brain that impair emotion and feeling detection can subsequently impair decision-making. Damasio concluded that "individuals make judgments not only by assessing the severity of outcomes, but also and primarily in terms of their emotional quality." This experiment demonstrates that emotions and thought processes are closely connected. Whatever notions we draw from our Stoic and Cartesian heritages, separating thinking and feeling is not necessarily more adaptive and may, in some cases, lead to disastrous consequences.

The Four-Branch Model

The term "emotional intelligence" was perhaps first used in an unpublished dissertation in 1986. One of us (Salovey), along with John D. Mayer of the University of New Hampshire, introduced it to scientific psychology in 1990, defining emotional intelligence as "the ability to monitor one's own and others' feelings, to discriminate among them, and to use this information to guide one's thinking and action."

Some critics have seen the concept of emotional intelligence as a mere outgrowth of the late-20th-century Zeitgeist—and indeed, as we reflect in the conclusion to this article, today the term has a vibrant pop-culture life of its own. But within psychology, the concept developed out of a growing emphasis on research on the interaction of emotion and thought. In the late 1970s psychologists conducted experiments that looked at a number of seemingly unrelated topics at the interface of feeling and thinking: the effect of depression on memory, the perception of emotion in facial expressions, the functional importance of regulating or expressing emotion.

Emotional intelligence is one of the concepts that emerged from this work. It integrates a number of the results into a related set of skills that can be measured and differentiated from personality and social skills; within psychology it can be defined as an intelligence because it is a quantifiable and indeed a measurable aspect of the individual's capacity to carry out abstract thought and to learn and adapt to the environment. Emotional intelligence can be shown to operate on emotional information in the same way that other types of intelligence might operate on a broken computer or what a photographer sees in her viewfinder.

Interested in helping the field of emotions develop a theory that would organize the numerous efforts to find individual difference in emotion-related processes, Salovey and Mayer proposed a four-branch model of emotional intelligence that emphasized four domains of related skills: (a) the ability to perceive emotions accurately; (b) the ability to use emotions to facilitate thinking and reasoning; (c) the ability to understand emotions, especially the language of emotions; and (d) the ability to manage emotions both in oneself and in others. This four-branch emotional intelligence model proposes that individuals differ in these skills and that these differences have consequences at home, school and work, and in social relations.

Perceiving and Using Emotions

The first domain of emotional intelligence, *perceiving emotions,* includes the abilities involved in identifying emotions in faces, voices, pictures, music and other stimuli. For example, the individual who excels at perceiving emotions can quickly tell when his friend is upset by accurately decoding his friend's facial expressions.

One might consider this the most basic skill involved in emotional intelligence because it makes all other processing of emotional information possible. In addition, our skill at reading faces is one of the attributes humans share across cultures. Paul Ekman of the University of California, San Francisco showed pictures of Americans expressing different emotions to a group of isolated New Guineans. He found that the New Guineans could recognize what emotions were being expressed in the photographs quite accurately, even though they had never encountered an American and had grown up in a completely different culture.

But emotion perception does vary across individuals. A study by Seth D. Pollak at the University of Wisconsin-Madison in 2000, for example, demonstrated that physical abuse might interfere with children's ability to adaptively perceive facial expressions.

Pollak asked abused and nonabused children, aged 8 to 10, to come into the laboratory to play "computer games." The children were shown digitally morphed faces that displayed emotional expressions that ranged from happy to fearful, happy to sad, angry to fearful, or angry to sad. In one of the games, the children were shown a single picture and asked to identify which emotion it expressed. Because all the faces expressed varying degrees of a certain emotion, the investigators were able to discover how the children perceived different facial expressions. They found that the abused children were more likely to categorize a face as angry, even when it showed only a slight amount of anger.

In addition, Pollak measured the brain activity of the children while completing this task using electrodes attached to their scalps. The abused children also exhibited more brain activity when viewing an angry face. This research shows that life experiences can strongly shape the recognition of facial expression. We can speculate that this difference in likelihood to perceive anger may have important consequences for the children's interactions with other people.

The second branch of emotional intelligence, *using emotions,* is the ability to harness emotional information to facilitate other cognitive activities. Certain moods may create mind-sets that are better suited for certain kinds of tasks.

In a clever experiment done during the 1980s, Alice Isen of Cornell University found that being in a happy mood helps people generate more creative solutions to problems. Isen brought undergraduates into the laboratory and induced either a positive mood (by showing them comedy clips) or a neutral mood (by showing them a short segment from a math film).

After watching one of the films, each student was seated at an individual table and given a book of matches, a box of tacks and a candle. Above the table was a corkboard. The students were given 10 minutes to provide a solution to the following challenge: how to affix the candle to the corkboard in such a way that it would burn without dripping wax onto the table. Those students who had watched the comedy films, and were therefore in a happier mood, were more likely to come up with

an adequate solution to the problem: They realized that the task can be easily accomplished by emptying the box, tacking it to the wall and using it as a platform for the candle. It appears that emotional intelligence can facilitate certain tasks; the emotionally intelligent person can utilize pleasant feelings most effectively.

Understanding and Managing Emotion

Mayer and Salovey classified the third and fourth branches of the emotional intelligence model as "strategic" (rather than "experiential") intelligence. The third branch, *understanding emotions,* is the ability to comprehend information about relations between emotions, transitions from one emotion to another, and to label emotions using emotion words. A person who is good at understanding emotions would have the ability to see differences between related emotions, such as between pride and joy. The same individual would also be able to recognize, for instance, that irritation can lead to rage if left unattended.

Boston College psychologist Lisa Feldman Barrett has demonstrated that the ability to differentiate one's emotional states has important implications for well-being. Feldman Barrett and her colleagues asked a group of 53 undergraduates to keep a daily diary of their emotions for two weeks. Specifically, they assessed the most intense emotional experience they had each day by rating the intensity of their experience of nine emotions, represented by words, on a scale from 0, *not at all,* to 4, *very much.* Four of the emotion words related to positive emotion (happiness, joy, enthusiasm, amusement); five related to negative emotion (nervous, angry, sad, ashamed, guilty).

Feldman Barrett and her colleagues then calculated the correlations between reported experiences of positive emotions and also looked at how correlated were reported experiences of negative emotions. A subject whose reports of positive emotions are highly correlated is perceiving less differentiation between positive states. Similarly, larger correlations between the reports of each negative emotion indicate less differentiation between negative states.

At the end of the study, all participants completed a questionnaire assessing the extent to which they engaged in various emotion-regulation strategies during the previous two weeks (for example, "talking to others"). Greater differentiation between positive emotional states had no effect on regulation strategies. But differentiation of negative states clearly did. That is, participants who were able to more specifically pinpoint *what* negative emotion they were feeling each day also engaged in more strategies for managing their emotions. This shows that the ability to distinguish and label emotions may represent an important skill in learning how to handle emotions successfully.

The fourth branch of emotional intelligence is the ability to manage one's emotions as well as the emotions of others. This skill of *managing emotions* is perhaps the most commonly identified aspect of emotional intelligence. Emotional intelligence is far more than simply being able to regulate bad moods effectively. It can also be important to maintain negative emotions when needed. For example, a speaker trying to persuade her audience of some injustice should have the ability to use her own outrage to stir others to action.

An example of how using different strategies for managing emotions can have different consequences is found in the work of James S. Gross of Stanford University, in experiments during the mid-1990s. Gross showed undergraduates video clips from medical procedures, such as amputation, that elicit disgust. The students were divided into three different groups. In the suppression condition, the students were instructed to hide their emotions during the film as much as possible by limiting their facial expressions. In the reappraisal condition, students were instructed to view the film as objectively as possible and to remain emotionally detached from what they were seeing. The third group was given no special instructions before viewing the film. All of the students' reactions to the films were recorded by video camera, and their physiological reactions, such as heart rate and skin conductance, were also measured. In addition, participants were asked to make self-reports of their feelings before, during and after watching the film.

The students in the suppression and reappraisal conditions had strikingly different experiences from watching the film. In the suppression condition, participants were able to successfully reduce the outward experience of their emotions by reducing their facial expressions and other behavioral reactions to the film. However, they showed heightened physiological arousal and reported feeling as much disgust as controls. The participants in the reappraisal condition reported lower levels of disgust upon watching the film while not displaying any heightened physical arousal (compared to controls). Gross's work demonstrates that there might be important, and sometimes hidden, physical costs for those individuals who chronically suppress expression of their negative emotions; nevertheless, monitoring and evaluating one's emotions may be strategically useful.

Measuring Emotional Intelligence

Any attribute being suggested as a form of intelligence must meet the standards of psychometrics, the field of psychological measurement. Scientists must be able to show that tests do not merely capture personality traits or information about other abilities. Three approaches to measuring emotional intelligence have been used: self-report tests, reports made by others and ability-based tests. Self-report tests were developed first and continue to be widely used, owing to the ease with which they can be administered and scored. Test-takers agree or disagree with items that attempt to capture various aspects of perceived emotional intelligence. For example, the popular Self-Report Emotional Intelligence Test (SREIT), authored by Nicola Schutte, asks respondents to rate how much they agree with such items as "I have control over my emotions," and "(other people find it easy to confide in me.)"

Reports made by others are commonly collected using "360" instruments. People who frequently interact with one another (such as friends and colleagues) are asked to rate one another's apparent degree of emotional intelligence. These instruments commonly contain items similar to those used in self-report tests, such as the statement "This person has control over his or her emotions."

Unfortunately, self-report tests assess self-estimates of attributes that often extend beyond definitions of emotional intelligence. They tend to incorporate facets of personality and character traditionally measured by existing personality tests.

Assessing emotional intelligence through self-report measures also presents the same dilemma one would face in trying to assess standard analytic intelligence by asking people, "Do you think you're smart?" Of course most people want to appear smart. Also, individuals may not have a good idea of their own strengths and weaknesses, especially in the domain of emotions. Similarly, although reports made by others seem more promising in providing accurate information, they are also highly vulnerable to biased viewpoints and subjective interpretations of behavior.

In an attempt to overcome these problems, the first ability-based measure of emotional intelligence was introduced in 1998 in the form of the Multi-factor Emotional Intelligence Scale (MEIS). An improved and professionally published version of the MEIS, from which problematic items were eliminated, was released in 2002 in the form of the Mayer-Salovey-Caruso Emotional Intelligence Test (MSCEIT, named for Mayer, Salovey and collaborator David R. Caruso of the EI Skills Group).

The MSCEIT consists of eight different tasks—two tasks devoted to each of the four branches of emotional intelligence. For example, the first branch, perceiving emotions, is tested by presenting participants with a photograph of a person and then asking them to rate the amount of sadness, happiness, fear etc. that they detect in the person's facial expression. Skill in using emotions is tested by having people indicate how helpful certain moods, such as boredom or happiness, would be for performing certain activities, such as planning a birthday party. The understanding-emotions portion of the test includes questions that ask participants to complete sentences testing their knowledge of emotion vocabulary and how emotions can progress from one to another. The test section addressing the fourth branch, managing emotions, presents participants with real-life scenarios. Participants are asked to choose, from several options, the best strategy for handling the emotions brought up in each scenario. After completing the MSCEIT, scores are generated for each of the four branches as well as an overall total score.

How Good Is the Test?

Marc A. Brackett of Yale University and Mayer calculated the extensive overlap between self-report tests of emotional intelligence and commonly used tests of personality. Many studies of personality are organized around The Big Five model of personality; they ask participants to self-rate how much they exhibit the following traits; neuroticism, extraversion, openness, agreeableness and conscientiousness.

Brackett and Mayer administered scales assessing The Big Five to a group of college students along with the MSCEIT and the SREIT. They found that scores on Big Five personality traits were more highly correlated with participants' scores on the SREIT than on the MSCEIT. The trait of "extraversion," for example, had a correlation of 0.37 with scores on the SREIT but only correlated 0.11 with scores on the MSCEIT. Therefore, it appears that self-report tests of emotional intelligence may offer limited information about a person above and beyond standard personality questionnaires.

The biggest problem one faces in trying to use an ability-based measure of emotional intelligence is how to determine correct answers. Unlike traditional intelligence tests, emotional intelligence tests can lack clear right or wrong solutions. There are dozens of ways one could handle many emotion-laden situations, so who should decide which is the emotionally intelligent way of doing things? Intrinsic to the four-branch model of emotional intelligence is the hypothesis that emotional skills cannot be separated from their social context. To use emotions in a useful way, one must be attuned to the social and cultural norms of the environment in which one interacts. Therefore, the model proposes that correct answers will depend highly upon agreement with others of one's own social group. Furthermore, experts on emotion research should also have the ability to identify correct answers, since scientific methods have provided us with good knowledge on correct alternatives to emotion-related problems.

Consequently, the MSCEIT is scored using two different methods: general consensus and expert scoring. In consensus scoring, an individual's answers are statistically compared with the answers that were provided by a diverse worldwide sample of 5,000 respondents aged 18 or older who completed the MSCEIT prior to May 2001. The sample is both educationally and ethnically diverse, with respondents from seven different countries including the United States.

In the consensus approach, greater statistical overlap with the sample's answers reflects higher emotional intelligence. In expert scoring, a person's answers are compared with those provided by a group of emotion experts, in this case 21 emotion investigators elected to the International Society for Research on Emotions (ISRE).

The amount of overlap between consensus and expert scoring has been carefully examined. Participants' responses have been scored first using the consensus method and then the expert method, and these results are then correlated with each other. The average correlation between the two sets of scores is greater than 0.90, indicating sizable overlap between the opinions of experts and the general consensus of test-takers. Laypeople and emotion experts, in other words, converge on the most "emotionally intelligent" answers. The scores of the experts tend to agree with one another more than do those of the consensus group, indicating that emotion experts are more likely to possess a shared social representation of what constitutes emotional intelligence.

The MSCEIT has demonstrated good reliability, meaning that scores tend to be consistent over time and that the test is internally consistent. In sum, given its modest overlap with

commonly used tests of personality traits and analytic intelligence, the MSCEIT seems to test reliably for something that is distinct from both personality and IQ.

Putting Research to Work

Research on emotional intelligence has been put to practical use with unusual speed. The reason may be simple: Experiments suggest that scores on ability-based measures of emotional intelligence are associated with a number of important real-world outcomes.

Emotional intelligence may help one get along with peers and supervisors at work. Paulo N. Lopes of the University of Surrey in the United Kingdom spearheaded a study conducted at a Fortune 500 insurance company where employees worked in teams. Each team was asked to fill out surveys that asked individuals to rate other team members on personal descriptors related to emotions such as, "This person handles stress without getting too tense," or "This person is aware of the feelings of others."

Supervisors in the company were also asked to rate their subordinates on similar items. Everyone who participated in the study also took the MSCEIT. Although the sample of participants was small, employees who scored higher on the MSCEIT received more positive ratings from both their peers and their supervisors. Their peers reported having fewer conflicts with them, and they were perceived as creating a positive atmosphere at work. Supervisors rated their emotionally intelligent employees as more interpersonally sensitive, sociable, tolerant of stress and possessing more leadership potential. Higher scores were also positively associated with rank and salary in the company.

Emotional intelligence may also be important for creating and sustaining good relationships with peers. A different study conducted by Lopes and his collaborators asked German college students to keep diaries that described their everyday interactions with others over a two-week period. For every social interaction that lasted at least 10 minutes, students were asked to record the gender of the person they interacted with, how they felt about the interaction, how much they had wanted to make a certain impression, and to what extent they thought they succeeded in making that impression.

Scores on the using-emotions branch of the MSCEIT were positively related to how enjoyable and interesting students found their interactions to be, as well as how important and safe they felt during them. Scores on the managing-emotions branch seemed most important in interactions with the opposite sex. For these interactions, students scoring high on managing emotions reported more enjoyment, intimacy, interest, importance and respect. In addition, managing emotions was positively related to the students' beliefs that they had made the desired impression on their opposite-sex partners (coming across as friendly, say, or competent).

Brackett also investigated how scores on the MSCEIT relate to the quality of social relationships among college students. American college students completed the MSCEIT along with questionnaires assessing the quality of their friendships and their interpersonal skills, In addition, these students were asked to recruit two of their friends to evaluate the quality of their friendship. Individuals scoring high in managing emotions were rated as more caring and emotionally supportive by their friends. Scores on managing emotions were also negatively related to friends' reports of conflict with them. In another recent study by Nicole Lemer and Brackett, Yale students who scored higher in emotional intelligence were evaluated more positively by their roommates; that is, their roommates reported experiencing less conflict with them.

Emotional intelligence may also help people more successfully navigate their relationships with spouses and romantic partners. Another study headed by Brackett recruited 180 young couples (mean age 25 years) from the London area. The couples completed the MSCEIT and then filled out a variety of questionnaires asking about aspects of the couples' relationships, such as the quality of the interactions with their partners and how happy they were with the relationship. Happiness was correlated with high scores for both partners, and where one partner had a high score and the other a low score, satisfaction ratings tended to fall in the intermediate range.

The Future of Emotional Intelligence

Context plays an important role in shaping how these skills are put into action. We can all name people—certain notable politicians come to mind—who seem extremely talented in using their emotions in their professional lives while their personal lives seem in shambles. People may be more adept at using the skills of emotional intelligence in some situations than in others. A promising direction for future research is a focus on fluid skills rather than crystallized knowledge about emotions.

Although it has proved valuable so far as a test of general emotional intelligence, the MSCEIT requires refinement and improvement. We view the MEIS and the MSCEIT as the first in a potentially long line of improved ways of assessing emotional abilities.

We believe research on emotional intelligence will be especially valuable if focused on individual differences in emotional processes—a topic we hope will continue to generate more empirical interest. The science of emotion thus far has stressed principles of universality. Ekman's work on faces, mentioned above, and similar cross-cultural findings offer important insights into the nature of human emotional experience. However, in any given culture, people differ from one another in their abilities to interpret and use emotional information. Because individual deficits in emotional skills may lead to negative outcomes, anyone interested in improving emotional skills in various settings should focus on how and why some people, from childhood, are better at dealing with emotions than others. Such knowledge provides the hope of being able to successfully teach such skills to others.

The Popularization of "EQ"

Media interest in emotional intelligence was sparked by *New York Times* science writer Daniel Goleman's bestselling book *Emotional Intelligence* in 1995. In October of the same year came the *TIME* magazine cover and additional media coverage proclaiming emotional intelligence the new way to be smart and the best predictor of success in life.

The late 1990s provided the perfect cultural landscape for the appearance of emotional intelligence. The latest in a string of IQ controversies had broken out with the 1994 publication of *The Bell Curve,* which claimed that modern society has become increasingly stratified not by money, power or class, but by traditionally defined intelligence.

The Bell Curve was read as advocating a view that intelligence is the most important predictor of almost everything that seems to matter to most people: staying healthy, earning enough money, even having a successful marriage. Yet half the population, by definition, has below-average IQs; moreover, IQ is seen as difficult to change over one's lifespan. For many readers, *The Bell Curve* contained an extremely pessimistic message. As if to answer the growing fear that a relatively immutable IQ is the primary predictor of success in life, Goleman's book on emotional intelligence included the phrase, "Why it can matter more than IQ," right on the cover. The public responded favorably to this new promise, and the book soon became a staple on airport newsstands worldwide.

Skepticism over narrow definitions of the word "intelligence" resonated powerfully with a public that seemed to agree that something else—something more intangible—may more strongly determine the quality' of one's life. Evidence that the Scholastic Aptitude Test (SAT), which is highly correlated with IQ, fails to predict academic success especially well beyond the first year of college continued to fuel interest in how emotional skills, or something else beside traditional intelligence, may more significantly determine one's future accomplishments. Americans have always prided themselves on a strong work ethic; the motto that "slow and steady wins the race" represents an attitude that fits well with public conceptions of emotional intelligence as a mark of good character. Americans also have a strong collective self-image of equality, which popular views of emotional intelligence support by characterizing success as dependent on a set of skills that anyone can learn.

Goleman's book continues to be one of the most successful and influential of its genre, and other trade books concerned with emotional intelligence (or EQ, as it is referred to in the popular literature) have appeared in recent years. More than just a passing fad, or temporary backlash against standardized testing, emotional intelligence has captured the long-term interest of employers and educators. In just a few years, what started as a somewhat obscure area of science-driven research in psychology burgeoned into a multi-million-dollar industry marketing books, tapes, seminars and training programs aimed at increasing emotional intelligence.

Popularization has in some cases distorted the original scientific definition of emotional intelligence. Many people now equate emotional intelligence with almost everything desirable in a person's makeup that cannot be measured by an IQ test, such as character, motivation, confidence, mental stability, optimism and "people skills." Research has shown that emotional skills may contribute to some of these qualities, but most of them move far beyond skill-based emotional intelligence. We prefer to define emotional intelligence as a specific set of skills that can be used for either prosocial or antisocial purposes. The ability to accurately perceive how others are feeling may be used by a therapist to gauge how best to help her clients, whereas a con artist might use it to manipulate potential victims. Being emotionally intelligent does not necessarily make one an ethical person.

Although popular claims regarding emotional intelligence run far ahead of what research can reasonably support, the overall effects of the publicity have been more beneficial than harmful. The most positive aspect of this popularization is a new and much needed emphasis on emotion by employers, educators and others interested in promoting social welfare. The popularization of emotional intelligence has helped both the public and research psychology reevaluate the functionality of emotions and how they serve humans adaptively in everyday life. Although the continuing popular appeal of emotional intelligence is both warranted and desirable, we hope that such attention will stimulate a greater interest in the scientific and scholarly study of emotion. It is our hope that in coming decades, advances in cognitive and affective science will offer intertwining perspectives from which to study how people navigate their lives. Emotional intelligence, with its focus on both head and heart, may adequately serve to point us in the right direction.

Bibliography

Bechara, A., H. Damasio and A. R. Damasio. 2000. Emotion, decision making and the orbitofrontal cortex. *Cerebral Cortex* 10:295–307.

Brackett, M. A., and J. D. Mayer. 2003. Convergent, discriminant, and incremental validity of competing measures of emotional intelligence. *Personality and Social Psychology Bulletin* 29:1147–1158.

Daniasio, A. R. 1994. *Descartes' Error, Emotion, Reason, and the Human Brain.* New York: Putnam.

Ekman, P. 1980. *The Face of Man: Expressions of Universal Emotions in a New Guinea Village.* New York: Garland STPM Press.

Feldman Barrett, L., J. Gross, T. Christensen and M. Benvenuto. 2001. Knowing what you're feeling and knowing what to do about it: Mapping the relation between emotion differentiation and emotion regulation. *Cognition and Emotion* 15:713–724.

Gardner, H. 1983. *Frames of Mind.* New York: Basic Books.

Goleman, D. 1995. *Emotional Intelligence.* New York: Bantam Books.

Gross, J. J. 1998. Antecedent and response focused emotion regulation: Divergent consequences for experience, expression, and physiology, *Journal of Personality and Social Psychology* 74:224–237.

Isen, A. M., K. A. Daubman and C. P. Nowicki. 1987. Positive affect facilitates creative problem solving. *Journal of Personality and Social Psychology* 52:1122–1131.

Lopes, P. N., M. A. Brackett, J. Nezlck, A. Schutz, I. Sellin and P. Salovey. 2004. Emotional intelligence and social interaction. *Personality and Social Psychology Bulletin* 30:1018–1034.

Lopes, P. N., S. Côté, D. Grewal, J. Kadis, M. Gall and P. Salovey. Submitted. Evidence that emotional intelligence is related to job performance, interpersonal facilitation, affect and attitudes at work, and leadership potential.

Mayer, J. D., and P. Salovey. 1997. What is emotional intelligence? In *Emotional Development and Emotional Intelligence: Educational Implications,* ed. P. Salovey and D. Sluyter, pp. 3–31. New York: Basic Books.

Mayer, J. D., P. Salovey and D. Caruso. 2002. *The Mayer-Salovey-Caruso Emotional Intelligence Test (MSCEIT).* Toronto: Multi-Health Systems, Inc.

Mayer, J. D., P. Salovey, D. R. Caruso and G. Sitarenios. 2003. Measuring emotional intelligence with the MSCEIT V2.0. *Emotion* 3:97–105.

Pollak, S. D., and S. Tolley-Schell. 2003. Selective attention to facial emotion in physically abused children. *Journal of Abnormal Psychology* 22:323–338.

Salovey, P. and J. D. Mayer. 1990. Emotional intelligence. *Imagination, Cognition, and Personality* 9:185–211.

Salovey, P., J. D. Mayer and D. Caruso. 2002. The positive psychology of emotional intelligence. In *Handbook of Positive Psychology,* ed. C. R. Snyder and S. J. Lopez, pp. 159–171. New York: Oxford University Press.

DAISY GREWAL is a doctoral student in the social psychology program at Yale University. She received her B.A. in psychology from the University of California, Los Angeles in 2002 and her M.S. in psychology from Yale in 2004. Her research focuses on gender stereotypes and prejudice, particularly in organizational contexts. **PETER SALOVEY,** who earned his Ph.D. from Yale in 1986, is Dean of Yale College and Chris Argyris Professor of Psychology at Yale, where he directs the Health, Emotion, and Behavior Laboratory and holds additional professorships in management, epidemiology and public health, and social and political studies. His research emphases are the psychological significance and function of mood and emotion, and the application of principles from social and personality psychology to promoting healthy behavior. Address for Salovey: Yale University, Department of Psychology, 2 Hillhouse Avenue, New Haven, CT 06520-8205. Internet for both: daisy.grewal@yale.edu.peter.salovey@yale.edu

Unconscious Emotion

Conscious feelings have traditionally been viewed as a central and necessary ingredient of emotion. Here we argue that emotion also can be genuinely unconscious. We describe evidence that positive and negative reactions can be elicited subliminally and remain inaccessible to introspection. Despite the absence of subjective feelings in such cases, subliminally induced affective reactions still influence people's preference judgments and even the amount of beverage they consume. This evidence is consistent with evolutionary considerations suggesting that systems underlying basic affective reactions originated prior to systems for conscious awareness. The idea of unconscious emotion is also supported by evidence from affective neuroscience indicating that subcortical brain systems underlie basic "liking" reactions. More research is needed to clarify the relations and differences between conscious and unconscious emotion, and their underlying mechanisms. However, even under the current state of knowledge, it appears that processes underlying conscious feelings can become decoupled from processes underlying emotional reactions, resulting in genuinely unconscious emotion.

PIOTR WINKIELMAN AND KENT C. BERRIDGE

To say that people are conscious of their own emotions sounds like a truism. After all, emotions are feelings, so how could one have feelings that are not felt? Of course, people sometimes may be mistaken about the cause of their emotion or may not know why they feel a particular emotion, as when they feel anxious for what seems no particular reason. On occasion, people may even incorrectly construe their own emotional state, as when they angrily deny that they are angry. But many psychologists presume that the emotion itself is intrinsically conscious, and that with proper motivation and attention, it can be brought into the full light of awareness. So, at least, goes the traditional view.

Our view goes a bit further. We suggest that under some conditions an emotional process may remain entirely unconscious, even when the person is attentive and motivated to describe his or her feelings correctly (Berridge & Winkielman, 2003; Winkielman, Berridge, & Wilbarger, in press). Such an emotional process may nevertheless drive the person's behavior and physiological reactions, even while remaining inaccessible to conscious awareness. In short, we propose the existence of genuinely unconscious emotions.

The Traditional View: Emotion as a Conscious Experience

The assumption that emotions are always conscious has been shared by some of the most influential psychologists in history. In his famous article "What Is an Emotion," James (1884) proposed that emotion is a perception of bodily changes. This perception forms a conscious feeling, which is a necessary ingredient of both simple affective states, such as pleasure and pain, and more complex emotions, such as love or pride. Conscious feeling is exactly what distinguishes emotion from other mental states. Without it, "we find that we have nothing left behind, no 'mind-stuff' out of which the emotion can be constituted . . ." (p. 193). For Freud (1950), too, emotions themselves were always conscious, even if their underprlying causes sometimes were not: "It is surely of the essence of an emotion that we should feel it, i.e. that it should enter consciousness" (pp. 109–110).

The assumption that affective reactions are conscious is widely shared in the contemporary literature on emotion. Explaining how most researchers use the term "affect," Frijda (1999) said that the term "primarily refers to hedonic experience, the experience of pleasure and pain" (p. 194). Clore (1994) unequivocally titled one of his essays "Why Emotions Are Never Unconscious" and argued that subjective feeling is a necessary (although not a sufficient) condition for emotion. In short, psychologists past and present generally have agreed that a conscious feeling is a primary or even a necessary ingredient of affect and emotion.

Implicit Emotion and Unconscious Affect

By contrast, it is now widely accepted that cognitive processes and states can be unconscious (occurring below awareness) or implicit (occurring without attention or intention). So, it may not require much of a leap to consider the possibility of uncon-scious or implicit emotion. As Kihlstrom (1999) put it,

> Paralleling the usage of these descriptors in the cognitive unconscious, "explicit emotion" refers to the person's conscious awareness of an emotion, feeling, or mood state; "implicit emotion", by contrast, refers to changes in experience, thought, or action that are attributable to one's emotional state, independent of his or her conscious awareness of that state. (p. 432)

Unconscious Elicitation of Conscious Affective Reactions

Research advances in the past few years challenge the tradi-tional view by demonstrating "unconscious emotion," at least in a limited sense of unconscious causation. Several studies have shown that stimuli presented below awareness can elicit an affective reaction that is itself consciously felt. An example is subliminal induction of the mere-exposure effect, that is, a positive response to repeatedly presented items. In one study, some participants were first subliminally exposed to several repeated neutral stimuli consisting of random visual patterns. Later, those participants reported being in a better mood—a conscious feeling state—than participants who had been sub-liminally exposed to neutral stimuli that had not been repeat-edly presented (Monahan, Murphy, & Zajonc, 2000). In other studies, changes in self-reported mood have been elicited by subliminal presentation of positive or negative images, such as pictures of snakes and spiders presented to phobic individuals (Öhman, Flykt, & Lundqvist, 2000).

But asserting that subliminal stimuli may cause emotion is different from asserting that emotional reactions themselves can ever be unconscious (Berridge & Winkielman, 2003; Kihlstrom, 1999). The research we just mentioned still fits into the con-ventional view that once emotions are caused, they are always conscious. In fact, these studies relied on introspective reports of conscious feelings to demonstrate the presence of emotion once it was unconsciously caused.

So the question remains: Can one be unconscious not only of the causes of emotion, but also of one's own emotional reaction itself—even if that emotional reaction is intense enough to alter one's behavior? Studies from our lab suggest that the answer is yes. Under some conditions, people can have subliminally triggered emotional reactions that drive judgment and behavior, even in the absence of any conscious feelings accompanying these reactions.

Uncorrected and Unremembered Emotional Reactions

In an initial attempt to demonstrate unconscious emotion, a series of studies examined participants' ratings of neutral stim-uli, such as Chinese ideographs, preceded by subliminally pre-sented happy or angry faces (Winkielman, Zajonc, & Schwarz, 1997). Some participants in those studies were asked to monitor changes in their conscious feelings, and told not to use their feelings as a source of their preference ratings. Specifically, experimental instructions informed those participants that their

feelings might be "contaminated" by irrelevant factors, such as hidden pictures (Study 1) or music playing in the background (Study 2). Typically, such instructions eliminate the influence of conscious feelings on evaluative judgments (Clore, 1994). However, even for participants told to disregard their feelings, the subliminally presented happy faces increased and sublimi-nally presented angry faces decreased preference ratings of the neutral stimuli. This failure to correct for invalid feelings indicates that participants might not have experienced any con-scious reactions in the first place. Indeed, after the experiment, participants did not remember experiencing any mood changes when asked about what they had felt during the rating task. Still, memory is not infallible. A skeptic could argue that par-ticipants had conscious feelings immediately after subliminal exposure to emotional faces, but simply failed to remember the feelings later. Thus, it is open to debate whether these studies demonstrate unconscious emotion.

Unconscious Emotional Reactions Strong Enough to Change Behavior

We agreed that stronger evidence was needed. Proof of uncon-scious emotion requires showing that participants are unable to report a conscious feeling at the same time their behavior reveals the presence of an emotional reaction. Ideally, the emotional reaction should be strong enough to change behav-ior with some consequences for the individual. To obtain such evidence, we assessed participants' pouring and drinking of a novel beverage after they were subliminally exposed to several emotional facial expressions (Berridge & Winkielman, 2003; Winkielman et al., in press). Participants were first asked if they were thirsty. Next, they were subliminally exposed to several emotional expressions (happy, neutral, or angry) embedded in a cognitive task requiring participants to classify a clearly visible neutral face as male or female. Immediately afterward, some participants rated their feelings on scales assessing emotional experience and then were given a novel lemon-lime beverage to consume and evaluate. Other participants consumed and evalu-ated the beverage before rating their feelings. Specifically, in Study 1, participants were asked to pour themselves a cup of the beverage from a pitcher and then drink from the cup, whereas in Study 2, participants were asked to take a small sip of the bever-age from a prepared cup and then rate it on various dimensions, including monetary value.

In both studies, conscious feelings were not influenced by subliminal presentation of emotional faces, regardless of whether participants rated their feelings on a simple scale from positive to negative mood or from high to low arousal, or on a multi-item scale asking about specific emotions, such as con-tentment or irritation. That is, participants did not feel more positive after subliminally presented happy expressions than after subliminally presented neutral expressions. Nor did they feel more negative after angry expressions than after neutral expressions. Yet participants' consumption and ratings of the drink were influenced by those subliminal stimuli—especially when participants were thirsty. Specifically, thirsty participants poured significantly more drink from the pitcher and drank more from their cup after happy faces than after angry faces (Study 1). Thirsty participants were also willing to pay about twice as much for the drink after happy than after angry expressions (Study 2). The modulating role of thirst indicates that unconscious emotional reactions acted through basic biopsychological mechanisms that determine reactions to incentives, such as a drink, rather than through cognitive mechanisms influencing interpretation of the stimulus (Berridge & Winkielman, 2003; Winkielman et al., 2002).

In summary, the studies just described show that subliminally presented emotional faces can cause affective reactions that alter consumption behavior, without eliciting conscious feelings at the moment the affective reactions are caused. Because the influence of emotional faces on consumption behavior was observed also for those participants who rated their feelings immediately after the subliminal presentation of the faces, these results cannot be explained by failures of memory. Thus, we propose that these results demonstrate unconscious affect in the strong sense of the term—affect that is powerful enough to alter behavior, but that people are simply not aware of, even when attending to their feelings.

Support From Evolution and Neuroscience

From the standpoint of evolution and neuroscience, there are good reasons to suppose that at least some forms of emotional reaction can exist independently of subjective correlates. Evolutionarily speaking, the ability to have conscious feelings is probably a late achievement compared with the ability to have behavioral affective reactions to emotional stimuli (LeDoux, 1996). Basic affective reactions are widely shared by animals, including reptiles and fish, and at least in some species may not involve conscious awareness comparable to that in humans. The original function of emotion was to allow the organism to react appropriately to positive or negative events, and conscious feelings might not always have been required.

The neurocircuitry needed for basic affective responses, such as a "liking" reaction[1] to a pleasant sensation or a fear reaction to a threatening stimulus, is largely contained in emotional brain structures that lie below the cortex, such as the nucleus accumbens, amygdala, hypothalamus, and even lower brain stem (Berridge, 2003; LeDoux, 1996). These subcortical structures evolved early and may carry out limited operations that are essentially preconscious, compared with the elaborate human cortex at the top of the brain, which is more involved in conscious emotional feelings. Yet even limited subcortical structures on their own are capable of some basic affective reactions. A dramatic demonstration of this point comes from affective neuroscience studies with anencephalic human infants. The brain of such infants is congenitally malformed, possessing only a brain stem, and lacking nearly all structures at the top or front of the brain, including the entire cortex. Yet sweet tastes of sugar still elicit positive facial expressions of liking from anencephalic infants, whereas bitter tastes elicit negative facial expressions of disgust (Steiner, 1973).

Even in normal brains, the most effective "brain tweaks" so far discovered for enhancing liking and related affective reactions all involve deep brain structures below the cortex. Thus, animal studies have shown that liking for sweetness increases after a drug that activates opioid receptors is injected into the nucleus accumbens (a reward-related structure at the base of the front of the brain). Liking reactions to sugar can even be enhanced by injecting a drug that activates other receptors into the brain stem, which is perhaps the most basic component of the brain. Such examples reflect the persisting importance of early-evolved neurocircuitry in generating behavioral emotional reactions in modern mammalian brains (Berridge, 2003; LeDoux, 1996). In short, evidence from affective neuroscience suggests that basic affective reactions are mediated largely by brain structures deep below the cortex, raising the possibility that these reactions might not be intrinsically accessible to conscious awareness.

Key Questions for Future Research

As we have argued, there are good theoretical reasons why some emotional reactions might be unconscious, and we suggest that our recent empirical evidence actually provides an example. However, several critical issues need to be addressed by future research.

The studies discussed here focused only on basic liking-disliking, so it is possible that the crucial property of unconscious emotion is simply positive-negative valence, rather than qualitative distinctions associated with categorical emotion (fear, anger, disgust, joy, etc.). However, evidence suggests that subcortical circuitry may be capable of some qualitative differentiation. For example, human neuroimaging studies reveal differential activation of the amygdala in response to consciously presented facial expressions of fear versus anger (Whalen, 1998). If future research shows that subliminally presented expressions of fear, anger, disgust, and sadness can create qualitatively different physiological and behavioral reactions, all without conscious experience, then there may indeed exist implicit affective processes deserving the label "unconscious emotion" in its strongest sense. Studies that simultaneously measure psychophysiology, behavior, and self-reports of emotion could be particularly useful to address such issues (Winkielman, Berntson, & Cacioppo, 2001).

The studies discussed here employed basic affective stimuli, such as subliminally presented facial expressions, to influence emotional behavior without eliciting conscious feelings. Future studies might address whether more complex stimuli that derive their positive or negative value from a person's cultural environment can also influence emotional behavior without eliciting any accompanying feelings. A related question concerns whether stimuli presented above the threshold of awareness can also change emotional behavior and physiology without influencing feelings.

The studies described here suggest that under some conditions emotional reactions are genuinely unconscious. But obviously many emotional states are conscious, even when elicited with subliminal stimuli (Monahan et al., 2000; Öhman et al., 2000). What determines when a basic emotional reaction is accompanied by conscious feelings? Is it possible for even a strong emotional reaction to be unconscious? What are the neural mechanisms by which emotion is made conscious? How do behavioral consequences of conscious and unconscious reactions differ?

Finally, a question of practical importance to many emotion researchers, as well as clinicians, concerns the meaning of people's reports of their own emotions. The existence of verifiable but unconscious emotional reactions does not mean that subjective feelings are merely "icing on the emotional cake." At least, that is not our view. We believe that self-reports of feelings have a major place in emotion research and treatment. However, it is also clear that psychologists should not limit themselves to subjective experiences. A combination of approaches and techniques, from psychology and human and animal affective neuroscience, will best lead to understanding the relation between conscious and unconscious emotions.

Note

1. We use the term "liking" to indicate an unconscious reaction, not a conscious feeling of pleasure.

References

Berridge, K. C. (2003). Pleasures of the brain. *Brain and Cognition, 52,* 106–128.

Berridge, K. C., & Winkielman, P. (2003). What is an unconscious emotion: The case for unconscious 'liking.' *Cognition and Emotion, 17,* 181–211.

Clore, G. L. (1994). Why emotions are never unconscious. In P. Ekman & R.J. Davidson (Eds.), *The nature of emotion: Fundamental questions* (pp. 285–290). New York: Oxford University Press.

Freud, S. (1950). *Collected papers,* Vol. 4 (J. Riviere, Trans.). London: Hogarth Press and Institute of Psychoanalysis.

Frijda, N. H. (1999). Emotions and hedonic experience. In D. Kahneman, E. Diener, & N. Schwarz (Eds.), *Well-being: The foundations of hedonic psychology* (pp. 190–210). New York: Russell Sage Foundation.

James, W. (1884). What is an emotion. *Mind, 9,* 188–205.

Kihlstrom, J. F. (1999). The psychological unconscious. In L.A. Pervin & O. P. John (Eds.), *Handbook of personality: Theory and research* (2nd ed., pp. 424–442). New York: Guilford Press.

LeDoux, J. (1996). *The emotional brain: The mysterious underpinnings of emotional life.* New York: Simon & Schuster.

Monahan, J. L., Murphy, S. T., & Zajonc, R. B. (2000). Subliminal mere exposure: Specific, general, and diffuse effects. *Psychological Science, 11,* 462–466.

Öhman, A., Flykt, A., & Lundqvist, D. (2000). Unconscious emotion: Evolutionary perspectives, psychophysiological data and neuropsychological mechanisms. In R. D. Lane, L. Nadel, & G. Ahern (Eds.), *Cognitive neuroscience of emotion* (pp. 296–327). New York: Oxford University Press.

Steiner, J. E. (1973). The gustofacial response: Observation on normal and anencephalic newborn infants. *Symposium on Oral Sensation and Perception, 4,* 254–278.

Whalen, P. J. (1998). Fear, vigilance, and ambiguity: Initial neuroimaging studies of the human amygdala. *Current Directions in Psychological Science, 7,* 177–188.

Winkielman, P., Berntson, G. G., & Cacioppo, J. T. (2001). The psychophysiological perspective on the social mind. In A. Tesser & N. Schwarz (Eds.), *Blackwell handbook of social psychology: Intraindividual processes* (pp. 89–108). Oxford, England: Blackwell.

Winkielman, P., Berridge, K. C., & Wilbarger, J. (in press). Unconscious affective reactions to masked happy versus angry faces influence consumption behavior and judgments of value. *Personality and Social Psychology Bulletin.*

Winkielman, P., Zajonc, R. B., & Schwarz, N. (1997). Subliminal affective priming resists attributional interventions. *Cognition and Emotion, 11,* 433–465.

PIOTR WINKIELMAN, University of California, San Diego, and **KENT C. BERRIDGE,** University of Michigan.

Ambition: Why Some People Are Most Likely to Succeed

A fire in the belly doesn't light itself. Does the spark of ambition lie in genes, family, culture—or even in your own hands? Science has answers.

JEFFREY KLUGER

You don't get as successful as Gregg Anddrew Shipp by accident. Shake hands with the 36-year-old fraternal twins who co-own the sprawling Hi Fi Personal Fitness club in Chicago, and it's clear you're in the presence of people who thrive on their drive. But that wasn't always the case. The twins' father founded the Jovan perfume company, a glamorous business that spun off the kinds of glamorous profits that made it possible for the Shipps to amble through high school, coast into college and never much worry about getting the rent paid or keeping the fridge filled. But before they graduated, their sense of drift began to trouble them. At about the same time, their father sold off the company, and with it went the cozy billets in adult life that had always served as an emotional backstop for the boys.

That did it. By the time they got out of school, both Shipps had entirely transformed themselves, changing from boys who might have grown up to live off the family's wealth to men consumed with going out and creating their own. "At this point," says Gregg, "I consider myself to be almost maniacally ambitious."

It shows. In 1998 the brothers went into the gym trade. They spotted a modest health club doing a modest business, bought out the owner and transformed the place into a luxury facility where private trainers could reserve space for top-dollar clients. In the years since, the company has outgrown one building, then another, and the brothers are about to move a third time. Gregg, a communications major at college, manages the club's clients, while Drew, a business major, oversees the more hardheaded chore of finance and expansion. "We're not sitting still," Drew says. "Even now that we're doing twice the business we did at our old place, there's a thirst that needs to be quenched."

Why is that? Why are some people born with a fire in the belly, while others—like the Shipps—need something to get

their pilot light lit? And why do others never get the flame of ambition going? Is there a family anywhere that doesn't have its overachievers and underachievers—its Jimmy Carters and Billy Carters, its Jeb Bushes and Neil Bushes—and find itself wondering how they all could have come splashing out of exactly the same gene pool?

Of all the impulses in humanity's behavioral portfolio, ambition—that need to grab an ever bigger piece of the resource pie before someone else gets it—ought to be one of the most democratically distributed. Nature is a zero-sum game, after all. Every buffalo you kill for your family is one less for somebody else's; every acre of land you occupy elbows out somebody else. Given that, the need to get ahead ought to be hard-wired into all of us equally.

"For me, ambition has become a dirty word. I prefer hunger."

—Johnny Depp

And yet it's not. For every person consumed with the need to achieve, there's someone content to accept whatever life brings. For everyone who chooses the 80-hour workweek, there's someone punching out at 5. Men and women—so it's said—express ambition differently; so do Americans and Europeans, baby boomers and Gen Xers, the middle class and the well-to-do. Even among the manifestly motivated, there are degrees of ambition. Steve Wozniak co-founded Apple Computer and then left the company in 1985 as a 34-year-old multimillionaire. His partner, Steve Jobs, is still innovating at Apple and moonlighting at his second block-buster company, Pixar Animation Studios.

Not only do we struggle to understand why some people seem to have more ambition than others, but we can't even agree on just what ambition is. "Ambition is an evolutionary product," says anthropologist Edward Lowe at Soka University of America, in Aliso Viejo, Calif. "No matter how social status is defined, there are certain people in every community who aggressively pursue it and others who aren't so aggressive."

Dean Simonton, a psychologist at the University of California, Davis, who studies genius, creativity and eccentricity, believes it's more complicated than that. "Ambition is energy and determination," he says. "But it calls for goals too. People with goals but no energy are the ones who wind up sitting on the couch saying 'One day I'm going to build a better mousetrap.' People with energy but no clear goals just dissipate themselves in one desultory project after the next."

"Ambition is like love, impatient both of delays and rivals."

—Buddah

Assuming you've got drive, dreams and skill, is all ambition equal? Is the overworked lawyer on the partner track any more ambitious than the overworked parent on the mommy track? Is the successful musician to whom melody comes naturally more driven than the unsuccessful one who sweats out every note? We may listen to Mozart, but should we applaud Salieri?

Most troubling of all, what about when enough ambition becomes way too much? Grand dreams unmoored from morals are the stuff of tyrants—or at least of Enron. The 16-hour workday filled with high stress and at-the-desk meals is the stuff of burnout and heart attacks. Even among kids, too much ambition quickly starts to do real harm. In a just completed study, anthropologist Peter Demerath of Ohio State University surveyed 600 students at a high-achieving high school where most of the kids are triple-booked with advanced-placement courses, sports and after-school jobs. About 70% of them reported that they were starting to feel stress some or all of the time. "I asked one boy how his parents react to his workload, and he answered, 'I don't really get home that often,'" says Demerath. "Then he handed me his business card from the video store where he works."

Anthropologists, psychologists and others have begun looking more closely at these issues, seeking the roots of ambition in family, culture, gender, genes and more. They have by no means thrown the curtain all the way back, but they have begun to part it. "It's fundamentally human to be prestige conscious," says Soka's Lowe. "It's not enough just to be fed and housed. People want more."

If humans are an ambitious species, it's clear we're not the only one. Many animals are known to signal their ambitious tendencies almost from birth. Even before wolf pups are weaned, they begin sorting themselves out into alphas and all the others. The alphas are quicker, more curious, greedier for space, milk, Mom—and they stay that way for life. Alpha wolves wander widely, breed annually and may live to a geriatric 10 or 11 years old. Lower-ranking wolves enjoy none of these benefits—staying close to home, breeding rarely and usually dying before they're 4.

Humans often report the same kind of temperamental determinism. Families are full of stories of the inexhaustible infant who grew up to be an entrepreneur, the phlegmatic child who never really showed much go. But if it's genes that run the show, what accounts for the Shipps, who didn't bestir themselves until the cusp of adulthood? And what, more tellingly, explains identical twins—precise genetic templates of each other who ought to be temperamentally identical but often exhibit profound differences in the octane of their ambition?

Ongoing studies of identical twins have measured achievement motivation—lab language for ambition—in identical siblings separated at birth, and found that each twin's profile overlaps 30% to 50% of the other's. In genetic terms, that's an awful lot—"a benchmark for heritability," says geneticist Dean Hamer of the National Cancer Institute. But that still leaves a great deal that can be determined by experiences in infancy, subsequent upbringing and countless other imponderables.

Some of those variables may be found by studying the function of the brain. At Washington University, researchers have been conducting brain imaging to investigate a trait they call persistence—the ability to stay focused on a task until it's completed just so—which they consider one of the critical engines driving ambition.

The researchers recruited a sample group of students and gave each a questionnaire designed to measure persistence level. Then they presented the students with a task—identifying sets of pictures as either pleasant or unpleasant and taken either indoors or outdoors—while conducting magnetic resonance imaging of their brains. The nature of the task was unimportant, but how strongly the subjects felt about performing it well—and where in the brain that feeling was processed—could say a lot. In general, the researchers found that students who scored highest in persistence had the greatest activity in the limbic region, the area of the brain related to emotions and habits. "The correlation was .8 [or 80%]," says professor of psychiatry Robert Cloninger, one of the investigators. "That's as good as you can get."

It's impossible to say whether innate differences in the brain were driving the ambitious behavior or whether learned behavior was causing the limbic to light up. But a number of researchers believe it's possible for the nonambitious to jump-start their drive, provided the right jolt comes along. "Energy level may be genetic," says psychologist Simonton, "but a lot of times it's just." Simonton and others often cite the case of Franklin D. Roosevelt, who might not have been the same President he became—or even become President at all—had his disabling polio not taught him valuable lessons about patience and tenacity.

I s such an epiphany possible for all of us, or are some people immune to this kind of lightning? Are there individuals or whole groups for whom the amplitude of ambition is simply lower than it is for others? It's a question—sometimes a charge—that hangs at the edges of all discussions about gender and work, about whether women really have the meat-eating temperament to survive in the professional world. Both research findings and everyday experience suggest that women's ambitions express themselves differently from men's. The meaning of that difference is the hinge on which the arguments turn.

"Ambition makes you look pretty ugly."

—Radiohead

Economists Lise Vesterlund of the University of Pittsburgh and Muriel Niederle of Stanford University conducted a study in which they assembled 40 men and 40 women, gave them five minutes to add up as many two-digit numbers as they could, and paid them 50¢ for each correct answer. The subjects were not competing against one another but simply playing against the house. Later, the game was changed to a tournament in which the subjects were divided into teams of two men or two women each. Winning teams got $2 per computation; losers got nothing. Men and women performed equally in both tests, but on the third round, when asked to choose which of the two ways they wanted to play, only 35% of the women opted for the tournament format; 75% of the men did.

"Men and women just differ in their appetite for competition," says Vesterlund. "There seems to be a dislike for it among women and a preference among men."

"Ambition, old mankind, the immemorial weakness of the strong."

—Vita Sackville-West

To old-line employers of the old-boy school, this sounds like just one more reason to keep the glass ceiling polished. But other behavioral experts think Vesterlund's conclusions

go too far. They say it's not that women aren't ambitious enough to compete for what they want; it's that they're more selective about when they engage in competition; they're willing to get ahead at high cost but not at any cost. "Primate-wide, males are more directly competitive than females, and that makes sense," says Sarah Blaffer Hrdy, emeritus professor of anthropology at the University of California, Davis. "But that's not the same as saying women aren't innately competitive too."

As with so much viewed through the lens of anthropology, the roots of these differences lie in animal and human mating strategies. Males are built to go for quick, competitive reproductive hits and move on. Women are built for the it-takes-a-village life, in which they provide long-term care to a very few young and must sail them safely into an often hostile world. Among some of our evolutionary kin—baboons, macaques and other old-world monkeys—this can be especially tricky since young females inherit their mother's social rank. The mothers must thus operate the levers of society deftly so as to raise both their own position and, eventually, their daughters'. If you think that kind of ambition-by-proxy doesn't translate to humans, Hrdy argues, think again. "Just read an Edith Wharton novel about women in old New York competing for marriage potential for their daughters," she says.

Import such tendencies into the 21st century workplace, and you get women who are plenty able to compete ferociously but are inclined to do it in teams and to split the difference if they don't get everything they want. And mothers who appear to be unwilling to strive and quit the workplace altogether to go raise their kids? Hrdy believes they're competing for the most enduring stakes of all, putting aside their near-term goals to ensure the long-term success of their line. Robin Parker, 46, a campaign organizer who in 1980 was already on the presidential stump with Senator Edward Kennedy, was precisely the kind of lifetime pol who one day finds herself in the West Wing. But in 1992, at the very moment a President of her party was returning to the White House and she might have snagged a plum Washington job, she decamped from the capital, moved to Boston with her family and became a full-time mom to her two sons.

"Being out in the world became a lot less important to me," she says. "I used to worry about getting Presidents elected, and I'm still an incredibly ambitious person. But what I want to succeed at now is managing my family, raising my boys, helping my husband and the community. In 10 years, when the boys are launched, who knows what I'll be doing? But for now, I have my world."

But even if something as primal as the reproductive impulse wires you one way, it's possible for other things to rewire you completely. Two of the biggest influences on your level of ambition are the family that produced you and the culture that produced your family.

Donald Trump
Achievements
Before he ever uttered the words "You're fired," Trump developed more than 18 million sq. ft. of Manhattan real estate, naming most of it after himself.
Early Signs of Ambition
While in college, Donald read federal foreclosure listings for fun. It paid off: he bought his first housing project before he graduated.

Bill Clinton
Achievements
Former U.S. President, current global celebrity.
Early Signs of Ambition
At 16, he beat out some 1,000 other boys to win a mock state senate seat and a trip to Washington, where he knew "the action was." Once in the capital, he got himself into position to shake hands with his idol, President John F. Kennedy.

Oprah Winfrey
Achievements
Her $1 billion media empire includes movies, a magazine and her talk show, now in its 20th year.
Early Signs of Ambition
She could read at 2, and although she was just 5 when she started school, she insisted on being put in first grade. Her teacher relented. The next year young Oprah was skipped to third grade.

Tiger Woods
Achievements
At 21, he was the youngest golfer ever ranked No. 1 in the world. Now 29, he holds the record for most prize money won in a career—$56 million and counting.
Early Signs of Ambition
At 6, he listened to motivational tapes—"I will make my own destiny"—while practicing his swing in the mirror.

Martha Stewart
Achievements
The lifestyle guru rules an empire that includes one magazine, two TV shows, a satellite-radio deal, a shelf full of best sellers and a home-furnishings line at Kmart.
Early Signs of Ambition
As a grade-schooler, she organized and catered neighborhood birthday parties because, she says, the going rate of 50¢ an hr. for babysitting "wasn't quite enough money."

Vera Wang
Achievements
She turned one-of-a-kind wedding gowns into a $300 million fashion business.
Early Signs of Ambition
Although from a wealthy family, she spent her high school summers working as a sales clerk in a Manhattan boutique.

After college, she landed a job at *Vogue* magazine, where she put in seven-day workweeks, rose quickly and became a senior editor at 23.

Condoleezza Rice
Achievements
The current Secretary of State and former National Security Adviser was 38 when she became Stanford University's youngest, and first female, provost.
Early Signs of Ambition
A gifted child pianist who began studying at the Birmingham Conservatory at 10, the straight-A student became a competitive ice skater, rising at 4:30 A.M. to spend two hours at the rink before school and piano lessons.

Sean Combs
Achievements
Diddy, as he's now known, is a Grammy-winning performer and producer and a millionaire businessman with a restaurant, a clothing line and a marketing and ad agency.
Early Signs of Ambition
During his days at Howard University, he learned about business by doing: he sold term papers and tickets to dance parties he hosted.

Jennifer Lopez
Achievements
The former Fly Girl dancer has sold 40 million records, is the highest-paid Latina actress in Hollywood and has launched fashion and perfume lines.
Early Signs of Ambition
When she signed with Sony Music, she insisted on dealing with its chief, Tommy Mottola. She told him she wanted "the A treatment. I want everything top of the line."

Britney Spears
Achievements
Her first single and first four albums made their debut at No. 1. Since then she has sold 76 million records and amassed a $150 million fortune.
Early Signs of Ambition
Spears used to lock herself in the bathroom and sing to her dolls. After each number, she practiced smiling and blowing kisses to her toy audience.

Tom Cruise
Achievements
He's a movie superstar who gets $25 million a film, an accomplished actor with three Oscar nods and a gossip staple who has sold a zillion magazines.
Early Signs of Ambition
After his first role in a high school musical, he asked his family to give him 10 years to make it in show business. Within four, he was starring in the surprise hit film *Risky Business.*

There are no hard rules for the kinds of families that turn out the highest achievers. Most psychologists agree that parents who set tough but realistic challenges, applaud successes and go easy on failures produce kids with the greatest self-confidence.

What's harder for parents to control but has perhaps as great an effect is the level of privilege into which their kids are born. Just how wealth or poverty influences drive is difficult to predict. Grow up in a rich family, and you can inherit either the tools to achieve (think both Presidents Bush) or the indolence of the aristocrat. Grow up poor, and you can come away with either the motivation to strive (think Bill Clinton) or the inertia of the hopeless. On the whole, studies suggest it's the upper middle class that produces the greatest proportion of ambitious people—mostly because it also produces the greatest proportion of anxious people.

When measuring ambition, anthropologists divide families into four categories: poor, struggling but getting by, upper middle class, and rich. For members of the first two groups, who are fighting just to keep the electricity on and the phone bill paid, ambition is often a luxury. For the rich, it's often unnecessary. It's members of the upper middle class, reasonably safe economically but not so safe that a bad break couldn't spell catastrophe, who are most driven to improve their lot. "It's called status anxiety," says anthropologist Lowe, "and whether you're born to be concerned about it or not, you do develop it."

> **"Ambition is so powerful a passion in the human breast that however high we reach, we are never satisfied."**
>
> —Niccolo Machiavelli

But some societies make you more anxious than others. The U.S. has always been a me-first culture, as befits a nation that grew from a scattering of people on a fat saddle of continent where land was often given away. That have-it-all ethos persists today, even though the resource freebies are long since gone. Other countries—where the acreage is smaller and the pickings are slimmer—came of age differently, with the need to cooperate getting etched into the cultural DNA. The American model has produced wealth, but it has come at a price—with ambition sometimes turning back on the ambitious and consuming them whole.

The study of high-achieving high school students conducted by Ohio State's Demerath was noteworthy for more than the stress he found the students were suffering. It also revealed the lengths to which the kids and their parents were willing to go to gain an advantage over other suffering students. Cheating was common, and most students shrugged it off as only a minor problem. A number of parents—some of whose children carried a 4.0 average—sought to have their kids classified as special-education students, which would entitle them to extra time on standardized tests. "Kids develop their own moral code," says Demerath. "They have a keen sense of competing with others and are developing identities geared to that."

Demerath got very different results when he conducted research in a very different place—Papua, New Guinea. In the mid-1990s, he spent a year in a small village there, observing how the children learned. Usually, he found, they saw school as a noncompetitive place where it was important to succeed collectively and then move on. Succeeding at the expense of others was seen as a form of vanity that the New Guineans call "acting extra." Says Demerath: "This is an odd thing for them."

That makes tactical sense. In a country based on farming and fishing, you need to know that if you get sick and can't work your field or cast your net, someone else will do it for you. Putting on airs in the classroom is not the way to ensure that will happen.

Of course, once a collectivist not always a collectivist. Marcelo Suárez-Orozco, a professor of globalization and education at New York University, has been following 400 families that immigrated to the U.S. from Asia, Latin America and the Caribbean. Many hailed from villages where the American culture of competition is alien, but once they got here, they changed fast.

As a group, the immigrant children in his study are outperforming their U.S.-born peers. What's more, the adults are dramatically outperforming the immigrant families that came before them. "One hundred years ago, it took people two to three generations to achieve a middle-class standard of living," says Suárez-Orozco. "Today they're getting there within a generation."

So this is a good thing, right? Striving people come here to succeed—and do. While there are plenty of benefits that undeniably come with learning the ways of ambition, there are plenty of perils too—many a lot uglier than high school students cheating on the trig final.

Human history has always been writ in the blood of broken alliances, palace purges and strong people or nations beating up on weak ones—all in the service of someone's hunger for power There's a point at which you find an interesting kind of nerve circuitry between optimism and hubris," says Warren Bennis, a professor of business administration at the University of Southern California and the author of three books on leadership. "It becomes an arrogance or conceit, an inability to live without power."

While most ambitious people keep their secret Caesar tucked safely away, it can emerge surprisingly, even suddenly. Says Frans de Waal, a primatologist at the Yerkes Primate Center in Atlanta and the author of a new book, Our Inner Ape: "You can have a male chimp that is the most laidback character, but one day he sees the chance to overthrow the leader and becomes a totally different male. I would say 90% of people would behave this way too. On an island with three people, they might become a little dictator."

But a yearning for supremacy can create its own set of problems. Heart attacks, ulcers and other stress-related ills are more common among high achievers—and that includes nonhuman achievers. The blood of alpha wolves routinely shows elevated levels of cortisol, the same stress hormone that is found in anxious humans. Alpha chimps even suffer ulcers and occasional heart attacks.

For these reasons, people and animals who have an appetite for becoming an alpha often settle contentedly into life as a beta. "The desire to be in a high position is universal," says de Waal. "But that trait has co-evolved with another skill—the skill to make the best of lower positions."

Humans not only make peace with their beta roles but they also make money from them. Among corporations, an increasingly well-rewarded portion of the workforce is made up of B players, managers and professionals somewhere below the top tier. They don't do the power lunching and ribbon cutting but instead perform the highly skilled, everyday work of making the company run. As skeptical shareholders look ever more askance at overpaid corporate A-listers, the B players are becoming more highly valued. It's an adaptation that serves the needs of both the corporation and the culture around it. "Everyone has ambition," says Lowe. "Societies have to provide alternative ways for people to achieve."

Ultimately, it's that very flexibility—that multiplicity of possible rewards—that makes dreaming big dreams and pursuing big goals worth all the bother. Ambition is an expensive impulse, one that requires an enormous investment of emotional capital. Like any investment, it can pay off in countless different kinds of coin. The trick, as any good speculator will tell you, is recognizing the riches when they come your way.

Eating into the Nation's Obesity Epidemic

ANN CONKLE

"What product does the slogan 'Melts in your mouth, not in your hand' belong to?" Kelly Brownell challenged his listeners. They chuckled and shouted in unison "M&Ms." The audience hadn't expected a pop quiz when coming to hear Brownell's invited address, "Changing the American Diet: Real Change Requires Real Change," at the APS 18th Annual Convention. Next came "They're Grrreat!," "I'm lovin' it," "Break me off a piece of that . . . ," and finally "I go cuckoo for . . ." Of course, the audience knew every one. But they couldn't answer one question, what departments create the federal government's nutrition guidelines and, most importantly, what are they? "Well," answered Brownell, an APS Fellow from Yale University, "The real question is who has done your nutrition education? And most startlingly, who will do the nutrition education of your children? There's no question that the answer is the food industry."

With that, Brownell, who is among this year's *Time* 100, a list of people whose actions and ideas influence the world, began his introduction into the reality of nutrition in America. As the quiz shows, "little effort goes in on the government's part to show people how to eat in a healthy way." Meanwhile the food industry bombards us with messages about cheap, tasty processed foods, which are, of course, high in sugars and fats. People are broadly trained that fruits and vegetables are good for them, but many Americans also believe sugary cereals are part of a nutritious breakfast and any drink with fruit in its name is healthy.

Over the last few decades, America has experienced an "absolutely startling increase [in obesity]. Pandemic or epidemic is not overstating the situation." Some see this as a failure of personal responsibility, but evidence suggests that something larger in the environment is spurring this trend. There is no evidence to suggest that we are less responsible eaters than our grandparents. Studies of developing nations show that when packaged foods such as soft drinks and snack foods replace traditional diets, obesity increases. The obesity epidemic could feasibly have a genetic or biological basis, but then why has it happened so quickly and recently when the gene pool has not changed? Recent studies about the economy of food give some insight into the food landscape. Five factors influence food choice: accessibility, convenience, taste, promotion and cost. Unhealthy foods win out on all five. They are more accessible, more convenient, tastier, more heavily promoted and cheaper. No wonder we all eat so badly.

What Psychological Scientists Can Do

So, what roles can psychology play to alleviate this crisis? Many people jump to say that psychology could help with clinical interventions of the already obese, but sadly, the only treatment with impressive results for obesity is surgery, which is too costly and invasive to be a viable solution for treating the vast number of obese people in America today. Clinical treatments also ignore the larger public health issue. According to Brownell, treating obesity without looking at the broader health issues would be like treating lung cancer without addressing the fact that smoking causes lung cancer. "For every case we successfully treat," said Brownell, "thousands more are created because of the environment." According to him, a social movement against unhealthy eating, similar to the movement against tobacco, is the only way to improve the way America eats.

To be effective, psychologists must change their thinking and make novel connections with people outside their field. Researchers should also realize that they may have more influence than politicians because they are not caught in political messiness (some would say quagmire) between the government, the food industry, subsidies and giant agribusiness.

Brownell outlined several key research questions that psychologists will be instrumental in answering. In a broad sense, psychologists can investigate the behavioral economics of food—why do people make the eating decisions that they do?

Psychologists should investigate attitudes about food supply and processing. Over the last several decades, there was an increasing distance from food sources to our tables. Food moved from coming from the ground or an animal to coming from the super market or vending machine and is now often filled with ingredients whose names we can't pronounce and whose chemical effects are not completely understood. How does this affect consumption and health? In addition, Americans seem to have an ingrained "more for less is good" value when it comes to food, as has been dramatically exploited by the "supersize it" marketing campaigns at fast food restaurants and ballooning portion sizes (Super Big Gulp, anyone?). The quest for value clearly affects what and how much we eat.

A related issue is marketing. How does promotion affect food choice, particularly among children? As shown by the quiz at the beginning of the talk, food marketing is highly effective. We all know the jingles and take them with us all the way to the supermarket aisle. Brownell asks whether we can equate the food industry's kid friendly advertising (Ronald McDonald, Tony the Tiger, Toucan Sam, and others) to the cigarette industries' now infamous advertising campaigns aimed at children. This advertising could have life-long impacts on food choice.

Finally, can food be addictive? Clearly, most severely obese individuals have a toxic relationship with food. What causes the cravings and the inability to stop when one has gone from nourishing her or his body to killing it? How can this cycle be stopped? What about food enhanced with sweeteners? High fructose corn syrup may be metabolized differently than other foods, creating unforeseen effects on bodies as well as minds. Addiction research could change the whole political landscape by changing how we think about eating as a simple choice.

Brownell offered a challenge to the audience and the broader public with five action steps: foster a social movement for nutrition, emphasize strategic science, target frequent contributors to obesity (starting with soft drinks), transform the economics of food, and pressure politicians to change the way Americans are educated about nutrition. Maybe then we would know the answers to all the questions in Brownell's pop quiz.

UNIT 7

Development

Unit Selections

Key Points to Consider

- Why do psychologists study human development?

- Can infants learn?

- What is plasticity and why is it important over the lifespan?

- What is resilience in children? Why do some children develop resilience while others don't?

- Do adolescents spend too much time on computers and cell phones? What can their behavior using these various media tell psychologists about them?

- What is Alzheimer's disease? Why is it so debilitating? Are there various forms of this disorder? Is there any treatment available?

- Is the United States a death-denying society? What is the best way to interact with someone who has recently experienced an important death?

Student Web Site

www.mhcls.com/online

Internet References

Further information regarding these Web sites may be found in this book's preface or online.

American Association for Child and Adolescent Psychiatry
http://www.aacap.org
Behavioral Genetics
http://www.ornl.gov/hgmis/elsi/behavior.html

The Garcias and the Szubas are parents of newborns. When the babies are not in their mothers' rooms, both sets of parents wander down to the hospital's neonatal nursery where pediatric nurses care for both babies—José Garcia and Kimberly Szuba. Kimberly is alert, active, and often crying and squirming when her parents watch her. On the other hand, José is quiet, often asleep, and less attentive to external commotion when his parents monitor him in the nursery.

Why are these babies so different? Are the differences gender-related? Will these differences disappear as the children develop, or will they become exaggerated? What does the future hold for each child? Will Kimberly excel at sports and José excel at art? Can Kimberly overcome her parents' poverty and succeed in a professional career? Will José become a doctor like his mother or a pharmacist as is his father? Will both of these children escape childhood disease, maltreatment, and the other misfortunes sometimes visited upon American children?

Developmental psychologists are concerned with all of the Kimberlys and Josés of our world. Developmental psychologists study age-related changes in language, motoric and social skills, cognition, and physical health. Developmental psychologists are interested in the common skills shared by all children, as well as the differences between children and the events that create these differences.

In general, developmental psychologists are concerned with the forces that guide and direct development. Some developmental theorists argue that the forces that shape a child are found in the environment, in such factors as social class, quality of available stimulation, parenting style, and so on. Other theorists insist that genetics and related physiological factors such as hormones underlie the development of humans. A third set of psychologists, in fact many psychologists, believe that some combination or interaction of all these factors, physiology and environment or nature and nurture, are responsible for development.

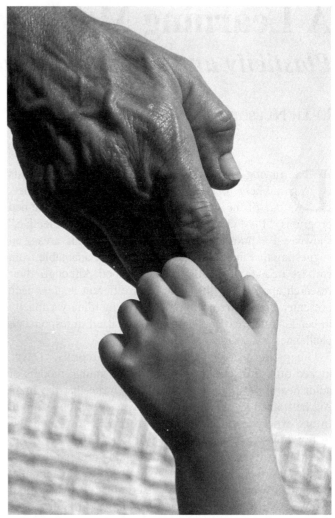

Photodisc

A Learning Machine
Plasticity and Change Throughout Life

LEAH NELSON

Drawing together five psychological scientists unlikely to cross paths outside of a conference, one of the APS 18th Annual Convention's themed programs, "Plasticity & Change: A Lifelong Perspective," showcased extraordinary research from various areas, all suggesting that the brain is almost infinitely adaptable from earliest infancy through latest adulthood Although their research approached the topic from different angles, each presenter demonstrated the brain's extraordinary capacity to bend, stretch, expand, and specialize itself in response to challenges.

Gregg Recanzone, University of California, Davis, kicked off the discussion with a talk on animal models of adult neural plasticity. His findings indicate that the brain can be trained to increase its sensitivity to various stimuli. In one experiment, Recanzone exposed adult owl monkeys to two tones and decreasing the difference between them over time. After several weeks of training at this relatively simple task, their auditory sensitivity sharpened to a point at which they were able to easily discriminate between tones that were indistinguishable at the beginning of training. This increased sensitivity, Recanzone found, corresponded with a functional reorganization of the cerebral cortex—meaning that the activity of large populations of neurons in the monkeys' brains adapted. This evidence of plasticity in animal subjects' brains, Recanzone said, suggests that long-term levels of performance may be related to changes in neural activity.

Purposes of Plasticity

As a "learning machine," said the next presenter, Michael Merzenich of the University of California at San Francisco, the brain "has the incredible task . . . of recapitulating what we've learned in the history of our species." Merzenich has recently been researching plasticity among the elderly. Adult brains, he said, use plasticity for "purposeful" reasons, based on specific needs. For example, a professional musician might find it useful to train her brain to recognize absolute pitches, while a mechanic's brain would be better served by expanding its sensitivity to the precise differences among types of rumbles from a troubled car's insides. In contrast, during the "critical period" of childhood, the brain experiences "anything-goes plasticity," adapting itself to sort and interpret a huge variety of incoming data from the world. As individuals master major skill sets, massive cortical changes occur, said Merzenich. It is only after the development of *selective attention control*—the ability to sort and focus on preferred input—that plasticity shifts into a more purpose-driven, adult mode.

Like the adult monkeys' brain in Recanzone's experiment, the adult human brain can be trained to accommodate new skills. Merzenich said that his research is about "shaping the machinery of your brain . . . to develop the capacities of your life." As people grow older, he said, their brains become "noisier" because they are filled with more information, the management of which causes them to slow down. Increased noise degrades brains' learning-control machinery. But these changes are reversible, Merzenich said. In one experiment, he used adaptive computer games to rejuvenate the learning machinery of elderly subjects. His findings are striking: Through auditory training, people between the ages of 70 and 95 were able to recover the cortical plasticity of people 10 to 15 years younger than they. Visual training resulted in increased plasticity equivalent to that of brains 25 years younger. Countering conventional wisdom, which says that brains simply slow down with age, Merzenich said that it is "very easy to change cortical dynamics by training."

The Logic of Imagination

Merzenich focused on the elderly; Alison Gopnik of the University of California, Berkeley talked about plasticity in children's brains. In "The Logic of Imagination: How Children Change the World," she offered insight on the potential connection between children's imaginative capacity and the patterns of human evolution. "Everything in the environment we live in now was completely imaginary at one point in time," she said. "The deepest part of our human nature is that we are trying to escape human nature."

Evolution, Gopnik said, requires that we discover new things about how the world works and use this knowledge to imagine new things, to change the world based on our imaginings. Cognitive stretches are made possible by the brain's ability to create abstract representations of the world, imagine things that don't exist yet in those representations, and build them. Our ability to develop coherent theories about how things work—or might work—is what allows us to turn imagined worlds into real ones. Gopnik proposed that young children behave like scientists exploring the world for the first time: making predictions, testing them, comparing data, and forming new theories. She discussed an experiment in which young subjects were encouraged to hypothesize about the nature of an object that seemed to respond to both physical stimuli and vocal requests. Based on their knowledge of the world, the children all assumed initially that the object could not respond to their vocal commands. When it appeared to do just that, the children were able to override their assumptions and theorize that the object did in fact understand them. "Children do seem to begin with assumptions about how the world works, but can very rapidly use data to learn," Gopnik said. "Children are able to use this powerful computational machinery to imagine new things in the world, and they can use that new information to do new things in the world. . . . What children are doing is discovering new things about the world, and later on using that machinery to change the world." Like little scientists—and like every human who has ever imagined and invented anything new—children hypothesize, experiment, and make changes based on new data. Their ability to reshape their assumptions according to reality and then reshape reality based on their imaginings reflects the course of human evolution as a whole. It is the capacity for plasticity that makes it possible for children to learn and for the species to evolve, build, change, and grow.

Controlling Desires

In "Delay of Gratification Over Time: Mechanisms and Developmental Implications," Columbia University's Walter Mischel discussed another outcome of imaginative ability. With temptations of every kind constantly surrounding us, he asked, how do we learn to delay gratification? He proposed that the brain can conceive of two representations of every object—a "cool" representation of its abstract aspects and a "hot" representation of its rewarding traits. Anticipatory responses, such as salivation at the thought of delicious food, are "hot." Delayed gratification, said Mischel, an APS Fellow, is possible because we can also conceive of that same food in abstract terms—as fattening, for example, or likely to give us a stomachache.

From birth, children want instant gratification. But by stretching their brains to encompass abstract concepts and counterfactuals, they are able to train themselves to control their desires. "What's important is what kids are doing in their heads," Mischel explained. He described an experiment in which children were shown a real cake and a picture of a cake. When he told the children to imagine that the real cake was only a picture, they reported "cool" reactions and a decreased desire to eat the dessert. When the children were asked to imagine that the picture was a real cake, they had "hot" reactions even though they knew the cake wasn't really there. The degree of a child's power to delay gratification at an early age is a good predictor of later coping ability. Early delay skills protect against later vulnerability, Mischel said, so training children in "cooling strategies," like using their imaginations, can have a significant payoff later in life. "Delay makes it possible for people to cool it if and when they want to," Mischel said.

Effects of Deprivation

The symposium's final presenter, Sir Michael Rutter of King's College, underscored the limits of cortical plasticity with a somber report on "Long-Term Effects of Early Institutional Deprivation: Findings from an Adoption Study and Implications of Causal Mechanisms." Rutter and his associates followed the behavioral development of children who were adopted from Romanian orphanages by UK families after the fall of the Ceausescu regime. After evaluating them at the time of adoption, they studied a sample of such children at ages four, six, and eleven years, deploying a battery of cognitive and psychological tests to construct a theory about the results of profound deprivation followed by above-average living environments.

Some of their findings surprised them. "Like much of science, one has a mix of the expected and the totally unexpected," Rutter said. At arrival, most of the children tested as mentally retarded, but by age eleven, they were nearly normal. Variations tended to correlate to the amount of time spent in deprived conditions: Children who had been in orphanages for less than six months recovered most completely, while those who were there longer displayed more severe and longer-lasting deficits. What surprised researchers was that the nature of the deficits varied among the children: Instead of consistently suffering a similar set of problems, each child showed a different pattern of disturbance. This finding suggested to Rutter that plasticity must vary from child to child—that individual brains will respond to similar extreme circumstances in completely different ways. Unable to find a strong connection between adaptive ability and the characteristics of the households that adopted the children, Rutter concluded that, although psychosocial deprivation was the main risk factor for all the deficits the children displayed, its effects are neither universal nor fixed—a challenge to what some developmental theories would predict most researchers would expect. "Whatever theoretical explanation we end up with," Rutter concluded, "we'll have to account for these huge individual differences." Rutter also delivered the Keynote Address at the APS annual meeting.

The five presenters were delighted at the similarities they saw among their diverse fields. "We should change the way we do business," said Mischel. "Psychological science is at the point that it should become a big science. We should think about the way that chemistry and physics became great sciences. The time of each person in his own lab should maybe be over."

LEAH NELSON is a writer who lives in New York.

Growing Up Online
Young People Jump Headfirst into the Internet's World

BRUCE BOWER

As a conversation unfolds among teenagers on an Internet message board, it rapidly becomes evident that this is not idle electronic chatter. One youngster poses a question that, to an outsider, seems shocking: "Does anyone know how to cut deep without having it sting and bleed too much?" An answer quickly appears: "I use box cutter blades. You have to pull the skin really tight and press the blade down really hard." Another response advises that a quick swipe of a blade against skin "doesn't hurt and there is blood galore." The questioner seems satisfied: "Okay, I'll get a Stanley blade 'cause I hear that it will cut right to the bone with no hassle. But . . . I won't cut that deep."

Welcome to the rapidly expanding online arena for teenagers who deliberately cut or otherwise injure themselves. It's a place where cutters, as they're known, can provide emotional support to one another, discuss events that trigger self-mutilation, encourage peers to seek medical or mental-health treatment, or offer tips on how best to hurt oneself without getting caught.

The conversation above, observed during a study of self-injury message boards, occupies a tiny corner of the virtual world that children and adolescents have aggressively colonized. Psychologist Janis L. Whitlock of Cornell University, the director of that study, and other researchers are beginning to explore how young people communicate on the Internet. The scientists are examining how various online contacts affect a youngster's schoolwork, social life, and budding sense of identity. Evidence also suggests that the Internet has expanded the reach of health-education efforts to teens in distant lands and provided unique leadership opportunities to a global crop of youngsters.

New findings, including six reports in the May *Developmental Psychology,* indicate that the Internet holds a special appeal for young people, says psychologist Patricia Greenfield of the University of California, Los Angeles (UCLA). That's because the Internet provides an unprecedented number and variety of meeting places, from message boards to instant messaging to so-called social networking sites such as *myspace.com.*

The one constant is that teens take to the Internet like ants to a summer picnic. Nearly 9 in 10 U.S. youngsters, ages 12 to 17, used the Internet in 2004, according to a national survey conducted by the Pew Internet & American Life Project in Washington, D.C. That amounted to 21 million teens, half of whom said that they go online every day. About three in four U.S. adults used the Internet at that time, Pew researchers found.

Teenagers, in particular, provide a moving target for Internet researchers, remarks psychologist Kaveri Subrahmanyam of California State University in Los Angeles. "By the time you publish research on one type of Internet use, such as blogging, teenagers have moved on to something new, such as *myspace,*" she says, with a resigned chuckle.

Express Yourself

Cyberspace offers a bevy of tempting opportunities to pretend to be who you're not. Yet teens don't typically go online to deceive others but to confront their own identities, according to recent studies. That's not surprising, Subrahmanyam notes, since adolescents typically seek answers to questions such as "Who am I?" and "Where do I belong?"

Consider the self-injury message boards studied by Whitlock's team. Five Internet search engines led the researchers to a whopping 406 such sites. Most of these attracted participants who identified themselves as girls between ages 12 and 20.

On message boards, as in chat rooms, participants register as members and adopt screen names, such as "Emily the Strange." In many cases, both members and nonmembers can view messages, although only members can post them.

> **"By the time you publish research on one type of Internet use . . . teenagers have moved on to something new."**
>
> —Kaveri Subrahmanyam,
> California State University

Whitlock and her coworkers studied the content of 3,219 messages at 10 popular self-injury message boards over a 2-month period in 2005. Many postings provided emotional support to other members. Participants also frequently discussed circumstances that triggered self-mutilation. These included depression and conflicts with key people in their lives. Some message senders detailed ways to seek aid for physical and emotional problems, but others described feeling addicted to self-injury.

More ominously, a substantial minority of messages either discouraged self-injurers from seeking formal medical or mental help or shared details about self-harm techniques and ways to keep the practice secret.

Online teen chat rooms generally don't have specific topics but, like message boards, attract a wide range of kids and present both helpful and hurtful communications. Subrahmanyam and her colleagues examined typical conversations at two online chat sites for teens. They monitored more than 5 hours of electronic exchanges selected at various times of the day during a 2-month stretch in 2003.

On one site, an adult monitored conversations for unacceptable language. The other site was unmonitored.

More than half of the 583 participants at both sites gave personal information, usually including sex and age. Sexual themes constituted 5 percent of all messages, corresponding to about one sexual comment per minute. Obscene language characterized 5 percent of messages on the unmonitored site and 2 percent on the monitored site.

One-quarter of participants made sexual references, which was not unexpected given the amount of daily sex talk that has been reported among some teens. In the chat rooms, however, all members were confronted with the minority's sexual banter.

The protected environment of the monitored chat room resulted in markedly fewer explicit sexual messages and obscene words than the unmonitored chat room did, Subrahmanyam says. Moreover, the monitored site attracted more participants who identified themselves as young girls than did the unmonitored venue, which featured a larger number of correspondents who identified themselves as males in their late teens or early 20s.

Much of the explicit sexuality on the unmonitored site amounted to degrading and insulting comments, adding to concerns previously raised by other researchers that youths who visit such sites are likely to encounter sexual harassment from either peers or adults.

Subrahmanyam's team also conducted in-person interviews with teens who hadn't participated in the chat room study. The results suggest that only a small minority ever pretend to be other people on the Internet.

Intriguingly, teens who write online journals, known as blogs, often forgo sex talk for more-mundane topics, such as daily experiences at home and school, Subrahmanyam adds. In 2004, she analyzed the content of 600 entries in 200 teen blogs.

Teen blogs offer an outlet for discussing romantic relationships and, especially for boys, disclosing hidden sides of themselves, says psychologist Sandra L. Calvert of Georgetown University in Washington, D.C. In a 2005 online report with David A. Huffaker of Northwestern University in Evanston, Ill., Calvert described entries in 70 teen blogs, evenly split between bloggers who identified themselves as girls and as boys. The ages given ranged from 13 to 17.

Bloggers routinely disclosed personal information, including e-mail addresses and other contact details, the researchers found. Half the blogs of both boys and girls discussed relationships with boyfriends or girlfriends. Ten boys, but only two girls, wrote that they were using the blogs to openly discuss their homosexuality for the first time.

"Teenagers stay closer to reality in their online expressions about themselves than has previously been suggested," Calvert asserts.

Net Gains

Give a middle school child from a low-income household a home computer with free Internet access and watch that child become a better reader. That's the conclusion of a new study that highlights potential academic consequences of the so-called digital divide separating poor kids from their better-off peers.

A team led by psychologist Linda A. Jackson of Michigan State University in East Lansing gave computers, Internet access, and in-home technical support to 140 children. The mostly 12-to-14-year-old, African-American boys and girls lived in single-parent families with incomes no higher than $15,000 a year. The researchers recorded each child's Internet use from December 2000 through June 2002.

Before entering the study, these children generally did poorly in school and on academic-achievement tests. However, overall grades and reading achievement scores—but not math-achievement scores—began to climb after 6 months of home Internet use. These measures had ascended farther by the end of the study, especially among the kids who spent the most time online.

Participants logged on to the Internet an average of 30 minutes a day, which isn't much in the grand scheme of teenage Internet use: Teens in middle- and upper-class families average 2 or more Internet hours each day. Only 25 percent of the children in the study used instant messaging, and only 16 percent sent e-mails or contributed to online chat. These low numbers probably reflect a lack of home Internet access among the kids' families and friends. Also, their parents forbade most of the participating kids from contacting strangers in chat rooms.

Still, text-heavy online sites seem to have provided reading experience that translated into higher reading scores and grades, the researchers suggest. Although participants remained below-average readers at the end of the study, their improvement showed promise, according to Jackson and her colleagues.

These findings raise the unsettling possibility that "children most likely to benefit from home Internet access are the very children least likely to have [it]," Jackson's team concludes.

In stark contrast to their poor peers, wealthier middle school and high school students spend much of their time on the Internet trading instant messages with friends, an activity with tremendous allure for young people trying to fit into peer groups, says psychologist Robert Kraut of Carnegie Mellon University in Pittsburgh.

For teens, instant messaging extends opportunities to communicate with friends and expands their social world, Kraut suggests. He and his colleagues probed instant messaging in interviews with 26 teens in 2002 and in surveys completed by 41 teens in 2004.

Instant messaging simulates joining a clique, without the rigid acceptance rules of in-person peer groups, in Kraut's view. Each user creates his or her own buddy list.

Within these virtual circles, teens become part of what they regard as a cool Internet practice and, at the same time, intensify feelings of being connected to friends, even when sitting by themselves doing homework, Kraut says.

Still, Internet-savvy youngsters typically have much to learn about the social reach and potential perils of online communication, says education professor Zheng Yan of the State University of New York at Albany.

Yan interviewed 322 elementary and middle school students in a New England suburb. Participants also drew pictures to show what the Internet looks like and, when told to think of the Internet as a city, what types of people one would see there.

By ages 10 to 11, children demonstrated considerable knowledge of the Internet's technical complexity, such as realizing that Internet sites act as data sources for many computers.

Not until ages 12 to 13, however, did youngsters begin to grasp the Internet's social complexity, such as the large numbers of strangers who can gain access to information that a person posts publicly. Even then, the kids' insight into the online social world's perils remained rudimentary compared with that previously observed in adults.

Children and teens plastering personal thoughts and images on Web sites such as *myspace.com* "often don't realize how many people have access to that information, including sexual predators," Yan asserts. He encourages parental monitoring of Internet activities and regular discussions of online dangers with children.

Worldwide Peers

Adolescents who form global Internet communities show signs of developing their own styles of leadership and social involvement, a trend that Northwestern University psychologist Justine Cassell and her coworkers view with optimism.

Cassell's team examined messages from an online community known as the Junior Summit, organized by the Massachusetts Institute of Technology. University officials sent out worldwide calls for youngsters to participate in a closed, online forum that would address how technology can aid young people. They chose 3,062 applicants, ages 9 to 16, from 139 countries.

Those selected ranged from suburbanites in wealthy families to child laborers working in factories. Computers and Internet access were provided to 200 schools and community centers in convenient locations for those participants who needed them.

During the last 3 months of 1998, children logged on to online homerooms, divided by geographic regions. Members of each homeroom generated and voted on 20 topics to be addressed by the overall forum. Topic groups then formed and participants elected a total of 100 delegates to an expenses-paid, 1-week summit in Boston in 1999.

Cassell's group found that delegates, whom the researchers refer to as online leaders, didn't display previously established characteristics of adult leaders, such as contributing many ideas to a task and asserting dominance over others. While the delegates eventually sent more messages than their peers did, those who were later chosen as online leaders—regardless of age or sex—had referred to group goals rather than to themselves and synthesized others' posts rather than offering only their own ideas.

> ## "Children most likely to benefit from home Internet access [may be] the very children least likely to have [it]."
>
> —Linda A. Jackson,
> Michigan State University

Without in-person leadership cues such as height or attractiveness, online congregants looked for signs of collaborative and persuasive proficiency, the researchers say.

Outside the controlled confines of the Junior Summit, teens even in places where few people own home computers find ways to obtain vital Internet information. Ghana, a western Africa nation in which adolescents represent almost half the population, provides one example.

Researchers led by Dina L.G. Borzekowski of Johns Hopkins Bloomberg School of Public Health in Baltimore surveyed online experiences among 778 teens, ages 15 to 18, in Ghana's capital, Accra.

Two-thirds of the 600 youngsters who attended high school said that they had previously gone online, as did about half of the 178 teens who didn't attend school. Among all Internet users, the largest proportion—53 percent—had sought online health information on topics including AIDS and other sexually transmitted diseases, nutrition, exercise, drug use, and pregnancy.

Out-of-school teens—who faced considerable poverty—ranked the Internet as a more important source of sexual-health information than the students did, the investigators say.

In both groups, the majority of teens went online at Internet cafés, where patrons rent time on computers hooked up to the Internet.

Internet cafés have rapidly sprung up in unexpected areas, UCLA's Greenfield says. She conducts research in the southeastern Mexico state of Chiapas, which is inhabited mainly by poor farming families.

Small storefronts, each containing around 10 Internet-equipped computers, now dot this hard-pressed region, Greenfield notes. Primarily young people frequent these businesses, paying the equivalent of about $1 for an hour of Internet surfing.

"Even in Chiapas, adolescents are in the vanguard of Internet use," Greenfield remarks.

Why Newborns Cause Acrimony and Alimony

"Differences in expectations of what parenting will bring to the marriage, and how to handle children, money, power, decisions, and chores all factor into the stresses that erode so many unions."

DOLORES PUTERBAUGH

Babies enter a couple's life through birth, adoption, or remarriage, creating new relationships, responsibilities, and joys. Whether a surprise, planned, or long sought, most babies are preceded with increased excitement, careful preparations, and growing hopes. Tiny clothing is bought; bedrooms are repainted; the best safety furniture and carriers obtained. Parents-in-waiting attend prenatal classes, scour books for information, and tolerate bushels of uninvited advice from family, friends, and strangers. Many couples seem overprepared, if such a thing is possible.

Yet, in the midst of this nearly obsessive planning and preparing, something often evades notice: about one in 10 couples divorce before their first child begins school. How can a baby generate such a series of emotional tidal waves that so often culminate in acrimony and alimony?

The changes in duties, income, and even the layout of the family home are anticipated; my experiences in the therapy room and with professional literature indicate that the true impact of these changes apparently strikes with little warning. If they are wise, aching new parents in hurting marriages will come for counseling before the damage is irreparable. At the beginning of counseling, Rebecca and Joshua (made-up characters) are angry, hurt, unappreciated, disappointed, and ashamed. "We always put the children first," they say proudly, but here they are, nearly dashed onto the rocks by an eight-pound tsunami.

The little tidal wave sweeps up both parents. Mom may be pulled up towards the crest, immersed in the profound relationship with the baby, while dad is swimming against the current under 20 feet water. These roles will shift as the waves crest, break, and rise again. Changes of all sorts—from money to time to perceptions of power and responsibility—drive those waves of emotional change.

If one parent, often the mother, provides full-time care for the infant, the loss of income creates emotional tension as well as financial stress. Betty Carter, founder and director at the Family Institute of Westchester (N.Y.), discovered in her research that the primary wage earner gradually takes on more financial decisionmaking rather than sharing decisions as when both were employed. In marriages where couples maintain separate finances, the difficulties may be compounded: "my money" and "your money" become one person's money.

When Rebecca left her job to care for the baby, she felt like a child having to ask Joshua for money each week; to her, it was like he had a checkbook and she had an allowance. Their eventual solution was to budget an amount each partner can spend on personal activities and purchases, while setting up two individual checking accounts in addition to the family account. This way, each has "my money" and there is adequate "our money." Neither Joshua nor Rebecca will have to ask permission to have lunch with a friend or get angry about ATM transactions not entered into the family checkbook.

Reducing any feeling of dependency will have to include an effort to discuss finances in terms of "us" rather than "mine and yours." Feeling dependent can lead to feeling powerless, to resentment and a cutoff of communication; we only can resent those whom we feel have power over us. It may be that the working parent solicits input on decisions but that the nonworking parent seemingly is reluctant to act as a full partner—but each perceives it differently; one feels stuck with full responsibility while the other feels marginalized.

Who has power over whom? While the stay-at-home parent may feel dependent and helpless, the working parent certainly is not riding the wave. According to a study published in the *Journal of Marriage and the Family,* men who are the primary or sole wage earner for a growing family often define themselves as successful parents if they provide financially for the family, while their wives define successful parenting based on relationships with the children and their satisfaction with parenting.

Dad is under pressure to work longer hours, earn more money, and increasingly be concerned about job security and benefits; a man who previously explored his options if his current position was not satisfactory may feel painted into a corner because others completely depend on him. Where his wife perceives power, he feels pressure. Separated by a wall of water, they are at odds, with fewer resources.

If they are typical, the couple has little time to discuss their differences. New parenthood correlates with less leisure time together, fewer positive interactions between the new parents, and a sense of reduced emotional availability for both spouses. Rebecca is preoccupied with managing the baby and household duties. Joshua is working longer hours and worrying about the bills and future expenses of childrearing. Like many couples, they may avoid addressing their problems—and tension will build between them. The financial freedom they had to go places has been reduced. Both are exhausted and stressed.

Angry that Joshua is "not helping," Rebecca turns more and more to her family and girlfriends for emotional support, discussing practical issues as well as her loneliness, need for adult companionship, and resentment towards her husband. Women, in particular, are likely to look for emotional support outside the marriage, from friends and family members. Turning primarily to outsiders for support, even extended family—rather than one another—can weaken the relationship, already challenged by financial stresses, interrupted sleep, and shifts in power and responsibility.

Differences in how men and women tend to define family roles, satisfactory parenting experiences, and their expectations for the marriage continue to foment trouble for many couples even after the first months of their child's infancy, when the parent on leave may have returned to work.

As introduced earlier, men often define themselves as successful parents based on how well they provide for their children. Society reinforces this perspective, from the marketing for the "best" infant equipment to the expectation that the parents of young adults should finance their offspring's education. Both men and women can fall victim to a societal message that children always must come first. Many men confess to resentment at the pressure to provide financially at the expense of getting to know and enjoy their kids, but, in line with cultural expectations, fathers often focus more on providing and less on hands-on parenting.

As published in the *Journal of Marriage and the Family*, William Marsiglio of the University of Florida found that over 10% of fathers never take their child (age four or under) anywhere on outings alone, while 15% never read to their young offspring. Men become more involved as their children mature. Fathers spend more time with sons and outgoing daughters; quiet daughters generally are more difficult for new dads. Mothers report consistent levels of interaction with their children regardless of temperament or parental satisfaction; indeed, the cultural pressure for mothers is to put the relationship with their children above everything else. However, the balance of the family and the relationship between spouses only can suffer when their primary commitment stops being to one another.

"For a woman . . . children in the home tend to bring more work, restricted freedom and privilege, and less pleasurable time with her husband."

The differences between fathers' and mothers' involvement do not appear to be entirely explained by mothers being the at-home parent, as working moms spend much more time with their children than fathers do. Even the morning commute tends to include more parenting-related concerns for mothers than fathers. In many marriages, then, husbands tend to perceive, and act on, a greater range of options in their level of involvement with their children, with their wives carrying the greater part of the burden regardless of whether both parents are wage earners. In such a situation, the wife may grow to resent her husband. She perceives him as wielding more financial power and then acting on his apparent freedom to pick and choose how much to engage with his offspring. He, meanwhile, sees his previous best friend, lover, and companion putting him second, third, fourth—or lower-on the priority list despite his efforts to be a good husband and father.

Joshua, working longer hours and cutting back on his own activities, begins to shut down in the face of Rebecca's apparent anger towards him. From his perspective, he cannot understand why she seems to be turning against him when he is doing his best to be a good husband and father. She cannot see why he does not want to spend more time with the baby. Didn't they agree to start a family? She is returning to work and expects him to start doing his share.

The breakdown of household tasks is a common topic for general discussion, women's magazines, and the occasional serious researcher. While many women stereotypically may complain that their husband does "nothing" around the house, research indicates this may be only a slight exaggeration. In 2004, surveys in the *Journal of Marriage and the Family* revealed that, on average, a full-time working married woman with children spent over 80 minutes per workday on household tasks, while her employed spouse spent under 30. He, however, probably is working two-and-a-half to five hours more per week at a full-time job than she is, making up for some of those missed housework hours. On weekends, her total time went up to almost 140 minutes, while his was just over 50. As time passes, the presence of daughters brings relief not to mother, but to father: The "mother's helper" tends to take over chores previously done by dad, reducing his duties rather than mom's!

Despite generally perceived changes in the inequality of male-female responsibility to children, moms still are spending more time than dads on household chores and tending to the kids. Youngsters under five require constant supervision: even a baby-proofed house can be dangerous when—if only for a moment—an adult's back is turned. Somehow, working mothers are managing to spend well over twice as much time on chores, and perform those chores while keeping a watchful eye on children. It is arguable that those chores might take less time were she not simultaneously managing a toddler or two.

For a woman, then, children in the home tend to bring more work, restricted freedom and privilege, and less pleasurable time with her husband. Meanwhile, her husband tends to be working extra hours, worrying about finances, and looking forward to when the children are old enough for him to enjoy. While it is not a picnic for anyone, it is not surprising that mothers report greater distress during the new parenting period. It is a warning alarm for marriages that, for women, greater unhappiness with parenting is correlated to marital dissatisfaction. Essentially, for women, parenting, marriage, and self-image are part of the same package, while for men, dissatisfaction in one area can have nothing to do with another.

Interestingly, fathers often report less satisfaction with their role as parents than women, but compartmentalize this from their feelings about marriage. As women become resentful of men's decisions about finances, family time, and chores, they seek social and emotional support outside the marriage from family and friends. As fewer confidences are exchanged between the couple, emotional distance develops. As typified by Joshua and Rebecca, the gap may become a chasm if the husband feels criticized, unappreciated, or overwhelmed by his wife's disappointment and expectations, or if her attempts to make things better are not met with some compromise.

Marital researcher John Gottman, co-founder of the Seattle Marital and Family Institute and author of a number of books, including *Why Marriages Succeed or Fail,* has identified this turning away from one another-rather than towards one another—in times of trouble as one of the danger signs of impending marital failure. Turning away may be a case of seeming to ignore one another's efforts to mend fences or by investing emotionally outside of the marriage for needs previously met within the union. When couples stop talking about their differences, and no longer turn first to each other in times of joy and sadness, they become emotionally disengaged.

Happy marriages are correlated with low levels of distress over the challenges of parenting. Many marriage and family researchers have asserted that the quality of the marriage itself predicts the satisfaction with parenting. Healthy relationships more easily withstand the burdens of parenting. As we consider the evidence that so many new parents' marriages devolve into quagmires of power struggles over finances, parenting, and chores, it becomes clear that differences in expectations are best addressed before the baby arrives.

Besides a healthy, honest dialogue about expectations for parenting styles, couples should address how money will be handled, division of chores, who will take family medical leave to provide care for the infant, etc. Whether through family members, professional therapists, or secular or worship communities, classes and guided discussions can provide useful assistance for new parents and help short-circuit the patterns that lead to divorce preceding kindergarten for so many families. Couples preparing for parenthood would do themselves a great service by learning about one another's actual expectations of what family life will be like. In this era of smaller families, many premarital programs include discussions with long-married couples that can enlighten young people (who may have grown up with one or no siblings) about childcare, time demands of

children, and some common pitfalls of early parenting. Those of us who have grown up in large families have few illusions about the time demands of parenting and are not shocked that a newborn can take control of a household or create emotional havoc. Inexperienced parents may have misconceptions about normal child development, leading to anger, frustration, and disappointment with the parenting role. How many of us have seen steely-eyed, clenched-jawed parents striding through an amusement park pushing a stroller with an over-tired, crying child far too young to appreciate a $75 per person, 12-hour day in what is advertised as a family heaven? A one-hour visit to a petting zoo can challenge a young family; heavily invested days of mega-amusement parks are out of line with most young children's energy and attention spans. Experienced parents or older children in large families know this. New parents from small families may not.

A primary complaint of many mothers is their mate's lack of involvement with the kids: not just in sharing the burdens of the household, but in actual engagement. One of Rebecca's main contentions is that Joshua never seems to do anything with the baby: she feels everything is left to her by default. If she does get help, she added, it is with household chores rather than spending time with the baby. Many experts cite men's relative inexperience and lack of confidence in handling babies and small children. Added to this may be a solicitous new mother's tendency to hover and correct based on what she would do; daddy may be within the bounds of correct care, but if different from mommy, she is likely to correct him. Providing training to new fathers, and encouraging new mothers to withhold all but constructive criticism can improve inexperienced fathers' confidence and comfort in accepting more responsibility for direct child care.

Coaching both parents can help them handle various situations and ease fears, perhaps unspoken, that they will "lose it" and make a terrible mistake with their child. Discussing household tasks and division of duties sounds simple, but most therapists familiar with couples' work will assert that such discussions tend not to occur under ideal circumstances. Differences in standards are a good area to seek a workable truce. This requires real listening and work: if one parent believes toddlers need daily activities (play dates, gymnastic classes, etc.) and that the house must be vacuumed daily, it may be necessary to compromise with a mate who believes that weekly—or perhaps twice-a-week—vacuuming is sufficient and that babies do not need expensive daily activities.

"Many couples [are dissatisfied] with the marriage because the intimate emotional relationship has been subsumed into a parent-child-parent triangle."

Bullied by the popular media's obsession with telling parents how to build the perfect child, Rebecca scheduled exercise classes, music and reading groups, and other activities, besides holding herself up to an unrealistic expectation of household cleanliness. Joshua, meanwhile, was more concerned with having a happy, relaxed family. He could not see the purpose in being frantic about activities that were supposed to be fun or in "driving ourselves crazy" with daily cleaning routines. Simplistic as it sounds, switching tasks for a few days can be a real eye-opener for everyone. Coaching mothers in asking for the help they need directly from theft spouse and in being proactive in arranging for breaks in childcare duties to pursue adult interests is another means to improving the situation. Mothers can take advantage of fathers' hands-on time by getting out of the house, having alone time in another room, or enjoying an uninterrupted phone call. In situations where the father is the full-time, at-home parent, the roles would reverse: he needs to spend time alone or with friends.

Many couples stop having couple time in exchange for family time, leading to dissatisfaction with the marriage because the intimate emotional relationship has been subsumed into a parent-child-parent triangle. This is unhealthy for the marriage and the children. Kids learn by observation. When they see parents putting one another last, they develop this as a template for their own future relationships. Children who later have difficulty maintaining truly intimate adult relationships should not be a surprise to parents who put family time far ahead of couple time.

I routinely "prescribe" a couple's night for every family I see, even if the problem is not the couple but a child's in-school behavior. The parents are urged to set aside one evening for themselves; they do not have to go anywhere or spend money. Couples with infants can schedule this around typical feeding times. If they have older kids, they are to send them to their rooms for an extra hour of reading before bedtime. This will provide a grown-ups' evening, as simple as a video and dinner, or a game of Scrabble, or pushing back the furniture for some dancing. Interestingly, my clients often report that their school-age children become enthusiastic about the parents' evening, for example, hearing a teenager explain to a friend, "No, we can't watch the game here. . . . It's my parents' date night. How about your house?" A kindergartner reminds the parents each Sunday, "Don't forget! It's your date night! We get to go to bed early and read." Children fear their parents divorcing. If Mom and Dad have a romantic night every week, it might be gross—but at least it's not a divorce, runs the child-logic. The youngster also is getting a powerful message about the importance of the marital relationship.

Differences in expectations of what parenting will bring to the marriage, and how to handle children, money, power, decisions, and chores all factor into the stresses that erode so many unions. A combination of education, support in seeking healthy ways to breach differences and strengthen the marital relationship, and, above all, turning towards one another to find solutions and support rather than turning separately to outsiders, serves to avoid and ameliorate the difficulties of early parenting that lead to so many fractured families before the first back-to-school night.

DOLORES PUTERBAUGH, a psychotherapist in private practice in Largo, Fla., is a member of the Advisory Board of the International Center for the Study of Psychiatry and Psychology.

From *USA Today* Magazine, by Dolores Puterbaugh, May 2005, pp. 27–29. Copyright © 2005 by Society for the Advancement of Education, Inc. Reprinted by permission. All rights reserved.

Ageless Aging:
The Next Era of Retirement

"Old age" and "retirement" must be rethought and redefined as the baby boomers surge through the later stages of life, according to a renowned authority on aging.

KEN DYCHTWALD

With the breakthroughs in medicine, public health, nutrition, and wellness in recent years, longevity has been steadily increasing. So what age should now be considered old?

Let's remember that the age selected to be the marker of old age was not sent from heaven or scripted in Moses' tablets. It was selected in the 1880s by Otto von Bismarck, who crafted Europe's first pension plan. Bismarck had to pick an age at which people would be considered too enfeebled to work and therefore eligible for state support and entitlement. He picked 65. At the time, the life expectancy in Europe and the United States was only 45 years. Now, life expectancy at birth for women has vaulted to nearly 80 and for men to about 74. In fact, if you were to craft a formula using a corresponding equation today, we would be retiring people at about 97. So to continue to use 65 as the marker of old age simply does not make any sense at all.

One misconception that people have about longevity is that it means more years added to the end of life. Few people would say, "If I could live longer, what I'd really like is to be old for twice as long." Rather, most people would say, "If I could live a little bit longer, I'd like to have a chance to reinvent myself. I'd like to have a chance to pursue some dreams that I might have put on the shelf when I was younger. I'd like to adjust the balance between work, leisure, and family, with the benefit of the kind of wisdom and experience that comes from having tried a few things out in the first half of my life." People don't want to be old longer. They want to be young and middle-aged longer. And many would prefer to live long, healthy lives without being any particular age at all, reflecting a new kind of ageless aging.

The Longevity Revolution: We've Only Just Begun

During the twentieth century, we did an excellent job of eliminating many of the diseases of youth, such as cholera, typhoid, smallpox, diphtheria, and pneumonia. Childbirth, once a major

cause of premature death, has become safer for most women, and more children are born healthier. The effect of these improvements is that more of us are living longer and longer.

Extraordinary advances are still ahead. The maximum biological potential age of the human body is somewhere between 120 and 140 years, so with significant breakthroughs in the next quarter century—whether they be in pharmaceuticals, hormone therapy, therapeutic cloning, or stem-cell research—we could add another five, 10, or even 20 years to a person's life.

The downside, of course, is that chronic health problems will also increase. We're living longer but not necessarily staying healthy longer. Unfortunately, 59 million Americans have one form or another of heart disease. Two-thirds of the American population is overweight. Up to 50 million people struggle with chronic pain due to conditions like arthritis and bursitis. There are about 18 million people with either Type 1 or Type 2 diabetes. These lifestyle-related chronic diseases have become the modern plagues.

In an ancient Greek fable, Eos, the beautiful goddess of the dawn, falls in love with the warrior Tithonus. Distraught over his mortality, she goes to Zeus's chamber and begs Zeus to grant her lover immortality. "Are you certain that is what you want for him?" Zeus challenges. "Yes," Eos responds. As Eos leaves Zeus's chamber, she realizes in shock that she forgot to ask that Tithonus also remain eternally young and healthy. With each passing year, she looks on with horror as he grows older and sicker. His skin withers and becomes cancerous. His organs rot, and his brain grows feeble. Ultimately, the once-proud warrior is reduced to a collection of pained, foul, and broken bones—but he continues to live forever.

The story of Tithonus is a fitting allegory for what is occurring in the U.S. health-care system today. While we have eliminated many of the childhood diseases that took our ancestors' lives, the health-care system is woefully inept at preventing or treating the chronic health problems that arise in life's later years. Age-related chronic conditions such as Alzheimer's disease, arthritis, osteoporosis, diabetes, prostate and breast cancer, and heart disease are reaching pandemic proportions.

The most troublesome challenges ahead, however, could be due to the rising incidence of the diseases among the oldest of the old. Although some of today's over-85 population are fit and independent, 62.5% are so disabled that they are no longer able to manage the basic activities of daily living without help. Currently, 47% of people over age 85 suffer from some form of dementia—a condition that already afflicts 4 million Americans.

Impacts of the Wellness Movement

Having participated in promoting the wellness movement since its beginnings 30 years ago, I am convinced that we could all be doing a much better job of both lowering health-care costs and creating a much healthier, more vital, independent life by practicing better health habits. With each birthday, the body struggles with a wider range of problems. For example, I am 55. I am a relatively healthy and fit person, but I've got a right shoulder that's troubled with bone spurs and arthritis. And even though I haven't eaten meat for about 25 years, I have high cholesterol that I grapple with. I also find that it's a little easier to gain weight now than when I was younger, so I'm always trying to keep an eye out for my calorie consumption. So even though I am still a youthful, healthy person, each birthday brings on more challenges to work against on a day-to-day basis.

When we're young, we tend to take our health for granted. When we're in our 40s or 50s, we begin to notice that there are some changes going on and we start to take them much more seriously. And as we look at our own moms and dads, we can see both the positive and the negative outcomes of how well or how badly they have taken care of themselves. As we grow a little bit older, the desire to be healthy, attractive, and potent doesn't diminish, but it becomes harder to stay well and to look youthful. These are very powerful motivations. You wouldn't expect your car to function well if you didn't take care of it. You wouldn't expect your clothes to look good if you didn't take good care of them. You wouldn't expect your computer to work well if you didn't maintain it the way it needs to be maintained. More people now realize that, to be healthy, look healthy, feel healthy, and have wellness prevalent in their lives as they age, they need to take charge of their wellness and practice the kinds of behaviors that will get them there.

As they age, baby boomers are likely to continue setting new trends in the United States. In my new book, *The Power Years,* I argue that, instead of viewing life after 40 as a time of decline, retreat, and withdrawal, boomers are coming to see this as a terrific new opportunity to reevaluate their lives and consider their new options. They will be empowered by a great deal more experience and wisdom and will plot new courses. Instead of limitation, I believe they'll choose liberation—it's their nature. Boomers are collectively reshaping the middle years of life into a new period for renewal and reinvention. "Middlescence"—an older and wiser version of adolescence—is emerging.

History provides us many role models for successful aging. Grandma Moses didn't start painting until she was almost 80. Galileo published his masterpiece, *Dialogue Concerning the Two New Sciences,* at 74. Frank Lloyd Wright designed the Guggenheim Museum in New York at 91. Mahatma Gandhi was 72 when he completed successful negotiations with Britain for India's independence. Society will be able to look forward to a multiplying pool of role models for this new, empowered maturity. Warren Buffett remains the world's most-respected investor at age 75. Film stars Sophia Loren and Sean Connery are still considered sexy in their seventh and eighth decades. And Federal Reserve Board Chairman Alan Greenspan remains capable and wise at 78.

Many people will reap the benefits of new freedoms as they grow older. As children leave home, parents' daily responsibilities are reduced. As busy schedules begin to let up, we'll have more free time than at any previous period of our lives. With these chunks of newfound leisure, we'll be free to pursue hidden passions and long-suppressed dreams: take a hike, write a novel, or sail the world.

As the boomer generation passes into maturity, now is the time for companies to adjust their thinking about men and women over age 50. When the leading edge of the baby boom first arrived, America and its institutions were totally unprepared. Waiting lists and long lines developed at hospitals across the country; facilities and staff were inadequate, and in some hospitals, hallways were used as labor rooms. Similarly, apartments and homes didn't have enough bedrooms for boomer kids, there was a shortage of baby food and diapers, and department stores couldn't keep enough toys in stock to meet the multiplying demand. When boomers took their first steps, the shoe, photo, and Band-Aid industries skyrocketed. Similarly, sales of tricycles, Slinkies, and Hula-Hoops exploded as the marketplace was flooded with products for kids.

When baby boomers reach any stage of life, the issues that concern them—whether financial, interpersonal, or even hormonal—become the dominant social, political, and marketplace themes of the time. Boomers don't just populate existing life stages or consumer trends—they transform them. On January 1, 1996, the first baby boomer turned 50. By the second decade of the twenty-first century, boomers will evolve into the largest elder generation in history. As the oldest members of the baby-boom cohort start turning 65 in 2011, they will swell the ranks of the "elderly" from approximately 40 million now to more than 70 million by 2030. But boomers will transform the look, meaning, experience, and purpose of maturity. As they reach age 65, it will not be viewed as "elderly."

Until recently, corporations, marketers, and entrepreneurs paid little attention to men and women over age 50. There was, after all, little to spark their interest in a group whose members tended to be financially disadvantaged, frugal, and perceived as set in their ways and uninterested in new products and ideas. But Americans in their 50s and older currently earn more than $2 trillion in annual income, own more than 70% of the nation's personal financial assets, and represent 50% of all discretionary spending power. In fact, their per capita discretionary spending is 2.5 times more than the average of younger households and is

New Opportunities for Aging Agelessly

In the years ahead, watch for growth in a wide variety of industries and services to meet the needs of a maturing marketplace, including:

- Specialty diagnosis and treatment centers for particular body parts, such as the eyes, ears, muscles, bones, or nervous system.
- Therapeutically cloned kidneys, livers, lungs, hearts, skin, blood, and bones for "tune-up" and replacement purposes.
- Nutraceuticals—foods and supplements engineered with macro- and micronutrients to fight aging.
- Cosmeceutical rejuvenation therapies for both men and women.
- Antiaging spas.
- High-tech exercise gear and equipment programmed to precisely "train" users to build stronger, healthier, and more youthful bodies.
- Smart acoustic systems in telephones, radios, and TVs that customize signals to accommodate the auditory range of each user's ears.
- Silver Seals—"for-hire" teams of elders with various problem-solving talents who are deployed to "fix" difficult community or business issues.
- Lifelong-learning programs at colleges, universities, churches, and community centers and on cable TV and the Internet.
- "Retirement Zone" stores featuring products and technologies appealing to older adults with free time.
- Adventure-travel services that send older adults to off-the-beaten-trail locations.

- Mature employment and career transition coordinators.
- Experience agents—similar to travel agents—that can be commissioned to orchestrate any type of request, whether it's a party, learning program, psychotherapy, sabbatical, travel adventure, spiritual retreat, introduction to new friends, or business partnerships.
- Mature dating services to help the tens of millions of single, mature women and men find new relationships.
- Longevity-oriented communities for health-minded elders.
- Intergenerational communes.
- Urban arts retirement communities that focus on cultural pursuits.
- University-based intergenerational housing for people who desire lifelong learning.
- Multinational time-share clubs for those who aren't interested in settling down in one location.
- Long-term care insurance financing to provide security against the possibility of late-life chronic health problems.
- Estate management and trust services to help families manage the $20 trillion inheritance cascade that is about to occur.
- Reverse mortgages to help people who are cash-poor but "brick-rich."

—Ken Dychtwald
Excepted from *The Power Years: A User's Guide to the Rest of Your Life* (Wiley, August 2005).

particularly strong in the financial services, health care, leisure, wellness, and beauty products categories.

The Challenge to Social Security

After studying aging issues for more than 30 years, I've concluded that the best way to guarantee a financially secure old age is to be a part of a very small generation and then give birth to a very large generation. That way, when you are in your 70s and they are in their 40s and 50s, they'll be paying enormous amounts of taxes for your support. That's exactly the situation for today's seniors.

In contrast, the baby boomers are part of a very large generation, who, relatively speaking, gave birth to a smaller number of kids to support them. Whereas the boomers' parents averaged four kids each, boomers themselves average around half that number. Because the boomers are also going to be living longer than anybody ever imagined, it's going to become increasingly difficult for government entitlements to support retirement at the age and level that we're seeing now. When Social Security was first created in the United States, the average life expectancy was only 63 years, and there were 40 workers supporting

each retiree. Now, there are only about 3.2 workers for each retiree. By the time I reach my middle 60s—about 10 years from now—there will only be about two workers supporting me, and I just don't think they're going to want to do that.

Many people are now choosing to continue working into their "retirement" years. We are on the verge of entering what I will call the "fourth era of retirement."

Four Eras of Retirement

The first era of retirement lasted for about 100,000 years and ended in the early twentieth century. During that era, you worked all of your life. That was not considered a bad thing, because work served a variety of purposes. In addition to providing a livelihood, work also offered a way of feeling worthwhile and productive. It was a great socialization activity, where you encountered people of all ages. You felt involved. If you had a very demanding job and your body was no longer able to conduct the work required to do that job, you would be transitioned to a more appropriate function. So if grandpa's job was to plow the fields and that became too hard, he might become involved with fixing the fences. But the idea that people were to retire was not a part of our consciousness. Working in maturity was viewed positively.

During the Industrial Revolution, all that abruptly changed. By the 1920s, the second era of retirement began and was well established with the crafting of Social Security in the 1930s. This wonderful program had two purposes: First, it was designed to create a thin safety net for older adults in a period of economic frailty. Second, with the unemployment levels skyrocketing to 25%, retirement provided an institutional process whereby older people would be removed from the workforce to make room for the young.

Then the third era of retirement emerged during the 1960s and 1970s, when we began to think of retirement as the "golden years" of life. In fact, the younger you retired, the more successful you were perceived to be. At the same time, longevity began to rise for adults, and so the post-work period became a stage lasting not two or three years, but 15 to 20 years or even longer. Ultimately, people began to think of retirement as a birthright—an entitlement. And that is the era in which we have been situated through the last quarter century. That era is fraying at the edges now, and I believe a fourth is now emerging.

The New Retirement Era: From Retirement to "Rehirement"

Recent research has shown that the modern retirement experiment is simply not working for most people. About half of all the retirees in the United States say they'd rather be working, though most don't want to work full time. Some might like to try doing something different and new, and most don't want all the pressure they had when they were young. Some even want to work for free as volunteers. A lot of people are now saying, "You know, this golden age thing is just not enough for me. While a few years of leisure is great—decades of nothing to do can be deadly!" So the new era of retirement will be "rehirement."

One reason for this growing interest in rehirement is that a lot of retirees are just plain bored: Last year, the average retiree watched 43 hours of television a week. Another reason is that most people simply cannot afford to live on a fixed income for 20 or more years. An increasing number of older adults are not interested in acting their age and retreating to the sidelines. Instead, they'd rather rebel against ageist stereotypes and are seeking to be productive and involved and even late-blooming in their maturity.

Again, we can look to a growing cadre of role models for the new style of aging. When you have John Glenn going up into space at 77, Sumner Redstone running Viacom at 80, and Lena Horne still on the concert circuit at 85, you are beginning to see the emergence of a new kind of lifestyle hero, an elder hero.

These forces are fueling the new, fourth era of retirement. People now do not really want to retire at all. Rather, they want a "turning point," a chance to step out of a full-time job or an exhausting career, take a break or sabbatical, and then reinvent themselves. Eventually, I believe, most people will want a better balance between work and leisure throughout their lives. As

they mature, they would like to be able to work at what they want, perhaps working fewer hours with more recreation and leisure interspersed. They will want to stay in the game—not relegated to the sidelines.

Retirement is in the midst of a sweeping transformation. In the years to come, more older men and women will be starting up their engines and jumping back into the workforce, maybe even having the most-productive years of their lives.

Ageless Explorers vs. The Comfortably Content

Generalizing about retirees is proving increasingly wrong-headed. Already we are seeing lifestyle or attitudinal differences among different retiree groups today.

My firm, Age Wave, in collaboration with Harris Interactive and sponsored by AIG SunAmerica, recently interviewed 1,000 retiree households to find out how folks were doing and whether there were differences in their experience of retirement. From this research, we discovered that there were four distinct types of mature adults, each with its own experience of retirement.

We've named one of the segments the Ageless Explorers—a group that makes up 27% of the older adult U.S. population. These are people who are becoming the new role models for retirement. They feel youthful and active. They want to contribute to their community. They like to learn and make new friends. They're very much alive—all their pistons are firing, and they want to keep working. They view themselves as aging in an ageless way. When we asked these people when they thought they'd feel elderly inside, they said "Never."

Another group of retirees we call the Comfortably Contents, comprising 19% of the older adult population. These people are essentially living their golden years—which may turn out to be yesterday's retirement dream. Their primary desire in this stage of their lives is to simply relax and be free of worry, stress, and obligation. When we asked members of this segment when they thought they'd feel elderly inside, they said "Soon." This may well be a pleasant retirement for some, but for many people, this life of pure leisure is just not exciting or vibrant enough. My guess is that most boomers will become Ageless Explorers rather than Comfortably Contents.

The third segment, making up 22% of the older adult population, are the Live-for-Todays. These folks define themselves as fun and adventuresome. They're interesting and lively people, and they love the idea of continuing to grow as individuals. The problem is that they spent so much of their lives living for today that they now don't have enough money to feel comfortable. They have an enormous amount of worry and regret about how they're going to make it, and they feel anxious that they may not achieve the level of pleasure and joy that they had hoped for, due to their lack of financial preparedness.

The fourth and largest category—32%—are the Sick-and-Tireds. These are people who have been beaten down by life, and most are having a miserable time in retirement. They've got the least amount of money and have done the least to prepare for retirement. The effect of it is that their unfortunate state leaves them feeling hopeless and unwilling to do nearly anything with their lives. When we asked these people if they would like to go to the community college, they said "No." Would they like to volunteer in their local church programs? "No." Would they like to spend more time with their family? "No." Take a trip? "No." They've pretty much resigned themselves to the fact that their lives are winding down, and they are suffering their way to the end.

Our "Re-Visioning Retirement" study also revealed that about 80% of the next generation of "retirees," the boomers, expect to be working at least part time in their retirement. They apparently do not want to be as disconnected as many of today's retirees seem to be. Instead, they want a different balance in their lives: They want to enjoy extended amounts of leisure time, but they also want to be doing some work—maybe two or three days a week of regular work, or helping out from time to time on a community project, or running a small business from home. Our respondents also said that they want to continue learning and growing in their maturity. They want to be developing their human potential rather than just sitting in the rocking chair and watching TV.

The Transformation of Retirement

We're currently at the tipping point in which retirement is transforming into a new model. It is becoming a time for personal reinvention—new beginnings, lifelong learning, and a cyclic blend of work and leisure.

In addition to their desire to postpone old age, the boomers' propensity for personal growth and new lifestyle challenges will also render obsolete the traditional "linear life" paradigm, in which people migrate in lockstep first through education, then work, then leisure/retirement. In its place, a new "cyclic life" paradigm is emerging in which education, work, and leisure are interspersed repeatedly throughout the life span. It will become normal for 50-year-olds to go back to school and for 70-year-olds to reinvent themselves through new careers. Phased retirements, part-time and flex-time work, and "rehirements" will become common options for elder boomers who'll either need or want to continue working.

Most discussions about increasing longevity have been focused on how to live longer rather than on why. I worry that without envisioning a new purpose for old age, we could be creating a future in which the young are pitted against the old.

In youth, boomers were self-indulgent in their priorities. In their late teens and 20s, many shared an idealistic commitment to bettering society. During the past several decades of career building and child-rearing, these boomers had to put aside many of their early ideals. In the decades ahead, the boomers will complete America's transformation into a gerontocracy, as they take control of the nation's social and economic power.

If they can step outside their generational tendency toward self-centeredness and wield this power wisely and productively, they could rise to their greatest height and make a remarkable success of history's first multiethnic, multiracial, and multigenerational melting pot. But if they use their numbers and influence to bully younger generations and gobble up all of the available resources, political "age wars" could erupt in which the young lash out in anger and frustration at the weighty demands placed on their increasingly strained resources.

However, if they can learn to exemplify a new kind of wise, mature leadership, when the boomers' time on earth is over, perhaps they will be remembered as not just the largest generation in history, but also the finest.

KEN DYCHWALD, founder of Age Wave, is a gerontologist, psychologist, public speaker, and best-selling author. His address is Age Wave, One Embarcadero Center, Suite 3810, San Francisco, California 94111. Web site www.AgeWave.com. His latest book, *The Power Years: A User's Guide to the Rest of Your Life,* will be published by Wiley in August.

Originally published in the July/August 2005, pp. 16–21 issue of *The Futurist*. Copyright © 2005 by World Future Society, 7910 Woodmont Avenue, Suite 450, Bethesda, MD 20814. Telephone: 301/656-8274; Fax: 301/951-0394; http://www.wfs.org. Used with permission from the World Future Society.

Blessed Are Those Who Mourn— and Those Who Comfort Them

In our death-denying society, all too often the message is: Get over it and get back to normal. The fact is, the bereaved's "normal" never will be the same.

Dolores Puterbaugh

Disbelief is the first thing you feel. The news does not make any sense. There is some mental scrambling around for an anchor. Is this real? How could this be? There is sadness and surprise and, perhaps hidden in the back of your mind, a sense of relief that it did not happen to you.

A friend, coworker, or extended family member has lost a loved one. Perhaps it was after a long illness, or maybe it was sudden and even violent: a crime, an accident, or suicide. The deceased may have been very old or an infant, perhaps not even yet born. Your friend's life has been irreparably changed, and you have an important role to play—even if you are "just" a coworker.

We live in a death-denying society. Most companies offer little time off for survivors, with many people using vacation days or even unpaid leave to accommodate vigils, funeral, and initial recovery. The physically and emotionally wounded survivors return to school or work within days, and often the expectation is that they will be "back to normal." The fact is, their "normal" has changed forever. Bereavement is a ripping away of part of one's heart. A hospice nurse told me the thing that strikes her most about bereavement counseling is that people always are taken by surprise at how powerful it is; the societal message of "getting over it" has infected most individuals.

Since we all will go through this—not once, but many times—it makes sense to figure out what to do to be helpful. Perhaps this will come back around to us, or perhaps we will just have the satisfaction of knowing that we tried to be supportive of a friend in need.

In *Healing Grief at Work: 100 Practical Ideas After Your Workplace Is Touched by a Loss,* clinician Alan Wolfelt reveals the experience of a client whose coworkers announced, one year after her child's death, that it was time to put away the picture on her desk and move on with her life. Knowing that this is shockingly inappropriate still does not provide guidance on how to behave. Of course, you would like to think you are more compassionate than that, but how can one act on that compassion?

Some simple aspects to being appropriately supportive are: be physically present; do not assume the "expert's" position; be a friend.

If a coworker has lost a loved one, you might not think it appropriate to go to the vigil or the funeral. Go! The vigil, visitation, and funerals, as well as the meal afterwards, not only are for the deceased—they are for the mourners, who need affirmation of their loss, recognition of their status as mourners, and support in their time of pain. Make sure you sign the guest book, greet the family, and participate in the rites whenever appropriate. Religious rites exist to help honor the deceased person and to provide comfort to the bereaved; every faith has developed rites to be celebrated in community, not alone. As part of the community of survivors, your role is to offer support.

In the weeks after the loss, continue to provide a physical presence. You may be rebuffed; deal with it and keep trying. This is not a time to keep score over whose turn it is to call whom, or who is next to invite whom to lunch. Prepare meals; invite the mourners over for food or call and invite yourself (with a prepared meal) over to their house. Show up with cleaning supplies or with a box of tissues. It can mean a lot to someone if you are able to help with the tasks that the deceased used to do. The survivor may be too upset or physically incapable of taking over the deceased's chores. Asking for help is difficult for most people, so volunteer your services.

Losing someone we love creates a tremendous void inside. The mourner may feel completely without anchor. This individual cannot be expected to hold up his or her end of the relationship with you at present. Saying, "Call me if you want to talk," is not good enough; be the one who calls and says, "How are you?" or "What about going out for breakfast on Saturday?" Evenings and weekends usually are hardest for those in mourning; make yourself available and be specific with your invitations.

Mourners often complain to me that friends, coworkers, and extended family analyze their (the mourners') grief process and mental health. This is not useful feedback. A common intervention by nonmourners is to provide unsolicited instruction on what stage of grief the mourner is experiencing. Some friends attempt to provide comfort by trying to put the loss into perspective. Another common error is to give mental health diagnoses and recommendations. Not only is this presumptuous, but it is self-aggrandizing on the friends', coworkers', or extended family's part. It is as if to say, "Let's look at you as a case study."

In a similar vein, more misused than any other expert is Elisabeth Kubler-Ross, whose 1969 work, *On Death and Dying,* was based on intensive interviews with the terminally ill and their families. She identified specific stages that occurred between the terminal diagnosis and death: denial and isolation; anger; bargaining; depression; acceptance; and hope. In the first stage, the reality is not accepted; the patient believes this is not happening. In the second stage, the reality begins to set in, but there is anger. From a psychological standpoint, anger is the emotion that accompanies the desire to change a situation; the dying person wants to fight the terminal condition. Next comes bargaining, generally with God: if you cure me, I'll never ——— or I'll always ———. This normal reaction can become paralyzing if the ill person is burdened with an ill-formed theology that believes in a higher power who doles out earthly experiences based on behavior. When bargaining fails, a depressed state of helplessness often ensues. It is beneficial if the dying are able to reach a stage of acceptance and hope. With all due respect to Kubler-Ross and her landmark work with the dying, many researchers and clinicians believe we cannot transfer her stages of dying on those in grief.

These normal reactions to terrible news often have been used to provide a template for grief. However, other researchers and specialists in the field offer different structures for making sense of the mourning process. J.W. Worden identified four primary tasks of grieving that assure a healthy outcome: accepting the fact of the death; working through the pain of the grief; adjusting to a world without the deceased; and renegotiating the internal relationship with the deceased so that the survivor can move forward with life.

Friends and coworkers should—at all costs—avoid announcing to the bereaved what stage, phase, or task they believe the mourner is experiencing at present, or should be. There are not very many "shoulds," if any, in grieving. Each person's experience of grief is unique and even experienced counselors are hesitant to assess any judgment on where someone "should" be at a given point in their grief. There are some specific things that must happen for a grief to become integrated into the person, but these happen gradually, with some overlapping, regressing, patience, and considerable pain.

Gaining Perspective

Another error often made by those trying to comfort grieving persons is attempting to put things into perspective. Survivors have been told to be grateful that someone who died unexpectedly "went quickly without suffering," while those whose loved ones died in hospice care are informed that they are fortunate that there was an opportunity to "say goodbye." Others who

nursed dying loved ones for weeks, months, or even years have confided that friends are less sympathetic because they presume they "had a chance to prepare and could do their grieving in advance." Each person's experience of grief is unique, shaped by the relationship as well as their history, spirituality, and physical, emotional, and mental resources. Friends and family should refrain from rating someone else's grief.

This also is not a time to diagnose. As a mental health professional, I sometimes am asked about this: When is grieving "depression"? This question most often comes from friends of a survivor. My response is that it is normal to feel depressed after a tremendous loss. For some months, the bereaved can expect to have disruptions in sleep, appetite, and energy. Some people will sleep often; a bereavement counselor with more than 20 years in the field describes the experience of grief like recovering from major surgery: sleep and healthy foods are imperative parts of healing; take naps every day, she recommends. Others may suffer lack of sleep. They feel exhausted and crave the escape of sleep, but are restless. Some lose their appetite while others may gain weight by eating for comfort. Concentration may be very poor, and short-term memory temporarily may become impaired. Most mourners can benefit from carrying a small notebook and writing down all tasks, even the simplest, for a few months after the death.

Some mourners will suffer a terrifying inertia. Taking the initiative to call you will be overwhelming. Simple tasks often take twice as long as usual. Doing any chores around the house will feel exhausting, and it especially can be difficult to take over the things that the deceased used to do. Others may fly into a frenetic pace, using busyness as a kind of drug to keep the emotional darkness at bay.

It is important to take some kind of action if the person shows signs of suicidal planning, such as talking about "when I'm gone," giving away personal items, and suddenly seeming upbeat (a sign that he or she has come to a decision about how to handle things—by dying). In this case, immediately go to other family members, clergy, or consult a mental health professional on what to do.

This is not a time to preach. Even ordained clergy assert that it is not recommended at this juncture to teach the mourning about your particular theology of life and death. Accept them where they are and help them find comfort within their own tradition. Encourage and let yourself be part of the rituals of grieving: prayer services, memorial Masses, candles, planting trees, or otherwise offering memorial are important means to express formally the process of separation and loss.

Being a good friend, coworker, or family member to someone who is mourning is simple, but not always easy. In many ways, you should continue whatever your relationship was before the death. If you had lunch together, continue to have lunch together; if you rotated card games at one another's home, keep up the routine.

Do not be afraid to say the deceased person's name. If tears come, it is not because you reminded the mourner of the dead person. He or she was in no danger of forgetting! Most people want to hear people talk about the person they love. They want to hear the funny stories and warm memories you may have, or be given the opportunity to share some of their own. Let them tell you the same stories over and over. This narration of the life they shared is part of the healing process. Ask to see photo albums and to hear the tales of times past. Listen to the story of the death and surrounding experiences as often as you have to. They are integrating the story of the person they love and have lost into their life in the present.

Mourners may ask if they are "going crazy" based on poor concentration, edginess, thinking they see or hear the deceased, and either great tearfulness or an inability to cry. It would help if friends and coworkers were patient and accepting of these aspects to grief.

Keep in mind the anniversaries of the death and, if you were close to the people, any significant dates such as birthdays or wedding anniversaries. Monthly anniversaries of the death are very difficult and mourners are well aware of these dates. Send a card, bring in flowers, or invite your friend over for a meal.

Holidays will be terribly difficult: Do not wait until the last minute to invite someone in mourning over for Thanksgiving, a concert, and other holiday (or nonholiday) religious or social activities. If the person is "taken" for Thanksgiving, ask them for the next day. That typical four-day holiday weekend can be torture if it seems like everyone else is with people they love.

Let's Talk—Or Not

For many, talking about their feelings is difficult. Our voyeuristic television shows may indicate otherwise, but it often is hard to discuss one's innermost feelings. Activities done side-by-side, rather than face-to-face, may encourage gradual conversation and sharing of thoughts, feelings, and memories surrounding the deceased's life, death, and the survivor's life since the death. Fishing, walking, and long drives are great ways to let someone have an opportunity for private conversation.

When conversation can occur, hold back trite sayings such as "He's in a better place," or "She's your guardian angel," or (perhaps worst of all), "It was God's will." Without intimate familiarity with the mourner's theology, you risk hurting that individual terribly. People in mourning do not need fortune telling about their future prospects ("You'll have other children" or "You're young . . . you'll find someone else"). They do not need to be advised about having a "stiff upper lip" or "toughing it out."

Do not singlehandedly take on responsibility to spare this person from grief. If you are very close with the individual in mourning, be sure you have a support system of your own. Spending a lot of time with someone who is grieving can be upsetting. You may find yourself recalling your own grief experiences and feelings of loss. Share these, at first, with someone else in your circle rather than with the bereaved. They are not ready to commiserate until later in the process.

Most important, do not take a grieving person's anger, tears, rebuffs, or rejection personally. It will be healthier for you and more helpful for your friend if you bear in mind that terrible pain sometimes interferes with polite behavior. Respect people's desire for some time and privacy but do not give up, walk away, or leave them alone.

DOLORES PUTERBAUGH is a psychotherapist in private practice in Largo, Fla.

UNIT 8

Personality Processes

Unit Selections

Key Points to Consider

- What is personality? Why do psychologists study it?

- What contributes to differences between people? Are people really all that different?

- What is self-concept? Is it the core of personality?

- How does being reared in one culture versus another influence the self-concept?

- What is a personality trait?

- How does a person high in the trait of sensation-seeking behave? Is this necessarily good or bad?

- In general, what is personality testing designed to do? How can we tell a good test from a weak one? Why are these tests controversial?

Student Web Site

www.mhcls.com/online

Internet References

Further information regarding these websites may be found in this book's preface or online.

The Personality Project
http://personality-project.org/personality.html

Sabrina and Sadie are identical twins. When the girls were young children, their parents tried very hard to treat them equally. The girls were dressed the same, fed the same meals and played with the same toys. Each had a kitten from the same litter. Whenever Sabrina received a present, Sadie received one. Both girls attended dance school and completed early classes in ballet and tap dance. In elementary school, the twins were both placed in the same class with the same teacher. The teacher also tried to treat them the same.

In junior high school, Sadie became a tomboy. She loved to play rough-and-tumble sports with the neighborhood boys. On the other hand, Sabrina remained indoors and practiced her piano. Sabrina was keenly interested in the domestic arts such as painting, needlepoint, and crochet. Sadie was more interested in reading novels, especially science fiction, and watching adventure programs on television.

As the twins matured, they decided it would be best to attend different colleges. Sabrina went to a small, quiet college in a rural setting, and Sadie matriculated at a large public university. Sabrina majored in English, with a specialty in poetry; Sadie switched majors several times and finally decided on a communications major.

Why, when these twins were exposed to the same early childhood environment, did their interests, personalities, and paths diverge later? What makes people—even identical twins at times—so unique, so different from one another?

The study of individual differences is the domain of personality. The psychological study of personality has included two major thrusts. The first has focused on the search for the commonalties of human behavior and personality. Its major question is: How are humans, especially their personalities, affected by specific events or activities? Personality theories are based on the assumption that a given event, if it is important enough, will affect almost all people in a similar way, or that the personality processes that affect people are common across events and people. Most psychological research into personality variables has made this assumption. Failure to replicate a research project is often the first clue that differences in individual responses require further investigation.

While some psychologists have focused on personality-related effects that are presumed to be universal among humans, others have devoted their efforts to discovering the bases upon which individuals differ in their responses to events. In its early history, this specialty was called genetic psychology, because most people assumed that individual differences resulted from differences in inheritance. By the 1950s the term genetic psychology had given way to the more current term: the psychology of individual differences.

Doug Menuez/Getty Images

Does this mean that genetic issues are no longer the key to understanding individual differences? Not at all. For a time, psychologists took up the philosophical debate over whether genetic or environmental factors were more important in determining behaviors. Even today, behavior geneticists compute the heritability coefficients for a number of personality and behavioral traits, including intelligence. Such coefficients are an expression of the degree to which differences in a given trait can be attributed to differences in inherited capacity or ability.

Most psychologists, however, accept the principle that both genes and the environment are important determinants of any type of behavior, whether it be watching adventure movies *or* sitting quietly and reading *or* caregiving to the elderly. Today, researchers devote much of their efforts to discovering how the two sources of influence interact to produce the unique individual. Given the above, the focus of this unit is on personality characteristics and the differences and similarities among individuals.

What is personality? Most researchers in the area define personality as patterns of thoughts, feelings, and behaviors that persist over time and over situations, are characteristic or typical of the individual, and typically distinguish one person from another.

Culture and the Development of Self-Knowledge

Although a great deal of work in the past decades has shown cultural variations in self-knowledge among adults, not until recently have researchers started to examine developmental processes and mechanisms that give rise to the variations. I discuss our research on the development of two kinds of self-knowledge: autobiographical memory and self-concept. Our findings indicate that children develop culture-specific self-knowledge early in life; the two kinds of self-knowledge reinforce each other at both individual and cultural levels; and early narrative practices constitute an important resource from which children draw cultural views about the self to incorporate into their self-understanding and remembering.

QI WANG

I am a wonderful and very smart person. A funny and hilarious person. A kind and caring person. A good-grade person who is going to go to Cornell. A helpful and cooperative girl.

I'm a human being. I'm a child. I like to play cards. I'm my mom and dad's child, my grandma and grandpa's grandson. I'm a hard-working good child.

The above self-descriptions were given by a Euro-American 6-year-old and a Chinese 6-year-old, respectively. While the first focuses on the child's own positive depositional traits and qualities, the second attends to the child's social roles and significant relations.

In the past two decades, a great deal of theoretical and empirical work has shown that self-knowledge in adults often integrates and reflects the prevailing cultural views of self (see Markus & Kitayama, 1991). In cultures that subscribe to an autonomous self and the inherent separateness of distinct persons, such as that of the United States, individuals often view themselves in terms of their unique personal attributes and qualities. In contrast, in cultures such as those of China and Japan, where prominence is given to interrelatedness and collectivity and the self is largely defined by one's place in a matrix of social networks, individuals tend to perceive themselves by focusing on their social roles and relationships. Yet not until recently have researchers started to examine the developmental origins of culture-specific self-knowledge.

Two Kinds of Self-Knowledge

My colleagues and I have studied the development of two kinds of self-knowledge: *autobiographical memory* and *self-concept* (Neisser, 1988). Autobiographical memory, or the "extended self," refers to long-lasting memory of significant personal experiences from an individual's life. Self-concept, or the "conceptual self," refers to an individual's conceptual representations of him- or herself. We view the development of self-knowledge as a process of cultural adaptation in which children, guided by socialization agents, internalize cultural views about the self into their own self-understanding and remembering (Wang, 2004; Wang & Ross, in press). This process is further facilitated by the interplay between the two kinds of self-knowledge: Self-concept enables privileged encoding of and access to autobiographical information that confirms the views about the self favored by the culture; autobiographical memory, in turn, sustains the development and maintenance of a self-concept that integrates cultural views about the self as its central component.

We use open-ended, free-narrative methods, which, compared with psychometric measures that have a preexisting norm often in favor of Western samples, allow children to describe themselves and their experiences in their own terms and from their own perspectives. Our findings address three interrelated questions, which I discuss in turn.

Does Culturally Construed Self-Knowledge Emerge Early?

Let's first consider self-concept. One important dimension of self-concept concerns whether individuals focus on their unique personal attributes or on their social roles and relationships in defining themselves. We have examined this self-dimension in children of different ages. Our youngest group was from an ongoing longitudinal study of Chinese families in China, first-generation Chinese immigrant families in the United States, and

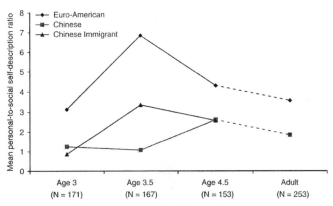

Figure 1 Mean personal-to-social self-description ratio as a function of culture and age. Children's responses were classified as "personal" when they referred to personal attributes, preferences, possessions, and behaviors unrelated to other people (e.g., "I'm happy," "I have a teddy bear") and as "social" when they referred to group memberships and interpersonal relations (e.g., "I am a girl," "I love my Mommy"). Some children did not provide any social self-descriptions, so the ratio was constructed for each child by dividing the number of personal self-descriptions by the number of social self-descriptions plus 1—that is, personal/(social + 1). The ratio represents a focus on personal relative to social aspects of self. The same ratio construct was used with the self-description data of Euro-American and Chinese adults. (The adult data come from Wang, 2001.)

Euro-American families. We interviewed children three times at home when they were 3, 3.5, and 4.5 years of age. We told children that we would like to write a story about them and asked them what things we should put in the story. Compared with their Chinese and Chinese immigrant peers, Euro-American youngsters were more likely to focus on their personal, as opposed to social, aspects of self across all age points (see Fig. 1). Interestingly, the pattern of cultural differences in preschool children's self-descriptions is not dissimilar to that of adults (Wang, 2001).

Cultural beliefs may also influence other dimensions of self-concept (Markus & Kitayama, 1991). The emphasis on autonomy in Euro-American culture endorses a context-independent self; such a self is defined by an individual's dispositional qualities and inner traits that are invariant over time and unconstrained by social situations. The high value placed on self-enhancement and self-esteem further encourages positive self-views that are considered crucial to one's psychological well-being. In contrast, the emphasis on social relatedness in Chinese culture advocates the situation boundedness of persons; in this view, the self is experienced and expressed in specific interpersonal contexts and characterized by an individual's overt behaviors. Self-criticism and humility are encouraged, to facilitate self-improvement and group solidarity.

In line with these analyses, I examined self-concepts in Euro-American and Chinese preschoolers, kindergartners, and second-graders (Wang, 2004). Children provided self-descriptions in a storytelling task. Across all age groups, Euro-American children described more abstract dispositions and inner traits (e.g., "I am smart") than did Chinese children, who referred to more situation-bound characteristics (e.g., "I play with my

friend Yin-Yin at school") and overt behaviors (e.g., "I practice the piano every day"). Euro-American children also gave more positive self-evaluations (e.g., "I'm beautiful") than did Chinese children, who more frequently described themselves in neutral terms. And again, Euro-American children focused more on their personal and less on their social aspects of self than did Chinese children.

Cultural views about the self can further shape how individuals sample, process, and retain autobiographical information; they thus affect memory *accessibility, style,* and *content.* An emphasis on autonomy may direct cognitive resources toward elaborate encoding of personal experiences, especially specific, one-moment-in-time events unique to the individual and focusing on the individual's own roles and perspectives (e.g., "the time I won the spelling-bee competition"). Such memories are likely to become richly represented and highly accessible during recall. They help individuals distinguish themselves from others and reaffirm their unique identity. An emphasis on relatedness may, instead, prioritize the retention of social knowledge critical for social harmony and group solidarity. Detailed remembering of one's own experiences may not be accentuated in this context. And when remembering the past, individuals may attend to generic routine events (e.g., "going to parties"), which, in contrast to memories of specific episodes, are often skeletal, have few sensory-emotional details, and generally serve to direct one's (appropriate) behavior in particular, oftentimes social, situations (Nelson & Fivush, 2004). Individuals may also focus on information about group activities and interactions, helping them relate to significant others and to the community.

Studies have supported this perspective. Compared with Asians, European and Euro-American adults are able to access more distant and more detailed very-long-term memories, such as early childhood experiences; retrieve more frequently unique, one-time episodes (as opposed to generic events); and focus more on their own roles and predilections (e.g., Mullen, 1994; Wang, 2001). We find the same pattern of cultural differences in children as young as age 3 or 4 (Han, Leichtman, & Wang, 1998; Wang, 2004). For instance, in Wang (2004), Euro-American and Chinese preschoolers, kindergartners, and second-graders were asked to recount four personal events such as a recent time when they did something special and fun. Across all age groups, Euro-American children provided lengthier, more detailed accounts and recalled more specific episodes than Chinese children did. They also more frequently commented on their preferences, opinions, and agency (e.g., "I liked the birthday present," and "My mom didn't let me go out but I did anyway") than did Chinese children, who more often spoke of other people relative to themselves (see Fig. 2).

Interestingly, Euro-Americans attend to specific episodes and focus on their own roles and perspectives not only when remembering events that happened to them personally but also when remembering things about other people. In a recent study (Wang, 2006), Euro-American and Taiwanese young adults were asked to recall their earliest childhood memories in response to cue words of self, mother, family, friend, and surroundings. Euro-Americans frequently reported specific events and focused on their own roles and predilections, even when recalling memories about their mother and their family. Taiwanese, in comparison, more often described generic events and emphasized the roles of others, across all memories.

How Are the Two Kinds of Self-Knowledge Related?

Given that self-concept and autobiographical memory are both culturally constructed from an early age, they may be linked not only at the cultural level but at the individual level as well. Thus, individuals with a greater autonomous sense of self should have more detailed, specific, and self-focused autobiographical memories. Consistent with this reasoning, our studies show that regardless of culture, children and adults who dwell more on personal attributes and qualities when describing themselves are more likely to provide detailed, specific, and self-focused memories, compared with those who dwell more on social roles and group memberships (Wang, 2001, 2004). In a more recent study, it was found that a focus on personal aspects of self in 3-year-olds uniquely predicted the amount of event details they recalled, independent of culture, gender, and language skills (Wang, in press).

Self-concept and autobiographical memory may further correspond across an individual's life periods. Theorists contend that individuals, no matter where they live, develop both personal (self-perceived distinctiveness) and social (self-perceived connectedness) identities in response to basic human needs and universal societal expectations (e.g., Kagitcibasi, 2005). The increasing autonomy and relatedness during ontogeny, then, should be reflected in individuals' lifespan retrieval. That is, when asked to recall personal experiences from their lives, individuals should exhibit an increase in both personal and social focuses in memories from earlier to later life periods. This prediction was confirmed in our study with Euro-American and Chinese middle-aged adults (Wang & Conway, 2004). Compared with participants' reported memories from childhood and youth, their memories from midlife periods were more likely to be specific episodes, focused more on the preferences and perspectives of the remember; midlife memories also attended more to social groups and significant others, independent of memory length. Thus, autobiographical remembering appears to be in concert with the lifespan development of personal and social identities.

If individuals possess both personal and social-relational aspects of self, it should be possible to prompt them to focus temporarily on either. We found that such shifts in attention can affect the content and accessibility of early memories (Wang & Ross, 2005). We asked European and Asian American adults to describe themselves by listing either ten unique personal attributes (personal prime) or ten memberships in social groups (relational prime). We then asked them to recall their earliest childhood memory. Regardless of culture, the personal prime elicited memories that focused more on the remember and less on social interactions than did the relational prime. The personal prime also helped Asians access more distant childhood memories, such that the first memories they reported were as early as those of Euro-Americans.

So, the focuses on autonomy and relatedness in self-views vary across individuals; they both increase within an individual with

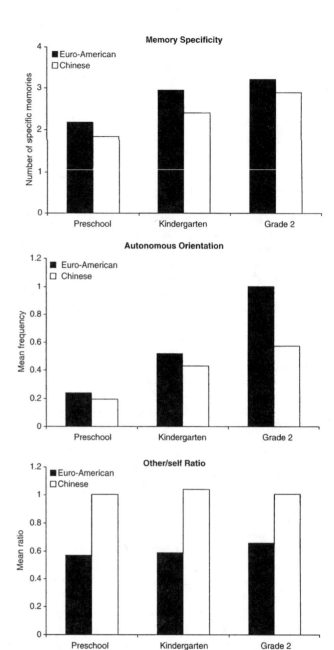

Figure 2 The specificity and content of children's autobiographical memories as a function of culture and age. Memory specificity (top panel) was scored based on the number of specific episodes (as opposed to generic events) children recalled, with a possible score range of 0 to 4. Autonomous orientation (middle panel) was scored by counting the number of instances children commented on their preferences, opinions, and agency per memory event. "Other/self ratio" (bottom panel), the number of times children mentioned other people over the number of times they mentioned themselves, captures the degree to which children attended to the roles of others versus themselves in their memories. The Euro-American group differed significantly from the Chinese group on all measures. From Wang (2004).

development; and they can change temporarily across circumstances, which further shape the content, style, and accessibility of autobiographical memories. These individual cognitive processes may elucidate how cultural differences in self-knowledge are formed and sustained: People incorporate into their self-concepts differing cultural views about the self that facilitate culture-specific forms of autobiographical remembering (i.e., which memories and which aspects of the memories are most likely to be accessible and enduring); their memories, in turn, support and regulate different modes of self-concept endorsed by their cultures.

Narrative Co-Construction of the Self

How do children come to incorporate cultural views of self into their own self-knowledge? Family memory sharing may serve as a critical forum for cultural transmission, in which parents model to children the appropriate ways of organizing, evaluating, and sharing their past experiences and further help children build the critical link between autobiographical memory and self-concept (Nelson & Fivush, 2004). This joint activity embodies rich cultural messages and parents' socialization goals pertaining to the self (Miller, Wiley, Fung, & Liang, 1997). A cultural emphasis on individuality and the use of memory to promote an autonomous sense of self may encourage memory sharing as a means of helping children construct elaborate personal stories to build a unique individual identity; a cultural emphasis on relatedness and collectivity may prioritize the use of memory sharing to instill social knowledge and a sense of belonging.

In a series of studies, we observed Euro-American and Chinese mothers sharing memories at home with their 3-year-olds in semi-structured interviews (see Wang & Ross, in press). Mothers selected past events in which both mother and child had participated, and then discussed the events with their children. Euro-American mothers frequently supplemented embellished information and commented and expanded on children's memory responses (e.g., "Yes, you got a balloon! A yellow balloon doggy. That was exciting."). In doing so, they scaffolded children's participation and meanwhile provided a narrative structure for the construction of elaborate personal stories. Furthermore, the conversations often centered on the child, and mothers frequently referred to the child's roles and predilections. Chinese mothers, in comparison, tended to take a directive role in posing pointed questions to children and provided less embellishment or feedback. They frequently referred to social norms and behavioral expectations and placed past events in a more social-relational context. These cultural differences are illustrated in the conversational excerpts about an emotionally salient event between two mother–son pairs (Table 1).

Here, both conversations were about an incident involving conflicts between the child and adults and, given the emotional nature of the events, both mothers referred to their children's feeling states. However, the style and content focus of the two conversations differed. The Euro-American mother frequently confirmed and elaborated on her child's speech. She focused the discussion on the child's actions and predilections, and further acknowledged the child's emotional tantrum as an expression of individuality. Such conversations facilitate children's detailed remembering of personal experiences that highlight their uniqueness and socialize children into an autonomous sense of self. In contrast, the Chinese mother initiated a directive and didactic talk with her child. The focus of the conversation was not to construct an elaborate personal story but to instill proper behavioral conduct in the child. The child's emotions were treated as part of his wrongdoing, which resulted in punishment so that a lesson could be learned. Such conversations situate children in a relational hierarchy, encourage them to abide by rules and develop a sense of belonging, and yet downplay the use of memory to construct a unique individual identity.

Table 1   Mother (M) and Child (C) Conversation Excerpts

Euro-American mother and son

M: Tell me about the craft fair. Mommy and Daddy went to the craft fair. What did we go there for, do you remember?

C: Yeah. Christmas time.

M: It was Christmas time, we were getting some Christmas presents. Did you want to be there?

C: No.

M: And what did you start to do?

C: Hit.

M: You started to hit and what else?

C: Scratch.

M: Do you remember why you were so mad?

C: Yell.

M: You were yelling very loud, I sure agree with that.

C: And crying.

M: And crying too. Why were you so mad?

C: Because I just want to do whatever I want to do.

M: You want to do whatever you want to do. I see.

Chinese mother and son

M: What story did Teacher Lin tell you at school?

C: "Qiu Shao-yun." He didn't move even when his body was on fire.

M: The teacher taught you to follow the rules, right?

C: Um.

M: Then why did you cry last night?

C: You and Grandma didn't let me watch TV.

M: Do you know why we didn't let you watch TV?

C: You were worried that my eyes would get hurt.
   I wanted to watch "Chao-Tian-Men."
   I was mad. I insisted on watching it.

M: So you got spanked, right?

C: Um.

These different narrative practices are mirrored in children's developing self-knowledge. Euro-American youngsters focus more on their unique attributes in defining themselves and provide more detailed and self-focused autobiographical accounts than their Chinese peers do (e.g., Han et al., 1998; Wang, 2004). Our longitudinal data (Wang, 2005) further showed that, regardless of culture, children whose mothers more frequently engaged them in the construction of elaborate personal stories came to recall more detailed and self-focused autobiographical memories. Maternal style further served as a potent mediator in explaining cultural differences in children's memories (Wang, in press). These findings suggest that family memory sharing directly contributes to the development of culturally construed self-knowledge.

Future Directions

The development of self-knowledge diverges early across cultures. It is a process taking place through individual cognitive processes and in adult-guided participation in the sharing of memory narratives. Our findings highlight the importance of studying developmental origins in order to understand cultural diversity in human cognition and behavior. Future research will continue to identify mechanisms for the development of culture-specific self-knowledge. For example, at which stage(s) of personal remembering (e.g., encoding, retention, retrieval) does culture exert an influence? How do children develop culture-specific self-knowledge in different life domains (e.g., family, school life)? How do language and culture interact in the process of narrative self-making? More specifically, which aspects of cultural self-knowledge most reflect the linguistic constraints of a language, and which aspects are relatively independent of language influences? It is also timely to study the impact of immigration and intercultural exchange on self-development to uncover the dynamic and adaptive nature of the cultural construction of the self.

References

Kagitcibasi, C. (2005). Autonomy and relatedness in cultural context: Implications for self and family. *Journal of Cross-Cultural Psychology, 36,* 403–422.

Han, J.J., Leichtman, M.D., & Wang, Q. (1998). Autobiographical memory in Korean, Chinese, and American children. *Developmental Psychology, 34,* 701–713.

Markus, H.R., & Kitayama, S. (1991). Culture and the self: Implications for cognition, emotion, and motivation. *Psychological Review, 98,* 224–253.

Miller, P.J., Wiley, A.R., Fung, H., & Liang, C.H. (1997). Personal storytelling as a medium of socialization in Chinese and American families. *Child Development, 68,* 557–568.

Mullen, M.K. (1994). Earliest recollections of childhood: A demographic analysis. *Cognition, 52,* 55–79.

Neisser, U. (1988). Five kinds of self-knowledge. *Philosophical Psychology, 1,* 35–59.

Nelson, K., & Fivush, R. (2004). The emergence of autobiographical memory: A social cultural developmental theory. *Psychological Review, 111,* 486–511.

Wang, Q. (2001). Cultural effects on adults' earliest childhood recollection and self-description: Implications for the relation between memory and the self. *Journal of Personality and Social Psychology, 81,* 220–233.

Wang, Q. (2004). The emergence of cultural self-construct: Autobiographical memory and self-description in American and Chinese children. *Developmental Psychology, 40,* 3–15.

Wang, Q. (2005, April). The socialization of self in Chinese and immigrant Chinese families. In R. Chao & H. Fung (Co-chairs), *Cultural perspectives of Chinese socialization,* Invited symposium conducted at the biennial meeting of the Society for Research in Child Development, Atlanta, Georgia.

Wang, Q. (2006). Earliest recollections of self and others in European American and Taiwanese young adults. *Psychological Science, 17,* 708–714.

Wang, Q. (in press). The relations of maternal style and child self-concept to autobiographical memories in Chinese, Chinese immigrant, and European American 3-year-olds. *Child Development.*

Wang, Q., & Conway, M.A. (2004). The stories we keep: Autobiographical memory in American and Chinese middle-aged adults. *Journal of Personality, 72,* 911–938.

Wang, Q., & Ross, M. (2005). What we remember and what we tell: The effects of culture and self-priming on memory representations and narratives. *Memory, 13,* 594–606.

Wang, Q., & Ross, M. (in press). Culture and memory. In H. Kitayama & D. Cohen (Eds.), *Handbook of Cultural Psychology.* New York, NY: Guilford Publications.

Address correspondence to Qi Wang, Department of Human Development, Cornell University, Ithaca, NY 14853 4401; e-mail: qw23@cornell.edu.

Acknowledgments—Part of the research was supported by NIMH Grant R01-MH64661 to the author. I thank Charles Brainerd, Lee Lee, and the Editor for helpful comments.

Frisky, but More Risky

High sensation-seekers' quest for new experiences leads some to the high-stress jobs society needs done but makes others vulnerable to reckless behavior.

CHRISTOPHER MUNSEY

In the early 1960s, University of Delaware psychology professor Marvin Zuckerman, PhD, and his fellow researchers noticed something unique about the young men volunteering for their sensory-deprivation experiments: Many were free-spirited types, wearing motorcycle jackets and favoring long hair over the close-cropped style still prevalent in those years. Yet it seemed to Zuckerman, initially at least, that the experiment couldn't have been more dull: Participants lay motionless for hours on an air mattress in a darkened, double-walled sound-proof room, the monotony broken only by restroom breaks and cold sandwiches.

Puzzled at the incongruity, Zuckerman then found out what was behind it: Some participants had supposedly experienced hallucinations during prior sensory-deprivation experiments conducted by other scientists, according to newspaper reports. Some of the volunteers now showing up for Zuckerman's experiments came seeking the same hallucinogenic sensations, he says.

He found that these volunteers scored high on a measure he developed to gauge sensation-seeking, and that high sensation-seekers also were more likely to volunteer for experiments on hypnosis and the testing of hallucinogenic drugs.

The discovery helped Zuckerman develop a new sensation-seeking construct for personality, one recognizing the role that an individual's desire for varied, complex, novel and intense stimulation plays in determining personality and behavior. In 1971 in the *Journal of Consulting and Clinical Psychology* (Vol. 36, No. 2, pages 45–52), he published the Sensation Seeking Scale Form IV, a personality test designed to measure a person's predilection for thrill- and adventure-seeking, experience-seeking, disinhibition and boredom susceptibility.

Subsequent research suggests that high sensation-seeking reaches into every aspect of people's lives, affecting engagement in risky sports, relationship satisfaction before and during marriage, tastes in music, art and entertainment, driving habits, food preferences, job choices and satisfaction, humor, creativity and social attitudes.

Compared with low sensation-seekers, high sensation-seekers are more likely to smoke, abuse alcohol and use drugs, and are more attracted to high-stress careers. Probing further, Zuckerman has found evidence for both a physiological and biochemical basis for the sensation-seeking trait: High sensation-seekers appear to process stimuli differently, both in the brain and in physiological reactions.

High sensation-seekers, who crave novel experiences, are at one end of the scale, while low sensation-seekers, who actively avoid excitement, are at the other end. Most people fall in the middle, with a moderate inclination to seek out new experiences, but a disinclination to push too far, he says.

What's Different

When presented with new stimuli, high sensation-seekers have a different orienting reflex (OR) than that of low sensation-seekers. As defined by Zuckerman, the OR is a measure of arousal and interest triggered by any novel object appearing in a perceptual field.

One study found that when subjects with high disinhibition scores were presented with a moderate-intensity tone, their heart-rates slowed down on the first exposure, while the heart rates of low sensation-seekers quickened.

Another of his studies, published in the *Journal of Personality* (Vol. 58, No. 1, pages 313–345) in 1990, indicates that the differences between high and low sensation-seekers extend to the cortex of the brain, with high sensation-seekers showing an "augmenting" electrochemical reaction, or increasing amplitude of cortical-evoked potentials (EPs) in response to increasing intensities of stimulation. Low sensation-seekers, however, demonstrate a reducing reaction, showing little EP increase in relation to increasing stimulus intensity, and sometimes showing a reduction in EP amplitudes at the highest intensities of stimulation.

The personality trait may have a biochemical basis as well. High sensation-seekers have lower levels of monoamine

Psychologists Are Thrill-Seekers Too

Come Memorial Day weekend, you can usually find Frank Farley, PhD, and a band of about a half-dozen devoted fellow psychologists in the stands at the Indianapolis 500 waiting for the green flag to signal the race's start.

"When those incredibly powerful engines start up, the roar is deafening, and the whole racetrack shakes and reverberates," says Farley, a Temple University professor.

Yet Farley sees something deeper at work than just spectacle at the Indy 500—namely, the human desire to pursue thrills for their own sake.

"It's kind of a focused example of thrill-seeking, of the vicarious enjoyment of thrills," he says.

He started coming to the race in part because of his friendship with Richard Hurlbut, PhD, a former president of the Wisconsin Psychological Association and clinical psychologist in Stevens Point, Wis. Hurlbut arranges the tickets and hotel rooms for psychologists making the annual pilgrimage.

Hurlbut's father owned an auto parts store and got free tickets to the race when he was a boy. Hurlbut stopped going for a while during his college years and first career as a high school English teacher, but started attending again with his psychologist colleagues in the early 1980s.

Together, they observe the full range of human behavior—"from the most classy things to the most debasing things," Hurlbut says—at what's been described as the largest regularly scheduled gathering of humanity in North America. It's all there, from drivers performing at their mental and physical peak, roaring more than 220 miles per hour six inches from the lip of a concrete wall, to the beer-belly bacchanalia among the tens of thousands of fans packed in the infield. There's slightly less inebriation than in years past, though, when at least one old, beat-up car would be doused with gasoline and ceremonially torched once the race started, he says.

Besides watching their fellow fans, the psychologists follow the careers of the drivers such as Rick Mears, a four-time Indy winner who has gone on to become a successful coach. Despite suffering a crushing foot injury during his driving career, Mears worked his way back into racing and recovered his ability to maintain a constant speed, completing lap after lap on the 2.5 mile track with times varying by as little as two-hundredths of a second.

"The people that get to that level are remarkably good, and remarkably devoted to what they're doing, and they risk their lives," Hurlbut says.

Back home at his practice, Hurlbut sometimes draws on Indy 500 lore to help treat people with chronic pain. His favorite is the tale of a 1920s race winner whose leg welded to the manifold after some protective metal ripped loose. It wasn't until after the driver completed the 200-lap, 500-mile race that he noticed that the heat had severely burned his leg.

Just like the driver, people can sometimes overcome their pain if they're intensely focused on something else, Hurlbut says.

—C. Munsey

oxidase (MAO) type B, an enzyme involved in the regulation of neurotransmitters, particularly dopamine, according to Zuckerman's book "Behavioral Expressions and Biosocial Bases of Sensation Seeking" (Cambridge University Press, 1994) and a research review chapter he wrote in the book "Biology of Personality and Individual Differences" (Guilford Press, 2006).

Moreover, research Zuckerman published with M. Neeb in *Personality and Individual Differences* (Vol. 1, No. 3, pages 197–206) in 1980 determined that sensation-seeking, which is higher in men than in women, peaks in the late teens and early 20s and gradually declines with age, along with levels of testosterone. MAO, which is low in high sensation-seekers, increases with age in the blood and brain.

Since the development of the sensation-seeking scale, Zuckerman has developed the Zuckerman-Kuhlman Personality Inventory measuring impulsive sensation-seeking as a major trait of personality, along with four other major traits: sociability, neuroticism-anxiety, aggression-hostility and activity.

Zuckerman emphasizes that high sensation-seeking is a normal personality trait, despite its association with risky behavior. For example, the trait plays a role in bringing people into pro-social occupations such as law enforcement, firefighting and emergency room medicine—high-stress jobs that would shut down low sensation-seekers.

"In a diverse society, you need both types," he says. "You need people to keep the books and make laws and have families, and you need your adventurers like Columbus to explore and find excitement."

Now a professor emeritus at Delaware, Zuckerman is preparing to publish his third book on sensation-seeking, "Sensation Seeking and Risky Behavior," through APA later this fall.

Looking to the future, Zuckerman says researchers need to learn more about how people's genetic makeup, family environment and social life interact to determine the sensation-seeking aspect of their personalities.

The Big T Personality

How a person's thrill-seeking traits fit into the larger society—and how society can channel positive aspects of thrill-seeking and dampen negative aspects—is a question that fascinates Temple University psychologist Frank Farley, PhD. A former APA president, Farley has developed a personality model that describes the Big T (thrill-seeking) personality.

"To me, one of the deepest motivations in the human spirit is to lead an exciting, interesting and thrilling life. It's not for everybody, but it's a powerful force," he says.

Farley's study of thrill-seeking has taken him to Nepal, where he interviewed Mount Everest climbers, to China and later to the Baltic states where he participated as a crew member in cross-country hot air balloon racing. He travels the world seeking extreme risk-takers, who provide him, he argues, a more valid profile than college students do.

"If I want to study major risk-taking, I've got to go to where the major risk-takers are," he says.

154

In Farley's model, the Big T "positive" personality can account for involvement in entrepreneurship, extreme sports such as parachuting and hang-gliding, or creative science and art. By contrast, the Big T "negative" personality may turn to crime, violence or terrorism "for the thrill of it"—embracing the destructive, dark side of the trait.

A Big T positive personality can find thrills in physical or mental activities. Albert Einstein, for example, was a Big T "mental" personality who found intellectual discovery thrilling.

Farley sees thrill-seeking everywhere, from special effects-laden Hollywood blockbusters to the hundreds of thousands of fans who gather annually at the Indianapolis 500 motor race, enjoying the vicarious thrill of watching hurtling race cars (see sidebar). It extends to the highest reaches of creativity and innovation in science, business and education, as he outlined in a chapter in "Fostering Creativity in Children, K–8: Theory and Practice" (Allyn and Bacon, 2001).

Farley theorizes that in a country such as the United States—a Big T nation built on the risky adventure of immigration—thrill-seekers are given more freedom to pursue their quest for bigger thrills and risks than in countries with more structured cultures, such as China.

Often democratic societies benefit economically, as risk-takers become ever more creative in their endeavors, says Farley. He cites as an example of a creative risk-taker Microsoft founder Bill Gates—a college dropout whose ideas helped revolutionize how society uses computers.

Despite America's tradition of thrill-seekers, Farley sees a constant tension between thrill-seekers and people who want stricter safety regulations, citing the ongoing debate over the toll of climbers killed on Mount Everest every year. Mountain climbers think the chance to reach the top is worth it, despite the risk of dying.

"Their view is, 'We're all going to die. I'd rather die undertaking a grand adventure than in bed with tubes running through my body,'" he says.

A Sense of Calm

While psychologists like Farley research thrill-seekers, others like Chris Carr PhD, focus their practice on them. Carr works with athletes who might be considered sensation-seekers and thrill-seekers by anyone not involved in their sports.

An Indianapolis-based sport psychologist, Carr served as team psychologist for the U.S. men's alpine skiing team from 1992 to 2002 and is currently working with the U.S. national diving team. He also consults with Rising Star Driver Development, a Chicago-based firm that helps younger race car drivers transition into professional racing. The skiers he's worked with rocket down icy slopes at speeds topping 70 miles per hour, while the divers leap off platforms more than 32 feet above a pool, twisting and turning to the water below.

Interestingly to him, the elite athletes he works with don't talk so much about the thrill of pulling off such physically challenging feats, but rather about the sense of calm they feel when performing at their peak, Carr says.

"I think they love the sensation of moving; they love the sensation of being in control when maybe everyone else would feel out of control," he says.

The Testing of America

CAROLINE HSU

A re you an introvert or an extrovert? A confronter? An idealist? An analytical Enneagram type 5, or a free-spirited orange? Or are you, like most people, just a good old ESTJ?

Whether you see the world through four-letter personality types, believe in ayurvedic *doshas,* or completed an online assessment before getting a job, chances are you've taken a personality test. If not, just wait: Personality tests are increasingly a part of American life, used to assess preschool applicants, match up college roommates, award promotions, and even match life partners. And they're big business: Personality testing companies make up a $400 million industry that's growing at an average of 10 percent a year. The tests are used in hiring, promotions, and professional development by a third of U.S. businesses. The Myers-Briggs Type Indicator, the most popular, is taken by an estimated 2.5 million people a year, and in the past three months alone, the online testing website *Tickle* administered 10 million personality tests.

Who are you? Yet despite some of the tests' scientific trappings, they may reveal less about "personality" than meets the eye. Within the field of psychology, there's not even a consensus on whether personality can be tested at all. While some psychologists regularly use tests to predict and understand behavior and guide individual change, others believe that personality is a moving target, determined by past experience and current environment. Some tests, like the Rorschach inkblots, are highly controversial yet still remain in use. And others, like the Myers-Briggs Type Indicator and its legions of imitators, have little academic support but are seen as largely harmless and sometimes very helpful in therapy and personal coaching.

"Personality tests are popular because they promise a shortcut," says writer Annie Murphy Paul, author of the forthcoming book *The Cult of Personality: How Personality Tests Are Leading Us to Miseducate Our Children, Mismanage Our Companies and Misunderstand Ourselves.* "There are now such large numbers of people in our schools, corporations, and legal system, we need a way to manage and screen them, and these tests ask what we're like as people and provide a neat, tidy label." While the SAT and IQ tests have been widely criticized and have adapted to meet those criticisms, personality tests have largely escaped serious examination. "The tests we use today reflect in large part the idiosyncratic and often eccentric personalities of their creators," says Murphy Paul. "Scientific proof of their effectiveness, however, is often lacking."

But John Putzier, a performance consultant and author of the new book *Weirdos in the Workplace,* argues that personality testing can be enormously valuable, precisely because often what is revealed as a weakness is actually a person's strength. "Someone who is analytical and likes to work by themselves all day might be a great engineer, planner, or accountant," says Putzier.

Ian Bilyj, 30, of Woodbridge, Va., first took the Myers-Briggs Type Indicator as part of a high school class. Students were assigned roles in a fictional company based on their four-letter type. Bilyj tested as a classic INTP, or an Introverted, Intuitive, Thinking Perceiver. In the world of Myers-Briggs, INTPs are often known as the Thinker, detached and analytical. Bilyj went on to become an engineer, a natural fit for his type, but also used college to work on his social skills. "I made a conscious effort to know people better, and when I took the test over after sophomore year of college, I had become an E," or Extrovert. Although personality type theory holds that core attributes such as introversion and extroversion don't change, in practice, as many as three quarters of Myers Briggs test takers have a different result upon retaking the test, according to a 1991 report by the National Research Council.

One of the newer uses of personality testing is electronic matchmaking. At the forefront is Neil Clark Warren, founder of the dating website *eHarmony.com.* Warren, a clinical psychologist, studied 2,000 married couples to devise his 436-question "compatibility index." *EHarmony* matches only couples who share similar levels in a minimum of 25 out of 29 areas of compatibility. Websites like *Tickle* and *Match.com* now have their own dating personality tests, too.

More controversial is the use of personality testing in high-stakes situations, like job interviews, parole hearings, and court cases. "One of the problems is there's no state or federal regulations on these tests," says Brad Seligman, a Berkeley, Calif., lawyer who has won clients million-dollar settlements for personality test questions that violated state law. In one particularly egregious case, welfare applicants in Contra Costa County were tested for substance abuse with queries like "True or False: I believe everything is turning out just the way the Bible said it would." Further investigation showed that the test incorrectly classified 44 percent of all applicants as addicts. The county paid $1.2 million to mislabeled test takers and stopped giving the test. In other cases, minorities have been able to show that tests were discriminatory.

Another controversy is brewing in the use of tests in custody disputes. The mmpi 2, a test designed to assess clinical mental disorders, is regularly administered in such cases. After taking the mmpi 2 as well as two other tests and undergoing a short interview, Tina Marie Camacho of Bay Shore, N.Y., was diagnosed with Munchausen syndrome by proxy, an illness where a parent seeking attention hurts or overmedicates a child. Despite the fact that Camacho's family pediatrician disagreed with the court-appointed psychologist's diagnosis, the personality test carried more weight, and Camacho lost custody of her two children.

"The worst test used well can be better than the best test used poorly."

Mo Therese Hannah was also forced to take the MMPI 2 as part of her court-ordered custody evaluation. Hannah, a psychology professor at Siena College in Loudonville, N.Y., knew the exact mechanics of the MMPI—she'd even taught classes about the test. She also knew that she was under a great deal of emotional stress from the trauma of the custody battle—stress that might make her appear an unstable mother. "I did try to take the test honestly," said Hannah, who was eventually awarded custody of her four children.

Bad behavior. But her situation also exemplifies the deep divide in psychology over just what personality is. "There's a tendency to think that everything a person does flows from his personality, but there are experiments that show what predicts behavior is not personality but situation," says John Darley, a social psychologist at Princeton University. A classic example is the infamous 1971 Stanford Prison Experiment, in which undergraduates chosen for their very "normalness" were randomly assigned roles as "prisoner" or "guard" and placed in a very realistic prison environment. In six days, the violence and cruelty had escalated to such levels that the study had to be called off.

"These tests are a snapshot, but life is a moving picture," says Ben Dattner, president of Dattner Consulting, a New York firm that administers personality tests. He cautions that tests can allow organizations to unfairly label an individual or allow an individual to rationalize faults that should be worked on. "To say that someone is an ENTP can be a stereotype that labels someone, 'You're a member of this group, and people like you are apt to have messy desks or be late for meetings," says Dattner. "Personality tests can offer one additional data point but shouldn't determine the outcome of decisions. The worst test used well can be better than the best test used poorly."

"Who am I? What should I do with my life? Why don't I get along with people who are different from me?"—these are all good questions, says Murphy Paul. As Americans live longer, change careers more often, and search for new ways to find life satisfaction, it's no surprise that they will continue to be drawn to such tests. "It gets the conversation going," concedes Murphy Paul. And yet the risk is that personality tests that purport to illuminate our true selves only create the illusion of insight.

UNIT 9
Social Processes

Unit Selections

Key Points to Consider

- Why are social behaviors the domain of psychologists and not just sociologists?

- Can the same person be both good and bad? What causes a person to flip-flop between the two?

- What is prejudice? Discrimination? An implicit bias? If people deny or are unaware of their own biases, how can psychologists possibly study them?

- From where does self-concept originate? How do others influence our self-concept?

- Are humans preordained to seek out the company of others? If yes, why?

- Is modern technology driving us away from or toward others? In what ways has technology changed how we interact with one another?

Student Web Site
www.mhcls.com/online

Internet References
Further information regarding these websites may be found in this book's preface or online.

National Clearinghouse for Alcohol and Drug Information
 http://ncadi.samhsa.gov
Nonverbal Behavior and Nonverbal Communication
 http://www3.usal.es/~nonverbal/

Getty Images

Everywhere we look there are groups of people. Your introductory psychology class is a group. It is what social psychologists would call a secondary group—a group that comes together for a particular, somewhat contractual reason, and then disbands after its goals have been met. Other secondary groups include athletic teams, church associations, juries, and committees. Can you think of more examples?

There are other types of groups, too. One is the primary group. A primary group has much face-to-face contact, and there is often a sense of "we-ness" in the group (cohesiveness, as social psychologists would call it.) Examples of primary groups include families, suite mates, sororities, and teenage cliques. What other primary groups have influenced your life?

Collectives, or very large groups, are loosely-knit, massive groups of people. A stadium full of football fans would be a collective. A long line of people waiting to get into a rock concert would also be a collective. A mob in a riot would be construed as a collective, too. As you might guess, collectives behave differently from primary and secondary groups. What examples of collectives can you think of?

Mainstream American society and any other large group that shares common rules and norms are also groups, albeit extremely large groups. While we might not always think about our society and how it shapes our behavior and our attitudes, society and culture nonetheless have a measureless influence on us. Psychologists, anthropologists, and sociologists alike are all interested in studying the effects of a culture on its group members.

In this unit we will look at both positive and negative forms of social interaction. Four articles comprise this section of the book on social aspects of human behavior. The first article provides a review of an interesting new psychological concept developed by noted psychologist Philip Zimbardo. Zimbardo's notion of the Lucifer Effect suggests that people can be both good and bad, like Jekyll and Hyde. The Hyde characterization would be tantamount to Lucifer. How can both of these sides coexist in a single individual? Zimbardo reveals the reasons or causes in this very interesting article. Several well-known social psychological phenomena can account for a person's seemingly sudden swing from good to bad.

We next move to other social behaviors. In "Mirror, Mirror: Seeing Yourself as Others See You," Carlin Flora provides information about how others shape our self-concept. Feedback from others is thought to fashion what we think of ourselves. Our self-awareness and sociability, for example, are determined in whole or in part by what others reflect back to us.

Finally, in "We're Wired to Connect," Mark Matousek writes about how modern technology is diminishing face-to-face interaction. The Internet and text messaging, for example, allow people to connect but not in thoroughly human and face-to-face ways. Important interpersonal cues such as facial expressions are missing from these forms of communication. Matousek suggests that these interactions are a bit "abnormal" because our brains are wired for us to actively and fully engage with others. The neuroplasticity of the brain, however, may help us adapt to these newer and less intimate forms of engagement with others.

Bad Apples or Bad Barrels?

Zimbardo on 'The Lucifer Effect'.

Eric Wargo

It is rare when a social scientist actually embraces theologically loaded words like "good" or "evil." Most prefer to speak in more muted terms of violence and aggression, or use the sanitized, judgment-free language of psychopathology—the language of disorders.

Not so, Philip Zimbardo.

"Psychologists rarely ask the big questions," the eminent Stanford psychologist said, addressing a standing-room-only crowd gathered to hear his talk, "The Lucifer Effect: Understanding How Good People Turn Evil," at the APS 18th Annual Convention. "We have all kinds of great techniques for answering small questions. We've never bothered to ask the big questions. It's time we asked the big questions like the nature of evil."

In a young century already dominated by iconic images of evil, the photographs with which he opened his presentation were both familiar and hard to watch. "This," he said, "is the ultimate evil of our time: The little shop of horrors, the dungeon, Tier 1A, the night shift, at Abu Ghraib." The pictures, a few of which had become well known from media reports of the prison, showed Army reservist guards torturing and humiliating Iraqi prisoners—naked prisoners stacked in pyramids or crawling on the floor with leashes; a prisoner standing in a black hood with electrodes on his fingertips; naked terrified prisoners being threatened with attack dogs or having guns pointed at their genitals by hideously masked guards; and worse.

"Pretty horrible," Zimbardo said, breaking the stunned silence in the room.

All of the photographs, he explained, were what he called "trophy photos" that had come from the guards' digital cameras. Zimbardo had access to them because he had served as an expert witness for the defense of one of the guards who had been tried for the atrocities. Despite the natural repulsion it was easy to feel toward those guards, Zimbardo's aim was to show how readily, given the right circumstances, almost any normal person can become an agent of evil.

Their accusers called them "bad apples"—a dispositional account that simply blames the individual for wrongdoing. But as psychologists, Zimbardo said, it is necessary to assume that the perpetrators of the abuses at Abu Ghraib and other prisons in Iraq "didn't go in there with sadistic tendencies, this is not part of their whole lifestyle, they are not serial murderers and torturers." Rather, they were transformed into perpetrators of evil by their situation, the "bad barrel" of war.

Known to everyone in the audience as the researcher who conducted the famous 1971 Stanford Prison Experiment, Zimbardo is probably the best-positioned psychologist in the world to deliver such a situational analysis of atrocity. "We imagine a line between good and evil," he said, "and we like to believe that it's impermeable. We are good on this side. The bad guys, the bad women, they are on that side, and the bad people never will become good, and the good never will become bad. I'll say today that's nonsense. Because that line is . . . permeable. Because sometimes, just like human cells, material flows in and out. And if it does, then it could allow some ordinary people like you to become perpetrators of evil."

From Jekyll to Hyde

Beginning with the classic studies of diffusion of responsibility, Zimbardo walked his engrossed audience through a great tradition of 20th-century social-psychological research seemingly tailor-made to understanding the situation at Abu Ghraib.

Ask a classroom of students who would be willing to pull the trigger to execute a condemned traitor; no one will raise their hands. Alter the conditions such that one would be part of a large firing squad in which there is only one real bullet, no one knowing who had fired the fatal shot, resistance to committing the deed lessens. "If you can diffuse responsibility, so people don't feel individually accountable, now they will do things that they ordinarily say 'I would never do that.'" This basic psychological principle is just one ingredient in the potion that can turn good Dr. Jekylls into sadistic Mr. Hydes.

Many of the other ingredients were revealed in Stanley Milgram's classic 1961 study of obedience to authority—in which over two thirds of subjects in a study ostensibly about memory went all the way in delivering what they thought was a lethal shock to another person (actually an actor feigning agony) when ordered to do so by an authority figure in a lab coat. Subsequent studies by other researchers in which male and female psychology students delivered actual nonfatal but painful shocks to a puppy (causing it to yelp and cry)—they were led to believe they would get a failing grade if they failed to condition the puppy—further revealed how easily people's scruples can evaporate when something even as minor as a grade is at stake.

From such studies, Zimbardo said, we can learn important principles about how to create obedience. He listed several, including the importance of a legitimate-sounding cover story (e.g., a memory study, or "national security"), a legitimate-seeming authority figure, and rules that are vague enough that they are hard to understand or remember. You also, he said, need a model of compliance that, ironically enough, allows room for dissent (" 'Yes, I can understand. Yeah, cry, go ahead and cry. Just keep pressing the button' "). Showing slides of the mass suicide/execution of 912 People's Temple cult members in Guyana in 1978, Zimbardo added that it is also important to "make exiting difficult. This is one of the big things all cults do: They literally create a barrier to leaving [by saying] 'If you exit, you're going to end up mentally impaired.' Literally a lot of people in practicing cults are there because they don't know how to exit."

Situations in which people are depersonalized are good breeding grounds for evil, Zimbardo said. Among the most disturbing of the Abu Ghraib photographs showed an Army reservist guard with his face painted like a hideous skeleton (modeled after the violent rock group "Insane Clown Posse"). "Can you imagine what it must have been like to be a prisoner, watching one of your guards look like this?" Zimbardo discussed a number of deindividution studies in which disguises such as hoods facilitated overcoming moral barriers to hurting another person. He also cited anthropological research showing that warriors in cultures that donned masks or costumes before engaging in battle were significantly more likely to torture, mutilate, and kill their enemies than warriors in cultures that didn't engage in self-disguise. "Masks have terrible power, they're a medium of terror. And of course the first terrorists in the United States were the Ku Klux Klan." Military uniforms, like disguises, are tools of deindividuating a person. And depersonalizing the enemy—if only through linguistic labels—is the flip side of the coin: He cited a study by Albert Bandura in which students delivered much higher electric shocks to another group of participants merely if they had overheard that those students from the other college seemed like "animals."

Zimbardo's famous Prison Study exemplifies all of the above principles and how they can be used to create evil. After randomly assigning 24 normal, psychologically healthy college students to roles of prisoner and guard, giving each group suitably depersonalizing attire (the guards wore reflective sunglasses, for example—an idea Zimbardo said he got from the movie *Cool Hand Luke*)—the students began very quickly to lose their everyday personalities and fulfill their assigned roles. Guards quickly began giving prisoners humiliating menial tasks, then forced them to strip naked and subjected them to sexual degradation. "Within 36 hours, the first normal, healthy student prisoner had a breakdown. . . . We released a prisoner

each day for the next five days, until we ended the experiment at six days, because it was out of control. There was no way to control the guards."

Ordinary People, Extraordinary Conditions

The parallels between the Stanford Prison Experiment and Abu Ghraib are striking. "What we've done is substituted social psychology for Dr. Jekyll's chemical—transforming good ordinary people into perpetrators of evil. So essentially we took the chemical out of Dr. Jekyll's hand. It's not necessary. You can do it using social psychology."

Thus Zimbardo's role as a witness for the defense of the reservist sergeant in charge of Tier 1A (where the infamous abuses were committed) made perfect sense. "This is Chip Frederick," he said. "He is the one who got the idea for the iconic image of torture, the hooded man"—referring to the now-famous photograph of a hooded Iraqi prisoner—"He put electrodes on his fingers, he put him on a box, and said, 'You get tired, you fall off, you get electrocuted.' Imagine the terror. But what was Frederick like before going out into the desert to do that terrible stuff?"

Like any of the students in Zimbardo's study, or any of the hundreds of participants in Milgram's or other similar studies, Frederick is—and was, before his fateful tour of duty—a normal healthy person. He had a distinguished work and military record and a healthy family life. "I had the army's permission to have a whole battery of psychological tests conducted by an assessment expert," Zimbardo said. "I interviewed him at my home. Normal. No evidence of any psychopathology. No sadistic tendencies. His only negatives were obsessive about orderliness, neatness, discipline, personal appearance—all of which was absent at Abu Ghraib." A series of slides of Frederick and his family taken both before and after his hellish experience in Iraq—including a charming photo of Zimbardo and Frederick embracing like old friends—drove his normality home.

According to Zimbardo, the inhuman conditions at the prison—which had been Saddam Hussein's torture chamber before the war—created the situation necessary to effect a Jekyll/Hyde transformation in Frederick's (and his fellow guards') character. Forced to work 12-hour shifts, seven nights a week, for 40 days without a break, in hellishly filthy conditions (without toilets or running water) and under constant enemy bombardment, it sounds like a picture of hell. "Frederick was in charge of 1,000 prisoner, 12 reservist guards, 60 Iraqi police guards who were smuggling weapons and drugs to the Iraqi prisoners. They had no training. There was never supervision on anyone's part. [Frederick] rarely left the prison. . . . Tier 1A became his total reference group, and we know what that means."

The situationist explanation does not absolve Frederick and the other guards from responsibility, Zimbardo emphasized. "What happened at Abu Ghraib was terrible. By understanding the processes we don't excuse it. These people are guilty." But for Zimbardo, the military leadership that had implicitly condoned torture and averted its eyes from what was happening at Abu Ghraib prison deserved the bulk of the blame. He made evident that in his analysis it was the military command and the Bush Administration that created the evil system that created the bad barrel that corrupted once-good American soldiers.

The more than a thousand attendees gladly stayed well over the allotted hour to hear Zimbardo finish his presentation. "I want to end on a positive note," he said, to relieved laughter. "Not all good people turn bad. People resist." Turning around Hannah Arendt's famous phrase "the banality of evil," Zimbardo coined the term "the banality of heroism" to describe the soldier—another otherwise undistinguished, normal guy—who blew the whistle on what was happening at Abu Ghraib by turning over a CD of the soldiers' trophy photographs to the authorities. "Heroic action by ordinary people . . . is more common than the few lifelong heroes," he said.

Zimbardo's address exemplified how social psychology—even the most depressing studies of human weakness—can actually be inspiring. "There will come a time in your life," he said, "when . . . you have the power within you, as an ordinary person, as a person who is willing to take a decision, to blow the whistle, to take action, to go the other direction and do the heroic thing." That decision is set against the decisions to perpetrate evil or to do nothing, which is the evil of inaction. Zimbardo concluded with a thought from Alexandr Solzhenitsyn, the Russian poet imprisoned under Stalin: "The line between good and evil lies at the center of every human heart." He added, "it is not an abstraction out there. It's a decision you have to make every day in here." With the last of Zimbardo's 150 slides and three video clips, came an extended standing ovation—rare among psychology audiences.

Young and Restless

Saudi Arabia's baby boomers, born after the 1973 oil embargo, are redefining the kingdom's relationship with the modern world.

Afshin Molavi

Scented smoke from dozens of water pipes mingled with Lebanese pop music at Al-Nakheel, a seaside restaurant in the Red Sea port of Jeddah. Saudi men in white robes and women in black *abayas,* their head scarves falling to their shoulders, leaned back on red cushions as they sipped tea and shared lamb kebab and hummus. Four young Saudi women, head scarves removed, trailed perfume as they walked past. Nearby, a teenage boy snapped photos of his friends with a cellphone. At an adjoining table, two young men with slicked-back hair swayed their heads to a hip-hop song echoing from the parking lot.

"Look around," said Khaled al-Maeena, editor in chief of the English-language daily *Arab News.* "You wouldn't have seen this even a few years ago."

Saudi Arabia, long bound by tradition and religious conservatism, is beginning to embrace change. You can see it in public places like Al-Nakheel. You hear it in conversations with ordinary Saudis. You read about it in an energetic local press and witness it in Saudi cyberspace. Slowly, tentatively, almost imperceptibly to outsiders, the kingdom is redefining its relationship with the modern world.

The accession of King Abdullah in August has something to do with it. Over the past several months he has freed several liberal reformers from jail, promised women greater rights and tolerated levels of press freedom unseen in Saudi history; he has reached out to marginalized minorities such as the Shiites, reined in the notorious religious "morals" police and taken steps to improve education and judicial systems long dominated by extremist teachers and judges. But a look around Al-Nakheel suggests another reason for change: demography.

Saudi Arabia is one of the youngest countries in the world, with some 75 percent of the population under 30 and 60 percent under 21; more than one in three Saudis is under 14. Saudi Arabia's changes are coming not only from the authorities above, but also from below, driven by this young and increasingly urban generation. Even as some of them jealously guard parts of the status quo and display a zeal for their Islamic faith unseen in their parents' generation, others are recalibrating the balance between modernity and tradition, directing bursts of new energy at civil society and demanding new political and social rights. "We must face the facts," said al-Maeena, who is 54. "This huge youth population will determine our future. That's why we need to watch them carefully and train them well. They hold the keys to the kingdom."

Saudi Arabia, home to a quarter of the world's known oil reserves, is one of the United States' key allies in the Middle East. Yet its baby boom was launched by an act of defiance—the 1973 oil embargo, in which King Faisal suspended supplies to the United States to protest Washington's support for Israel in its war with Egypt and Syria. As oil prices rose, cash-rich Saudis began having families in record numbers. The kingdom's population grew about 5 percent annually from 6 million in 1970 to 16 million in 1989. (The current growth rate has slowed to about 2.5 percent, and the population is 24 million.)

Those baby boomers are now coming of age. And as Saudi analyst Mai Yamani writes in her book *Changed Identities: The Challenge of the New Generation in Saudi Arabia,* "Their numbers alone make them the crucial political constituency."

Their grandparents largely lived on subsistence farms in unconnected villages where tribe, clan and ethnicity trumped national identity. Their parents (at least the men) worked in the burgeoning state bureaucracy and trained with the foreign engineers and bankers who flocked to the kingdom; they lived in an era when television, foreign travel, multilane highways, national newspapers and mass education were novelties. But the boomers live in a mass culture fed by satellite TV and the Internet, consumerism, an intellectual glasnost and stirrings of Saudi nationalism. "I'm not sure young Saudis grasp the enormity of the changes in just three generations," al-Maeena told me. "It is like night and day."

The boomers, however, did not grow into fantastic wealth. In 1981, the kingdom's per capita income was $28,000, making it one of the richest countries on earth. But by 1993, when I first met al-Maeena in Jeddah during a year I spent there on a journalism exchange program, the kingdom was recovering from both a long recession (oil prices had dwindled) and a war on its border (the Persian Gulf war of 1991). Per capita income was declining rapidly; and boomers were straining the finances of a largely welfare-driven state. Government jobs and scholarships for foreign study grew scarce. (In 2001, per capita income was a quarter of what it had been in 1981.)

Arabic satellite television was in its infancy and state censorship was pervasive—in August 1990 the Saudi government prohibited the media from publishing news of Iraq's invasion of Kuwait for three days. But as the '90s progressed, technology forced change.

Long-distance telephone service became affordable. The Internet began to shrink the world, Aljazeera became a boisterous news channel breaking social, political and religious taboos: Many young Saudis began to feel they were living in a country with outdated institutions: an education system that favored rote learning over critical thinking, a religious establishment that promoted an intolerant brand of Islam and a government that was falling behind its neighbors in economic development.

"I'm not sure young Saudis grasp the enormity of the changes in just three generations. It is like night and day."

"The 1990s were not a good decade for young people," said one young Saudi civil servant, who asked not to be named because he works for the government. "We didn't have the secure jobs of our parents' generation, and our government was basically incompetent and getting too corrupt." In the private sector, employers preferred skilled foreigners to newly minted Saudi college graduates. "We were just sitting still while everyone else seemed to be moving forward," the civil servant added.

Then came September 11, 2001, and with it the revelation that 15 of the 19 men who launched the attacks on the United States were Saudis—acting under the auspices of another Saudi, Osama bin Laden. "That event and the [West's] anti-Saudi reaction made me feel more nationalist," said Khaled Salti, a 21-year-old student in Riyadh. "I wanted to go to America and defend Saudi Arabia in public forums, to tell them that we are not all terrorists. I wanted to do something for my country."

Ebtihal Mubarak, a 27-year-old reporter for the *Arab News,* said the attacks "forced us to face some ugly truths: that such terrible people exist in our society and that our education system failed us." She called May 12, 2003, another infamous date for many Saudis: Al Qaeda bombed an expatriate compound in Riyadh that day, killing 35, including 9 Americans and 7 Saudis. A series of attacks on Westerners, Saudi government sites and Arabs ensued, leaving hundreds dead. (In late February, Al Qaeda also took responsibility for a failed attempt to blow up a Saudi oil-processing complex.)

Most violent opposition to the ruling al-Saud family comes from boomers—jihadists in their 20s and 30s—but those extremists are hardly representative of their generation. "When we think of youth in this country, two incorrect stereotypes emerge," Hani Khoja, a 37-year-old business consultant and television producer, told me. "We think of the religious radical who wants to join jihadist movements, like the 9/11 guys, or we think of extremist fun-seekers who think only of listening to pop music and having a good time. But the reality is that most young Saudis are somewhere in the middle, looking for answers, curious about the world and uncertain of the path they should take."

In dozens of conversations with young Saudis in five cities and a village, it became obvious that there is no monolithic Saudi youth worldview. Opinions vary widely on everything from internal reform to foreign policy to the kingdom's relations with the United States and the rest of the West. Regional, ethnic and religious differences also remain. Young Saudi Shiites often feel alienated in a country whose religious establishment often refers to them as "unbelievers."

Residents of Hijaz, a cosmopolitan region that encompasses Mecca, Jeddah and Medina, regularly complain about the religious conservatism and political domination of the Najd, the province from which most religious and political elites hail. Some Najdis scorn Hijazis as "impure Arabs," children fertilized over the centuries by the dozens of nationalities who overstayed a pilgrimage to Mecca. And loyalty to tribe or region may still trump loyalty to the state.

But despite these differences, the kingdom's baby boomers seem to agree that change is necessary. And collectively they are shaping a new national identity and a common Saudi narrative.

Ebtihal Mubarak is one of several talented female reporters and editors on the *Arab News* staff. That in itself is a change from my days at the paper more than a decade ago. In recent years the *News* has doubled its full-time Saudi female staff and put more female reporters out in the field. Mubarak reports on the small but growing movement for greater political and social rights for Saudis. Persecution by extremists is a common theme in her work. As she surfed Saudi Internet forums one day last fall, she came across a posting describing an attack on a liberal journalist in the northern city of Hail. "A journalist's car had been attacked while he was sleeping," she said. "A note on his car read: 'This time it's your car, next time it will be you.'"

"The *hijab* is such an overexamined issue in the West. I like wearing it. We as women face more serious issues."

A few years ago, such an episode would probably have ended with the Hail journalist intimidated into silence. But now, Mubarak worked the phones, speaking with the journalist, the police and outside experts, and put together a story for the next day's paper, quoting the journalist: "What happened to me is not just a threat to one individual but to the whole of society." Thanks to the Internet, the episode became a national story, and the subject of vigorous debate.

And yet: after Mubarak exercised the power of the press, she faced the limited power of Saudi women. Once she filed her story, she hung around the newsroom, glancing at her watch—waiting for a driver, because under a patriarchal legal system Saudi women may not drive. "I feel like I'm always waiting for someone to pick me up," she said. "Imagine a reporter who cannot drive. How will we beat the competition when we are always waiting to be picked up by someone?"

Mubarak reflects how much Saudi society has changed, and how much it hasn't. Like her generational peers, she comes from the urban middle class. Yet as a working woman, she represents a minority: only 5 percent of Saudi women work outside the home. Most are stifled by a patriarchal society and a legal system that treats them like children.

Beyond matters of mobility and employment opportunity is the issue of spousal abuse, which, according to Saudi newspapers, remains prevalent. In one high-profile case, the husband of Rania al-Baz, the country's first female broadcaster, beat her nearly to death in 2004. Saudi media covered the case with the zeal of British tabloids, creating widespread sympathy for the victim and sparking a national debate on abuse. The case even made it to

"Oprah," where al-Baz was hailed as a woman of courage. Once the spotlight dimmed, however, the broadcaster succumbed to pressure from an Islamic judge and from her own family to forgive her husband.

Tensions between the old and the new aren't always so consequential, but they persist. Hani Khoja, the TV producer, told me that he "wanted to show that it is possible to be religious and modern at the same time" on the popular youth-oriented show "Yallah Shabab" ("Let's Go Youth"). Another program that promotes a more modern view of Islam is "Kalam Nouam" ("Speaking Softly"). One of its hostesses, Muna Abu Sulayman, embodies that blend. Born in 1973, Abu Sulayman followed her father, a liberal Islamic scholar, around the globe, including nine years in the United States, where she studied English literature. (Saudi universities opened their doors to women in 1964.) Today, in addition to her television work, she advises billionaire businessman Prince Al-Waleed bin Talal on philanthropic activities that seek to build links between the Islamic world and the West.

The prince's company, Kingdom Holdings, has the only known Saudi workplace that allows Muslim women to choose whether to wear the *hijab* (the Islamic veil and other modest apparel) or Western dress. (The prince also employs the only female Saudi pilot.) Kingdom Holdings' quarters look more Beirut than Riyadh, with fashionable women in corporate attire shuffling between offices. Abu Sulayman, however, chooses to wear the hijab—on the day I met her, a striking green head scarf and shirt ensemble. "The hijab is such an over-examined issue in the West," she told me. "I like wearing it. We as women face more serious issues."

And even as she acknowledges that "the opportunities available to me today were unavailable a generation ago," she says, "We are hopeful to achieve more. I expect my daughter to be living in an entirely different world."

"I want to get things done. . . . I will try to do it quietly and not just to score political points against the extremists."

"I am from Burayda, that famous city you Western journalists are curious about," Adel Toraifi said when we met at a Holiday Inn in Riyadh. He was smiling—Burayda is the heartland of Wahhabi Islam. Toraifi, now 27, came of age in one of the most conservative regions of the kingdom.

More than two centuries ago, Sheikh ibn Abd al Wahhab emerged from the desert there with a puritanical vision of Islam focused on the concept of *tawhid,* or the oneness of God. At the time, he made a key alliance with the local al-Saud ruler, who pledged to support the passionate preacher in return for support from the religious establishment. Eventually, Wahhabism spread across central Arabia, even when the al-Sauds lost power twice in the 19th century (to regain it again in the early 20th). When King Abdulaziz ibn Saud, the founder of modern Saudi Arabia, began his march across the Arabian Peninsula in the early 20th century to reclaim his tribal lands, he revived the bargain with the descendants of Sheikh ibn Abd al Wahhab, known today as the al-Alsheikh family.

The essential outlines of that relationship remain intact. Wahhabi preachers hold the highest positions of religious authority while the al-Sauds hold political authority. Today's Saudi Wahhabist is quick to condemn those who belong to other schools of religious thought as impure or, worse, kufr, unbelievers. That explains part of the political radicalism of young Saudi jihadists—but only part.

Another explanation might lie in the evolution of Saudi Arabia's education system. In the 1960s and '70s, the kingdom fought a rear-guard battle with Egypt for regional hearts and minds. To counter Gamal Abdel Nasser's secular pan-Arab nationalism, the Saudis promoted a conservative pan-Islamism. While Egypt, Syria and Jordan were expelling Islamist radicals, many of whom were college graduates, Saudi Arabia welcomed them as teachers.

When Toraifi was 13, he decided to become a religious scholar in the Wahhabi tradition. For five years, he led an ascetic life, studying the Koran and the sayings of the Prophet Muhammad several hours a day. "I was not a radical," he said, "but my mind was not open, either. I dreamed of becoming a respected scholar, but I had never read a Western book or anything by an Islamic modernist or Arab liberal."

As he walked home from evening prayer one day, he was hit by a car. After three months in a coma, he spent more than a year recuperating in a hospital, thinking and reading. "I thought to myself: I did everything right. I prayed. I fasted. I learned the Koran by heart, and yet I got hit by a car. It was troubling to me."

Once recovered, Toraifi took to reading Western philosophy and Arab liberals with a seminarian's zeal. He studied engineering, but political philosophy was his passion. After taking a job as a development executive with a German technology company, he began writing articles critical of Wahhabism—including one published shortly after the May 12, 2003, attacks warning that a "Saudi Manhattan" was coming unless religious extremism was checked. He was excoriated in some religious Internet forums, but the government largely let it pass.

Then Toraifi repeated his views on Aljazeera, whose coverage had often been critical of the royal family. That, apparently, crossed a line: afterward, Toraifi said, Saudi intelligence detained him for several days before letting him go with a warning. Then an establishment newspaper offered him a column—writing about foreign, but not domestic, affairs. The gesture was seen as an attempt to bring a critic into the mainstream. But he dismisses concerns that he might have been co-opted. "I will continue speaking about the importance of democracy;" he told me. (In December, he accepted a fellowship at a British think tank, where he is writing a paper on Saudi Arabia's reform movement.)

The Al-Sauds number some 7,000 princes and princesses. The most senior princes are sons of the late Ibn Saud, who died in 1953, and most are in their 60s, 70s and 80s. Their sons include Prince Bandar bin Sultan, the former Saudi ambassador to the United States, and Prince Turki al-Faisal, the former director of Saudi intelligence and the current ambassador to the United States. Third- and fourth-generation princes have just begun to make their marks, and while the occasional rumor about corruption or a wild night in a European disco makes the rounds, several third-generation princes are becoming important drivers of modernization.

"I was not radical but my mind wasn't open, either. . . . I had never read a Western book or anything by an Islamic modernist."

Mohammed Khaled al-Faisal, 38, is one of them. The Harvard MBA runs a conglomerate of diverse businesses, including a world-class industrialized dairy farm. When I visited his Riyadh office, he proudly described an initiative that his company had taken to hire village widows and unmarried women to work at the dairy.

"In order to circumvent protest from local religious authorities, we reached out to them and asked them to consult with us on the proper uniforms the women should wear on the job," he said. "We didn't ask them if we could employ women; we simply brought them into the discussion, so they could play a role in how we do it. I am a businessman. I want to get things done. If my aim is to employ more women, I will try to do it quietly and not just to score political points against the extremists."

Economic reform, he went on, is "the chariot that will drive all other reforms." What Saudi Arabia needs, in his judgment, is more small and medium-sized businesses and the jobs they would provide.

"I see my older brother unemployed," said Hassan, a dimpled 14-year-old. "I'm afraid that will happen to me too." The four other students in the room, who ranged in age from 13 to 16, nodded their heads in agreement.

They and their teacher met me in an office in Qatif, in the oil-rich Eastern Province—home to most of Saudi Arabia's Shiite Muslims. Some of the most vitriolic abuse from Saudi religious authorities and ordinary citizens is directed at Shiites, who make up only 15 percent of the population. Though they share job anxiety with their Sunni peers, they feel that upward mobility belongs primarily to Sunnis.

Two of the youths attend a village school several miles away; while the other three go to the local public high school. The lack of a college in Qatif, many Shiites say, is an example of the discrimination they feel.

I asked if teaching had improved since 9/11. "The new teachers are good," said Ali, a smiling 15-year-old, "but the old ones are still around and still bad." The students said their teachers praised bin Laden, ridiculed the United States or described Shiites as unbelievers.

Recently, Ali said, he had brought sweets to school to celebrate the birthday of a prominent Shiite religious figure, and his teacher reprimanded him with anti-Shiite slurs.

I asked if they ever thought of leaving Saudi Arabia.

"No, Qatif is my home," said Hassan. "I am proud to be from Qatif."

Are they proud to be from Saudi Arabia?

Mohammad, who had spoken very little, answered: "If the government doesn't make us feel included, why should we be proud to be from Saudi Arabia? If they did include us more, then I think we would all be proud."

"I see my older brother unemployed," says one of the students in the room. "I'm afraid that will happen to me too."

Public pop concerts are banned in the kingdom, so musically inclined young Saudis gather at underground events or in small groups. Hasan Hatrash, an *Arab News* reporter and musician, took me to a heavy-metal jam session in Jeddah.

Hatrash, who abstains from drink and covers the hajj, the annual Islamic pilgrimage, for local papers, had spent the past two years in Malaysia, waiting tables and playing guitar in bars. When I asked about his eclectic tastes, he said, "I am a Hijazi. We have DNA from everywhere in the world!"

At a walled villa in Jeddah, young men were tuning guitars and tapping drums. Ahmad, who is half-Lebanese and half-Saudi, is the lead singer of a band known as Grieving Age. He introduced me around. A few of the musicians, including Ahmad, had long hair and beards, but most did not. One wore a Starbucks shirt—for his job, afterward. Another worked as an attendant on Saudia, the national airline, and a third worked in insurance. All seemed exceedingly polite.

They played songs from the genre heavy-metal fans call "melodic death." It had a haunting appeal, though the lyrics were, predictably unintelligible amid the heavy bass. On the wails, a poster of the British band Iron Maiden competed for space with one of Mariam Fares, a sultry Lebanese pop star.

When Hatrash took the stage, he played a series of guitar favorites, such as Jimi Hendrix's Purple Haze and softer rock, to the seeming delight of the heavy-metal aficionados. Throughout the evening, more young men arrived—but no women. Some took turns playing; others just watched. By midnight, the jam session had wound down. "This is a tame event, as you can see," Hatrash said. "There is no drinking or drugs. We are just enjoying the music."

I asked if he could envision a day when he could play in public, instead of behind closed doors.

He just smiled and launched into another song. Someone jumped up to accompany him on the bass, and Ahmad mouthed the lyrics. The guy in the Starbucks shirt rushed out the door, late for his shift.

AFSHIN MOLAVI, a fellow at the New America Foundation, has covered the Middle East for many publications.

Mirror Mirror: Seeing Yourself as Others See You

To navigate the social universe, you need to know what others think of you—although the clearest view depends on how you see yourself.

CARLIN FLORA

I gave a toast at my best friend's wedding last summer, a speech I carefully crafted and practiced delivering. And it went well: The bride and groom beamed; the guests paid attention and reacted in the right spots; a waiter gave me a thumbs-up. I was relieved and pleased with myself. Until months later—when I saw the cold, hard video documentation of the event. * As I watched myself getting ready to make the toast, a funny thing happened. I got butterflies in my stomach all over again. I was nervous for myself, even though I knew the outcome would be just fine. Except maybe the jitters were warranted. The triumph of that speech in my mind's eye morphed into the duller reality unfolding on the TV screen. My body language was awkward. My voice was grating. My facial expressions, odd. My timing, not quite right. Is this how people saw me? * It's a terrifying thought: What if I possess a glaring flaw that everyone notices but me? Or, fears aside, what if there are a few curious chasms between how I view myself and how others view me? What if I think I'm efficient but I'm seen as disorganized? Critical, but perceived as accepting?

While many profess not to care what others think, we are, in the end, creatures who want and need to fit into a social universe. Humans are psychologically suited to interdependence. Social anxiety is really just an innate response to the threat of exclusion; feeling that we're not accepted by a group leaves us agitated and depressed.

Others always rate you one point higher than you rate yourself on a scale of physical attractiveness.

The ability to intuit how people see us is what enables us to authentically connect to others and to reap the deep satisfaction that comes with those ties. We can never be a fly on the wall to our own personality dissections, watching as people pick us apart after meeting us. Hence we are left to rely on the accuracy of what psychologists call our "metaperceptions"—the ideas we have about *others'* ideas about us.

The Bottom Line: It Comes Down to What You Think about Yourself

Your ideas about what others think of you hinge on your self-concept—your own beliefs about who you are. "You filter the cues that you get from others through your self-concept," explains Mark Leary, professor of psychology at Wake Forest University in Winston-Salem, North Carolina.

Our self-concept is fundamentally shaped by one person in particular: Mama. How our mother (or primary caregiver) responded to our first cries and gestures heavily influences how we expect to be seen by others. "Children behave in ways that perpetuate what they have experienced," says Martha Farrell Erickson, senior fellow with the Children, Youth and Family Consortium at the University of Minnesota. "A child who had an unresponsive mother will act obnoxious or withdrawn so that people will want to keep their distance. Those with consistently responsive mothers are confident and connect well with their peers."

As an infant scans his mother's face he absorbs clues to who he is; as adults we continue to search for our reflections in others' eyes. While the parent-child bond is not necessarily destiny, it does take quite a bit to alter self-concepts forged in childhood, whether good or bad. People rely on others' impressions to nurture their views about themselves, says William Swann, professor of psychology at the University of Texas, Austin. His research shows that people with negative self-concepts goad others to evaluate them harshly, especially if they suspect the person likes them—they would rather be right than be admired.

The Top Line: You Probably Do Know What People Think of You

But it's likely you don't know any one person's assessment. "We have a fairly stable view of ourselves," says Bella DePaulo, visiting professor of psychology at the University of California at Santa Barbara. "We expect other people to see that same view immediately." And they do. On average there is consensus about how you come off. But you can't apply that knowledge to any one individual, for a variety of reasons.

For starters, each person has an idiosyncratic way of sizing up others that (like metaperceptions themselves) is governed by her own self-concept. A person you meet will assess you through her unique lens, which lends consistency to her views on others. Some people, for example, are "likers" who perceive nearly everyone as good-natured and smart.

Furthermore, if a particular person doesn't care for you, it won't always be apparent. "People are generally not direct in everyday interactions," says DePaulo. Classic work by psychologist Paul Ekman has shown that most people can't tell when others are faking expressions. Who knows how many interactions you've walked away from thinking you were a hit while your new friend was actually faking agreeability?

And there's just a whole lot going on when you meet someone. You're talking, listening and planning what you're going to say next, as well as adjusting your nonverbal behavior and unconsciously responding to the other person's. DePaulo calls it "cognitive busyness."

Because of all we have to contend with, she says, we are unable to effectively interpret someone else's reactions. "We take things at face value and don't really have the means to infer others' judgments." Until afterward, of course, when you mull over the interaction, mining your memory for clues.

Context is Key

While our personalities (and self-concepts) are fairly consistent across time and place, some situations, by their very structure, can change or even altogether wipe out your personality. You might feel like the same old you wherever you are, but the setting and role you happen to be playing affect what people think of you. Suppose you describe yourself as lighthearted and talkative. Well, no one could possibly agree if they meet you at your brother's funeral.

What Type of Person Can Handle Feedback . . .

Are you open to experience? Are you, say, perennially taking up new musical instruments or scouting out-of-the-way neighborhoods? If so, your curiosity will drive you to learn new things about the world and yourself. You'll be inclined to ask people how you're doing as you embark on new challenges, and you will gather a clearer idea of how you come off to others, says David Funder, professor of psychology at the University of California at Riverside.

How to Solicit a Character Critique (Yours!)

Muster your courage and set up an "exit interview" if you're left wondering why a relationship went south, in a spirit of fact-finding—that is, without hostility—contact your ex and ask for an honest and kind discussion of how things went awry. You're not looking to get your ex back (or get back at your ex) but to gather information to prevent lightning from striking twice. Ask questions ("What could I have done better?") and listen. Be sure you don't use the conversation to justify your old behavior.

People endowed with the trait of physical awareness have a keen sense of how they present themselves. If you are concerned with the observable parts of personality—voice, posture, clothes and walk—as an actor would be, says Funder, "you will control the impression you give, and your self-perception will be more accurate." If, for example, you slouch but don't know it, your droopy posture registers in the minds of those you meet and enters into how they see you—unbeknownst to you.

If you are someone who craves approval, you will tend to think you make a positive impression on other people. And generally, you will, says DePaulo.

People who have learned to regulate their emotions are in a much better position to know what others think of them, says Carroll Izard, professor of psychology at the University of Delaware: "They are able to detect emotions on others' faces and to feel empathy." If you are either overwhelmed with feelings or unable to express them at all, it becomes difficult to interpret someone else's response to you. Learning to give concrete expression to your feelings and to calm yourself in highly charged moments will give you a much better grip on your own and others' internal states.

Those with personalities that feed the accuracy of their metaperceptions are handsomely rewarded. "The more accurate you are about how others perceive you, the better you fare socially," says Leary. "Think of a person who thinks he's really funny but isn't. He interprets polite laughter as genuine laughter, but everyone is on to him and annoyed by him."

. . . And What Kind of Person Rejects Feedback

There are people who behave in ways that prevent them from getting direct feedback from others, which renders them less able to know how they come off. Maybe you're a boss who is prickly and hostile in the face of criticism. Or a student who bursts into tears over a bad evaluation. Either way, coworkers and teachers will start leaving you in the dark to fumble over your own missteps.

Such demeanor may even encourage others to lie to you, says DePaulo. You may project a fragility that makes others afraid they will break you by offering honest criticism.

Too much concern about what others think of you can only constrict behavior and stifle the spirit.

Narcissism also blocks metaperception. Instead of wincing, as "normal" subjects do, when forced to see themselves onscreen, narcissists become even more self-biased, finds Oliver John, professor of psychology at the University of California at Berkeley. When he and his team videotaped people diagnosed as pathological narcissists, a group absorbed with themselves, their subjects loved watching the footage and uniformly thought they came off beautifully! The finding underscores how fiercely we defend our self-concepts, even if they reflect psychological instability.

Shyness: A Double Whammy

If you are socially anxious (otherwise known as shy), you likely fret that you don't come off well. Unfortunately, you're probably right. Shy people convey unflattering impressions of themselves, says DePaulo. But not for the reasons they think. People don't see them as lacking in smarts, wit or attractiveness but as haughty and detached. When you're anxious, you fail to ask others about themselves or put them at ease in any way, which can be seen as rude and self-centered.

In a way, many shy people are self-centered, points out Bernie Carducci, psychologist at Indiana University Southeast and author of *Shyness: A Bold New Approach*. They imagine that everyone is watching and evaluating their every move. They think they are the center of any social interaction, and because they can't stand that, they shut down (unlike an exhibitionist, who would relish it). Socially anxious people are so busy tracking what others think that they can't act spontaneously. Still, many people find them endearing, precisely because they don't hog attention.

The Powerful and the Beautiful

Neither group gets accurate feedback. "People are too dazzled or intimidated to react honestly to them," says Funder. Michael Levine, the head of a Hollywood public relations agency, has run up against many such people, who end up with a deluded sense of self thanks to a coterie of sycophants. If you are among the bold and the beautiful, he says, you must invite feedback by playing on the fact that people want desperately to be liked by you. "You must let them know that your approval is conditional upon their honesty with you."

Don't Worry—You're Not See-Through

The traits others judge us on fall roughly into two categories—visible and invisible. Funder has found that others notice our visible traits more than we ourselves do (the eye, after all, can't see its own lashes, as the Chinese proverb goes). You would rate yourself higher on the characteristic of "daydreams" than

others would—simply because they cannot easily discern whether or not you're a daydreamer. They'll tend to assume you're not.

There's always a trade-off between how good you want to feel—and what you want to know.

The good news, however, is that on a scale of physical attractiveness, others always rate you about one point higher than you rate yourself. This applies to "charm," too—another characteristic you can't easily convey to yourself, one that others naturally have a better window onto. "Imagine trying to be charming while alone on a desert island," Funder observes.

One common concern is that internal states are evident for all to see. In a study where subjects did some public speaking and then rated their own performances, the anxious ones in the group gave themselves a low rating, thinking that their inner churning was apparent to all. But audiences reported that they did just fine.

"Invisible" traits aren't entirely invisible—at least not to close friends. But an anxious friend would still rate herself higher on worry than we would.

The invisible/visible trait divide helps explain why people agree more on your positive attributes than your negative ones, says Eric Turkheimer, professor of psychology at the University of Virginia.

"First of all, people are less honest about their own negative traits," he says, "and many of these are 'stealth' traits. You'd have to know someone really well to have any thoughts on whether or not he 'feels empty inside,' for example."

Self-Awareness: A Blessing and a Curse

There is one sure way to see yourself from others' perspective—on videotape (as I did post-toast). But remem-ber, the image is still filtered through your self-concept—it's still you watching you. Paul Silvia, assistant professor of psychology at the University of North Carolina at Greensboro, points to an experiment in which psychologically healthy adults watched tapes of themselves giving group presentations. They described it as quite sobering. They cued into their faults and judged themselves much more harshly than they would have had they relied on their own impressions of the experience. You evaluate yourself much more critically when you are self-aware, because you are focused on your failure to meet internal standards.

If I watch myself on tape, I'm not only viewing with my self-concept in mind, I'm comparing "me" to my "possible selves," the "me's" I wish to become. Here is where an unbridgeable gap opens up between people: I will never have a sense of anyone else's possible selves, nor they mine.

So, should we just rely on our memories of events, protective of self-esteem as they are, and eschew concrete documentation of ourselves? Not necessarily, says Silvia. But the dilemma reveals how self-awareness is a double-edged sword. Self-awareness furnishes a deep, rich self-concept—but it also can be paralyzing, warns Leary, author of *The Curse of the Self. Self-Awareness, Egotism and the Quality of Human Life*. "It leads you to overanalyze others' reactions to you and misinterpret them."

Many of the most unpleasant shades on our emotional palettes—embarrassment, shame, envy—exist solely in the interpersonal realm. We cannot feel them until we are self-aware enough to worry what others think about us. These emotions are supposed to motivate us to cut out potentially self-destructive behaviors. But, Leary points out, given the brain's natural bias toward false alarms, people feel overly embarrassed. Too much concern about what others think can only constrict behavior and stifle the spirit.

Do You Really Want to Know How You Come off?

Report cards and annual reviews give you information on your performance in school and at work. But you'll rarely be treated to a straightforward critique of your character—unless someone blurts one out in a heated argument or you solicit it directly. "You could always ask a family member or someone else who knows you are stuck with them to tell you honestly what they think of you," says Funder. Publicist Levine took this approach a bit further when he asked several ex-girlfriends to each list three positive and three negative aspects of being in a relationship with him. "There was some consistency in their answers," he says. "It was challenging to take it in, but really helpful."

"There's always a trade-off between how you want to feel and what you want to know," says DePaulo. If ignorance is bliss, maybe it's best to trust someone's instinct to protect you. "But there are times when you really need accurate feedback," she says, "such as when you are trying to decide if you would be good in a certain career."

Perhaps the delicate balance between feeling good about yourself and knowing exactly how you come off is best maintained not by all those elusive "others." Maybe it's maintained by your most significant ones, the people who will keep you in line but appreciate you for who you are, not just for the impressions you leave behind.

We're Wired to Connect

Our brains are designed to be social, says bestselling science writer Daniel Goleman—and they catch emotions the same way we catch colds.

MARK MATOUSEK

Have you ever wondered why a stranger's smile can transform your entire day? Why your eyes mist up when you see someone crying, and the sight of a yawn can leave you exhausted? Daniel Goleman, Ph.D., has wondered, too, and just as he helped revolutionize our definition of what it means to be smart with his 1995 blockbuster, *Emotional Intelligence*, the two-time Pulitzer nominee and former science reporter for *The New York Times* has dropped a bombshell on our understanding of human connection in his startling new book, *Social Intelligence* (Bantam).

For the first time in history, thanks to recent breakthroughs in neuroscience, experts are able to observe brain activity while we're in the act of feeling—and their findings have been astonishing. Once believed to be lumps of lonely gray matter cogitating between our ears, our brains turn out to be more like interlooped, Wi-Fi octopi with invisible tentacles slithering in all directions, at every moment, constantly picking up messages we're not aware of and prompting reactions—including illnesses—in ways never before understood.

"The brain itself is social—that's the most exciting finding," Goleman explains during lunch at a restaurant near his home in Massachusetts. "One person's inner state affects and drives the other person. We're forming brain-to-brain bridges—a two-way traffic system—all the time. We actually catch each other's emotions like a cold."

The more important the relationship, the more potent such "contagion" will be. A stranger's putdown may roll off your back, while the same zinger from your boss is devastating. "If we're in toxic relationships with people who are constantly putting us down, this has actual physical consequences," Goleman says. Stress produces a harmful chemical called cortisol, which interferes with certain immune cell functions. Positive interactions prompt the body to secrete oxytocin (the same chemical released during lovemaking), boosting the immune system and decreasing stress hormones. As a doting grandparent himself (with author-therapist wife Tara Bennett-Goleman), the author often feels this felicitous rush. "I was just with my two-year-old granddaughter," he says. "This girl is like a vitamin for me.

Being with her actually feels like a kind of elixir. The most important people in our lives can be our biological allies."

The notion of relationships as pharmaceutical is a new concept. "My mother is 96," Goleman goes on. "She was a professor of sociology whose husband—my father—died many years ago, leaving her with a big house. After retiring at 65, she decided to let graduate students live there for free. She's since had a long succession of housemates. When she was 90, a couple from Taiwan had a baby while they were living there. The child regarded her as Grandma and lived there till the age of two. During that time, I swore I could see my mother getting younger. It was stunning." But not, he adds, completely surprising. "This was the living arrangement we were designed for, remember? For most of human history there were extended families where the elderly lived in the same household as the babies. Many older people have the time and nurturing energy that kids crave—and vice versa. If I were designing assisted-living facilities, I'd put daycare centers in them and allow residents to volunteer. Institutions are cheating children," he says. "And we older people need it, too."

Positive interactions can boost the immune system: "The most important people in our lives can be our biological allies."

Young or old, people can affect our personalities. Though each of us has a distinctive temperament and a "set point of happiness" modulating our general mood, science has now confirmed that these tendencies are not locked in. Anger-prone people, for example, can "infect" themselves with calmness by spending time with mellower individuals, absorbing less-aggressive behavior and thereby sharpening social intelligence.

A key to understanding this process is something called mirror neurons: "neurons whose only job is to recognize a smile and make you smile in return," says Goleman (the same goes for frowning and other reactions). This is why, when you're smiling, the whole world does indeed seem to smile with you. It also explains the Michelangelo phenomenon, in which long-term partners come to resemble each other through facial-muscle mimicry and "empathic resonance." If you've ever seen a group with a case of the giggles, you've witnessed mirror neurons at play. Such mirroring takes place in the realm of ideas, too, which is why sweeping cultural ideals and prejudices can spread through populations with viral speed.

This phenomenon gets to the heart of why social intelligence matters most: its impact on suffering and creating a less crazy world. It is critical, Goleman believes, that we stop treating people as objects or as functionaries who are there to give us something. This can range from barking at telephone operators to the sort of old-shoe treatment that long-term partners often use in relating to each other (talking at, rather than to, each other). We need, he says, a richer human connection.

Unfortunately, what he calls the "inexorable technocreep" of contemporary culture threatens such meaningful connection. Presciently remarking on the TV set in 1963, poet T.S. Eliot noted that this techno-shredder of the social fabric "permits millions of people to listen to the same joke at the same time, and yet remain lonesome." We can only imagine what the dour writer would have made of Internet dating. And as Goleman points out, this "constant digital connectivity" can deaden us to the people around us. Social intelligence, he says, means putting down your BlackBerry, actually paying full attention—

showing people that they're being experienced—which is basically what each of us wants more than anything. Scientists agree that such connection—or lack of it—will determine our survival as a species: "Empathy," writes Goleman, "is the prime inhibitor of human cruelty."

And our social brains are wired for kindness, despite the gore you may see on the nightly news. "It's an aberration to be cruel," says Goleman. Primitive tribes learned that strength lay in numbers, and that their chances of surviving a brutal environment increased exponentially through helping their neighbors (as opposed to, say, chopping their heads off). Even young children are wired for compassion. One study in Goleman's book found that infants cry when they see or hear another baby crying, but rarely when they hear recordings of their own distress. In another study, monkeys starved themselves after realizing that when they took food, a shock was delivered to their cage mate.

Perhaps the most inspiring piece of the social-intelligence puzzle is neuroplasticity: the discovery that our brains never stop evolving. "Stem cells manufacture 10,000 brain cells every day till you die," says Goleman. "Social interaction helps neurogenesis. The brain rises to the occasion the more you challenge it."

MARK MATOUSEK'S *The Art of Survival* (Bloomsbury) will be published next year.

UNIT 10
Psychological Disorders

Unit Selections

Key Points to Consider

- What is a mental disorder? Are some individuals more prone to disorders than other individuals?

- What disorders do you think are the most debilitating?

- How does a mass murderer's mind function or malfunction? What factors contribute to a mass murderer's violence?

- What is post-traumatic stress disorder? Who is likely to suffer from it? How can such individuals be treated?

- What is an anxiety disorder? Is phobic disorder an instance of anxiety disorder?

- What role does the brain play in these disorders? What role does learning play?

Student Web Site
www.mhcls.com/online

Internet References
Further information regarding these websites may be found in this book's preface or online.

American Association of Suicidology
http://www.suicidology.org
Ask NOAH About: Mental Health
http://www.noah-health.org/en/mental/
Mental Health Net Disorders and Treatments
http://www.mentalhelp.net/
Mental Health Net: Eating Disorder Resources
http://www.mentalhelp.net/poc/center_index.php/id/46
National Women's Health Resource Center (NWHRC)
http://www.healthywomen.org

Jay and Harry were two brothers who owned a service station. They were the middle children of four. The other two children were sisters, the oldest of who had married and moved out of the family home. Their father retired and turned the station over to his sons.

Harry and Jay had a good working relationship. Harry was the "up-front" man. Taking customer orders, accepting payments, and working with parts distributors, Harry was the individual who dealt most directly with the public, delivery personnel, and other people accessing the station. Jay worked behind the scenes. While Harry made the mechanical diagnoses, Jay was the mastermind who did the corrective work. Some of his friends thought Jay was a veritable mechanical genius; he could fix anything.

Preferring to spend time by himself, Jay had always been a little odd and a bit of a loner. Jay's friends thought his emotions had been more inappropriate and intense than other people's emotional states, but they passed it off as part of his eccentric talent. On the other hand, Harry was the stalwart in the family. He was the acknowledged leader and decision-maker when it came to family finances.

One day Jay did not show up for work on time. When he did, he was dressed in the most garish outfit and was laughing hysterically and talking to himself. Harry at first suspected that his brother had taken some illegal drugs. However, Jay's condition persisted and, in fact, worsened. Out of concern, his family took him to their physician, who immediately sent Jay and his family to a psychiatrist. After several visits, the diagnosis was schizophrenia. Jay's maternal uncle had also been schizophrenic. The family somberly left the psychiatrist's office and traveled to the local pharmacy to fill a prescription for anti-psychotic medications. They knew they would make many such trips to retrieve the medicine that Jay would likely take the rest of his life.

What caused Jay's drastic and rather sudden change in mental health? Was Jay destined to be schizophrenic because of his family tree? Did competitiveness with his brother and the feeling that he was less revered than Harry cause Jay's descent into mental disorder? How can psychiatrists and clinical psychologists make accurate diagnoses? Once a diagnosis of mental disorder is made, can the individual ever completely recover?

These and other questions are the emphasis in this unit. Mental disorder has fascinated and, on the other hand, haunted

us for centuries. At various times in our history those who suffered from these disorders were persecuted as witches, tortured to drive out demons, punished as sinners, jailed as dangers to society, confined to insane asylums, or at best hospitalized for simply being too ill to care for themselves.

Today, some psychologists and psychiatrists propose that the notion of mental disorders as "illnesses" has outlived its usefulness. We should think of mental disorders as either biochemical disturbances, brain malfunctions, or disorders of learning in which the person develops a maladaptive pattern of behavior that is then maintained by the environment. At the same time, we need to recognize that these reactions to stressors in the environment or to inappropriate learning situations may be genetically preordained; some people may be more inherently susceptible to disorders than others. The propensity for mental disorder lies within all of us, stronger or weaker depending on the individual, and then the environment triggers the disorder.

Mental disorders are serious problems and not just for the individual who has been diagnosed with one. The impact of mental disorder on the family (just as for Jay's family) and friends deserves our full attention, too. Diagnosis, symptoms, and the implications of the disorders are covered in some of the articles in unit ten. The following unit, eleven, will explore further the concept of treatment of mental disorders.

175

Inside a Mass Murderer's Mind

JEFFREY KLUGER

If you want a sense of just how terrible Monday's crimes were, here's something to try: imagine yourself committing them. It's easy enough to contemplate what it would feel like to rob a bank or steal a car; you might even summon a hint of the outlaw frisson that could make such crimes seem appealing. But picture yourself as Cho Seung-Hui, the 23-year-old student responsible for the Virginia Tech bloodbath, walking the halls of the school, selecting lives to extinguish and then . . . extinguishing them. It is perhaps a measure of our humanity that we could sooner imagine ourselves as the killed than as the killer, and find it easier to conjure up what it would feel like to plead for our lives than to take someone else's.

That is where the hard work of trying to make sense of a crime like that at Virginia Tech always hits a wall. We can debate, as we predictably do in these cases, what an incident like this means for our endless national argument about guns and violence and the coarsening of the culture. That's well-mapped ground. What remains uncharted is the unlit places in the minds of the people who are capable of doing these things—and, by extension, in all our minds. What is it that makes individual members of a usually empathetic species turn rogue? How does one of our most primal faculties—the ability to understand that things that cause me pain or fear would do the same to you and that I therefore ought not do them—get so completely shut down? Is empathy optional, at least in some people, and if so, how does that emotional decoupling take place? More important, if we can figure out that part of the question, can we figure out how to prevent such things from happening? "We always ask ourselves, 'Is this a person who has no conscience at all?'" says Stanton Samenow, a forensic psychologist and author of the 2004 book *Inside the Criminal Mind*. "They seem to have an unfathomable ability to shut off knowledge of the consequences, of the difference between right and wrong. It's critical for us to try to understand that worldview and mental makeup."

For all the ink and airtime that follow an attack like the one at Virginia Tech, mass murder is an exceedingly rare crime. The rate of killings in the U.S. involving five or more victims—one generally accepted definition of a mass killing—represented less than 1% of all homicides 25 years ago, and still does today. Among kids, the overall violence figures are actually plummeting, with the number of children under 17 who commit murder falling 65% between 1993 and 2004. Mass killing, says Diane Follingstad, a professor of clinical and forensic psychology at the University of South Carolina, "is a low-rate-base thing. It just does not happen very often."

When it does happen, the people likeliest to commit the crime fall into a drearily predictable group. They're 95% male, and 98% are black or white—not a big surprise since more than 87% of the population is made up of those two races. Cho, a native of South Korea, is a rare exception. If the killers' profiles are all more or less the same, however, their crimes aren't. The best known—or at least most lurid—of the mass killers are the Ted Bundys and Jeffrey Dahmers, the serial murderers whose crimes often play out over decades. In most cases, people who commit such murders are driven by a dark, even sexual pleasure, and while remorse is often associated with the acts—which accounts for the long lapses that can occur between them—those tuggings of conscience are quickly overcome by the impulse to kill again. "There is a charge and a thrill associated with the murders," says Samenow.

That does not seem to be the case with a mass murderer who kills at once. Few people who are in a position to observe a Dahmer at work survive to talk about it, but plenty of people present at shootings like those at Virginia Tech or Columbine High School in Littleton, Colo., in 1999 make it out alive. And what they describe about the killer's mien as the shooting is taking place sounds nothing like a person who's thrilled by—or even much enjoying—what he's doing. There is, survivors report, a cold joylessness to the proceedings, something that in its own way is a lot harder to parse than the perverse pleasure of a serial killer. What makes mass murderers do it? Trying to find the much-looked-for snapping moment—the one inciting incident that pushes a killer over the edge—rarely gets you very far. Cho's lethal outburst, by all accounts, may have been simmering for months, if not years. In 2005, after Cho sent harassing messages to two female students, a Virginia court ruled him a danger to himself and others. His package of angry, self-pitying videos, stills and text, sent to NBC News on the day of the killings, probably took days to prepare.

"Snapping is a misnomer," says Dr. Michael Welner, associate professor of psychiatry at New York University School of Medicine. "These people plan to carry out a mass killing without any indication of when they will do it. Instead of snapping, imagine a cage that someone has the capacity to unhinge. They simply decide that today is the day."

Mass murder, in short, is not a random act. There are things that explain it. Psychosis, for one, can never be ruled out. Russell Weston, a 41-year-old killer who went on a shooting spree in the Capitol Building in Washington in 1998, was a paranoid schizophrenic. Brain injury in an otherwise healthy person can lead to similar violence. Damage to the frontal region of the brain, which regulates what psychologists call the observing ego, or the limbic region, which controls violence, reflection and defensive behavior, can shut down internal governors and trigger all manner of unregulated behavior. "Somebody who had damage to both regions would be a bad player for sure," says forensic psychiatrist Neil Kaye, a faculty member at Jefferson Medical College in Philadelphia.

From everything we know so far, however, Cho was suffering from none of these things. Any wounds that he carried were deeper, psychic ones—and in all likelihood, he shared them with most of the mass shooters who have gone before him. In many ways, the profile of the mass killer looks a lot like the profile of the clinical narcissist, and that's a very bad thing. Never mind the disorder's name, narcissism is a condition defined mostly by disablingly low self-esteem, requiring the sufferer to seek almost constant recognition and reward. When the world and the people in it don't respond as they should, narcissists are not just enraged but flat-out mystified. Cho's multimedia postmortem package exuded narcissistic exhibitionism, and the words he spoke into the camera left no doubt as to what he believed—or wanted to believe—was his own significance. "Thanks to you," he said in one of his many indictments of his victims, "I die like Jesus Christ."

Narcissism is not the only part of the psychic stew that leads to mass murder. Among the additional risk factors experts look for is a history of other kinds of emotional turmoil, such as depression, substance abuse or some kind of childhood trauma. After the Columbine killings in 1999,

the Federal Government commissioned a study of 37 incidents of school violence from 1974 to 2000 in an attempt to sketch some kind of profile of likely campus killers. In general, the investigators found that more than half of all attackers had documented cases of extreme depression, and 25% had had serious problems with drugs and alcohol. "People will often say that the killer was such a quiet boy," says Follingstad. "Then you talk to the family and find out he's had three previous hospitalizations and was mumbling something he was angry about for weeks."

A less well-documented percentage of mass killers have also been physically or sexually abused. Just a day after the Virginia Tech killings, Cho's graphically awful writings—playlets that deal with the molestation of young boys—began appearing on websites. The writings are not proof that he experienced similar mistreatment, but they certainly raise questions. "These things can percolate for years," says N. G. Berrill, a forensic psychologist and professor at John Jay College of Criminal Justice in New York City. "Quite often there is an early event where they are submitted to violence or are marginalized."

That last feeling can be the real problem. Where there's marginalization, there's a profound sense of powerlessness, and powerless people tend to hit back. More worryingly, it doesn't take grave abuses like molestation to leave people feeling so minimized. Parental or spousal indifference or dismissal—or at least the belief that it exists—can have a similar effect. If the world outside the home seems to be conspiring in the mistreatment, the sense of invalidation grows worse still. It may be true that none of us suffer a lost job, a busted romance or a failed exam easily, but to someone already highly sensitized to such setbacks, they can be intolerable. "These are people who are already angry," says Samenow, "and when things don't go the way they want them to, they personalize it. They take out their rage not on the person who hurt them last, but on the whole world."

Something like this is what appears to have happened with Cho. When he blew, he blew savagely. Not only was the sheer body count on the campus horrific, but so was the relish with which the victims were killed. Doctors in the hospital where the survivors were treated described their injuries as "brutal," with each of the victims sustaining at least three bullet wounds. Of course, plenty of people fail tests and end romances and even suffer unspeakable abuse as children. And while there are a lot of narcissists in the world, many of whom crash and burn in their personal and professional lives, only an infinitesimal fraction of even the most unstable people lash out in remotely as violent a way as mass killers do. So what should we look for in people for whom such a homicidal rage is a real risk?

Age is an indicator, but an imperfect one. Adolescents and people in their early 20s are not famous for good judgment and sober reflection. Indeed, recent neurological studies reveal that the brain doesn't even finish laying down all its wiring until deep into the second decade of life—far beyond the babyhood years in which scientists once believed this basic work got done. "Adolescents tend to take more risks in general and tend to be more impulsive," says psychologist William Pollack, of McLean Hospital in Boston. "Boys [especially] are socialized into the idea that such behavior is OK."

While teens lack wisdom, however, they're generally spared the long lifetime of frustrations and setbacks that can contribute to murderous rampages in older killers—the fired post office employee or office worker who suddenly reappears and guns down his former colleagues. "We see people with a job or a relationship that defines them," says Dr. Anthony Ng, assistant professor of psychiatry at George Washington University. "When that is shattered, they decide that they have nothing else." Opportunity and unlucky serendipity play a big role too. People with ready access to guns are likelier to use them than people who have to work to get their hands on a weapon. A household in which problems are settled violently, or at least in a volatile fashion, makes acting out less alien as well. What your culture—national, ethnic, religious—teaches you about how to handle rejection or, worse, humiliation can be critical too.

As these factors accumulate, killers in the making remain surprisingly cool, all the while strolling toward the edge. That is what makes mass murder especially chilling. Eric Harris and Dylan Klebold planned the Columbine assault for months, buying guns, practicing their aim, even designing their own shabby bombs that were intended to blow up the building. Cho bought the first of the two pistols he used in his killings on March 13, then bought the second just days before the murders—decorously observing the 30-day waiting period the state of Virginia requires between handgun purchases.

Throughout the slow, deliberate smolder that leads up to the shootings, all mass killers also tend to disengage from the people around them. More and more of their emotional energy becomes consumed with planning their assault and, tellingly, with what often appears to be a new-found fascination with firearms and other weapons. "The quiet is the problem," says Welner. "The anger and rage just get bigger and bigger and seep into a fantasy life, and the person becomes increasingly alienated and isolated and contemptuous."

The fully annealed killer who emerges from this process is a cold and deliberate thing. The time he's spent rehearsing his carnage is a big part of what causes the actual execution of it to appear so disciplined and free of emotion—or even pleasure. That, however, does not mean that mass murder is conducted entirely without feeling. For the killer, the powerlessness that came from a sense of victimization has been replaced by its perfect opposite—a heady experience that may produce an implacable serenity on the one hand, or the eerily jocular banter that surveillance tapes picked up between Harris and Klebold in Columbine on the other. Making the gunman calmer still is the fact that he has long since convinced himself that the world brought the carnage on itself. Because nobody is exempt from membership in that world, nobody's exempt from the line of fire either. "You forced me into a corner. The decision was yours," were among the most disturbing lines in the suicide videos that Cho left behind, but they may also have been the least original.

However long it takes the killing to play out, when the crime is finally over, the shooter almost never expects to survive. Indeed, he typically doesn't want to. Achieving the state of nihilistic certainty that's necessary to commit the killings is one thing; crossing back to the world of the living afterward may be well-nigh impossible. "They are both homicidal and suicidal," says Pollack. "After the attack they are simply waiting for the next step, which they assume is the police shooting them." Most killers don't wait even that long, taking their own lives before whatever killing room they have barricaded themselves inside can be stormed.

If there is a hopeful lesson to be drawn from this week's tragedy, it's that people planning mass murder sometimes seem to recognize the dark place they're headed toward and, even as they're cooking up their carnage, send out warning signals. The federal school study after Columbine found that in more than 75% of cases, at least one person had knowledge of the killer's plans. In 40% of cases, that knowledge actually included detailed descriptions of precisely where and when the attacks would happen. Klebold and Harris went so far as to post their lethal ruminations on the Web. The key, Pollack insists, is for friends and family members to be alert to these and other cues and to act on them—fast. "Connection, connection, connection," he says. "It's through these connections that people in authority, when they hear certain things, can provide the appropriate help."

The larger culture can help as well—particularly the media. It may be uncomfortable for any journalist to admit it, but the flood-the-zone coverage that usually follows mass murders simply confirms a potential killer's belief that what he sees as his small and inconsequential life can end on a large and monstrous chord, even if he won't be around to enjoy the transformation. "We glorify and revere these seemingly powerful people who take life," says Kaye. "Meanwhile, I bet you couldn't tell me the name of even one of Ted Bundy's victims."

Sadly, Kaye's indictment is well founded. But he's also right in his choice of words. People like Cho are indeed only seemingly powerful. In an open culture with cheap and plentiful guns, any fool can kill a lot of people. For all the loss and suffering such a shooting sparks, it is in fact a weak and furtive act, one that masquerades as a gesture of sublime power but is really an act of confusion and cowardice. The very purpose of the murders, Welner explains, is to give the shooter the last word. Unfortunately, what he says when he at last has that chance to be heard is: "I surrender."

With reporting by Barbara Kiviat, Alice Park and Carolyn Sayre/ New York

Treating War's Toll on the Mind

Thousands of Soldiers Have Post-traumatic Stress Disorder. Will They Get the Help They Need?

BETSY STREISAND

As they take their seats in the movie theater, Eric and Raquel Schrumpf could be any young couple out on a summer night in Southern California. No one notices as Schrumpf, 31, a former Marine sergeant who served in Iraq, scans the rows for moviegoers who may be wired with explosives under their jackets. No one pays attention as a man who appears to be Middle Eastern, wearing a long coat with bulging pockets, takes a seat in the same row as the Schrumpfs and Eric starts watching him intently. No one listens as Schrumpf instructs his wife to "get as low to the ground as you can if something happens." Then something does. Schrumpf hears metal jangling as the man reaches into his pocket. Convinced he is a suicide bomber about to strike, Schrumpf lunges at him. The man jerks away and his deadly weapon falls to the floor: a can of Coke.

Schrumpf has everyone's attention now, as he and his wife quickly leave the theater. The Schrumpfs can't even remember what movie they went to see. Not that it would have mattered. Eric Schrumpf had room for only one movie in his head, the one where he is in Iraq. Now, more than two years later, Schrumpf has a good job, a strong marriage, a couple of pets, and a life that looks startlingly like everyone else's in Orange County, Calif. But he is still never more than a sound, smell, or thought away from the war. He gets anxious in a crowd, has been known to dive for cover, even indoors, at the sound of a helicopter, reaches for nonexistent weapons to be used in nonexistent circumstances, and wakes up screaming from nightmares about burning bodies and rocket-propelled grenades. "I'll never be the same again," says Schrumpf, who as a weapons and tactics instructor with the 5th Marine Regiment was part of the initial push into southern Iraq in 2003. "The war will be part of my life and my family's life forever."

Reliving the war. Like thousands of soldiers who have returned from Iraq and Afghanistan, Schrumpf is suffering from post-traumatic stress disorder, a chronic condition whose symptoms include rage, depression, flashbacks, emotional numbness, and hypervigilance. It can be brought on by a single event, such as when a grenade landed next to Schrumpf, ticking off his death and then failing to explode. Or it can be the result of repeated exposure to trauma such as house-to-house firefights or the accidental killing of civilians. "Soldiers who are routinely exposed to the trauma of killing, maiming, and dying are much more likely to bring those problems home," says Army Col. Kathy Platoni, a clinical psychologist and leader of a combat stress-control unit that works with soldiers on the battlefield. At its most basic, PTSD is the inability to flip the switch from combat soldier to everyday citizen and to stop reliving the war at so high a frequency that it interferes with the ability to function.

The problem is as old as war itself. But this time, American soldiers have been assured by the government and the military that the solution will be different: Iraq will be nothing like Vietnam, with its legacy of psychologically scarred veterans whose problems went unrecognized, undiagnosed, and untreated. "The hallmark of this war is going to be psychological injury," says Stephen Robinson, a Gulf War vet and director of government relations for Veterans for America in Washington, D.C. "We have learned the lessons of Vietnam, but now they have to be implemented."

Since the war began, the departments of Defense and Veterans Affairs have stepped up efforts to address the mental health needs of soldiers before, during, and after they are deployed. And more effective treatments for PTSD have been developed. But as the war drags on, the psychological costs are mounting and so is the tab for mental health care. Troop shortages are driving already traumatized soldiers back into combat for three and sometimes four tours of duty. Those who make it home often feel too stigmatized to ask for treatment lest they jeopardize their military careers. And if they do ask, they often can't get the care they need when they need it.

In addition, there are concerns among veterans groups that the Bush administration is trying to reduce the runaway cost of the war by holding down the number of PTSD cases diagnosed (and benefits paid), and that the promise to protect the mental health of nearly 1.5 million troops is not being kept.

"Throughout this war, everything has been underestimated–the insurgency, the body armor, the cost, and the number of troops," says Paul Rieckhoff, an Iraq war vet and founder of Iraq and Afghanistan Veterans of America in New York. "Now, the psychological problems and the needs of these soldiers are being underestimated, too."

Just how many troops will bring the war home with them is impossible to know at this point. But the numbers could be substantial. In a study published in 2004 in the *New England Journal of Medicine,* researchers at the Walter Reed Army Institute of Research found that nearly 17 percent of soldiers who have returned from Iraq, or nearly 1 in 6, showed signs of major depression, generalized anxiety, or PTSD. A report in the *Journal of the American Medical Association* earlier this year found that 1 in 5 soldiers met the risk for concern. And those numbers are virtually certain to grow as the war enters its fourth year. "I do think we're going to see a whole lot more PTSD as time goes on," says Platoni.

The VA, short of doctors, therapists, and staff in some areas, is straining to meet the mental health needs of the troops who have already returned from Iraq and Afghanistan. Soldiers often wait weeks or even months to see a psychiatrist or psychologist. A 2004 study by the Government Accountability Office found that six of the seven VA medical facilities it visited "may not be able to meet" increased demand for PTSD. "I don't think anybody can say with certainty whether we are prepared to meet the problem because we don't know what the scope is yet," says Matthew Friedman, a psychiatrist and executive director of the VA's National Center for PTSD in White River Junction, Vt. "What we do know is that the greater the exposure to trauma, the greater the chance that someone will have PTSD."

PTSD is the inability to flip the switch from combat soldier to everyday citizen.

Danger zone. There may be no war better designed to produce combat stress and trauma. Operation Iraqi Freedom is a round-the-clock, unrelenting danger zone. There are no front lines, it's impossible to identify the enemy, and everything from a paper bag to a baby carriage is a potential bomb. Soldiers are targets 24–7, whether they are running combat missions or asleep in their bunks. "There is no moment of safety in Iraq," says Andrew Pomerantz, a psychiatrist and chief of the Mental Health and Behavioral Science Service at the VA Medical Center in White River Junction. "That's one of the things we're seeing in people when they come back–a feeling of an absolute lack of safety wherever they are."

Stories of vets who sleep with guns and knives and patrol the perimeters of their homes obsessively are as common as tales of valor. Marine Lt. Col. Michael Zacchea, 38, who trained Iraqi troops and was in about 100 firefights, knows that paranoia all too well. "Every time I get on the road," says Zacchea,

who commutes from Long Island to Wall Street, "it's like I'm back in the streets of Baghdad in combat, driving and running gun battles, with people throwing grenades at me." Zacchea, a reservist, is now being treated for PTSD at a VA hospital, but had it not been for chronic dysentery, migraines, and shrapnel wounds in his shoulder, he says he probably would have been redeployed in September, emotional scars and all.

And he still may be. The military's need to maintain troop strength in the face of historic recruiting lows means many service members, including some suffering from psychological problems like Zacchea, have no choice but to return. President Bush recently authorized the Marine Corps to call up inactive reservists, men and women who have already fulfilled their active-duty commitment. "They're having to go deep into the bench," says Robinson, "and deploy some people who shouldn't be deployed."

Multiple tours. Robinson is referring to the increasing number of reports of service members who stock antidepressants and sleeping pills alongside their shampoo, soap, and razor blades. The Defense Department does not track the number of soldiers on mental health medications or diagnosed with mental illnesses. But the military acknowledges that service members on medication who may be suffering from combat-induced psychological problems are being kept in combat. "We're not keeping people over there on heavy-duty drugs," says Army Surgeon General Kevin Kiley, who estimates that 4 to 5 percent of soldiers are taking medications, mostly sleeping pills. "Four to five percent of 150,000, that's still a lot of troops. But if it's got them handling things, I'm OK with that."

Handling things is a relative term. Army Pvt. Jason Sedotal, 21, a military policeman from Pierre Part, La., had been in Iraq six weeks in 2004 when he drove a humvee over a landmine. His sergeant, seated beside him, lost two legs and an arm in the explosion. Consumed by guilt and fear, Sedotal, who suffered only minor injuries, was diagnosed with PTSD when he returned from his first tour in early 2005 and given antidepressants and sleeping pills. Several months later, while stationed at Fort Polk, La., he sought more mental health care and was prescribed a different antidepressant.

Last November, Sedotal was redeployed. "They told me I had to go back because my problem wasn't serious enough," Sedotal said in an interview from Baghdad in mid-September. Sedotal says he started "seeing things and having flashbacks." Twice a combat stress unit referred him to a hospital for mental health care. Twice he was returned to his unit, each time with more medication and the second time without his weapon. "I stopped running missions, and I was shunned by my immediate chain of command and my unit," says Sedotal, who returned to Fort Polk last week.

Cases like Sedotal's prompted Congress earlier this year to instruct the Department of Defense to create a Task Force on Mental Health to examine the state of mental health care for the military. It is expected to deliver a report to Secretary of Defense Donald Rumsfeld in May 2007 and make recommendations for everything from reducing the stigma surrounding disorders to helping families and children deal with the traumatized soldier.

Sending military members who suffer from PTSD back into combat goes straight to one of the toughest issues of the war: how to protect soldiers' mental health and still keep them fighting. It is well-established that repeated and prolonged exposure to combat stress is the single greatest risk factor in developing PTSD.

At the same time, there is tremendous resistance to sending home soldiers who are suffering from psychological wounds, in all but the most severe cases. "If a soldier has some PTSD symptoms," says Kiley, "we'll watch him and see how he does." The expectation "is that we're all in this boat together and we need to drive on to complete the mission," he says, adding that if the situation gets worse, the soldier would most likely be given a couple days of rest to see if he recovers. Once soldiers are evacuated, "they are much less likely to come back."

There are no front lines, it's impossible to identify the enemy, and everything from a paper bag to a baby carriage is a potential bomb.

With that in mind, the DOD has designed a program to manage combat stress and identify mental health problems when they occur. It will include so-called battle-mind training for recruits, which focuses on the emotional fallout of seeing and contributing to the carnage of war and how to deal with it. Once they are in Iraq, there are psychologists and combat stress-control teams, such as Platoni's, who work side by side with troops to help them deal with their emotions and decompress immediately after battle. "Soldiers suffering from combat stress do better if they are treated early, efficiently, and as close to the battlefield as possible," says Col. Charles Hoge, chief of the Department of Psychiatry and Behavioral Sciences at Walter Reed Army Institute of Research.

Currently, there are more than 200 psychiatrists, therapists, social workers, and other mental health experts working with soldiers "in theater." They lend an ear, encourage soldiers to talk about their experiences with each other, and administer whatever short-term remedies they can, including stress-reduction techniques, anger-management strategies, or medications. However, their mission, first and foremost, is to be "force multipliers" who maintain troop strength. Their success is judged by their ability to keep soldiers from going home for psychological reasons. Soldiers are often their allies in this effort, as they feel such guilt and shame over abandoning their units they'll most likely say anything to keep from leaving. "It's a very sticky wicket," says Platoni. "We don't know if our interventions are enough to help them stay mentally healthy, or if they'll suffer more in the long term."

Last year, for instance, Platoni spent four months in Ar Ramadi, near Baghdad, where her battalion was under constant attack by insurgents. "They were watching their fellow soldiers burning to death and thinking they might be next," says Platoni. When a break came, one platoon was removed from combat for 48 hours so they could rest, shower, have a hot meal, and talk to psychologists about what they'd been through. "When they returned to the fighting," says Platoni, "they were able to deal with their fears better and focus on what needed to be done."

When soldiers do return home, the true emotional trauma of war is often just beginning. They go through a cursory post-deployment medical screening and a quick interview with a healthcare worker, who may or may not specialize in mental health. And returning soldiers are far more likely to downplay emotional problems for fear of being shifted from the "go home" line into the "further evaluation" line and being prevented from seeing families and friends.

Macho warrior. Three to six months after they return–the time when PTSD symptoms are the most likely to start becoming obvious–troops are given another mental health screening and may be referred for further evaluation, although the chances are slim. A GAO report issued in May, for instance, found that of the 5 percent of returning veterans between 2001 and 2004 who tested as being at risk for PTSD, fewer than one quarter were referred for further mental health evaluations. William Winkenwerder, assistant secretary of defense for health affairs, took issue with the study: "We're doing more than any military in history to identify, prevent, and treat mental health concerns among our troops. It is a top priority for us." Even with a referral, many veterans and active-duty soldiers will not seek help for fear of being stigmatized. To help break down the barriers, the DOD has begun encouraging high-ranking soldiers to openly discuss the effects that combat and killing can have on a person's psyche. Even so, the military remains dominated by the image of the macho warrior who sucks it up and drives on. According to the VA, the number of PTSD cases has doubled since 2000, to an all-time high of 260,000, but fewer than 40 percent of veterans from Iraq and Afghanistan have sought medical treatment. "This is the military culture," says Schrumpf, who now gets regular therapy and takes medication to help with his PTSD. "If it gets out that you even went to see the medical officer, and it always does, then you're done as a career marine."

In a surprising admission, former Georgia Sen. Max Cleland, who lost three limbs in Vietnam, announced in August that he is being treated for PTSD in the hopes of encouraging other vets to do the same. One of the biggest problems for Vietnam veterans, for instance, was that their psychological wounds went unrecognized and unattended for so long that, by the time they got treatment, many were past of the point of being helped. Cleland is one of a growing crowd of Vietnam vets who are finally seeking help–and competing for VA services–as a result of long-buried feelings stirred up by the Iraq war.

In the past few years, in part because of events such as September 11, there have been advances in therapies for PTSD. "Just because you have PTSD, it doesn't mean you can't be successful in daily life," says Harold Wain, chief of the psychiatry consultation and liaison service at Walter Reed Army Medical Center in Washington, D.C., the main Army hospital for amputees. Many of the patients Wain sees have suffered catastrophic injuries and must heal their bodies as well as their minds.

As the war drags on, psychological costs are mounting and so is the tab for mental health care.

Reimagining the trauma again and again, or what's known as exposure therapy, has long been believed to be the most effective way of conquering PTSD. It is still popular and has been made even more effective by such tools as virtual reality. However, therapists are increasingly relying on cognitive behavior therapy or cognitive reframing, putting a new frame around a thought to shift the way a soldier interprets an event. A soldier who is racked with guilt because he couldn't save an injured buddy, for instance, may be redirected to concentrate on what he did do to help. Other approaches such as eye movement desensitization and reprocessing use hypnosis to help soldiers.

For some soldiers, simply talking about what happened to them can be therapy enough. When Zachary Scott-Singley returned from Iraq in 2005, he was haunted by the image of a 3-year-old boy who had been shot and killed accidentally by a fellow soldier. With a son of his own, Scott-Singley couldn't get the picture of the child and his wailing mother out of his head and became increasingly paranoid about his own child's safety. "I was constantly thinking about how people were going to attack me and take him," he says. Scott-Singley twice sought mental health care from the Army. The first time he says he was told that since he wasn't hurting anybody, he didn't have PTSD. The next counselor suggested he buy some stress-management tapes on the Internet and practice counting to 10 whenever he felt overwhelmed. (The VA is legally precluded from discussing a soldier's medical records.) Ironically, Scott-Singley found his therapy on the Web anyway, with his blog A Soldier's Thoughts (*misoldierthoughts.blogspot.com*). "It feels so much better to know I am not alone."

Outcry. Many veterans say they would also find it therapeutic to hear Bush acknowledge PTSD and the psychological costs of the war instead of downplaying them. Earlier this year, for instance, the Institute of Medicine was asked by Congress to re-evaluate the diagnostic criteria for PTSD, which was established by the American Psychiatric Association in 1980. Critics claim the review was ordered by the Bush administration in an effort to make it harder to diagnose PTSD, which would in turn reduce the amount of disability payments. The number of veterans from all wars receiving disability payments for PTSD, about 216,000 last year, has grown seven times as fast as the number receiving benefits for disabilities in general, at a cost of $4.6 billion a year. And that figure does not include most of the more than 100,000 Iraq and Afghanistan veterans who have sought mental health services. The IOM report, released in June, supported the current criteria for diagnosing PTSD.

Now the institute is looking at the accuracy of screening techniques and how to compensate and treat vets with PTSD, widely regarded as an easy condition to fake. And in another move that infuriated veterans groups, the VA late last year proposed a review of 72,000 cases of vets who were receiving full disability benefits for PTSD to look for fraud. The move prompted such an outcry that it was called off.

Studies and reviews aside, there isn't enough help available to veterans with PTSD. According to a report from the VA, individual veterans' visits to PTSD specialists dropped by 20 percent from 1995 to 2005–"a decrease in capacity at a time when the VA needs to reach out," the report stated. Secretary of Veterans Affairs James Nicholson says the VA sees 85 percent of new mental health patients within 30 days. "But that still leaves 15 percent and that's a big number. Could we do better? Yes."

Bush has called for a record $80.6 billion in the 2007 VA budget. That includes $3.2 billion for mental health services, a $339 million increase over this year's budget. However, those increases are being met by increasing demands for care, as well as rising cost-of-living allowances and prescription drug prices. "The bigger budget doesn't really add up to much," says Rieckhoff.

However frustrating and exhausting the process, most vets can avoid getting help only so long before friends and family push them into counseling or they get in trouble with the law. "It's almost like your family has its own form of PTSD just from being around you every day," says a former Army sergeant who worked as an interrogator in Iraq and asked that his name be withheld. "When I came back I was emotionally shut down and severely paranoid. My wife thought I was crazy and my son didn't realize who I was. Because of them, I got help."

Like many soldiers, he found it at one of more than 200 local Veterans Centers, which offer counseling for PTSD and sexual assault, a growing concern for women in the military. Vet Centers are part of the VA but operate like the anti-VA, free of the delays and bureaucracy. There is almost no paperwork, and the wait to see a counselor is rarely more than a week. It's no coincidence that when *Doonesbury* character B.D. finally went for help with his PTSD, he went to a Vet Center (story, Page 182). The centers are small and staffed mostly by vets, which creates the feel of a nurturing social environment rather than an institutional one. The free coffee is strictly decaf, and the approach is laid back. "Someone may come in asking about an insurance problem, and as we answer their questions, we ask them how are they feeling," says Karen Schoenfeld-Smith, a psychologist and team leader at the San Diego Vet Center, which sees a lot of Iraq vets from nearby Camp Pendleton. "That's how we get them into it." Many come just to talk to other vets.

It is that same need to talk that keeps Schrumpf E-mailing and phoning fellow marines and returning to Camp Pendleton every couple of weeks to hang out. "It is the only place I can talk about the killing," he says. Next month, Schrumpf will leave California for his home state of Tennessee, where he says it will be easier to raise a family. He's not worried about taking the war with him. In fact, in many ways he is more worried about leaving it behind. "The anger, the rage, and all that is just there," says Schrumpf. "And honestly, I don't want it to leave. It's like a security blanket." Or a movie, that just keeps on playing.

Soldier Support

**Psychologists help troops handle the stresses
of combat in Iraq and the anxieties of coming home.**

CHRISTOPHER MUNSEY

Last fall near the city of Ar Ramadi in Iraq, the strain of combat was beginning to overwhelm a platoon from an Army unit supporting infantry pursuing insurgents, says Lt. Col. Kathy Platoni, PsyD, an Army psychologist. The soldiers were worn down by a constant toll of attacks from insurgents, pushed close to the edge of panic by fear.

"They were afraid to die, because so many of them had," Platoni says.

The insurgents' most frequent method of attack came via improvised explosive devices (IEDs), bombs planted by insurgents on roads and highways used by U.S. forces, but other soldiers had been killed or wounded by small arms fire, rocket-propelled grenades and sniper bullets. "They watched their beloved fellow soldiers being blown up all the time, burning to death right in front of them," she says.

Concerned about the soldiers' ability to continue functioning given their level of fear and sheer physical exhaustion, Platoni worked with the unit's leadership to give many of them a 48-hour reprieve from operations.

During the break, the soldiers got a chance to sleep, take a shower, eat a hot meal and talk to mental health professionals about their experiences, if they wanted to talk. Following the brief respite, the soldiers returned to their duties, still facing constant danger, but better able to manage their fears and concentrate on the job at hand.

Platoni, a mobilized Army reservist and private practitioner in Beavercreek, Ohio, organized the reprieve project with fellow soldier and mental health specialist Sgt. George McQuade during a 10-month stint working at forward operating bases in Iraq last year. Nicknamed FOBs in military lingo and scattered across Iraq, the bases are where U.S. servicemen and-women live and operate from while serving in the country.

The need for psychological services, she says, is evident in the sobering statistics: As of mid-March, 2,302 service members had been killed in action in Iraq and more than 17,124 had been wounded. Every day in Iraq, psychologists like Platoni are helping soldiers, Marines, sailors and airmen cope with the traumatic effects of combat and the stresses of living and working far from home and family in austere, dangerous conditions. They're also helping service members adjust to life after Iraq when they return home.

How Therapy Is Delivered

In fact, the Army has redoubled its mental health efforts, making psychologists and combat stress-control teams more accessible to deployed soldiers, instituting more stress-control training for deploying soldiers and surveying individual units for problems.

For example, working with the Marines, Navy medicine has adopted a new approach called OSCAR, for Operational Stress Control and Readiness. Instead of assigning a Navy psychologist from outside the unit's existing medical support staff, the program matches psychologists with Marine regiments in the months before a deployment, continuing during a rotation in Iraq, then back home, so that closer relationships can be built between psychologists and a unit's leadership.

Psychologists across military branches say their goal is keeping service members mentally focused during deployment and fostering resilience that encourages service members to rely on both their individual and unit strengths. Keeping soldiers or Marines focused can help them stay sharp in a hazardous environment requiring constant vigilance, psychologists say.

Often, doing that requires psychologists to get out from behind a desk in the larger, relatively more secure FOBs and experience firsthand what some service members see patrolling the roads and neighborhoods of Iraqi cities and towns every day.

**"Just living in this environment can
be overwhelming."**

Bret Moore
U.S. Army

Different Types of Stress

Psychologists say service members encounter two broad kinds of stress in Iraq. The first is combat stress, created by directly experiencing roadside bomb explosions, suicide vehicle bomber attacks and combat operations. Besides the threat of IEDs, service members also have to deal with the unnerving threat of lethal mortar and rocket attacks targeting service members where they work and sleep.

The second is operational or deployment stress, created by being deployed overseas and working in harsh conditions. Service members live with very little privacy and typically sleep jammed together in tents, trailers and bunkers, all while enduring an outside environment with temperatures topping 130 degrees in the summer and cold rain and mud in the winter.

And while the immediacy of e-mail makes it much easier for family members to stay in touch, it sometimes exacerbates stress when spouses relay bad news and expect help with financial problems and kids in trouble back home.

Psychologists say they help service members cope with the different types of stress in a number of ways. Working from a FOB in northern Iraq, Army Capt. Bret Moore, PsyD, is the officer-in-charge of a three-person preventive team from the 85th Medical Detachment, making care available to about 5,000 soldiers. "Just living in this environment can be overwhelming," Moore says.

The Army deals with soldiers experiencing combat stress using a set of precepts, BICEPS. The acronym stands for:

- *Brevity.* Treatment will be short, addressing the problem at hand.
- *Immediacy.* An intervention will take place quickly, before symptoms worsen.
- *Centrality.* Treatment will be set apart from medical facilities, as a way to reduce the stigma soldiers might feel about seeking mental health services.
- *Expectancy.* A soldier experiencing problems with combat stress is expected to return to duty.
- *Proximity.* Soldiers are treated as close to their units as possible and are not evacuated from the area of operations.
- *Simplicity.* Besides therapy, the basics of a good meal, hot shower and a comfortable place to sleep ensure a soldier's basic physical needs are met.

All told, Moore says about 98 percent of soldiers sent to restoration areas come back to their units.

If a soldier isn't sent to a restoration area for 48- to 72-hour respite, Moore says he's only got enough time for between five and six therapy sessions with each soldier. The therapy's goal is keeping the soldier with his or her unit and functioning, he says. Moore uses a variety of techniques, ranging from cognitive-behavioral therapy to handing out CDs explaining deep breathing and other relaxation practices. To strengthen resiliency, he advises soldiers to exercise every day—preferably through a team sport—to eat balanced meals and to sleep when they can, he says.

It's not just Army psychologists helping care for soldiers. Another psychologist, Air Force Capt. Michael Detweiler, PhD, runs a life skills support center at an overseas base in Southwest Asia.

Detweiler describes himself as the only mental health provider for about 10,000 service members, mostly Army and Air Force personnel. Besides assisting soldiers in dealing with trauma, he often helps service members get along better.

"We live with the same people we work with . . . so the same people who drive you crazy at work are the same people you live with," Detweiler says.

Other important roles for psychologists in Iraq are helping leaders understand morale problems or handle interpersonal difficulties within units. Navy psychologist Lt. Cmdr. Gary Hoyt, PsyD, served with two Marine regimental combat teams in 2004 in Iraq, during which he regularly went out on patrols. Being present and exposed to the same dangers helped him earn the trust of junior enlisted Marines.

If the tempo of operations was too high, if they weren't getting enough sleep or if they were struggling with the big-picture "whys" of their mission in Iraq, Hoyt says he heard about it. With his access to leaders, Hoyt served as a conduit for those concerns, letting battalion-level officers know what was bothering junior Marines.

"There's no way they're going to hear this input directly from the junior ranks," he says. Besides talking to senior leadership, Hoyt says he stressed education and training of small-unit leaders about combat stress so Marines could spot problems themselves and help each other tackle them before the problems worsened.

Follow-up Care Strengthened

Besides offering mental health treatment for deployed soldiers, the Army also seeks to detect symptoms of post-traumatic stress disorder or other combat-related psychological problems when they return home, says Col. Bruce Crow, PsyD, the Army's chief psychologist. Currently, the best estimates are that about 15 percent of soldiers returning from Iraq will show symptoms of post-traumatic stress, Crow says.

As part of a militarywide initiative, all service members receive a health screening about 90 days after they return home. In addition, all soldiers and their families can tap into counseling through the Deployment Cycle Support Program.

Aiding in this effort is Lt. Col. Platoni, who works with returning combat soldiers on adjusting to life in the civilian world.

We Love to Be Scared on Halloween

But fears and phobias are no laughing matter

RICHARD HÉBERT

It seems we humans spend a good deal of time and energy in pursuit of thrills, chills, and spills, especially at this time of year. From haunted houses to ghoulish get-ups, we love to be scared.

Even when it's not Halloween, scary pursuits are commonplace. For fun we jump off bridges tethered to bungee cords or drive fast cars or swim with sharks. Or watch others do it. On the face of it, these fear-seeking behaviors seem contrary to our basic instincts of self-preservation. But it could be that they are vestiges of our genetic and environmental past.

"Many individuals are motivated to seek increased arousal," explains Fordham University's Dean McKay, whose research focuses on obsessive compulsive disorder and anxiety disorders. "Intense experiences such as bungee jumping or extreme rock climbing satisfy this need. Most individuals seek this out in some way, whether by direct experience or (vicariously) by observation."

High jinks and thrills aside, fear is an excellent survival tool handed down by our cave-dwelling ancestors who probably learned fear in order to avoid saber-toothed tigers and woolly mammoths. Today's world can be quite scary, too; we teach life-preserving fears to our children—warning them about cliff edges and hot stovetops and talking to strangers.

So, fear is a good thing. But like so many good things, too much of it can be a problem. Too much fear can be debilitating, and the result can be an anxiety disorder or phobia.

At some point in our lives, about three in 10 of us experience an anxiety disorder severe enough to meet diagnostic criteria for impairment, according to APS Fellow and Charter Member David Barlow, Director of Boston University's Center for Anxiety and Related Disorders. And 11 percent of us meet criteria for a specific phobia.

Control is the key, McKay says. Halloween revelers and thrill-seekers have it; phobics and victims of anxiety disorder don't. When systems that serve a critical need malfunction, the result is disease. Think of phobias and anxiety disorders as "diseases" of the brain's "fear system."

Our understanding of phobias has been undergoing a revolution. "For a long time," says Barlow, "we thought that people with phobias must have had some traumatic experience that

created the fear. Now we know that's not true. Only a minority of people with specific phobias have actually had a bad incident."

Fear of water can show up in children too young to have any meaningful experience with water, he says. And when you compare people who have a fear of dogs with others who don't, about the same number in each group have had a bad experience with a dog. The dog attack might precipitate phobia in those already vulnerable, but it doesn't cause it.

It's more often quite the opposite, according to research by Ross Menzies, University of Sydney, Australia. Most stuntmen, he found, have histories of serious childhood accidents. Far from making them phobic, they embraced the wellspring of their fear and built a livelihood around mastering it.

> **Phobias are not learned: We're born with them and "events previously thought to bring about phobias actually lead to greater approach for the object."**

McKay says this demonstrates that phobias are not learned: We're born with them and "events previously thought to bring about phobias actually lead to greater approach for the object."

But don't go looking for a "phobic gene." According to Barlow, the inherited DNA codings are a bit more complex than that. "We're now learning that they're not single genes, they're variations in genetic structure, certain genes with certain patterns of alleles that, when they're turned on by events in the environment, would make us more susceptible."

So yes, genetic inheritance does play a role, accounting for perhaps a third to half of the variance between those who develop phobias and those who don't, "but it's misleading to talk like that. The genetic piece means nothing unless it's part of the feedback system."

He likens that system to an "intricate dance" of "triple vulnerabilities," genetics being only one dancer. The other two are psychological vulnerabilities—one generalized, based on early experiences developing a sense of control over events or lack of it, and the other more specific, in which one learns to focus anxiety on specific objects or situations. "When these three vulnerabilities line up, then you're at substantial risk for developing a phobia," Barlow says. "If they don't line up, if you just have one and not the others, you're at much less risk.

"There was always this myth that somehow anxiety disorders were due to chemical imbalance and could be treated with pills, whereas the psychological myth was that it was some distorted cognition or learning. We now know all these things are in it and interrelated. It's all a system. You have to change the whole system, not just neurotransmitter endings."

One of the most successful ways to counter the genetic vulnerability, he says, is by changing the internal and external environment. This "could be behavior, regulating your emotions, or learning new ways to respond to stress, which in turn will influence brain functioning."

Not All Phobias Are Alike

Of course, not all phobias are alike. They are typically grouped under three headings: specific phobias (like fear of heights, dogs, or water); social phobias, now more often called social anxiety disorders; and panic disorders—inexplicable panic attacks.

More than simple fear is involved, McKay says. It's also disgust, "a pretty powerful emotion for engendering avoidance. In the past two or three years, we've seen a big upswing in this kind of work, where an effort is being made to isolate the way disgust contributes to phobias." He is currently co-editing a book on the subject with Bumni Olatunji of Vanderbilt University, to be published in 2007.

How phobias are treated is another of the major turnarounds prompted by psychological research over the past few years. "Up until recently," Barlow says, "the usual approach was to see patients once a week and have them do a lot of prescribed exercises between sessions." Treatment lasted 10 to 12 weeks. The innovation, pioneered by Lars-Göran Öst, Stockholm University, "was simply to do it all at once in an intensive fashion," says Barlow, who now treats phobic patients using Öst's method—in a single four- to six-hour session, "more equivalent to doing surgery."

In that session, a patient gets intensive exposure to the thing or situation that triggers the terror. A patient might be shown insects, or small animals brought in from a pet store. The acrophobe may be taken to high places and a claustrophobe to enclosed spaces. Guided by the psychologist, the patient learns to "extinguish" the fear by learning to control it.

"The success rates, particularly for adults, seem to be up in the 80 to 90 percent range," Barlow says, "so it's clearly the treatment of choice" for specific phobias. Only about 10 to 15 percent of the patients relapse, and even then "it's fairly easy to go back and have a booster session."

More generalized social anxiety and panic disorders still require long-term therapy or medication, which are about equally effective, says Barlow. The drugs are either antidepressants, such as selective serotonin reuptake inhibitors (SSRIs), or high-potency tranquilizers, although the latter are used much less and typically as adjuncts to therapy because patients can develop dependence on them.

While some patients prefer the "quick fix" of a pill, especially when they see it promoted on television, surveys have shown that around 75 percent prefer therapy that teaches them to master their fears. This is due primarily to the side effects of the medications, but also because relapse is more common with drugs.

"Psychological treatments are more durable," Barlow says. "The patients actually seem to learn something that has lasting benefit." As for combining drugs and therapy for anxiety disorders, he says, "Surprisingly, there does not seem to be any advantage to combining the two. It's more expensive and there's no evidence that the treatments are additive."

> **"Psychological treatments are more durable," Barlow says "The patients actually seem to learn something that has lasting benefit."**

Exposure therapy teaches patients to regulate and master their emotional response "and to accept that there has to be some confrontation with both the internal and external situation that provoked the phobic response," Barlow says.

The main disadvantage of the new one-day treatments is that they aren't readily available. "These intensive treatments came into their own in the past five years, but are still not widespread," he says. "Our biggest obstacle is actually getting them out there to the consumers. They require a lot of training, and that expertise is just not widely available yet."

Barlow's center at Boston University is now experimenting with intensive exposure therapy for panic disorders and social phobias as well. It recently received a five-year National Institute of Mental Health grant of $2 million to test one-day exposure therapy on 50 adolescents with panic disorders, comparing their results to patients who received more traditional care. The investigators are beginning with adolescents because the need is greater: It's harder for schoolchildren to get to a clinic every week than for adults.

A similar study using adult patients has also been started, and the center has a pilot project to treat severe social anxiety by putting small groups of patients together for several hours a day for a week. After their group interactions, they are sent out on assignments to interact socially in public, such as at a coffee shop.

Relapse is Tied to Context

The therapy springs from intriguing results in animal research. Mark Bouton, University of Vermont, has been working with laboratory rats since 1979, building on Pavlov's work on conditioned responses in dogs almost a century ago. Bouton demonstrated that a rat learns to fear a certain sound because it is always accompanied by an electric shock, then "extinguishes" that fear response by repeatedly hearing the tone without the shock. But he never "unlearns" the original fear; it lives on alongside the new learning, ready to spring alive again—in the right context.

He discovered this by teaching rats fear in one chamber, teaching them to extinguish it in a different chamber, then putting them back in the original chamber. When the tone sounded in the original chamber, the rats once again froze in fear, even after the fear was extinguished in the second chamber. It also happened if they were placed in a neutral third chamber and received the shock with the bell tone. The fear came rushing back to the fore.

"The fact that the original performance can recover after extinction may be an important insight into understanding relapse after therapy," Bouton and his colleagues write in their chapter in a newly published book on fear and learning (Bouton 2006). "(M)any manipulations of the context can cause an extinguished fear . . . to recover or return."

Their recent research has focused on how to take advantage of this context-dependency to prevent relapse into the original fear reaction, without much success. "(A)s far as we have been able to determine," they write, "extinction can often still remain surprisingly sensitive to the context (and the original responding thus susceptible to relapse) even after extinction procedures that have been designed to optimize the new learning."

The one approach they say "appears especially promising" at preventing relapse is building treatment "bridges," such as conducting therapy in the very situations that usually trigger the fright.

They offer multiple ways of doing this: "Conducting exposure therapy in the context where relapse is going to be a problem provides the most direct bridge," they write. "Retrieval cues for extinction provide another kind of bridge in the sense that they bring a piece of therapy to the relapse context. Occasional reinforced trials in extinction are another kind of bridge because they allow extinction in the presence of a cue (a new reinforced trial) that may be a strong stimulus for relapse."

Bouton is now studying time as context. "Extinction is specific to the temporal context in which it is learned," he explains, "just as it appears to be specific to the room in which it is learned. We are therefore looking at a lot of implications of this idea that are leading us in some interesting new directions. One practical implication is that extinction trials—therapy sessions—that are widely spaced in time should protect the system from relapse that might otherwise occur at intervals shorter than the interval between extinction trials."

Given that relapse rates for specific phobias are so low, the research appears to have greater significance for social anxiety and panic disorders, where relapse is more common. "I think of our research as a kind of caution sign," Bouton says.

A Clearer Picture in the Brain

Thanks both to animals like Bouton's rats and brain-imaging research, we now also have a better idea of what's happening in the brain when phobias strike. "It's very clear that the amygdala is a central player from the animal research," says Scott Rauch, MD, Associate Chief of Psychiatry for Neuroscience Research at Massachusetts General Hospital, "but it's just one part of a larger network. At least two other key areas play a role. The ventromedial prefrontal cortex (vmPFC) probably plays a critical role in the capacity to recall extinction memory, whereas the hippocampus plays an important role in the context" in which that memory was acquired.

Raffael Kalisch and colleagues at the University of Hamburg, Germany, are looking in the other direction—removing context from the equation. They have conducted the first study of fear extinction's context-dependence in humans. "A key feature of this study," they write in the *Journal of Neuroscience* (in press), "is that our design allows delineation of the neural circuitry involved in that function, using a psychological manipulation that engenders recall of extinction memory in the appropriate context.

"Clinically, contextual restrictions on extinction can considerably complicate anxiety therapy. . . . For therapeutic purposes, therefore, it often may be desirable to create non-contextualized extinction memories." They say their data suggest this might be achieved by making the vmPFC-dependent recall of the extinction memory—the therapy—independent of the hippocampus.

A clearer picture of how the three realms of the brain interact is slowly emerging, says Rauch. In patients with post-traumatic stress disorder (PTSD), "quite an array of data from a variety of imaging tools" shows that "the amygdala is hyper-responsive, and that the vmPFC and hippocampus are both structurally small and of reduced function. It is hypothesized (but not yet shown) that the reduced function results in insufficient inhibition of the amygdala."

The amygdala also plays a role in learning about safety, he says, but "it seems to take the prefrontal cortex to recall that extinction learning and to suppress the amygdala's response."

Rauch and colleague Mohammed Milad also have shown that the thickness of an individual's vmPFC correlates with the ability to recall the fear-extinction, and that may link it to personality as well. "The thicker the area, the more extroverted a person might be. The idea being, if you're able to extinguish these adverse associations effectively, it enables you, when you have a bad experience, to limit that to the situation in which it occurred and not to over-generalize it. It allows you to be somebody who is more courageous or outgoing in the way you attack life."

There are differences, of course. It's generally believed that anxiety disorders and PTSD have similar brain mechanisms, he says, "but we also know these disorders are distinct one from another, and there ought to be some differences. That's precisely where the science is right now, trying to understand what the similarities and differences are."

For example, data from imaging studies "suggest that PTSD and panic subjects show exaggerated amygdala responses to general threat-related stimuli as well as stimuli related to their particular fears, whereas for (specific) phobias, exaggerated amygdala responses may be limited to the stimuli related to their particular fears."

Panic attacks are also being re-examined in light of human imaging studies, Rauch says. Historically, panic disorder attacks were thought to arise spontaneously, but research shows the amygdala can be activated subconsciously. This opens the door to reinterpreting "spontaneous" panic attacks. "It opens the possibility that, even though the individual is not aware of what stimulus in the environment tweaked their amygdala, it doesn't mean there wasn't any stimulus, just that they didn't know what it was."

For the most disabling cases that require more aggressive treatments—panic disorders, PTSD, obsessive-compulsive disorder—Rauch says, "as we come to understand underlying mechanisms and brain circuitry, it may be possible to develop newer and better medications, or use treatments to influence the limbic system circuitry, known to play a critical role in anxiety disorders."

Experimental procedures being investigated include lesions that cut the circuitry at targeted locations; "deep brain stimulation," in which implanted electrodes modulate the circuitry; electro-convulsive therapy; and trans-cranial magnetic stimulation—putting a magnet against the head to create a magnetic field that influences brain activity.

Whatever technology comes along for extreme cases, however, it is clear that for the foreseeable future behavioral therapy, and especially the innovative intense exposure therapies being developed by psychological science, will be called upon to carry the load in treating most patients with phobias and anxiety disorders.

Reference

Bouton, M.E., Woods, A.M., Moody E.W., Sunsay, C. & García-Gutiérrez, A. (2006). "Counteracting the Context-Dependence of Extinction: Relapse and Some Tests of Possible Methods of Relapse Prevention," In *Fear and Learning: Basic Science to Clinical Application* (175–196). In M.G. Craske, D. Hermans, & D. Vansteenwegen (Eds.), Washington, DC: American Psychological Association.

RICHARD HÉBERT is an *Observer* contributor.

UNIT 11

Psychological Treatments

Unit Selections

Key Points to Consider

- How are jails and mental institutions similar? Different? Should we be housing people with mental disorders in either of these places?

- How essentially does psychotherapy work? Is one form of "talking" therapy better than another?

- If the brain or something biochemical creates the symptoms of a mental disorder, how can the individual be treated? Should psychologists or physicians be in charge of the treatment?

- What is depression? What are some of the recent advances in the understanding and treatment of depression?

- What do you think of using the Internet to find and experience treatment for a mental disorder? Do you see any dangers in doing so?

Student Web Site
www.mhcls.com/online

Internet References
Further information regarding these websites may be found in this book's preface or online.

The C.G. Jung Page
   http://www.cgjungpage.org
Knowledge Exchange Network (KEN)
   http://www.mentalhealth.org
NetPsychology
   http://netpsych.com/index.htm
Sigmund Freud and the Freud Archives
   http://plaza.interport.net/nypsan/freudarc.html

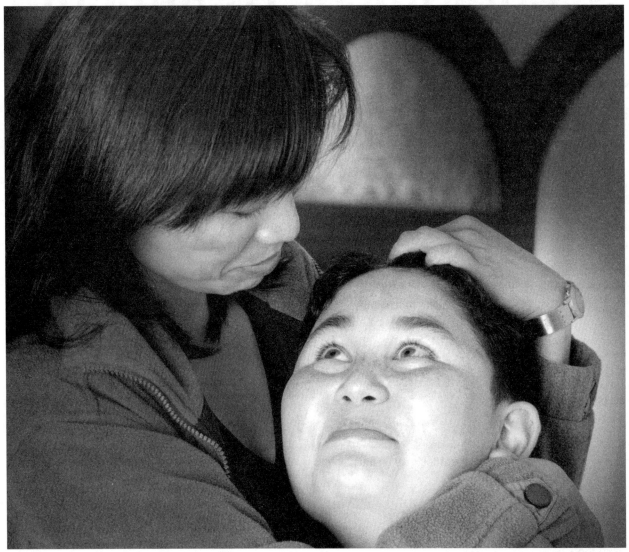

CORBIS/Royalty-Free

Have you ever had the nightmare that you are trapped in a dark, dismal place? No one will let you out. Your pleas for freedom go unanswered and, in fact, are suppressed or ignored by domineering authority figures around you. You keep begging for mercy but to no avail. What a nightmare! You are fortunate to awake to your normal bedroom and to the realities of your daily life. For the mentally ill, the nightmare of institutionalization, where individuals can be held against their will in what are sometimes terribly dreary, restrictive surroundings, is a reality. Have you ever wondered what would happen if we took perfectly normal individuals and institutionalized them in such a place? In one well-known and remarkable study, that is exactly what happened.

In 1973, eight people, including a pediatrician, a psychiatrist and some psychologists, presented themselves to psychiatric

hospitals. Each claimed that he or she was hearing voices. The voices, they reported, seemed unclear but appeared to be saying "empty" or "thud." Each of these individuals was admitted to a mental hospital, and most were diagnosed as being schizophrenic. Upon admission, the "pseudopatients" or fake patients gave truthful information and thereafter acted like their usual, normal selves.

Their hospital stays lasted anywhere from 7 to 52 days. The nurses, doctors, psychologists, and other staff members treated them as if they were schizophrenic and never saw through their trickery. Some of the real patients in the hospital, however, did recognize that the pseudopatients were perfectly normal. Upon discharge almost all of the pseudopatients received the diagnosis of "schizophrenic in remission," meaning that they were still clearly defined as schizophrenic; they just weren't exhibiting any of the symptoms at the time of release.

What does this study demonstrate about mental illness? Is true mental illness always readily detectable? If we can't always pinpoint mental disorders (the more professionally accepted term for mental illness), how can we appropriately treat them? What treatments are available, and which treatments work better for various diagnoses? The treatment of mental disorders is a challenge. The array of available treatments is ever increasing and can be downright bewildering—and not just to the patient or client! In order to demystify and simplify your understanding of treatments and interventions for mental disorders, we will look at them in this unit.

We commence with a general article about mental disorders and treatments. There are as many forms of treatment as there are mental disorders. The heated debate about what constitutes a mental disorder and which treatments are appropriate or effective are the focus of this controversial article by noted critic Thomas Szasz. Szasz claims that the mental health care system is nothing more than a branch of the criminal justice system. In many respects, he may be correct; today, with the closing of so many psychiatric hospitals (which offered another form of confinement), it is not unusual to find an individual with a mental disorder in jail. Ask yourself, "Are jails designed to house and treat these individuals?"

In the final essay, author Norbert Myslinski offers up a treatise on depression, a very common mental disorder. He takes the approach that depression may be a brain disorder rather than something purely psychological, so, therefore, the most promising treatments may lie mostly in the realm of medical interventions.

People are turning more and more to the Internet to search for help with mental health issues. Researchers are just now examining whether this trend bodes well for the future. As you will read in the last article of this anthology, much more research is needed on the usefulness and safety of cyber-therapy.

Psychiatry: A Branch of the Law

Thomas Szasz

Medicine and law are independent but intimately interacting social institutions. Medicine guards its autonomy jealously and relates to the legal system as an equal partner. Psychiatry, in contrast, submits slavishly to being dominated by the law and obediently meets its demands. Herewith some examples.

On July 3, 2006, Orin Guidry, M.D., president of the American Society of Anesthesiologists, appealed to his colleagues to refuse to assist the states in carrying out a death sentence by means of lethal injection. "Lethal injection," Guidry reminded anesthesiologists, "was not anesthesiology's idea. American society decided to have capital punishment as part of our legal system and to carry it out with lethal injection. The fact that problems are surfacing is not our dilemma. The legal system has painted itself into this corner and it is not our obligation to get it out."

The American Medical Association's code of ethics, Guidry continued, declares: "A physician, as a member of a profession dedicated to preserving life when there is hope of doing so, should not be a participant in a legally authorized execution." Guidry urged the Association's 37,000 members "not to attend executions of death sentences by lethal injection, even if called to do so by a court. The court cannot modify physicians' ethical principles to meet its needs" (www.asahq.org/news/asanews063006.htm).

Evidently many, perhaps most, American anesthesiologists reject rescuing the criminal justice system from the consequences of its decision to deprive certain persons of life. Depriving persons of liberty is only one rung down the ladder of harms that the state may legally inflict on certain individuals. Nevertheless, most American psychiatrists feel it is their professional privilege to assist the justice system in depriving certain individuals of liberty; indeed, they insist that loss of liberty under psychiatric auspices constitutes a form of medical treatment for the imprisoned individuals. In fact, the assertion of this claim—as medical "fact"—was the very first resolution enacted in 1844 by the newly formed American Psychiatric Association (APA; then more descriptively named the Association of Medical Superintendents of American Institutions for the Insane): "Resolved, that it is the unanimous sense of this convention that the attempt to abandon entirely the use of all means of personal restraint is not sanctioned by the true interests of the insane."

Ever since, psychiatrists have clung to their privilege to imprison innocent persons like drowning men cling to life-preservers.

Indeed, psychiatrists never tire of asserting and reasserting their right to deprive people of liberty. In 2005 Steven S. Sharfstein, president of the APA, reiterated his and his profession's commitment to coercion: "We must balance individual rights and freedom with policies aimed at caring coercion." The term "caring coercion" would have fit perfectly into the Nazi lexicon, along with *Arbeit macht frei* ("labor liberates") and *Gnadetot* ("mercy death").

Because the ideas about psychiatry I have been presenting in these columns differ radically from what people read in the newspapers or see on television, I always present the evidence for my view. The reader is free to judge the information and come to his own conclusion. In support of my contention that psychiatrists have an unappeasable appetite for assisting the legal system in imprisoning individuals who irritate and upset society, I offer the following evidence.

The history of mental-health laws and of standard psychiatric practices illustrates that psychiatric confinement has nothing to do with psychiatric treatment. In 1851 an Illinois statute specified that "married women . . . may be received and detained at the hospital on the request of the husband of the woman . . . without the evidence of insanity or distraction required in other cases."

Today the desire to psychiatrically incarcerate persons who are not committable by the lawyers' and psychiatrists' own criteria looms large in connection with the popular pressure and political need to keep so-called sex offenders confined *after they have served their sentences*. In 1997 the U.S. Supreme Court declared this practice to be constitutional. In *Kansas v. Leroy Hendricks* the Court declared: "States have a right to use psychiatric hospitals to confine certain sex offenders once they have completed their prison terms, even if those offenders do not meet mental illness commitment criteria."

In November 2005 New York Governor George Pataki made the headlines when he initiated "an administrative program to commit sexual predators to public psychiatric hospitals indefinitely." Pataki's order pulls back the curtain. The state's mental-health system is like an army. The governor is the general. The foot soldiers, the psychiatrists, are expected to follow the orders of their superiors. "As citizens, most of us would be comfortable seeing people properly incarcerated if these are considered crimes," said Barry Perlman, M.D., president of the New York State Psychiatric Association (NYSPA). "What we are concerned about is using the mental health system to solve a problem that seems to spill over to it because the criminal justice system cannot adequately handle it."

Perlman acts as if he had just discovered that the mental-health system is an arm of the criminal justice system. But even after discovering it, he does not suggest that psychiatrists, individually or as a group, defy the governor's orders.

Politicians have no illusions about psychiatry; they know that it is an extension of the state's law-enforcement apparatus and use it as such. According to one report, "The governor [Pataki] directed the Office of Mental Health and the Department of Correctional Services to push the envelope of the state's existing involuntary commitment law because he couldn't wait any longer for the Assembly leadership to bring his legislation to the floor for a vote. . . . The state has begun to identify 'appropriate models for treatment' and to hire staff to treat these patients. . . . To date, 16 states and the District of Columbia have enacted laws to allow authorities to confine violent sexual offenders in psychiatric hospitals after their prison terms."

Mental Hospitals as Prisons

It is important to note here that as far back as in 1988 the APA's Council of Psychiatry and Law explicitly approved the use of mental hospitals as prisons. In a document dated November 11–13, 1988, the Council declared: *"Psychiatric patients who no longer require active psychiatric treatment or who are untreatable can still be best managed in a psychiatric setting. . . . Acquittees who are unable to be discharged to outpatient status should remain under psychiatric care in a hospital environment."* Note that the psychiatric prisoner longing for freedom is treated as if he has power over his own discharge but is "unable" to exercise it: he is termed "unable to be discharged." Not surprisingly, psychiatrists resent being considered jailers. Confronted with the reality that the mental hospital is a prison and that the psychiatrist who works there is a jailer, they deceive themselves, no less than they deceive the public, with a rhetoric of "care."

It is obvious that as long as law, psychiatry, and society define destructive and self-destructive behaviors as mental diseases and assign the duty to control persons who display such behaviors to psychiatrists, who eagerly embrace that responsibility, "seclusion and restraint"—in plain English, psychiatric coercion—will remain a characteristic feature of psychiatric practice.

The definition of psychiatry as a medical specialty concerned with the diagnosis and treatment of mental diseases is a monumental falsehood. Psychiatry is a branch of the law, combining features of criminal, civil, and family law: its primary function is to promote and ensure domestic tranquility.

THOMAS SZASZ (tszasz@aol.com) is professor of psychiatry emeritus at SUNY Upstate Medical University in Syracuse. His forthcoming book is *Coercion as a Cure: A Critical History of Psychiatry* (Transaction).

From *The Freeman: Ideas on Liberty,* December 2006, pp. 19–20. Copyright © 2006 by Foundation for Economic Education. Reprinted by permission.

The Quandary over Mental Illness

RICHARD E. VATZ

In 2001, there was an important event concerning the decades-old struggle between critics of psychiatry and worldwide institutional psychiatry. The Fifth International Russell Tribunal on Human Rights in Psychiatry—of which the author was a member of the jury—a concept based on the Vietnam War Crimes Tribunal of the 1960s, heard accusations regarding the historical, legal, and rhetorical abuses of human rights committed in the name of psychiatry, particularly in the mid 20th century.

Individuals who believed they were victimized by psychiatric coercion provided testimony relevant to their experiences, which consisted of events regarding forced drugging, electroshock, involuntary hospitalization, etc. The accused (international psychiatry), which could be construed as establishmentarian institutional psychiatry, was not represented at the hearings.

The findings of the Tribunal's jury concluded with the statement, "We find psychiatry guilty of the combination of force and unaccountability, a classic definition of totalitarian systems. Compensation should be made for harms . . . done. Public funds should be made available for humane and dignified alternatives to coercive psychiatry."

Some of the hearings would have been protested as an anachronism by representatives of American psychiatry. Indeed, the verdict represented a compromise worked out by the disparate members of the jury.

In the present-day U.S., there are millions who have engaged in talk therapy, as well as 20,000,000 or so who are using—or have used—Prozac, other selective serotonin reuptake inhibitors, and various psychoactive drags through prescription. This widespread usage constitutes the normalization of pharmacological mood enhancers; normalization marked by the extensive prescribing of these drags, often by nonpsychiatric physicians, arguably, in some cases, merely for the enhanced happiness of their users. This is called cosmetic psychopharmacology, a term coined by psychiatrist Peter Kramer in his landmark work, *Listening to Prozac.*

This brave new world hardly puts to rest the tension among those who dispute the concept, if not the experience, of mental illness. Even some traditional psychiatrists deplore the casual use of pharmacological measures to solve the problems in living that are an inescapable part of life. The battles between mental health advocates and critics generally seem not only to be endless, but completely irresolvable.

We wish to stipulate that, by the following attempt at a partial meeting of the minds, if not a rapprochement, between psychiatry and its critics, we do not include many in the latter group often referred to as "anti-psychiatry." Although, at times, the amorphous anti-psychiatric movement is depicted by some as including almost anyone critical of psychiatry, the term is more accurately associated specifically with the late R.D. Laing and, to a lesser degree, with David Cooper (who invented the term) as well as Gregory Bateson.

Szasz Steps Up

Thomas Szasz, who often is erroneously labeled as personifying anti-psychiatry, promotes views that are, in fact, antithetical to some of the seminal views held by authentic anti-psychiatry scholars. Szasz's positions correctly are distinguished from those of the anti-psychiatry movement by his conservatism and belief in individual responsibility and control, and it is that perspective of psychiatric criticism for which we are trying to create a limited reconciliation. The views of Szasz, Peter Breggin, Ron Leifer, Jeffrey Schaler, and others are not all, we maintain, completely irreconcilable with each and every view of modern-day psychiatry.

[Before we procede further, however, let us be clear: Szasz is a personal friend and subject of a book of ours, but he was not consulted regarding this piece, nor has he approved any of the text which follows.]

The major tenets of Szasz's approach are the following, with apologies for our somewhat oversimplifying his arguments: mental illness is a myth because the mind is not an organ; the mind is a construct, and a construct cannot be diseased, except metaphorically. Further, there are no pathological correlates specific to any given mental illness. As he has argued in several of his works, texts in pathology make no reference to mental illness; therefore, mental illness is a bogus disease.

Many psychiatrists—even those with some sympathy for the argument that much of what is called mental illness reflects no more than common difficulties in living—insist, as does eminent psychiatrist E. Fuller Torrey, that there can be no brooking the fact that schizophrenia, which Szasz calls psychiatry's sacred symbol, is a disease. To this argument, Szasz no longer responds—he does not like the word "concedes"—that schizophrenia is not a disease. Instead, using the pathological criterion of demonstrable lesion as disease, Szasz puts forth that, if schizophrenia validly could be attributed to a brain lesion—as Parkinsonism, for example, can be—then it would be an authentic illness. His point is that some schizophrenia—only that which is linked to a brain lesion—then would be a neurological illness, not a psychiatric disorder.

Thus, although Szasz does consider some cases of schizophrenia to be authentic diseases, his concern is that any concession of this point would lead to the rampant definition of virtually all those whom psychiatrists wish to label as "mentally ill" as "schizophrenic," especially for the purpose of qualifying for third-party payments for insurance.

Indeed, some of the diseases that the American Psychiatric Association calls "severe mental illness" may be seen by psychiatrists and their critics as "illness." Again, it is Szasz's contention that, what is called mental illness never is authentic mental disease, since the mind is not an organ, but may, in some cases, be authentic brain disease when it meets certain objective and scientific criteria.

For the vast majority of untoward behaviors labeled as mental illness, Szasz contends that they are freely chosen behaviors for which the agent must take responsibility; psychiatry tends to ascribe responsibility for only socially-approved actions. In Pharmacracy, Szasz deplores "the seemingly unappeasable thirst to medicalize, pathologize, and therapeutize all manner of behaviors manifesting as personal or social problems." Moreover, while behavior may be the cause or consequence of a disease—a possible area of some limited agreement between psychiatrists and critics—"behavior, per se, cannot, as a matter of definition, be a disease." Practically speaking, no responsible critic of psychiatry denies that unwanted behaviors are "treatable" in the nonmedical sense that persuasion can influence behavior, but that does not make the feeling or behavior a "disease."

Historically, the rhetoric of mental illness has conflated the most dubious of alleged psychiatric illnesses (*e.g.*, adjustment, dysthymic, social anxiety, and body dysmorphic disorders), with the most compelling the "severe mental illnesses," such as schizophrenia. Parenthetically, the use of the term "disorder" surely will remain a sticking point between psychiatry and its critics— Szasz considers it a "weasel term" which allows psychiatry to assert and deny that it is treating "illnesses" simultaneously. To some extent, it is the inclusion of minor mental illnesses (critics would say "problems in living") with outrageously large estimates of incidence of mental illnesses which has created such widespread incredulity at psychiatric pretensions.

One of the reasons that an objective observer must be pessimistic regarding hopes for reconciliation between psychiatry and its critics are the estimates of the number of mentally ill people in the U.S., a number which has increased precipitously over the years. In a brochure on its web page, the American Psychiatric Association states: "During any one-year period, up to 50 million Americans—more than 22 percent—suffer from a clearly diagnosable mental disorder." Moreover, the National Institute of Mental Health approximates that 52,000,000 adults have a diagnosable mental illness. The APA and NIMH both claim that over 50% of all Americans will be mentally ill at some time in their lives. There is no way to disconfirm any of these statistics. Rex Cowdry, former head of the National Institute of Mental Health, notes that such high estimates of the incidence of mental illness simply do not "pass the laugh test." Perhaps, but there is little public dissent against the psychiatric profession concerning this data.

Simultaneous with the concerns regarding promiscuous diagnosis of mental illness is the proliferation in the use of psychiatric drugs. Not only is there long-term concern regarding the effects of such medication, as in the use of Ritalin in children, there is the rising conviction that chemicals are no better than placebos in many cases. *The Washington Post* reports that, "After thousands of studies, hundreds of millions of prescriptions and tens of billions of dollars in sales, two things are certain about pills that treat depression: Antidepressants like Prozac, Paxil and Zoloft work. And so do sugar pills. . . . In the majority of trials conducted by drug companies in recent decades, [placebos] have done as well as—or better than—antidepressants. Psychiatrist Arif Kahn, in trials for the Food and Drug Administration, found that in a majority of trials that 'the effect of antidepressants could not be distinguished from that of the placebo.' "

Surely, there must be some common ground here among psychiatrists, primary care physicians (who provide most of the antidepressant drug prescriptions to patients), and critics of psychiatry. If there is a current prototype of what Szasz calls "the manufacturing of mental illness" and the attending pharmacological issues, including their costs, it could well be with respect to "social anxiety disorder" (also known as "social phobia"), although it is not the only one that we suspect even some psychiatrists disbelieve. (A few years ago, a psychiatrist confided to us that whenever he had a patient who was troubled, he just wrote down "adjustment disorder" as a catch-all psychiatric diagnosis to facilitate third-party payments.)

We first criticized social anxiety disorder years ago in an op-ed piece in the *Baltimore Sun*. Often criticized as a medicalized version of "shyness," it rapidly was normalized into the psychiatric-pharmaceutical complex. The *Washington Post* detailed in an exposé of the selling of this alleged disorder that the significant consequence of false disorders is what even conventional mental health sources claim is "blurring the line between normal personality variation and real psychiatric conditions [which] can trivialize serious mental illness."

What's more, the conflation of personality differences with alleged brain disorders creates a broad market not only for talk therapy, but pharmacological prolificacy. The *Post* documents social anxiety disorder proponents' covering and promoting the condition as part and parcel of a public relations campaign. There were "pitches to newspapers, radio and TV, satellite and Internet communications, and testimonials from advocates and doctors who said social anxiety was America's third most common mental disorder with more than 10 million sufferers." As the *Post* pointed out, the campaign was so successful that "media accounts of social anxiety rose from just 50 stories in 1997 and 1998 to more than 1 billion references in 1999 alone." All of this publicity was to promote the selling of Paxil, with sales rising 18%.

It should be pointed out that the selling of social anxiety disorder transpired at the behest of the makers of Paxil, Glaxo SmithKline, not physicians.

Psychiatrist Paul McHugh's work could provide some grist for a partial meeting of the minds between the psychiatric establishment and Szasz. McHugh maintains that, too often, psychiatry proceeds on a disease by disease basis; an alleged mental disorder becomes what often is derided as the "mental illness du jour"—such as, again, body dysmorphic disorder a few years ago or multiple personality disorder, which McHugh abjures. Many critics judge such disorders to be false, but atypical.

The point probably is best made in McHugh's trenchant December, 1999, *Commentary* article, "How Psychiatry Lost Its Way." This piece—its brilliance somewhat lessened due to its insufficient citing of Szasz—opines that "Proposals for new psychiatric disorders have multiplied so feverishly that the DSM [Diagnostic and Statistical Manual of Mental Disorders] itself has grown from a mere 119 pages in 1968 to 886 pages in the latest edition."

This prolific creation of new mental disorders is due to the emphasis on "appearances." In response to McHugh's article, we penned a correspondence reply, saying that McHugh was "right on the mark in . . . many areas . . ." but that "many of the points argued by [him] have been articulated by Dr. Szasz over the years." Some of these include McHugh's contentions that, as stated above, there is a substantial increase in "new, nonorganic, bogus" mental illnesses; psychiatry utilizes a criterion of reliability rather than validity; there is collusion between some pharmaceutical companies and some psychiatric diagnosticians; there is a significant role in self-fulfilling prophesy in the evidence put forth for the public's "suffering" from mental illness (a point often made by Jeffrey Schaler, author of *Addiction's a Choice*); and the changing of behaviors by psychotropic drugs ("Everyone is more attentive when on Ritalin") affects anyone who takes them, and therefore, said changes cannot be validly used as indicative of the existing psychiatric disorders.

Prescription Pressure

Regardless, the gravamen of the piece—that there is a proliferation of new, scientifically unverified psychiatric disorders and a "thoughtless prescription of medication for them"—is one of the bases for building some understanding, if not wholesale agreement, between psychiatry and its detractors.

None of this gainsays the differences—and some might claim they are unbridgeable—between Szasz and McHugh, as well as psychiatry and Szasz, such as the overriding importance Szasz attributes to free will, which only is partially recognized by McHugh. He, for example, speaks of some drugs as being "addictive," whereas Szasz argues that, while a person can become reliant on them, individuals always maintain the ability to refuse to continue to take substances.

So, where would Szasz have to yield if we are forging a compromise? He insists that no psychiatric diagnosis can be "pathology-driven" since all psychiatric illnesses are human creations. To the extent that schizophrenia and other now so-called major psychiatric illnesses have consistent pathological correlates, he would say that they may be illnesses. Where would psychiatry have to yield on the same issues? The American Psychiatric Association would have to revamp its diagnostic manual to include only those mental disorders which, when medically analyzed, are brain diseases that have consistent pathological definitions. Psychiatry would be the study and practice of the

attention—pharmacological and counseling—given those with behaviorally-affected neurological disorders.

One of Szasz's central concerns always has been the involuntariness of psychiatric clients. This is a critically important aspect of his views because if it were well-understood, people would not lump him in with anti-psychiatry, which, again, he considers an irresponsible movement since he does not oppose, as he calls it, "psychiatric practice between consenting adults."

One of the most irreconcilable areas of disagreement between psychiatry and its critics is the question of legal responsibility for one's actions; most strikingly, the insanity plea. In an article several years ago in Liberty, "The Trouble with Szasz," Ralph Slovenko, a respected writer on psychiatry and the law, notes that psychiatry gets a bad rap insofar as its interaction with the criminal justice system is concerned. Slovenko points out that, it is the court which rules, not the psychiatrist. This is a profoundly disingenuous argument, for it merely asserts without proof a hierarchically inferior role of the psychiatrist. One easily could argue that it is repeatedly psychiatric expertise to which courts typically turn to make final dispositions in the "law-psychiatry axis."

Speaking of which, Slovenko unquestioningly parrots the new received wisdom that "Not Guilty by Reason of Insanity" represents the "rare" case, ignoring the deep involvement that psychiatry wields in the criminal justice system in alternative sentencing, mitigation of sentences, plea bargains, and the like. Moreover, the "low" percentage of successful NGRI cases, generally accepted to be one-quarter of one percent, masquerades the fact that, over the years, this translates into thousands of cases.

There are areas of psychiatry that simply are irreconcilable due to intervening institutional issues. A major tenet of Szasz's views is his opposition to the threat of the "Therapeutic State," the use of psychiatry through the misleading rhetoric of therapy to deprive people of their life, liberty, and property rights. Szasz would argue against any extra-legal interference in depriving people of their freedom, while many psychiatrists want the power, among other things, to declare people incompetent or dangerous to themselves and others. While we may side with Szasz on the issue of people's freedom to pose a not illegal danger to others, the weakness of the criminal justice system in protecting such people, say, for example, wherein stalking is not illegal, often leaves people at the mercy of predators. We might—although Szasz would not—concede that psychiatry might be useful in depriving dangerous people of their freedom, but only as a method of last resort.

The foregoing attempt at some agreement between psychiatry and its critics is consistent with a rhetorician's persuasive duty to find "common ground" between those who profoundly disagree with one another. Admittedly, though, there will be those who say that the disagreements between responsible psychiatrists and responsible critics of psychiatry are irreconcilable.

RICHARD E. VATZ, Associate Psychology Editor of *USA Today,* is professor of rhetoric and communication, Towson (Md.) University and 2004 winner of the "President's Award for Distinguished Service to the University."

Computer- and Internet-Based Psychotherapy Interventions

Computers and Internet-based programs have great potential to make psychological assessment and treatment more cost-effective. Computer-assisted therapy appears to be as effective as face-to-face treatment for treating anxiety disorders and depression. Internet support groups also may be effective and have advantages over face-to-face therapy. However, research on this approach remains meager.

C. BARR TAYLOR AND KRISTINE H. LUCE

In recent years, the increasing number of users of computer and Internet technology has greatly expanded the potential of computer- and Internet-based therapy programs. Computer- and Internet-assisted assessment methods and therapy programs have the potential to increase the cost-effectiveness of standardized psychotherapeutic treatments by reducing contact time with the therapist, increasing clients' participation in therapeutic activities outside the standard clinical hour, and streamlining input and processing of clients' data related to their participation in therapeutic activities. Unfortunately, the scientific study of these programs has seriously lagged behind their purported potential, and these interventions pose important ethical and professional questions.

Computer-Based Programs
Information
A number of studies have demonstrated that computers can provide information effectively and economically. An analysis of a large number of studies of computer-assisted instruction (CAI) found that CAI is consistently effective in improving knowledge (Fletcher-Flinn & Gravatt, 1995). Surprisingly, few studies evaluating the use of CAI for providing information related to mental health or psychotherapy have been conducted.

Assessment
Traditional paper-based self-report instruments are easily adapted to the computer format and offer a number of advantages that include ensuring data completeness and standardization. Research has found that computer-administered assessment instruments work as well as other kinds of self-report instruments and as well as therapist-administered ones. Clients may feel less embarrassed about reporting sensitive or potentially stigmatizing information (e.g., about sexual behavior or illegal drug use) during a computer-assisted assessment than during a face-to-face assessment, allowing for more accurate estimates of mental health behaviors. Studies show that more symptoms, including suicidal thoughts, are reported during computer-assisted interviews than face-to-face interviews. Overall, the evidence suggests that computers can make assessments more efficient, more accurate, and less expensive. Yet computer-based assessment interviews do not allow for clinical intuition and nuance, assessment of behavior, and nonverbal emotional expression, nor do they foster a therapeutic alliance between client and therapist as information is collected.

Recently, handheld computers or personal digital assistants (PDAs) have been used to collect real-time, naturalistic data on a variety of variables. For example, clients can record their thoughts, behaviors, mood, and other variables at the same time and when directed to do so by an alarm or through instructions from the program. The assessment of events as they occur avoids retrospective recall biases. PDAs can be programmed to beep to cue a response and also to check data to determine, for instance, if responses are in the right range. The data are easily downloaded into computer databases for further analysis. PDAs with interactive transmission capabilities further expand the potential for real-time data collection. Although PDAs have been demonstrated to be useful for research, they have not been incorporated into clinical practice.

Computer-Assisted Psychotherapy

Much research on computer-based programs has focused on anxiety disorders (Newman, Consoli, & Taylor, 1997). Researchers have developed computer programs that direct participants through exercises in relaxation and restfulness; changes in breathing frequency, regularity, and pattern; gradual and progressive exposure to aspects of the situation, sensation, or objects they are afraid of; and changes in thinking patterns. Although the majority of studies report symptom reduction, most are uncontrolled trials or case studies and have additional methodological weaknesses (e.g., small sample sizes, no follow-up to assess whether treatment gains are maintained, focus on individuals who do not have clinical diagnoses).

Computer programs have been developed to reduce symptoms of simple phobias, panic disorder, obsessive-compulsive disorder (OCD), generalized anxiety disorder, and social phobia. In a multi-center, international treatment trial (Kenardy et al., 2002), study participants who received a primary diagnosis of panic disorder were randomly assigned to one of four groups: (a) a group that received 12 sessions of therapist-delivered cognitive behavior therapy (CBT), (b) a group that received 6 sessions of therapist-delivered CBT augmented by use of a handheld computer, (c) a group that received 6 sessions of therapist-delivered CBT augmented with a manual, or (d) a control group that was assigned to a wait list. Assessments at the end of treatment and 6 months later showed that the 12-session CBT and the 6-session CBT with the computer were equally effective. The results suggested that use of a handheld computer can reduce therapist contact time without compromising outcomes and may speed the rate of improvement.

An interactive computer program was developed to help clients with OCD, which is considered one type of anxiety disorder. The computer provided three weekly 45-min sessions of therapy involving vicarious exposure to their obsessive thoughts and response prevention (a technique by which clients with OCD are taught and encouraged not to engage in their customary rituals when they have an urge to do so). Compared with a control group, the clients who received the intervention had significantly greater improvement in symptoms. In a follow-up study with clients diagnosed with OCD, computer guided telephone behavior therapy was effective; however, clinician-guided behavior therapy was even more effective. Thus, computer-guided behavior therapy can be a helpful first step in treating patients with OCD, particularly when clinician-guided behavior therapy is unavailable. Computers have also been used to help treat individuals with other anxiety disorders, including social phobia and generalized anxiety disorder, a condition characterized by excessive worry and constant anxiety without specific fears or avoidances.

CBT also has been adapted for the computer-delivered treatment of depressive disorders. Selmi, Klein, Greist, Sorrell, and Erdman (1990) conducted the only randomized, controlled treatment trial comparing computer- and therapist-administered CBT for depression. Participants who met the study's criteria for major, minor, or intermittent depressive disorder were randomly assigned to computer-administered CBT, therapist-administered CBT, or a wait-list control. Compared with the control group, both treatment groups reported significant improvements on depression indices. The treatment groups did not differ from each other, and treatment gains were maintained at a 2-month follow-up.

Little information exists on the use of computer-assisted therapy for treating patients with complicated anxiety disorders or other mental health problems. Thus, further study is needed.

The Internet

Internet-based programs have several advantages over stand-alone computer-delivered programs. The Internet makes health care information and programs accessible to individuals who may have economic, transportation, or other restrictions that limit access to face-to-face services. The Internet is constantly available and accessible from a variety of locations. Because text and other information on the Internet can be presented in a variety of formats, languages, and styles, and at various educational levels, it is possible to tailor messages to the learning preferences and strengths of the user. The Internet can facilitate the collection, coordination, dissemination, and interpretation of data. These features allow for interactivity among the various individuals (e.g., physicians, clients, family members, caregivers) who may participate in a comprehensive treatment plan. As guidelines, information, and other aspects of programs change, it is possible to rapidly update information on Web pages. The medium also allows for personalization of information. Users may select features and information most relevant to them, and, conversely, programs can automatically determine a user's needs and strengths and display content accordingly.

Information

Patients widely search the Internet for mental health information. For example, the National Institute of Mental Health (NIMH) public information Web site receives more than 7 million "hits" each month. However, the mental health information on commercial Web sites is often inaccurate, misleading, or related to commercial interests. Sites sponsored by nonprofit organizations provide better and more balanced information, but search engines often list for-profit sites before they generate nonprofit sites. Furthermore, education Web sites rarely follow solid pedagogical principles.

Screening and Assessment

Many mental health Web sites have implemented screening programs that assess individuals for signs or symptoms of various psychiatric disorders. These programs generally recommend that participants who score above a predetermined cutoff contact a mental health provider for further assessment. The NIMH and many other professional organizations provide high-quality, easily accessible information combined with screening instruments. Houston and colleagues (2001) evaluated the use of a Web site that offered a computerized version of the Center for Epidemiological Studies' depression scale (CES-D; Ogles, France, Lunnen, Bell, & Goldfarb, 1998). The scale was completed 24,479 times during the 8-month study period. Fifty-eight percent of participants screened positive for depression, and fewer than half of those had previously been treated for depression. The Internet can incorporate interactive screening, which already has been extensively developed for desktop computers. Screening can then be linked to strategies that are designed to increase the likelihood that a participant will accept a referral and initiate further assessment or treatment.

On-Line Support Groups

Because Internet-delivered group interventions can be accessed constantly from any location that has Internet access, they offer distinct advantages over their face-to-face counterparts. Face-to-face support groups often are difficult to schedule, meet at limited times and locations, and must accommodate inconsistent attendance patterns because of variations in participants' health status and schedules. On-line groups have the potential to help rural residents and individuals who are chronically ill or physically or psychiatrically disabled increase their access to psychological interventions.

A wide array of social support groups is available to consumers in synchronous (i.e., participants on-line at the same time) or asynchronous formats. The Pew Internet and American Life Project (www.pewinternet.org) estimated that 28% of Internet users have attended an on-line support group for a medical condition or personal problem on at least one occasion. After a morning television show featured Edward M. Kennedy, Jr., promoting free on-line support groups sponsored by the Wellness Community (www.wellness-community.org), the organization received more than 440,000 inquiries during the following week! The majority of published studies on Internet-based support groups suggest that the groups are beneficial; however, scientific understanding of how and when is limited. Studies that examine the patterns of discourse that occur in these groups indicate that members' communication is similar to that found in face-to-face support groups (e.g., high levels of mutual support, acceptance, positive feelings).

Only a few controlled studies have examined the effects of Internet-based support programs. One such study investigated the effects of a program named Bosom Buddies on reducing psychosocial distress in women with breast cancer (Winzelberg et al., in press). Compared with a wait-list control group, the intervention group reported significantly reduced depression, cancer-related trauma, and perceived stress.

On-Line Consultation

On-line consultation with "experts" is readily available on the Internet. There are organizations for on-line therapists (e.g., the International Society for Mental Health Online, www.ismho.org) and sites that verify the credentials of on-line providers. However, little is known about the efficacy, reach, utility, or other aspects of on-line consultation.

Advocacy

The Internet has become an important medium for advocacy and political issues. Many organizations use the Internet to facilitate communication among members and to encourage members to support public policy (e.g., the National Alliance for the Mentally Ill, www.nami.org).

Internet-Based Psychotherapy

The Internet facilitates the creation of treatment programs that combine a variety of interactive components. The basic components that can be combined include psychoeducation; social support; chat groups; monitoring of symptoms, progress, and use of the program; feedback; and interactions with providers. Although many psychotherapy programs developed for desktop computers and manuals are readily translatable to the Internet format, surprisingly few have been adapted in this way, and almost none have been evaluated. Studies show that Internet-based treatments are effective for reducing symptoms of panic disorder. Compared with patients in a wait-list control group, those who participated in an Internet-based posttraumatic stress group reported significantly greater improvements on trauma-related symptoms. During the initial 6-month period of operation, an Australian CBT program for depression, MoodGYM, had more than 800,000 hits (Christensen, Griffiths, & Korten, 2002). In an uncontrolled study of a small subsample of participants who registered on this site, program use was associated with significant decreases in anxiety and depression. Internet-based programs also have been shown to reduce symptoms of eating disorders and associated behaviors. Users consistently report high satisfaction with these programs.

Treatment programs for depression, mood swings, and other mental health disorders are being designed to blend computer-assisted psychotherapy and psychoeducation with case management (in which a therapist helps to manage a client's problems by following treatment and therapy guidelines) and telephone-based care. These programs might also include limited face-to-face interventions, medication, and support groups. The effectiveness of these programs remains to be demonstrated.

Eventually, the most important use of the Internet might be to deliver integrated, home-based, case-managed, psychoeducational programs that are combined with some face-to-face contact and support groups. Unfortunately, although a number of such programs are "under development," none have been evaluated in controlled trials.

Ethical and Professional Issues

Web-based interventions present a number of ethical and professional issues (Hsiung, 2001). Privacy is perhaps the most significant concern. The Internet creates an environment where information about patients can be easily accessed and disseminated. Patients may purposely or inadvertently disclose private information about themselves and, in on-line support groups, about their peers. Although programs can be password-protected, and electronic records must follow federal privacy guidelines, participants must be clearly informed that confidentiality of records cannot be guaranteed.

Internet interventions create the potential that services will be provided to patients who have not been seen by a professional or who live in other states or countries where the professionals providing the services are not licensed to provide therapy. Professional organizations are struggling to develop guidelines to address these concerns (e.g., Hsiung, 2001; Kane & Sands, 1998).

Because of its accessibility and relative anonymity, patients may use the Internet during crises and report suicidal and homicidal thoughts. Although providers who use Internet support groups develop statements to clearly inform patients that the medium is not to be used for psychiatric emergencies, patients may ignore these instructions. Thus, providers need to identify ancillary procedures to reduce and manage potential crises.

Given the continuing advances in technology and the demonstrated effectiveness and advantages of computer- and Internet-based interventions, one might expect that providers would readily integrate these programs into their standard care practice. Yet few do, in part because programs that are easy to install and use are not available, there is no professional or market demand for the use of computer-assisted therapy, and practitioners may have ethical and professional concerns about applying this technology in their clinical practice. Thus, in the near future this technology may primarily be used for situations in which the cost-effectiveness advantages are particularly great.

Conclusion

Computers have the potential to make psychological assessments more efficient, more accurate, and less expensive. Computer-assisted therapy appears to be as effective as face-to-face therapy for treating anxiety disorders and depression and can be delivered at lower cost. However, applications of this technology are in the early stages.

A high priority is to clearly demonstrate the efficacy of this approach, particularly compared with standard face-to-face, "manualized" treatments that have been shown to be effective

for common mental health disorders. Studies that compare two potentially efficacious treatments require large samples for us to safely conclude that the therapies are comparable if no statistically significant differences are found. Kenardy et al. (2002) demonstrated that multi-site, international studies sampling large populations could be conducted relatively inexpensively, in part because the intervention they examined was standardized. If a treatment's efficacy is demonstrated, the next step would be to determine if the therapy, provided by a range of mental health professionals, is useful in large, diverse populations. Examination of combinations of therapies (e.g., CBT plus medication) and treatment modalities (Taylor, Cameron, Newman, & Junge, 2002) should follow. As the empirical study of this technology advances, research might examine the utility and cost-effectiveness of adapting these approaches to treating everyone in a community who wants therapy.

Continued use of the Internet to provide psychosocial support and group therapy is another promising avenue. As in the case of individual therapy, research is needed to compare the advantages and disadvantages between Internet and face-to-face groups, determine which patients benefit from which modality, compare the effectiveness of professionally moderated groups and self- or peer-directed groups, and compare the effectiveness of synchronous and asynchronous groups.

As research progresses, new and exciting applications can be explored. Because on-line text is stored, word content can be examined. This information may teach us more about the therapeutic process or may automatically alert providers to patients who are depressed, dangerous, or deteriorating.

Although research in many aspects of computer-assisted therapy is needed, and the professional and ethical concerns are substantial, computers and the Internet are likely to play a progressively important role in providing mental health assessment and interventions to clients. Thus, mental health professionals will need to decide how they will incorporate such programs into their practices.

References

Christensen, H., Griffiths, K. M., & Korten, A. (2002). Web-based cognitive behavior therapy: Analysis of site usage and changes in depression and anxiety scores. *Journal of Medical Internet Research, 4*(1), Article e3. Retrieved July 16, 2002, from http://www.jmir.org/2002/1/e3

Fletcher-Flinn, C. M., & Gravatt, B. (1995). The efficacy of computer assisted instruction (CAI): A meta-analysis. *Journal of Educational Computing Research, 3,* 219–241.

Houston, T. K., Cooper, L. A., Vu, H. T., Kahn, J., Toser, J., & Ford, D. E. (2001). Screening the public for depression through the Internet. *Psychiatric Services, 52,* 362–367.

Hsiung, R. C. (2001). Suggested principles of professional ethics for the online provision of mental health services. *Medinfo, 10,* 296–300.

Kane, B., & Sands, D. Z. (1998). Guidelines for the clinical use of electronic mail with patients: The AMIA Internet Working

Group, Task Force on Guidelines for the Use of Clinic-Patient Electronic Mail. *Journal of the American Medical Informatics Association, 5,* 104–111.

Kenardy, J. A., Dow, M. G. T., Johnston, D. W., Newman, M. G., Thompson, A., & Taylor, C. B. (2002). *A comparison of delivery methods of cognitive behavioural therapy for panic disorder: An international multicentre trial.* Manuscript submitted for publication.

Newman, M. G., Consoli, A., & Taylor, C. B. (1997). Computers in assessment and cognitive behavioral treatment of clinical disorders: Anxiety as a case in point. *Behavior Therapy, 28,* 211–235.

Ogles, B. M., France, C. R., Lunnen, K. M., Bell, M. T., & Goldfarb, M. (1998). Computerized depression screening and awareness. *Community Mental Health Journal, 34* (1), 27–38.

Selmi, P. M., Klein, M. H., Greist, J. H., Sorrell, S. P., & Erdman, H. P. (1990). Computer-administered cognitive-behavioral therapy for depression. *American Journal of Psychiatry, 147,* 51–56.

Taylor, C. B., Cameron, R., Newman, M., & Junge, J. (2002). Issues related to combining risk factor reduction and clinical treatment for eating disorders in defined populations. *The Journal of Behavioral Health Services and Research, 29,* 81–90.

Winzelberg, A. J., Classen, C., Alpers, G., Roberts, H., Koopman, C., Adams, R., Ernst, H., Dev, P., & Taylor, C. B. (in press). An evaluation of an Internet support group for women with primary breast cancer. *Cancer.*

Address correspondence to C. Barr Taylor, Department of Psychiatry, Stanford University Medical Center, Stanford, CA 94305-5722; e-mail: btaylor@stanford.edu.

From *Current Directions in Psychological Science,* February 2003, pp. 18–22. Copyright © 2003 by the Association for Psychological Science. Reprinted by permission of Blackwell Publishing, Ltd.

Test-Your-Knowledge Form

We encourage you to photocopy and use this page as a tool to assess how the articles in *Annual Editions* expand on the information in your textbook. By reflecting on the articles you will gain enhanced text information. You can also access this useful form on a product's book support Web site at *http://www.mhcls.com/online/*.

NAME: _____   DATE: _____

TITLE AND NUMBER OF ARTICLE: _____

BRIEFLY STATE THE MAIN IDEA OF THIS ARTICLE:

_____

LIST THREE IMPORTANT FACTS THAT THE AUTHOR USES TO SUPPORT THE MAIN IDEA:

_____

WHAT INFORMATION OR IDEAS DISCUSSED IN THIS ARTICLE ARE ALSO DISCUSSED IN YOUR TEXTBOOK OR OTHER READINGS THAT YOU HAVE DONE? LIST THE TEXTBOOK CHAPTERS AND PAGE NUMBERS:

_____

LIST ANY EXAMPLES OF BIAS OR FAULTY REASONING THAT YOU FOUND IN THE ARTICLE:

_____

LIST ANY NEW TERMS/CONCEPTS THAT WERE DISCUSSED IN THE ARTICLE, AND WRITE A SHORT DEFINITION:

We Want Your Advice

ANNUAL EDITIONS revisions depend on two major opinion sources: one is our Advisory Board, listed in the front of this volume, which works with us in scanning the thousands of articles published in the public press each year; the other is you—the person actually using the book. Please help us and the users of the next edition by completing the prepaid article rating form on this page and returning it to us. Thank you for your help!

ANNUAL EDITIONS: Psychology Update 08/09

ARTICLE RATING FORM

Here is an opportunity for you to have direct input into the next revision of this volume.
We would like you to rate each of the articles listed below, using the following scale:

1. **Excellent: should definitely be retained**
2. **Above average: should probably be retained**
3. **Below average: should probably be deleted**
4. **Poor: should definitely be deleted**

Your ratings will play a vital part in the next revision.
Please mail this prepaid form to us as soon as possible.
Thanks for your help!

RATING	ARTICLE	RATING	ARTICLE
	1. Why Study Psychology?		22. Unconscious Emotion
	2. Does Psychology Make a Significant Difference in Our Lives?		23. Ambition: Why Some People Are Most Likely to Succeed
	3. The 10 Commandments of Helping Students Distinguish Science from Pseudoscience in Psychology		24. Eating into the Nation's Obesity Epidemic
	4. How to Spot Bias in Research		25. A Learning Machine
	5. The Amazing Brain: Is Neuroscience the Key to What Makes Us Human?		26. Growing Up Online
	6. Genetic Influence on Human Psychological Traits		27. Why Newborns Cause Acrimony and Alimony
	7. From Discovery to Translation		28. Ageless Aging: The Next Era of Retirement
	8. The Structure of the Human Brain		29. Blessed Are Those Who Mourn—and Those Who Comfort Them
	9. Sensational Tune-Ups		30. Culture and the Development of Self-Knowledge
	10. Extreme States		31. Frisky, but More Risky
	11. A Matter of Taste		32. The Testing of America
	12. What Dreams Are Made Of		33. Bad Apples or Bad Barrels?
	13. Teaching for Understanding		34. Young and Restless
	14. What Studies of Actors and Acting Can Tell Us About Memory and Cognitive Functioning		35. Mirror, Mirror: Seeing Yourself As Others See You
	15. Memory Flexibility		36. We're Wired to Connect
	16. Theory of Multiple Intelligences		37. Inside a Mass Murderer's Mind
	17. Shouldn't There Be a Word . . . ?		38. Treating War's Toll on the Mind
	18. What Was I Thinking?		39. Soldier Support
	19. The Culture-Cognition Connection		40. We Love to be Scared on Halloween
	20. The Structure of Emotion		41. Psychiatry: A Branch of the Law
	21. Feeling Smart: The Science of Emotional Intelligence		42. The Quandary Over Mental Illness
			43. Computer- and Internet-Based Psychotherapy Interventions

BUSINESS REPLY MAIL
FIRST CLASS MAIL PERMIT NO. 551 DUBUQUE IA

POSTAGE WILL BE PAID BY ADDRESSEE

McGraw-Hill Contemporary Learning Series
501 BELL STREET
DUBUQUE, IA 52001

ABOUT YOU

Name   Date
_____

Are you a teacher? ❏ A student? ❏
Your school's name
_____

Department
_____

Address   City   State   Zip
_____

School telephone #
_____

YOUR COMMENTS ARE IMPORTANT TO US!

Please fill in the following information:
For which course did you use this book?
_____

Did you use a text with this ANNUAL EDITION? ❏ yes ❏ no
What was the title of the text?
_____

What are your general reactions to the Annual Editions concept?
_____

Have you read any pertinent articles recently that you think should be included in the next edition? Explain.
_____

Are there any articles that you feel should be replaced in the next edition? Why?
_____

Are there any World Wide Web sites that you feel should be included in the next edition? Please annotate.
_____

May we contact you for editorial input? ❏ yes ❏ no
May we quote your comments? ❏ yes ❏ no